Nights in the Big City

D0370901

TOPOGRAPHICS

# Nights in the Big City

Paris · Berlin · London 1840–1930

## *Joachim Schlör*

*Translated by*
PIERRE GOTTFRIED IMHOF
*and* DAFYDD REES ROBERTS

REAKTION BOOKS

Published by Reaktion Books Ltd
11 Rathbone Place, London W1P 1DE, UK

First published in English 1998

First published in German as *Nachts in der großen Stadt*
© Artemis & Winkler Verlag 1991

English translation © Reaktion Books, 1998

Translated by Pierre Gottfried Imhoff and Dafydd Rees Roberts

Printed and bound in Great Britain by
Biddles Limited, Guildford and King's Lynn

British Library Cataloguing in Publication Data

Schlör, Joachim
Nights in the big city: Paris, Berlin, London, 1840–1930.
– (Topographics)
1. Cities and towns – Europe – History 2. Paris (France) –
Description and travel 3. Berlin (Germany) – Description and
travel 4. London (England) – Description and travel
I. Title
914
ISBN 1 86189 015 X

# Contents

# 1 Contradictory Reports from Night in the Big City

Fear and fascination meet us as we approach the nocturnal city and accompany us along our way. We enter a world that is both familiar and strange, a landscape full of light and rich with shadows, the receptacle of our desires and of our hidden, unspeakable fears. What a challenge to the senses: hesitant perhaps, often full of curiosity and hopeful of reward after a day of normality, we feel our way forward in the darkness, and eyes, ears and nose quicken to the new and different impressions of the night.

The idea of 'night life' comes to mind, with its promising associations: pleasure, escape from the everyday, secret get-aways. It would be tempting, delightful and only too easy to write about this 'night life', to craft garish, colourful phrases, paint images of the 'intoxication of the night'. We will talk about night life, but night in the big city has other dimensions. It is worth digging deeper, questioning clichés and stereotypical images: the riches of the night do not disclose themselves at first glance, but lie buried in little-known sources, texts and stories.

With the fall of darkness the other half of the metropolitan **day** begins, ending with the dawn, the first light of the new day. The transitions are fluid: slowly and gradually the urban workings change, submitting little by little to the conditions of the night. But many functions and habits of the diurnal city simply go on uninterrupted, little influenced by light or dark. It would probably be off-putting if someone were to take 'day in the big city' as a topic of research; the day calls for facts and realities, the structural elements of the urban mechanism: work, economy, environment, traffic. Themes and problems are so multi-layered and complex that no concept like 'Berlin am Tage' or 'Paris le jour' could even begin to encompass them. All these are still at work in the nocturnal city, yet there does seem to be an overarching unity that allows us to speak of *night in the big city*.

'Paris la nuit', 'Berlin bei Nacht', 'London by night' – the sound of the words conjures up a broad field of associations, images and memories, an almost infinite ensemble of attitudes and behaviours. Two images in particular spring up before our eyes: on the one hand the nocturnal city as celebration, as the place of pleasure and entertainment, and on the other the nocturnal city as the place of terror, of threatening danger. Both images describe and characterize, in contradictory fashion, *one single* world. Entertainment, lively streets, bright window displays, neon signs with their colourful promises, cinemas and restaurants, the parade of the many who 'go out' to recover from the strains of work – and empty streets, dark corners, the play of shadow on sinister doorways, disturbing noises, and single, apprehensive, solitary wanderers.

Both images present nocturnal reality, but they awaken totally different feelings: temptation, desire and fascination on the one hand; intimidation, fear and terror on the other. Fascination and terror are the two sides of the night, inseparably linked. By themselves these images show only one aspect of the nocturnal city, and it is only together that they form a whole.

News about the city at night is marked by the same contradiction. What we see in newspapers and other media has a dual face: here, news of assaults and nocturnal attacks; there, reports on the entertainment business of the nocturnal city. The contradiction finds expression in numerous word-pairs – light and shadow, dream and nightmare, wealth and poverty – antonyms which construct a wide field from real news and fabulous stories, a world of its own.

What does this world look like? Günter Kunert attempted a first appraisal: 'At the approach of darkness something strange and extraordinary happens to a city which cannot be exhaustively explained by such cursory formulations about aesthetic appearance. Something becomes apparent which I will dare to call the "mythical quality" of the city'.[1]

This is the *beauty of the night*, a beauty 'rooted in atmosphere'[2] that is not easily explained. We sometimes think too of the *intoxication of the night*, an intoxication that Paul Nizon describes in Paris:

> I didn't know what night life was about, I had never experienced it, and now I was overwhelmed, devoured by the life of the night. The streets glittered with the reflections of the most varied illuminations, the colourful adverts, neon signs and decorative lights of bars and night-clubs, restaurants and shops, the doors of the bars opening and closing like pumps, letting out floods of music, noise, gossip and people, and in front of the bars half-dressed girls, bar-girls, night-girls

wriggling in time to the different musics, and promenading all along, the crowd of lascivious pleasure seekers.[3]

Male fantasy? Dream or nightmare? A third image to close the kaleidoscope for the time being – here life has left the city, and *darkness rules*:

City jungle, at night and in the milky light of dawn. The pavement gleams wet and dirty. In tenement yards, scum gathers, human refuse. The air vibrates with the ringing of countless burglar alarms. Neon signs flicker monotonously through the night, reflected in shrill lightning on the tarmac.[4]

This is very evidently an image from a film, but such a cinematic imagination can also be found in literary texts. Once seen, once read, these images accompany our nocturnal walks through the city. In our luggage too we carry information about the growing lawlessness of the city, and we fear the night as a possible scene of crime.[5] We are aware of the debate about extending shop-opening hours, and share the hope that nocturnal dreariness and unpeopled inner cities may come enticingly alive. We have heard about the difficult living conditions of night-workers – waiters, taxi drivers, nurses and night-security staff[6] – and sometimes we hear of arguments about the 'town-planning factor in nocturnal insecurity'[7] (and the difficulty of making improvements), and about the problems women face out-of-doors at night. In 1976 a young woman working in Paris explained:

The street at night is also the place and the time when the prostitutes work, so you get asked: 'C'est combien?'. What am I supposed to say to that, how can I explain that I like to go walking at night? Why do I still do it? Because it's a world of its own, despite everything. It's a break from daily routine, something might happen.[8]

There are a series of relationships and frames of reference in which the essence, the peculiarity of the nocturnal city emerges in rough approximation: night and violence, night and sexuality, night and pleasure, night and solitude. These clusters of motifs cannot however be clearly separated. Here too imagination and reality merge, combining in an ensemble of associations, metaphors and images.

Is it nevertheless possible to gain an overall view? The subject of this book is not night in the contemporary city, but the history of its creation. The present, however, is constantly at hand. History does not interest me in itself, but only as the basis of the contemporary, its

The scenery of the night, Montmartre: lonely streets and tempting night-spots together make up the picture of 'night life'. Photograph by André Kertész. *Montmartre, 1930.*

latest manifestation. The images that form in our minds have been historically created, and we will find out more about ourselves and our imagined worlds if we have a better knowledge of those of the past. This is a truism which however acquires a new importance in the context of the nocturnal city: we have to enter into dialogue with those who wandered the nights of the past if we want a better understanding of the landscape in which we ourselves move.

Two fundamental orientations, in space and time, are necessary. Night in the big city itself is a space-time model, needing to be measured and paced out in temporal and spatial dimensions. The *temporal* framework in which the story is told extends from 1840 to 1930. The chapters, dedicated to the most important points of content and chronologically arranged, have been framed with observations on the 'beginning' of the story around 1840 and its 'end' around 1930. The opening chapter sets the scene, setting the themes of the night into the more general context of the years around 1840. After these have been presented under the categories of security, morality and accessibility, the closing chapter takes them all up once again, re-establishing the context anew for the period around 1930.

## 1 *Access to the night*

The business of writing a book about this cluster of motifs, events and 'images' could itself be compared to a visit to a nocturnal city. Where should we start? What should we visit? The entertainment districts, the deserted neighbourhoods, the industrial areas? All of them, preferably, but in what order, and under whose guidance?

Access to the nocturnal city is often obstructed. Whoever wants to get to know a city 'by night' – Berlin, Paris or London – will come across a number of obstacles, the first of which has to do, very literally, with the problem of restrictions on access: big cities, at night too, are nowadays not very pedestrian-friendly.

Walking is a mode of locomotion very appropriate to humans, a true art form in these days of four-laned or even wider breaches in the fabric of the 'car-oriented city'. When walking one gains insights into the essence of the nocturnal city that remain hidden from the hurried driver. But for walkers too, strollers who do have the time, access to the city is often obstructed; they are driven into pedestrian zones, the native reserves of an overtaken form of locomotion. There are greater and greater restrictions placed on the possibility of appropriating the urban environment, of checking out in the *whole city* what has changed and what ought to change. The city's *mental topography* changes together with the real: greater 'clarity' and functional separation restrict the possible routes we can take, and limit our imagination too. The 'other side' of accessibility is the *limit*. It is a matter not just of what the possibilities are for moving around, but also of the obstructions that stand in the way of autonomous perambulation.

On our walks through the past of the nocturnal city we will meet the most varied people: policemen and missionaries, nocturnal revellers and *flâneurs*, sociologists and solitary walkers. They have all left behind reports of their night-time travels, reports with whose help I will try to write a history of the nocturnal city – and to rediscover in our contemporary urban nights the existence of elements one had thought were lost.

## 2 *Sources and reporters*

Who reports on the nights of the past? First of all, without a doubt, the police. For them, as will be shown, the city night was a *terrain interdit*, a prohibited area, and they fought desperately for every minute of time, every inch of space they could control – which little by little escaped them. Police records are an interesting source if they are read against the grain. The nocturnal world is not as the police see it, and even less as they would like it to be. In their files one finds clues to a nocturnal behaviour inconsistent with the conception of order entailed by such ideas as *nocturnal security*; lovers of the nocturnal city often move about it in opposition to the authorities' attempts to rule and regulate. This leads over and over again to tensions and conflicts, and we must also read, in contrast to the reports of the authorities, the far less unambiguous documents, reports and accounts by night-walkers of various shades, literary and journalistic texts that report on their 'penetration' of the nocturnal city.

Among the cognoscenti of the city belong, not surprisingly, its enemies. There are a number of sources of various provenance that can be grouped under the idea of the 'anti-metropolitan'.[9] Here belong the papers of the clerical night-critics of the 'morality' movement and the home mission; they provide us with texts which above all struggle to defend a *nightly threatened morality*. Security and morality are the two principal images of order, and the discourse about their possible endangerment in the night is reflected in the most varied sources of different origins.

Finally there is a third group of sources for a history of the city night, which may be subsumed under the idea of 'curiosity'. Above all these are newspaper reports and feature articles, stories about life in the nocturnal city. Here too belong the texts of the sociologists, those interested in the night, who often believe they can provide insights into the functioning of the whole city – and of life under modern conditions – through the description of city life at night.

For me, the most interesting are sources that tell of the city 'in movement', for I fear that all attempts to halt urban life and force it under a microscope are condemned to failure. Those who plunge into this vast field of associations can very quickly get lost; but those who, fearful of this danger, too quickly introduce emphasis and structure, developing rigid analytical models, not only lull themselves into a false sense of security which the subject-matter does not so easily allow, but also give up the possibility of noticing and reflecting upon the importance of the blurred, the unclear, and the non-comprehensible.

While walking, insights are admittedly gained more by chance than by system. They are necessary, but unreliable, inexact and difficult to grasp. In this way they come quite close to the nature of the nocturnal city itself, or at least to our image of it. The informants whom we can ask for advice are all those who – for very different reasons – were abroad in the city night. Their reports are only very approximate as regards dates, figures and other solid facts. This is not such a problem. Together they still form a picture, if one can succeed in arranging the different sources and the different perspectives unfolded therein in an intensive and polyphonic dialogue.

## 3 *Methods of research*

Sources do not 'speak' for themselves; they have to be found, uncovered, selected and arranged. From the material I have seen, a choice has been made, which, I hope, makes possible an approach to our subject. There are, however, certain methodological guidelines with whose help I try to track the mix of empirically verifiable realities and abstract but nonetheless persistent images which form their own 'reality'. In this the weight and valency of both realms, reality and imagination, must be properly taken into account.

The concept of 'internal' urbanization, as developed by Gottfried Korff,[10] is concerned with inner life, with *mentality*, 'as it has been formed in the communicative relational system of the metropolis', with the role of 'acting, thinking and feeling in the process of urbanization.' Here the focus is on the effects of 'external', material urbanization on the way of life, views and behaviour of people who experience the process – and on the repercussions of these mentalities on the ongoing process itself.

In the few investigations so far that have adopted this approach, it has become clear that 'internal' urbanization can *also* be thought of as the creative process of formation of urban behaviours necessary for survival in the city: among these are mobility, flexibility in dealing with new forms of work and life, accustoming oneself to a new praxis of time. Changes in the city night form an important chapter in the ensemble of new challenges to behaviour, perception and attitude. External changes have repercussions on 'internal' experience. The process of 'internal' urbanization, however, does not at all develop in linear fashion, as it affects and involves different groups of the urban population at different times and in different ways; nor does it develop mechanically and one-sidedly, but in simultaneous dialogue between *the city* and *the people*, more precisely between the specific challenges of the urban environment and its inhabitants' possibilities of reacting to it appropriately – where their reactions and their behaviour in turn influence and even shape the urban environment. This point is important: the history of the urban night shows that there are quite different ways of experiencing the urbanization process, and the tension between different ways of reacting contains within it elements of freedom.

THE DEBATE WITH THE MODERN

The 'urbanist discourse'[11] which emerges in the 1840s is also a discourse, a social debate openly conducted, on urbanization as part of social *modernization*. Where metropolitan experiences have been thematized, we may read and interpret them as evidence of the *modern experience*. The city is the arena of the modern, its stage, its location; the symbol of 'modernity' is, in all the cities investigated, the street. For critics as well as apologists of the city, it is the central figure of the urban description, as metaphor and as material reality; it is the site of encounter and confrontation. The city as *ensemble of challenges* demands the adoption of 'modern', temporally appropriate behaviours, at the same time making available ways and means of meeting these challenges.

In my view, many previous investigations of the 'metropolis as the site of the modern'[12] too quickly take their leave of the material reality of the city and its development. Even conventional archival sources can be successfully questioned as to the form of debate with the modern that is manifested within them. Literary texts, on the other hand, may be interrogated for the real urban experience they contain.

Guy de Maupassant's story, *La nuit. Un cauchemar*, for example, in which 'a lover of the metropolitan night becomes its victim', is one of the key texts of the literature of the city:

> At some point the gas-lights go out, and eventually the solitary walker, nocturnal counterpart of the *flâneur*, finds that his watch has stopped. He is robbed of orientation in space and time, and thus of his last connection with functioning civilization; the sleeping city appears deserted and dead, and at the Seine the metropolitan citizen discovers the horror of a nature emptied of humanity, where an archaic and elemental death awaits him, from hunger, tiredness, and cold.[13]

The topography of this 'night piece' is in no way imaginary. What is described, though in literary distancing, is the nocturnal Paris that we find in contemporary police reports and newspaper articles: the boulevards, the Champs Elysées, the Bastille, the faubourg Montmartre, the Halles – way-stations of a prototypical walk through the nocturnal city, of a 'déambulation nocturne'[14] which leads out of the light and deeper and deeper into the darkness. Knowledge of this topography, of the material anchorage of certain signals deliberately placed by Maupassant, increases the appeal and the documentary value of the text.

The German folklore movement has often conducted its debate with the modern as a debate with life in the city. It is itself a *child of the modern*: the various traditions and precursors of folkloristic thinking and research – cameralistics (the science of government)[15] and statistics, travel-writing, the collection of accounts of 'popular' culture – merged at a certain point to constitute folklore studies as a science as the investigation of tradition and custom turned into a flight from the reality of the present.

It was a field of historical study marked by 'cultural pessimism and distance from the city'.[16] In the distinctly delineated social picture drawn by Wilhelm Heinrich Riehl, the 'father' of German folklore studies, new, modern cultural forms and practices can only be seen as 'decadence' and 'decay'. Even for this conservative point of view, the big cities are *laboratories of the modern*, places in which the ways of life and work of industrialized society are presented in exemplary fashion.

The changes in the life-world are extensive, touching on all areas of existence, even opinions, attitudes, forms of dealing with the environment, temporal rhythms and spatial feeling. In the social picture drawn by the conservative cultural critic these changes are seen as artificial – and reversible: 'The world of the metropolis will break down and these cities . . . will remain standing as skeletons.'[17] Night life, together with all the negative elements from which – according to this view – it is formed, soon emerges as one of the areas vehemently attacked by the critique of the metropolis. This ideological battle, and there is no gentler word to describe it, against 'moral decay in the big cities'[18] often made use of the metaphor of the night to attack the city as a place to live. Individual manifestations of life in the city are intensified through repetition and omission to become 'characteristics', symbols of the urban. This form of 'research' into the big city has indeed created its own reality,[19] an ever more free-standing horror-museum of 'excesses' and extremes, distorted pictures taken to represent the whole city, and, above all, modern society.

Folklorists too were among those who went into the big city with research – and preconceptions – in mind, reporting back on it to an interested public. In their publications they took the traditions of earlier images of the city and transformed them in accordance with their own knowledge and imagination, making their own contribution to the formation of the horror-picture of the city night.

In the discussion so far there has been much talk of 'images'; this is a labile concept. What is metropolitan perception? In texts which deal with this subject-matter, two formulations of the question have often been mixed up: on the one hand it is a question of the city as a 'perceptual scandal',[20] of the sensual stimulation represented by the city itself; on the other hand it is about a general perceptual disposition of the inhabitants of the big city, about changes in their ways of seeing brought about by the new living conditions. In both cases the night offers an interesting field of investigation: it presents 'images' which often condense into solid metaphors, into signals for a particular attitude towards the city; and it challenges perceptual capacity in special ways. At the same time it also offers an opportunity to tie the imagination closer to practical knowledge, experience and everyday life.

> Our German capital has the unhappy reputation of being the city that offers the most pleasures and thus the most temptation in the world. Just look at the night life in the 'arcade', on the street-corners, in the 'Scheunenviertel'! Between 11 and 2 o'clock in the morning you see the playhouses and cinemas, the musical theatres and variety clubs, the dance halls and beer-cellars empty out, delivering the sensually excited youth to the temptations of the nocturnal street.[21]

> 'A lot of bad things (says Thomas Edison) are said about night life. It comes in for far too much criticism. For night life means progress . . . night life and stupidity don't get along. So the growth of night life also means increasing mental freshness . . . electric light, though, means night life, and night life means progress. Berlin is on the way to becoming the most progressive city in Europe'.[22]

It isn't a matter of deciding who is right. What is much more interesting is the fact that the same phenomenon, at the same time, in the same city, can be perceived in such different ways.

The regular succession of day and night, night and day, belongs among the most secure commonplaces of our existence. Such recurring and predictable basic structures[23] form our everyday, everynight life to a greater extent than we would think: particularly because we do not think any more about them. It gets dark, and then it gets light again; we know this, or at least believe it.

It is not my intention to write a philosophy of the night, nor is there any thought of returning to a romantic 'nocturnal view of life'.[24] It is much more a question of analysing the development of a curious confrontation: in the hundred years from 1830 to 1930 the long-familiar night is subjected to a process of terrific change, of accelerating transformation. The phenotype of the night changes a great deal, first of all through progress in street and shop-window lighting, and the increase in traffic, and the *manner of speaking* about the night takes on new – modern – forms. Nevertheless the basic structure is preserved, and from the relationship between this ponderous and firmly rooted basic structure and its so decisively altered appearance numerous conflicts, contradictions and non-simultaneities arise.

*Non-simultaneities*: various groups within a society, within a city, for example, develop different conceptions, forms of perception and behaviour regarding (not only) the night, on the basis of their respective experiences and living conditions. Some welcome the new light, the new forms of entertainment, or new ways of organizing the police; others recoil from the new possibilities and the new challenges, seeing *their image of the city* endangered.

It is particularly interesting to observe this process in the metropolis at the time of its formation. As a rule new technological achievements reached the 'city' – though only certain of its areas and regions! – quicker than they did the 'countryside'. In the cities there existed forms of public discussion (and they spread) in which the advantages and disadvantages of the new developments were discussed. In the course of the formation of the modern city, there emerge individual regions in which 'modernization' is achieved with varying speed and varying intensity – and in which it is also perceived in different ways. This *production of non-simultaneity* is more than a side effect, it is a constituent element of the modernization process.

*Contradictions*: in many parts 'the night' remains, let us say in 1840, what it had been for generations, a time of retreat from the outside to the inside, from the street to the house, a time for sleep, rest and regeneration – and also the time for ghost stories. At the same time, in other parts, the night is already taking on other forms: one goes out, in search of pleasure, entertainment, distraction. The word 'parts' should not be understood only geographically. Individuals' and groups' relationships with the city are marked by many factors: attachment to a particular class, sex or religion, their roots in different traditional worlds and their regulations, their situation in terms of work-place and residence.

On closer inspection 'the night' in Paris or Berlin in the 1840s dissolves into many different views of the night. Rich and poor, men and women, young and old, immigrants and old-established inhabitants, those who live in central areas and those who live at the periphery, the single and the married – they all have different images of the night and they experience it in different ways.

This is why we find numerous 'contradictions' in the sources of the day. In the same year and in the same city one author describes the night as friendly, another as hostile, here one is (still?) speaking about the 'terror', there (already?) about 'fascination'. These contradictory findings are part of the public debate about night in the cities, a fundamental precondition of the social discourse. The aim of research cannot be to iron out these contradictions; on the contrary, it has to make them speak.

*Conflicts*: different views about how the hours of night are best to be organized and fitted into the daily routine almost inevitably come into conflict. Public struggles break out early on between those who (still?) see the night as a closed-off time of retreat and those who want to open it up for life – for pleasure and work; a fight develops between the representatives of a strict nocturnal order and those who question it. It is a fight that lasts a long time, and accompanies the history of the nocturnal city; the arguments used in it, the images of the city developed by the adversaries, are keys to an understanding of the discussion about modernity.

The night – and the ways of dealing with it, ways of talking about it – draws our attention to the unfinished, not quite perfect modernization of our society, our cities. Here the two-sided nature of the social process we call modernization becomes apparent. On the one hand industrialized society presents its acquisitions and achievements in a particularly lustrous, 'glowing' fashion: out of an almost inaccessible, in many ways 'forbidden' terrain it creates a realm of (almost) universal accessibility, a gigantic leisure and entertainment business; on the other hand there also emerges in the night of the cities a field of new, 'modern' dangers and obstacles.

Henri Lefèbvre equated the process of modernization with the 'image of the city', 'which tends towards a concept (that is, towards knowledge)':[25] many phenomena which present a challenge to perception can in time be rationally explained, captured in concepts and composed into a realist picture. But this happens slowly and irregularly, precisely in the city, because there are always new phenomena coming along that demand explanation, and there are always individuals left behind who cannot cope with the new demands. The process by which the 'moonlit magic night' becomes the 'miserable darkness of the big city', which is then itself illuminated by the 'luxury and security lights of the public lighting system',[26] does not come about at the flick of a switch, and the earlier conditionings are preserved alongside the new forms of perception.

Science often deals, without acknowledging it, with subjects that have something of the 'uncanny' about them, covering this up with a veneer of rationality which gives the appearance of transparency without really producing it. In this way the fantastical, irrational part of things, stories and behaviours, which is difficult to understand, remains largely unexplored. There is a form of 'enthusiasm for the night' which obviously belongs to the past. Those who deal with the modern night are well advised to take seriously the texts in which the *fascination of the nocturnal* lives on. The texts of the 'night-enthusiasts' make one aware of the relativity of the 'enlightenment' process. What could be read as 'irrational' and thus be disqualified has a special place in the history of the night. The conjurors of magic who succumb to the fascination of the nocturnal, the story-tellers and solitary nocturnal ramblers who again and again dare to cross over onto the 'night side' of the city testify to the permanence of a deeply rooted desire.

## 4 *Themes of the night: security, morality, accessibility*

There are three fundamental areas in which conflicts are played out: *security*, *morality*, and – lying across the other areas, and penetrating both – *accessibility*.

In the years around 1830 to 1840 a process begins in which the nocturnal city 'opens up'; in the same way as the outer walls of the city are falling, the solid barriers within it that have existed for centuries are also dissolving. At first the authorities see every step along this road as a *security problem*: if there are more people about at night than before, and there are then also potentially more of them who make use of the opportunities of the night for their own dark purposes, then new steps must be taken to (re)establish security. This is how the authorities see it, in London no differently than in Paris or Berlin, and as a consequence there develop new forms of organization of nocturnal security, which in turn change the picture of the night. It is not surprising that other groups of urban society see it differently; they hope for and demand a new freedom of movement in the city, even at night, and they experience the measures taken by the authorities as restrictions. The conflict between the desire for freedom on the one hand and the desire for order on the other accompanies the debate about the metropolitan night, generating interesting materials which provide information not just about the various organizational possibilities but also about the different images of the night.

The gradually extended freedom of movement leads to a second change: 'prostitution is a nocturnal animal', as it was put concisely by the criminologist Gotthold Lehnerdt,[27] and the 'new' night promotes new forms of public sexuality, which pose a considerable challenge and danger to the existing conception of morality. This is how the situation is seen by the representatives of the 'morality movement', the church people, city fathers, guardians of morality of various provenance. Here too, not everyone sees it the same way, and for many the promise of greater freedom counts for more than the supposed danger to morality and decency. The image of the city night is marked by this conflict and public debate about prostitution and the way to deal with it and all its 'side effects'. We can also learn much from these conflicts and from this debate, about how contemporaries imagined the night – what they hoped for, what they feared.

When regulations which strictly regulated access to the city are dropped or relaxed, there finally comes about a third change and the question of *access* to the city night leads back to a realization of inequalities and non-simultaneity. The poor and the rich, men and women, migrants and locals have different possibilities of access, see themselves confronted by different limits. The conflicts around

23

security and morality in the night also relate to the fundamental question of for whom – when, with what rights, and with what restrictions – is access to the nocturnal city open: to whom does the night belong? Who can dispose of it? Here too we can follow over the years a long-drawn-out social debate freighted with metaphors, images, and associations, and it is in many ways an instructive one.

## 5 *Ways of speaking about the night*

In these debates, which were mostly conducted in public, there crystallized over the years certain *ways of speaking* about the night, 'languages of the night'[28] rich in metaphors and stories. But these languages are not reliable; various concepts always make their appearance, but often bearing different meanings. This is not the place for an extensive presentation of all the connotations and associations that have since long ago been linked with the word 'night'; the Grimm brothers' *Deutsche Wörterbuch* as well as the controversial yet informative *Handwörterbuch des deutschen Aberglaubens* provide an enormous amount of evidence on this.[29] In our context, the decisive thing is that the imaginary world and associations of the word 'night' still have a hold on the minds of those who lived through the beginnings of the *modern* night. The talk of 'secrets' and 'wonders' of the night that we find in fairy tales and legends, and also in Romantic literature, could not be extinguished by the rise of electric lighting. The ghosts remained in memory, even if reason is little by little killing them off. 'The electric light bulb in a room now robbed of shadows did far more to rob the night of its terrors than did Voltaire, for example', said Ernst Bloch.[30] But the fears and terrible imaginings traditionally linked to the night do not disappear so quickly, not as quickly as the new, 'rational' forms of dealing with the night come into being. In November 1819 the *Kölnische Zeitung* vehemently agitated against the new forms of lighting, amongst others

> for theological reasons: because it appears as an interference with God's order, according to which night is for darkness, only interrupted at certain times by moonlight; . . . for philosophical and moral reasons: morality is worsened by street lighting. The artificial brightness chases from the mind the horror of darkness that keeps the weak from many a sin.[31]

When in November 1965 the first big blackout 'darkened' New York, the most modern city in the world (what a reversal: as if the artificial light was the natural one, as if darkness had to be created artificially), the fears one had thought banished returned:

> We were all told again and again that it could never happen . . . We could go about our business without fear of the dark . . . With the blackout these fears came back, and stronger, because our experts had proved to be so wrong . . . One way or another it made most of us in the dark realize acutely that the dilemma of modern man is that he lives in a society he does not really understand and cannot really control.[32]

This is how far one had from the moment when the inhabitants of the early nineteenth-century city were confronted for the first time by the artificial light of the gas lamps, to the moment when the inhabitants of the brightest city unexpectedly and quite unprepared found themselves in darkness. Contrary to what we are asked to believe by a history of 'illumination' written from the point of view of the light, what lies between is no history of forward-storming progress. It is the story of changing relations between light and dark, in which the beauty *and* the terror of the night function as bearers of memory.

## 6  *Excursions into the city night*

'Nocturnal home-comers to the Hansa quarter always look as if they wanted to go somewhere else'.[33] For Wolf Jobst Siedler and his co-authors Elisabeth Niggemeyer and Gina Andress in 1964, the town planning and urban development of the post-war period have 'killed off, with the night life, the disreputable charm of the metropolitan'.

Is 'night life' now dead? This sounds quite improbable, particularly in Berlin. It is more the case that a certain form of nocturnal life and experience has been lost. There are of course the tours from one bar to the next, undertaken in larger groups, but the peculiarities of the night are no hindrance to those who take part in them. The uncontrollable aspects that were feared – 'disorder, vice, indecency, unfathomability'[34] – were as a rule ascribed to the street, and this is why organized night tours prefer to lead their visitors from one closed *place*, from one establishment to the next.[35] References in the media refer exclusively to events within closed spaces, and reports on 'night life' follow the same schema.

The reading of such texts leads to a picture of the nocturnal city made up of many points that change from time to time – but the connections, the paths between these places, do not play any part in it. This domination of *places* has led to the fact that they and what happens in them are seen as representative of 'night life'. This promotes the creation and spread of clichés: 'Sometimes one has the impression that the tourists are moving in a gigantic theatrical production that has been arranged specially for them.'[36]

Those who deal with the big city of the nineteenth century think inevitably of Paris, 'La Ville Lumière', the 'capital' of the period,[37] and the capital of light as well. London on the other hand, the biggest city in the world, the metropolis of commerce and the markets, was the city with the first gas lights and ahead of Paris in many technical developments. Berlin became a metropolis only from 1870 onwards, but then experienced many changes in a very short time. A comparison of London, Paris and Berlin gives one a picture of different stages in the history of the night, the lags and leads that generated a real competition: which was the most modern, most safe, most lively, which was the 'true' world city? The attraction of the mythical night-places remains unbroken despite all the changes since, and it is maintained in the excursions which lead tourists through 'Paris-by-night'. As György Konrad put it, in the European cities 'there is the opportunity to look around', 'the unfathomable and inexhaustible enigma of the cities, their density an accumulation of mysteries – a first-class European fortune'.[38] Is this fortune accessible, obtainable? Can we imagine the night of the 1840s, 1870s, 1900s or 1930s, for example, during a walk through the nocturnal city of the present? The attempt might be worth it, and in this way we may familiarize ourselves with the landscape in which the events of the following chapters are played out.

PARIS

'In this great city', enthused the cultural historian Alexander von Gleichen-Rußwurm, 'the cultivated reader is never alone.'[39] Particularly 'on the boulevards', he says, the curious stroller may meet the 'figures of literary immortality'; it is indeed literature, like no other medium, that stimulates the imagination of the city rambler: do cities 'tell stories', do stones 'speak' – or do they serve only as the echo of our own promptings?

Let us go 'on the boulevards': a possible starting-point for our excursion would be the Palais Royal, the former city residence of the Dukes of Orléans and until 1836 the centre of Parisian nocturnal activities:[40] its arcades were once *the* prostitutes' catwalk. Today at night it is quiet and deserted. If we follow Julien Lemer's description and trace the path of a small group of nocturnal revellers, of 'noctambules', after their meeting place closed down for the night, it leads along the avenue de l'Opéra, today mostly a shopping street, and the boulevard des Italiens, passing the Printemps and Lafayette department stores, to the northern part of the inner ring of boulevards which surrounds the old centre of the city and separates it from the 'faubourgs', the former artisans' and workers' suburbs.

Along this stretch, which changes its name three times – boulevard de Montmartre, boulevard Poissonière, boulevard de Bonne-Nouvelle – on the way to the porte Saint-Martin, where we will take a break, there stood the most famous theatres, cafés and varieties, and of course the passage des Panoramas and the passage Jouffroy, the most splendid arcades of the heyday of the boulevards.[41] This was the stage for the aristocratic and bourgeois *flâneurs*, as it has been described hundreds of times in literature[42] and as we will encounter it many times again.

As on the Champs Elysées further west, we also see here the transformation of cafés into fast-food restaurants, small theatres into action and porno cinemas, and second-hand bookshops into new bookshops and poster supermarkets. Particularly during the evening hours, the traffic flows incessantly, pushing pedestrians to the edge and making it difficult to cross the street. Here one can see 'night life' in its etiolated form as the 'supply of goods for self-gratification'.[43]

A second starting-point for our imaginary excursion through Paris by night could be the site of the Halles Centrales, the former central market. The 'belly of Paris' described by Emile Zola had already lost its original function at the end of the 1960s when the market moved to Rungis. But it was only the demolition in 1972, amidst much protest, of the halls themselves, a steel and glass construction by the architect Victor Baltard, in which a nocturnal subculture had very quickly developed, that radically changed the character of the area.[44] A kind of nocturnal entertainment lives on in the shadow of the largely subterranean concrete construction of the Forum des Halles, but the market halls' function as the 'melting-pot' of Paris has been lost. From here the route leads in the direction of the Centre Beaubourg, and then onwards to the north: running parallel to each other there are the rue Saint-Denis, with its small side alleys, the traditional area for street prostitution, and the boulevard Sébastopol, driven through in the course of Haussmann's trans-formations of the 1860s as a means of military access to the revolu-tionary faubourgs.[45] Today the 'Sébasto' almost exclusively serves traffic, and leads to the Northern and Eastern train stations. The rue Saint-Denis is above all frequented by foreign tourists who prefer to view rather than actually sample the supply of an increasingly industrialized and brutalized form of prostitution. Here too a process of change is taking place, with old-established inhabitants, café tenants and shop-keepers no longer being able to afford the rising rents – 'histoires de la nuit parisienne' can hardly any longer be gathered from people who know them at first hand.[46]

A third possible starting-point for a nocturnal stroll is the neigh-bourhood around the place de la Bastille. In recent years what had earlier been an artisan area has become chic, with the construction of the *Opéra populaire* and its inauguration in the anniversary year of 1989. The old workshops are being converted into 'lofts', and the departure of the furniture manufacturers is accelerating the process. Today the area is more lively during the hours of night than it used to be, but an entertainment industry imported from the 5th and 6th arrondissements (which in turn have lost in nocturnal activity because of the relocation of the universities to peripheral districts) is bringing greater uniformity, and has also reached a street of great significance in the history of Paris: the rue de Lappe, a narrow alley which was for decades the meeting point of the 'apaches', small-time gangsters and pimps, the scene of knifings (and even more the scene of countless films about knifings), but also the street of the *bals musettes*, the traditional dance halls – all in all a street which had considerable appeal for the rich and for foreigners who wanted to take a peek at the 'underworld' without coming to grief. There are still many 'Paris-by-night' tours which take in the rue de Lappe, but the magic of the past is hard to find.

From here the Eastern Boulevards lead over the place de la République and the boulevard Saint-Martin to the porte Saint-Martin. We can still follow the route along the rue du faubourg Montmartre and the rue Notre-Dame-de-Lorette which Parisian revellers used to take in the late 1880s, away from the boulevards and up to Montmartre, to the place Pigalle, a centre of nocturnal entertainment since the establishment of the Moulin Rouge in 1889. On the whole of the place Pigalle there is only one bar left, Les Noctambules, which has not yet given up its claim to be the starting-point and contact-point for all nocturnal pleasures. Elsewhere the rip-off rules, and bus-loads of tourists are dragged through the production of 'Paris-by-night' specially arranged for them. Nevertheless the streets here, like those around the Bastille and the Centre Beaubourg, remain lively until late at night, and here you can also meet people whose greatest pleasure is a night-time walk.

LONDON

There are two paths through nocturnal London. They mark an inter-esting historic change, because today the appearance of the various areas at least partially contradicts their earlier function. On the one hand there is the West End, with Soho and the area around Covent Garden. The 'Sin Map of London in Victorian Times'[47] which locates the focal points of nocturnal life there and in the Haymarket has become of only limited use as guide. In the 1860s, suffering from insomnia, Charles Dickens sketched the nocturnal goings-on in Covent Garden, a centre of nocturnal London, and around 1900 Robert Machray described Piccadilly Circus as follows: 'The Circus suddenly buzzes with life; it hums like a giant hive. Here are move-ment, colour and a babel of sounds.'[48] In the 1920s the theatres and night-clubs attracted people hungry for entertainment to Soho. As an entertainment area Soho has developed in a similar way to Times Square in New York, to St Pauli in Hamburg (and the way it will probably happen to the Place Pigalle): with the arrival of the sex industry with its peep-shows and live-shows in the 1970s the area lost some of its reputation and the inhabitants left the area. In the 1980s one saw more of the dark side of 'Swinging London', the image of the night-time street being characterized by the presence of homeless people. According to an observer of 1989, the life of leisure withdrew more and more from the street into private spaces and closed societies, leaving the impression that 'in comparison to other world cities London has only a very limited social life'.[49] In the 1990s this has changed again, and Soho seems to have been successfully

29

rehabilitated. Today the streets of the area are once again attractive to a wider public, very much like Covent Garden where the traditional central market has been swept away but its character as a place of evening entertainment has been retained.

A second walk takes us to an area which is also undergoing dramatic changes. While Soho was threatening to change from a place of brilliance to a place of misery, the East End underwent a 'revaluation' which attempted to alter its character completely. Even today this area is not to be found on the visitors' maps of Central London; for tourists London ends at Tower Bridge, though for night researchers this is where it starts. The areas of Whitechapel, Limehouse, Bethnal Green, Poplar and Wapping include the London docks – white patches on the map. As a result of the decline of the old port the former wharves and warehouses are being transformed into expensive flats, artists' studios and office complexes, and new subway connections are being built. But as yet this process has only reached a small part of Wapping and Tower Hamlets; the others are still areas of poverty, joblessness, hopefully a half-way house for emigrants on the way to America but often enough the end of the road, regions of social unrest. They are nonetheless the places where the new (sub)cultures of the immigrants from the Commonwealth are being developed.

This was the field of investigation for Henry Mayhew's journalistic study of *London Labour and the London Poor*,[50] for the scientific analysis of *Life and Labour of the People in London* by Charles Booth[51] and for Beatrice Webb's *My Apprenticeship*,[52] and it was here that William Booth founded the Salvation Army. Hardly any tourists find their way here, with one exception: there are excursions on the tracks of 'Jack the Ripper', for the murders of 1888 all took place in Whitechapel. This is why almost daily in the early evening hours one finds groups of tourists moving along the streets of the East End, grouped almost fearfully around their guide. The tours end up in a pub called the 'Jack the Ripper', with historic newspaper cuttings on the walls, a true horror museum of all the clichés of the city night: criminality, prostitution, police, insecurity and fear.

BERLIN

Excursions into the night have been easier to organize since the whole of Berlin has become accessible, though some elements of nocturnal life in the East are threatening to go under soon, under the onslaught of 'Western' night culture. Our route starts in the Mitte, the central district. The alley An der Königsmauer has not existed for a long time, being sacrificed in 1887 to the construction of the Kaiser-Wilhelmstrasse, the extension of the Unter den Linden towards Alexanderplatz (today still Karl-Liebknechtstrasse). This was the old centre of Berlin prostitution until its role was taken over by the Friedrichstrasse. While the area behind the former royal palace has been destroyed and altered beyond recognition, the Friedrichstrasse follows its old course; we will have to wait to see what will happen to it in this new period that has erupted in Berlin. In the years around 1900, after being relieved by the new shopping streets and entertainment streets in the West, it was *the* symbol of Berlin by night; its history, from a GDR point of view, has been partially documented in recent years.[53]

If one walks along the Friedrichstrasse to the Oranienburger Tor, and from there again in the direction of the Alexanderplatz, then one will have more or less walked an area of the city which played an important role in the history of the Berlin night: in front of the Rosenthaler Tor and the Hamburger Tor was the Vogtland described by Bettine von Arnim, the largest concentration of paupers in Berlin. The Scheunenviertel followed, which in the years of industrialization accommodated the 'overflow' of the Berlin proletariat, the quarter soon coming to stand, according to Eike Geisel, for 'poverty, immorality and crime'.[54] Geisel described the difficulties of searching for traces in the former Scheunenviertel: one finds façades and empty rooms, and it is for the imagination of the melancholic rambler to fill the gaps with the cast and scenery of a long-gone night life.

In 1930 WEKA (Willy Pröger) published a report on a 'truly not very easy walk'[55] through the sites of Berlin prostitution; it took him from the Schlesische Bahnhof (today the Ostbahnhof) along the Krautstrasse, Berlin's proletarian "Chinese quarter", to the Alexanderplatz, and then through Mulackstrasse into the former Scheunenviertel – 'The first port of call going west is the area around the Oranienburger Tor' – then continuing through the Friedrichstrasse and the 'Passage' in the direction of the Hallesches Tor, then the Potsdamer Strasse in the direction of Bülowbogen and the Nollendorfplatz, and finally into the middle of the 1920s city of light, with the Tauentzien, the Gedächtniskirche and the Kurfürstendamm. It is a walk from darkness into light, from the East to the West, from the 'old' Berlin night from before the turn of the century into the 'new' night of the 1920s.

Today the road from East to West is open and WEKA's route can be walked again. The old West Berlin was (and is) famous for its nocturnal attractions – the only German city without fixed closing-times – while at night the former East Berlin, with the exception of certain small enclaves, counted as one of the most closed areas in Europe. There is however a common trait to be observed: in both halves of the city today (or until today?), unlike in Paris, nocturnal *street* life for various reasons does not play a significant role. In the last few years a new entertainment district has developed out of the ruins and remnants of the 'alternative' places that thrived during 1989/90 around Hackescher Markt and the Mitte district. 'Night life' was (and is?) on both sides linked to closed locations, to fixed (even if changing) institutions, to 'establishments'. This finding prompts a question about the relationship, the reciprocal influence between 'places' and streets – and about how this development away from the street and towards enclosed spaces came about, how the idea developed that nocturnal entertainment is to be found in enclosed spaces, while the terrors of the night are linked to the street.

# 11 A Beginning: Big City Nights Around 1840

> Too much life, badly canalized, makes for fear. It is urgently
> necessary that order should prevail in the city if one is no
> longer to fear going out in the evening.
>
> ARLETTE FARGE (1979)[1]

News of the nocturnal metropolis from the time before the nineteenth
century generally comes to us in the form of reports on disturbances
of a well-established order: *l'ordre urbain* stands for an ideal of
control that extends a fine-spun web of permitted and prohibited
pathways over the city, assigning all its inhabitants to determinate
places within this labile functional framework and providing institutions to monitor and sanction breaches of the regulations.

Breaches of order endanger control, and deviations from the prescribed paths challenge their exclusive jurisdiction over the organization of life in the city. Absolute control over the city could only be
achieved if all life and all movement in it were to freeze – and then it
would no longer be the city; so it is a question of channelling movements as much as possible and keeping as close a watch as possible
on the 'arteries' through which life pulsates. Control of the city is in
particular control of the street, because it is here rather than in the
more easily supervised indoor spaces that the threat of disorder is
greatest. What can be pressed into a rigid order there, the police fear,
may break free and 'pour out' onto the street.[2]

The street is the site of confrontation between the different social
groups in the city, and between these groups on the one hand and
the forces of order on the other. From the point of view of the
custodians of the law there is always *trop de vie*, too much life on
the street. They therefore develop mechanisms which are supposed
above all to restrict the manifold functions of the street, strategies to
produce clarity and order-creating spatial division. This idea of the
street as *site of confrontation* allows one to see the existence of many
different groups, many different ways of life in the city. In the eyes of

The old night was quiet: the night-watchman was in control, protecting the sleeping city, his calls providing a sense of security. Soon enough, however, the city would 'come out of its shell', even at night. *Job as Night-watchman*, lithograph after a painting by J. P. Hasenclever, 1852.

the authorities there is a danger that conflicts could arise from the clash of various groups (and interests) on the streets: disturbances of order. So their agents mix 'with the people', they patrol the streets, making themselves visible. The sight of the police officer who tries to control – from the centre of the action – what cannot be controlled by decree 'from the top', is part of the picture of the street. He symbolizes the claim that power reaches into the furthest corners. But the claim cannot ever be totally made good, for the supervised find means – and ways! – to elude supervision, and they discover the street as an ally.[3]

Both sides – if we maintain this polarity for the moment, for there are of course intermediary forms and transitions – form for themselves a picture of the city according to their own interests, a *mental topography of paths of flight and pursuit*, of *spaces of security and of insecurity*, of confidence and fear, of domination and subordination.

At night this struggle achieves a dimension of its own. The danger of the development of uncontrolled spaces increases with darkness. Even more strictly than during the day the regulations insist that at night all inhabitants of the city should stay where they belong. Those who abandon the prescribed paths at night even more clearly throw order into question.

## 1 *Signals of the night*

The arrival of night is announced by cries or other acoustic signals, signs that the inhabitants are to close off the city from the outside and, within it, 'to close their shutters and retire into their houses'.[4] The voices of the night-watchmen are evidence of the constant presence of the authorities: 'Through the whole night, in all the cities of the world, the night-watchmen reassure the inhabitants with their punctual cries'.[5] Here the functions of reassurance and control can hardly be separated, because without a doubt the security measures met a widespread need.[6] Retreat into one's own home, so far as it is available, provides the necessary protection from the dangers of the night, which are 'locked out', banished to the street – and so ascribed to it. At night, one's habitation is invulnerable, as a rule not even accessible to the police.[7] Those who leave the protection of home not only place themselves in danger but also render themselves suspect. The ideal of power is the separation between the good

35

citizen lying in his bed and the 'wicked schemer who sneaks around in the dark'.[8]

Stories about the deviationists, the *night-walkers*, construct a repellent picture from suggestions of immorality, disruption of order and work-shyness:

> When some lucky devil's carriage rolls thundering into the yard, bringing him home from a night of partying, the industrious artisan tears himself from the arms of sleep in order to earn by a whole day's labour as much for himself and his numerous family as his first-floor neighbour's coachman spent on wine and brandy that night out of sheer boredom.[9]

This introduces a motif which will become firmly established in the ongoing debate about the big city, the *image of the meeting at dawn* – but the division into 'good' sleepers and industrious early-risers on the one hand and 'bad' night-revellers on the other does not quite come off. The image also provoked envy in many an 'industrious artisan' and pride in the 'lucky devils', who appropriated the story for themselves and retold it as proof of their greater freedom.

## 2 First transgressions and centres of nocturnal activity

The phrase 'the sleeping city' is not however entirely accurate, and with the growth of the big cities it becomes more and more of a myth: the boundaries of the night are burst open very early on both sides. On the one hand the creation and development of *markets*,[10] and on the other the establishment of *centres of entertainment and extravagance*,[11] leads to the emergence of centres of nocturnal activity in the heart of the cities. Both types of centre extend their circles of influence, establishing off-shoots in other places, and communicating pathways are established between these focal points: there crystallizes a new topography of the nocturnal city.

The growing population of the city has increasingly to be supplied from outside, and in the market halls the beginning of work shifts earlier and earlier into the night hours. Near the markets public houses are opened which are given permission to stay open until the early morning hours or to start selling wine at that time.[12] Markets and taverns in turn attract a swelling number of casual workers, who make themselves at home in this 'little world' and make it their own. In Paris this world emerges in the middle of the old, overcrowded city centre, and in the eyes of the authorities the city appears endangered from within, its old core becoming a potential seat of fire. The inner-city space, the area around the market halls, becomes, in real terms, the space of the night, street after street becoming involved in the web of nocturnal public activity.

At the same time, in the last years of the eighteenth century, there begins to form a second focal point of urban life, which also puts the existing equilibrium into question: the Palais Royal. The transformation of the 'favoured rendezvous of the aristocracy'[13] into a *Palais marchand* with high-class shops and promenades was already complete in 1784, but after the Revolution and in the first years of Napoleonic rule in particular it was described in the literature of Paris as the centre of elegant social life. According to contemporary reports it became particularly lively in the evening hours. Life in the Palais Royal, much described, stands for one side of the nocturnal history of Paris: splendour and pleasure congregated here and functioned as a pole of attraction. Here visitors were to a certain extent safe from the adversities of the street. The clientèle of the shops and promenades, however, also proved a strong attraction for prostitutes. It is they who created the *pathway between both nocturnal focal points* in Paris, and their provocative presence is mentioned in every contemporary guide or travelogue.

In the descriptive accounts of cities which were becoming increasingly numerous at the end of the eighteenth century, there gradually developed from concrete observations a tendentially abstract 'concept of the metropolis detachable from individual phenomena'.[14] In travels and city descriptions, of course, the particularities of different cities are described, but at the same time the travellers noticed that there were typical *motifs of metropolitan life* that could be found in many places. The authors of these early reports worked like journalists, like reporters: they would consciously and deliberately transgress the limits that had been until then established; they would go themselves to the places and locations within the city that were seen as taboo. The ambiguity of their mode of operation is visible in the fact that they themselves were not so sure of their ground, that they often drew moralizing pictures of manners as something of a deterrent and with the intention of emphasizing their own courage – or wrote 'books of advice and instruction' ('how to go about the streets in the daytime, and whether one should go out at night?')[15] –

travel guides to the newly discovered jungle which fed on the 'old' fears and pre-modern intimidations.

The ideal map of nocturnal Paris changed on two sides. The Halles and the Palais Royal are not even a kilometre apart; in contemporary reports the road from the place of elegant pleasure to the place of work and of rougher entertainment is described as a gradual descent from light into darkness. The metaphor had its real basis in the different state of street-lighting,[16] but quickly became independent, a topos of 'light and shadow', of 'splendour and misery'.

'But the significance of the large city in relation to the development of luxury', says Werner Sombart in his study of the spirit of extravagance, 'lies chiefly in the fact that it suggested new possibilities in gay and opulent living, creating thereby novel forms of luxury. The city is responsible for making available to large sections of the populace the enjoyment of festivities which heretofore had been the privilege only of members of the ruling court.'[17] As evidence Sombart quotes the story of the Prince of Monaco, who at the end of the eighteenth century went to London and thought that 'the many lights in the street as well as in the windows of the shops, which were kept open until 10 o'clock,' had been lit in his honour. Sombart concedes that in these years the 'fundamental transformation' of the strictly private development of luxury into a collective development is only beginning. Nevertheless, it is not surprising that the reference is to the evening, to the lights; evening life – and particularly night life – is luxury, the privilege of the few, it has its place in the residences of the mighty and in their environs. From there it spreads out.

The places where, according to Sombart, the life of luxury takes place – theatres, music halls, ballrooms, restaurants, hotels and shops – display certain common characteristics: here various forms of entertainment, of sociability and of the organization of leisure are raised to a new level, and here we may indeed observe the slow generalization of lifestyles formerly restricted to the privileged and aristocratic. Through imitation a gradually forming stratum of urban bourgeoisie is finding its own forms of entertainment; the partly public display of wealth worked for (rather than inherited) plays a central role in this, demonstrating the new self-confidence of an industrialized generation which in its leisure borrows from the aristocracy, but which is at pains to differentiate itself from the 'top' as well as from the 'bottom': *to have time and to organize one's time,*

38

according to one's own inclinations and one's own possibilities, is to have achieved something.

The imitation of upper-class entertainment, however, is only one element that nourishes bourgeois urban entertainment life. Another is the forms of celebration and entertainment of the lower social classes; the English variety show, according to Ernst Günther, clearly has its prehistory in the street ballads and 'music-hall songs' performed in simple taverns, distinguished not only by their coarseness and humour, but in particular by a critical treatment of political and social ills. The more the music halls turned towards the bourgeois public the more their shows and performances lost piquancy and directness; Charles Morton, who opened the Saint George Tavern and after that another half dozen theatres, 'banished vulgarity and anything too primitive, "organized" the spectacle and made demands on his public in terms of dress, nobility and discipline'.[18] Perhaps Günther's Marxist interpretation tends to ascribe too elevated a theme to proletarian entertainment, but he is probably correct in his assessment: bourgeois amusement also drew on the rich fund of pre- or even anti-bourgeois forms of entertainment and transformed them in accordance with its own needs. To do this some elements of this culture had to be polished and 'bourgeoisified', while others were retained, at least as pastiche, as for example the habit of insulting the elegant audience that was cultivated as part of their performance by such as Aristide Bruant in Paris or Hans Hyan in Berlin.

Hotels, shops, restaurants, playhouses and variety theatres share a further common trait: all of them also represent spaces of withdrawal. They may be for the public, but they nevertheless refuse direct contact with the street. It was in this form of 'night life' rather than in wholly public space that the *time of night* was first used in a new way. The evening and night life of these closed spaces is created within a contradiction that will accompany it: it is a life *in* the night, and at the same time a life *without* it. One leaves the security of one's own home only in order to enter as quickly as possible into other buildings, in which is presented or served up some-thing different from home: a little freedom, a little rudeness perhaps, made consumable, without terror. What threatens the domestic framework, or cannot develop its potential within it, is transferred outside – luxury seeks a public – but it is not taken onto the street, which remains a dangerous place. It is taken – new clothes, new mores, new ideas – to the meeting places of similarly situated people, where these are exchanged, traded, demonstrated, and what has just developed is reduced to a tolerable scale (that is also acceptable to the authorities). Nevertheless, even in these closed spaces evening life is developed and multiplied, which in turn has an effect on the outside: illuminated windows, shop-fronts at least, generous and lavishly decorated entrances, and the noises from inside these establishments little by little open up the restaurants and shops onto the street.

The authorities face the problem of how to keep the focal points under control in various ways. In this they also encounter social differentiation: one cannot deal with the noble and bourgeois public in the same way as with the 'plebs' in the neighbourhood of Les Halles; and threatening confrontations between the two groups have to be avoided as well.

## 3 Under the eye of the police: rag-merchants, beggars, prostitutes

At the same time as the early journalists and city travellers, the state authorities also 'discover' – through their representatives, the police – the changes occurring in the areas to be policed; their attention is directed towards the same places and the same people that have captivated the interest of the reporters, and like them the police at first have at their disposal an anachronistic apparatus of concepts and possibilities of action. Only little by little do the powers that be form a total picture of the 'new' night, painfully pieced together from individual events and localities.

To begin with the police are dealing with groups and places of the night with which they are already familiar, and at first they classify 'new' developments only in terms of categories already formulated before their appearance.

A good example of this is the way the *chiffonniers*, the Paris rag-merchants, are treated in the documents of the Paris Prefecture of Police. They were familiar from the days before the Revolution, fulfilling, on the edge of society but not beyond it, an important function in keeping the city clean; they also functioned as a focal point for other socially marginal groups. Traditionally they went about their business at night, and they moved through it with

40

natural ease. This made them suspect; 'the story went about that under *cover of night* they were using their trade to commit all sorts of crimes as they roamed through the streets of Paris'.[19]

The police not only kept voluminous files on individual rag-merchants (and whole family dynasties of them)[20] but also followed their traces, getting to know the nocturnal city better in the course of these expeditions through the Paris streets. The areas where the rag-merchants lived in the peripheral quarters of the city were early on identified as the 'hiding-place' of criminals and prostitutes. The authorities, however, were completely unaware of the drastically worsening social conditions of the rag-merchants in the first years of the nineteenth century;[21] in the course of the sanitary reorganization of the city their work was to be gradually taken over by communal services, and from 1 September 1828 they were prohibited by police ordinance from exercising their trade between midnight and 5 a.m. They were dispossessed of the night that belonged to them. At the same time, the authorities saw everyone on the streets during these hours as possible *chiffonniers* contravening the regulations.

A second group on whom the authorities had always concentrated were the beggars. In the process of opening the nocturnal cities to new groups their presence on the street was seen as disturbing; already in 1800 it was said in Berlin: 'As soon as it starts getting a little dark, you cannot walk 50 paces in the main streets of the city without being molested by intrusive beggars of all shapes, ages and sexes'.[22]

It only becomes 'disturbing' when other social groups discover the need 'to go out into the night themselves – without being molested, and without being lumped together with beggars and rag-merchants. The author of this complaint about beggars suggests the establishment of 'pauper guard patrols' in order 'to keep the streets clear of beggars'. Until then this had not been necessary, because for the police they were a constituent part of the nocturnal city, easily recognizable, easy to control. Now a reorganization was needed. Reorganization however meant that the established boundaries of nocturnal life had to be redefined, and possibly extended.

The police were also disturbed by the growth in prostitution. This trade and the locations where it was 'pursued' had always been the object of the authorities' vigilance. The prostitutes were known elements of the nocturnal city, they too could be localized and relatively easily supervised; the danger ascribed to prostitution referred above all to its typical *mobility*: 'The prostitute embodied movement,

41

instability, turbulence, excitement.'[23] As long as this danger was kept within topographical bounds the supervision could limit itself to the partial restrictions that marked these limits. When prostitution begins to leave the places assigned to it, however, and spreads across the city, then the *organizational fantasy* of the authorities is challenged in novel ways, and they are forced to follow along the new paths that prostitution has established.

## 4 *The nocturnal locations are recorded*

Already in 1818 the Prefect of the Paris police was instructing his superintendents to record systematically the 'mauvais lieux' of the city. He identified *prostitution* as the 'main cause' of all the disturbances of nocturnal order: 'In this single word the saddest and most shameful sides of our society are linked'.[24] The intensified supervision was less for the existing 'maisons de tolérance' than for the 'prostitution publique', for which there were not yet any specific categories: taverns, tobacco-divans, cafés, late-closing shops and the streets in the immediate vicinity of these establishments became potentially 'bad places'.

In a further circular of 1819 the Prefect writes that closing times should be closely checked, because the spread of premises for dancing and drinking until the late hours of the night 'leads to turmoil and to nocturnal gatherings that disturb the peace of the citizen'.[25]

More and more often the disturbances concern the street, public space. Individual areas have emerged, for example in the neighbourhood of Les Halles, in which so many taverns and other *établissements* have been opened that control of these places themselves is no longer sufficient: in the years between 1820 and 1840 in Paris demands mount for an efficient 'night-watch service', a nocturnal street patrol.

## 5 *New images of the night*

Documents of the Paris police from the years around 1840 – and in the early stages also those from the Berlin police – give the impression of a city night before an explosion, before the beginning of a new era: contemporary writers also register the changes, first in

Paris. Eugène Briffault bemoans the numerous patrols of the night-watch, who disturb the quiet of the night with their presence.[26] He remembers the nights of the period *before* 1830 as pleasant and full of interesting events; but the times have changed and with them the nights as well. The old picture of the night from the time before 1830 or 1840 is already no longer true. The same goes for Berlin, which in 1831 Joseph Alois Mercy still describes as idyllic:

> The moonlight gives beauty to the perspective of the long, wide streets, the diverse forms of the tall buildings, and the view of the great squares of Berlin. I start my nocturnal walk with pleasure, and my pulse beats slower in this pleasant darkness, which I find an agreeable exchange for the burning heat, the deadly dust and rushing noise of mid-day.[27]

Here the night is still very clearly the *counterpart of the day*, reason and opportunity for contemplation; the streets are empty, 'the intrigues and passions of the inhabitants of the royal city have followed them under their roofs and show themselves only in the airy forms of their dreams'. Mercy describes 56 nights of walking peacefully through his area of the city without anything happening to him. At the beginning of the 1830s the volume *Berlin wie es ist* appears, by C. von Kertbeny. At first glance not much has changed:

> The squares and markets a few hours ago full of vivacious life are now quiet and calm, and only a few people pass through them. If the evening is pleasant and the sky without clouds, strollers pass by, but quietly and seriously, occupied partly with themselves, partly with what presents itself to them at the moment.[28]

But in fact the idyll is already broken: 'Certain areas of the city where retail trade is carried on' are lively during the evening hours, and 'wine and ale houses' also occasionally interrupt the nocturnal quiet:

> And in a few areas of the suburbs, and particularly in those parts of Berlin where loose women have taken up residence, it is particularly this hour which becomes the most lively with fights or other disturbances. To prevent all this disorder and the consequences arising from it, from the fall of dusk there are patrols from the different watches going the whole night through, changing from hour to hour and continuing their service until the break of dawn.[29]

Still, these interruptions are occasional, and with 'the arrival of the middle of the night there is the deepest silence over the whole city'. As before, the nature of the night is silence. Those who disturb it are questioning 'holy law'. But it is already noticeable in different parts of the city – where retail trade is carried on, where wine and ale houses invite the stroller to prolong the night, where the 'loose women' live – that order is in dissolution.

In this period perception of the city is confronted by particularly great challenges. The view over the *whole city*, as presented by Adalbert Stifter in Vienna in 1841, becomes a nostalgic documentation, because in fact he is no longer capable of capturing 'everything' that presents itself to the eye. Stifter's idea, in 'view and contemplation from the top of the St Stephan's tower', 'to encompass the history of a single day, a single night',[30] only succeeds as a glance into the past that is in the process of being overcome. Everything that happens before 'the day comes up, and the sun, so mild and innocent rises over the city, as over a green carpet of grass, on which the little animals play or slumber',[31] everything that characterizes the new night has been frozen in a wistful parable. In Vienna, the nocturnal city is still capable of provoking the ideal; the image of the Biedermeier city which can assign its mysterious aspect to the night – and thus control it – is, however, already endangered.

## 6 *On the street*

Contemporaries clearly locate the entertainment life of the royal city of Berlin in the Biedermeier period – 'absolutely a small town'[32] – in *definite places*, theatres, wine and coffee houses and ballrooms; the nocturnal street appears as the space of threatening dangers and conflicts, its function limited to ensuring transport from one place to the next, finally providing the way home. In the description of the city the figure of the night-watchman is often introduced to reassuring effect:

> Nocturnal security is guaranteed by the patrols sent out by the military guard and the civilian night-watch. The latter consists of 150 night-watchmen, under the supervision of ten sergeants. The night-watchmen have blue uniforms and are armed with a long staff. A whistle serves to announce the hours and a horn the outbreak of fire. They are responsible for nocturnal peace on the streets, the closing of buildings etc., and for watching over the public peace.[33]

The night-watch – whose organization will be discussed in detail – develops into a moral institution, the point of intersection between order and evasion, the testing ground for the city's capacity to maintain overview and control. The image of the night-watchman stands for this claim. In 1842, Adolf Glassbrenner draws a peaceful, carefree picture of the dreaming watchman:

> Billiard balls click against each other in the restaurants, glasses ring together in liquor-stores and wine taverns, carriages rattle and roll along, and aesthetic teas and jolly family parties *gradually rob the streets of their life*. Under the lime trees the hands of the bright Academy clock point to 9 o'clock; a significant hour for those ladies walking alone who shoot fiery glances from the fading embers of their eyes, and even address the men, when there are no police near by. At 10 o'clock it is already getting quiet and empty; the night-watchman blows his whistle and shouts: 'It strikes ten!', closes the buildings and lies on the steps close by to dream of his duties.[34]

There does exist an evening entertainment life, but it takes place indoors. For a brief moment and 'when no police are near by' the street belongs to prostitution, then there is silence.

Glassbrenner's dreaming night-watchman does not see the other side of the city. The counter-image to this is created by Max Kretzer's naturalistic novel *Meister Timpe* (1888), which treats of the 1840s in retrospect. Timpe junior sneaks home through the sleeping city in the early morning hours: '. . . it was between 3 and 4 o'clock on one of the last days of April – at that hour, *when the streets suddenly seem empty of people*, as if even the most ardent roisterer had felt the need to reach home under the protection of darkness, before the abrupt change of night and day.'[35] Timpe junior is unlucky and he is observed: night-watchman Krusemeyer and constable Liebegott are the real masters of this eastern part of the city, because they know the night and all who move in it; and he who knows the night knows the whole city: 'On his lonely walks through the dark streets he [Krusemeyer] had in time become a philosopher.' Bernhard Hesslein had found the catchy formula in his one-act play *Berlin at Midnight* (c.1844): 'Berlin is under the night-watchman.'[36]

These are literary images of the city. But they do catch something of the contradictory nature of the city night in these years around 1840. Concepts like 'metropolis' and 'metropolitan' are now used more often; for 'the Berliner too the urbanity typical of the big city is not something alien',[37] and the night becomes more important among the factors that are considered to make a city – even if the

45

judgements made on this basis are widely divergent, depending on the point of view of the observer.

For example, although in 1854 Karl Gutzkow still felt that evening in Berlin was like being in 'Herculaneum and Pompeii',[38] by 1846 Ernst Dronke could already see 'life becoming more concentrated in the city . . . toward the evening ',[39] even if this was in the tobacco and coffee houses rather than on the streets. Many activities of the city night appear in the sources, but only as the broken-mirror image of police reports and moral pamphlets. Of course they had their own reality, their own internal lives, which would be seen differently by the critical observer in the street than by one of the participants and guests at the entertainment. Forms of metropolitan entertainment like visiting a revue[40] or a ball distinguish themselves through the fact that 'going out' and 'stopping off', daring and retreat, can form into a new ensemble of experiences. The *Illustrirte Zeitung* gives us a nice example in 1844 from Kroll's Garten:

> He who sits around for hours, listening to the music and making eye contact with pretty girls, is entertaining himself in Berlin fashion. You only open your mouth in order to drink, to greet, and to let out the sudden outpourings of the heart. Because there is here so much that is surprising that the ahs and ohs stream out, and so many diverse things that you have to point out the details to each other. Almost all the nations are represented, and the different facial features and dresses are so attractive to Berliners that even without witty conversation, the spice of life, the hours fly by.[41]

Kroll's Garten was outside the centre in the Tiergarten, a favourite excursion destination, and after the visit one drove back to the city. The journey there and back was not yet part of the entertainment, least of all at night. But even for the daytime, it was only in the 1840s that the significance of the public space of the street was recognized. In his project, submitted in 1840, for 'Ornamental and boundary features for Berlin and its immediate environs', Peter Joseph Lenné, the planner of modern Berlin, wrote: 'The more a people progress in culture and prosperity, the more diverse become their sensuous and spiritual needs. This calls for public pedestrian paths whose construction and multiplication is to be urgently recommended, for reasons not only of pleasure but also of health.'[42]

This marks the beginning of the planning of modern Berlin, in which the needs of the 'working and trading classes' were to be taken into consideration, with a clear aim of their improvement. The newly forming urban society creates for itself its own 'public geography',[43] a space for public activity. With this Berlin also embarks on what has already found articulation in London and Paris as an urbanistic discourse: a public debate on the further development of the big cities, generated by the perception of pressing social problems. It is worth noting that *themes and questions of the night* play a significant role in this from the start, and also that the question of *accessibility* is already being raised.

## 7 *The city night and 'modernity'*

In the late 1830s and early 1840s the English public started to become interested in the problems of the cities, particularly those of London and the industrial regions; the Victorians, according to the historian Asa Briggs, were both 'horrified and fascinated by the new quality of the cities, which were the best evidence for the fact that in this time 'a new life' was beginning, 'based on totally new principles'.[44]

The Parisian historian Louis Chevalier puts a similar temporal emphasis; in his depiction of the city, the Paris of the first half of the nineteenth century is as alien to us today as the Paris of the Middle Ages. The transition happens in the Paris described by Baudelaire – but it is only the Paris of the 1840s and 1850s, 'that flourishes in the light of the gas lamps, illuminated by this light and as if drunk on it',[45] only this Paris that is still well known to us today; we recognize it and recognize ourselves in it.

Looking back to the years before the foundation of the Reich, the Royal Police Authority also dates the elevation of Berlin into a metropolis 'to the days of the '40s', when Berlin (partly as a result of the growing traffic on the railways) 'came *out of itself* and into lively contact with the wider world'.[46]

In all three cities in those years – and so under totally different economic and political conditions – there emerge *metropolitan* questions and problems, no doubt with locally varying emphasis, but still comparable in their new urban quality: the big cities 'come out of themselves'. One of the spaces where this process can be observed, if by no means the only one, is the nocturnal city.

In 1844, the first *Medical Topography and Statistics* of the city to appear for 50 years was published in Berlin.[47] Much space was devoted to questions of public *welfare* and public *control*; and here too the lack of public pedestrian paths was bemoaned: 'the great majority also fail to compensate in the evening hours of leisure for the adverse effects of sedentary strain through movement in the open air.' There is, however, the author continues, a legitimate need for evening relaxation; and if this need cannot be properly met, the ordered system comes apart at the seams. The doctor notices an increasing 'tendency towards sensual pleasures and sexual enjoyment', which itself corresponds to a growing 'advertisement of depravity'.

The authors of such texts do not overlook the connection with industrialization and the consequences of daily factory work; but their interest is first directed towards the city, as the location where these consequences become visible: the search for *places* in which the need for evening entertainment can be met finds an answer in the fact that 'the opportunity is paraded day and night' – on the street. According to Karl Rosenkranz in his *Topography* of Berlin, the promenade Unter den Linden represents the 'highest level of the life of sensual pleasure in Berlin' – and for the Berliner it is the badge of the 'modernity' of their city.[48]

At the same time as the places of (nocturnal) entertainment, two other areas of the public geography of Berlin move to the centre of public attention: the Vogtland, the pauper colony by the Hamburger Tor, sign of the growing misery in the city, and the narrow streets behind the royal castle, places of noticeable public indecency. Two descriptions of these very different spaces clarify the urgency of the debates:

In front of the Hamburger Tor, in the so-called Vogtland, a virtual pauper's colony has been created . . . It seems however a matter of indifference that the poorest members of a great society are herded together, more and more fenced off from the rest of the population, and *developing into a terrible counterweight.*[49]

When in 1839 prostitution in Berlin was allocated a certain hiding-place, that it had in a way delimited for itself, in the little street 'An der Königsmauer', our city's legislators were guided by the most correct views in as it were *amputating its moral disease from the body of Berlin, and isolating the diseased limb.*[50]

Misery and 'moral disease' appear as signs for the existence of an 'other' side, a *night side* of the city. At the same time and in parallel with the formation of the actual city – a process which is accompanied by pride – a 'counterweight' emerges from it, and in the process of growth of the 'body' of Berlin, an internal disease develops alongside it. The images speak unambiguously: the danger is in the fact that the counterweight might take the upper hand, and that the diseased limb, were it not radically 'amputated', might destroy the healthy body.

The debate about the future development of the city is in the main a debate about the appropriate measures – and about the responsibility for their implementation – for controlling this challenge to order. The pro-active urban planning oriented towards the future that Lenné, for example, had striven for, fell by the wayside in the face of the pressing urgency of reactive policies. In Berlin the development of a dynamic urban policy was made more difficult by the fact that 'the actual regent of the city . . . was for the whole of the nineteenth century the Chief of Police',[51] matters pertaining to security and morality being the responsibility of the police, even as they had a say in street-cleaning and urban lighting.

## 8 *The discovery of the dangerous classes*

From 1840 onwards Berlin's civic administration was able to extend its field of activities only with difficulty. For in the eyes of the police authority public poverty and public immorality were signs of a disturbance of order; and their method of dealing with the disturbing elements was indiscriminate, aimed only at their removal from the ordered cityscape. Socio-political research on causes and on the development of differentiated preventative and welfare programmes inevitably remained marginal. Significant here is a debate held in 1845–6 on the Berlin workhouse. This institution had been attacked in a book published in 1845, *Voyage en Prusse*, because criminals were thrown together with innocent people. The preacher Andrae defended the 'general purpose' of the institution, which was 'to create a great depository for the moral and possibly also physical misery of our capital city. It thus welcomes in its confines all these different classes of the unfortunate. . .',[52] while the Berlin paupers' directorate pointed out that the situation already acknowledged by Andrae was so serious 'that in this alone the Workhouse already appears to be a totally inappropriate institution'.[53]

49

Because a differentiated perception of poverty and its causes could hardly develop, the concept of 'classes dangereuses dans la population des grandes villes'[54] was adopted in Berlin too. H. A. Frégier, the Chef de Bureau of the Préfecture de la Seine, tried to answer the question set in a writing competition of what means there were for the 'bettering' of the dangerous classes. His assessment was absolutely suited to give rise to fear and terror among the wealthy. The danger, Frégier declared, lay particularly in the fact that certain parts of the population were leaving the place allocated to them, that they were wandering about the city, *errants*, without work, and so evading control. The search for their present places of residence and the paths by which they travelled the city, bringing misery and immorality in their wake, is turned by the author into a *topographie morale* of his city of Paris: no area, not even the most noble, is without its 'dark corners'; everywhere in the city one finds *quelques rues étroites*, a few narrow and out-of-the-way little streets – the city has weak points everywhere, starting-points for the destructive life form of the dangerous classes.

Certain quarters, however, are particularly dangerous: there is the *domaine particulier des prostituées, des vagabonds et des malfaiteurs*, the particular domain of prostitutes, vagabonds and malefactors: immorality, rootlessness and lawlessness are united in an impenetrable mix of danger. The great interest in these themes is an essential element of the new mentalities which crystallize with life in the big cities; it is shaped by *model experiences* like the confrontation with the 'dangerous classes' in the dark corners of the city. In 1843–4, in his serialized novel *Les Mystères de Paris*, Eugène Sue presented such model experiences and disseminated them by the thousand. Sue made the 'accidental' or 'imprudent' walk into the dark region of the city into a principle and systematized it. Critics have often noted that Sue the 'dandy'[55] supplied the 'wilderness' of the city with an aura of exoticism (and that this form of presentation was successful); at the same time he created what was to be for a long time the pattern for the description of the 'nocturnal sides' of big cities.

Not only did numerous imitators and 'mystery' writers of other cities follow in his footsteps – 'so too, as was to be expected, the mystery-fever found a particularly receptive and fertile ground in Berlin . . . that is the interest in the state of today's society, in its so-called "nocturnal sides", its lower spheres'[56] – but he also provided the impulse for the recording of social misery on a scale unknown until then.

## 9 *Ambiguous night sides*

The growing misery of the proletarian classes of the population, especially, was seen as something specifically metropolitan. In the *Mysterien von Berlin* published in 1844, the author August Brass writes that 'luxury, with its expensive companion, vice, do more and more to smudge the stamp of nationality'.[57] Although Berlin had not yet reached the 'state' in which we find Paris, Brass's introduction could be read as saying that if Berlin wanted to emulate the example of Paris and develop into a metropolis, then it had to recognize the existence of its own night sides.

In those years, however, the concept of 'night sides' was already shifting and unclear. It does not necessarily always refer to night itself, but soon the negative side of the city's development is nevertheless attributed to it. F. Gustav Kühne described the Berlin of 1843 in categories of increasing contradiction:

> The life of the streets has grown louder, the traffic of the citizens more lively. Luxury has grown, and the opulence of wealth and the misery which digs and burrows through the lower classes *confront each other more sharply*; here are now more nobility and more rabble than was usual, more perfumed arrogance and more naked crime.[58]

The place and time of this confrontation is the night. It also plays an important role in the Berlin books of the two democratic revolutionaries, Ernst Dronke and Friedrich Sass – and provides the background for their social accusations. Friedrich Sass starts his book *Berlin in seiner neuesten Zeit und Entwicklung* (1846) directly with a night scene:

> Those who wander the broad deserted streets with a heart full of despair and sorrow, while everywhere the doors are shutting . . . these will soon be discovered in their nakedness, and in the person of a night-watchman or policeman, bourgeois society will take care of them, although not in the gentlest fashion.[59]

Ejected onto the nocturnal streets and helplessly at the mercy of the authority: this is the metaphor for despair and sorrow. For the police the proof of a home, a legal nocturnal place to stay, is the precondition for the recognition of existence, and so the situation of *homelessness*, of roaming the night without aim and without rest, represents exclusion from bourgeois society.

## 10 *The mystery of the urban night*

From the beginning of this history there developed in London a different form of perception of the nocturnal city. Here too in 1832 a book was published, *The Mysteries of London* by George Reynolds, but it had a different character, and it carried a different message. In his preface, Reynolds deals with the subject of civilization, which 'withdrew from Egypt and Syria' and from there conquered the world. 'For centuries has Civilisation established, and for centuries will maintain, its headquarters in the great cities of Western Europe; and with Civilisation does Vice go hand-in-hand.'[60] The relationship between civilization and vice is the thread of his long story, and it is also linked, more strongly than in Paris or Berlin, with the contradictory pairing of wealth and poverty: 'Among these cities there is one in which contrasts of a strange nature exist. The most unbounded wealth is the neighbour of the most hideous poverty; the most gorgeous pomp is placed in strong relief by the most deplorable squalor; the most seducing luxury is only separated by a narrow wall from the most appalling misery.' Whatever the contradictions may be here, they can be traced back to the one fundamental contradiction: '. . .there are but two words known in the moral alphabet of this great city; for all virtues are summed up in the one, and all vices in the other,' and those words are

WEALTH / POVERTY

As in the biblical image of the broad and the narrow way, here too there are only two ways that start within the city, one leading to the haunts of crime, of lust and decadence; the other, full of danger, leading in the end to justice and virtue. In the mystery story which is to unfold, the paths of two brothers who start at the same point will cross, but will go in very different directions. And this story too, obeying the unwritten law of the mysteries, can only begin like this:

Our narrative opens at the commencement of July, 1831.
The night was dark and stormy. . .

Reynolds, an active Chartist who also works a positive view of the French Revolution into his novel, identifies the cause of crime as the unequal distribution of wealth and poverty.[61] At about the same time as the novel there appeared Friedrich Engels' analysis of *The Condition of the English Working Class*. The novelist sees the city differently from the political analyst, as 'an accumulation of secrets' – but his view of the world and the city is defined by the same antithesis. Reynolds, like Sue in France, became the most popular author of his day, and the image he communicated, which was almost free of any romanticization of the nocturnal urban landscape, came in time to catch the imagination of the English public. At a political level, an 'association between crime and political subversion'[62] can be seen at least in the criticism of those who saw their rule threatened by the emerging genre of the *social novel*; it was only 'in the '50s, with the end of the Chartist threat to the political system', that crime came to be seen as a structural problem of advanced industrial society. The social factor, however, is still present in the early development of the crime novel, and it is so strong that the romanticized representation of the 'underworld' that we know from Paris is here almost completely absent.

What does grow, on the other hand, is an interest in social questions that still finds political justification in the concrete social picture of the growing city. In his novel *Dombey and Sons*, published in 1848, Charles Dickens still dealt with the London of the 1820s and 1830s; *David Copperfield* also belongs to the old London. With his journalistic writing in *Household Words*, and above all with the novel *Bleak House*, however, Dickens turns to the new social questions, which can no longer be answered with a simple rejection of the workhouse system, but demand a creative imagination. Dickens's brother-in-law Henry Austin was employed by the Board of Health, as F. S. Schwarzbach tells us.[63] Working earlier as a railway engineer, he had become acquainted with the living conditions of the poor in the slums alongside the new railway lines, and he now convinced Dickens to take part in the campaign for better sanitary conditions in these areas, and even to meet Edwin Chadwick.

The years between 1830 and 1840 were a time of decisive social change for London too. 'The accession of Queen Victoria marks the commencement of an era of social legislation and of systematic efforts to improve the condition of the poorer classes hitherto unparalleled.'[64] At the start of this period there is a change in the perception of urban misery and want.

Reynolds had used the word 'mysteries' in connection with a description of poverty, overcrowding and disease in an inner-city working-class district; in the context of open and very visible poverty it seems strange and inappropriate, and so the use of this word in this instance may say something about the author and his origins. Reynolds describes the filth of the courtyards in which animals were often slaughtered: 'As if nothing should be wanting to render that district as filthy and unhealthy as possible, water is scarce.' Pigs were kept in the yard, whole families slept together in one room, the dead were not buried quickly enough, and diseases spread. The everyday, everynight horror was accompanied by violence and incest. This is a forcefully drawn exaggeration, but without any doubt such scenes could indeed be witnessed in the London of the 1830s and 1840s. But what is it that brings the author to sum it up like this?

> These are the fearful mysteries of that hideous district in the very heart of this great metropolis. From St John Street to Saffron Hill – from West Street to Clerkenwell Green, is a maze of narrow lanes, choked up with dirt, pestiferous with nauseous odours, and swarming with a population that is born, lives, and dies, amidst squalor, penury, wretchedness, and crime.[65]

This is too much: too strong, too lacking in nuance to have a real basis in statistical fact. The image has become independent as an *image*, and remains fixed in the social imagination, which is shy of real contact, exciting and reassuring itself at the same time with these 'mysteries'. Thanks to its distance from reality, the image hardly changes in the course of decades. Our visual imagination of this life is very strongly marked by the illustrations of Gustave Doré. For him night also reigns over the scenes of day; so all-encompassing is the torment of poverty, so fundamental the appeal from the darkness, that the days too seem darkened by it. In 1872 the book *London, a Pilgrimage* appeared with texts by Blanchard Jerrold, in which the visual beauties of the city, the icons of London, are presented side by side with descriptions of 'unspeakable' misery.

## 11 *First steps into the night*

While Friedrich Sass thought of street life as the 'colourful shell' of life – 'it deceives' – Ernst Dronke put the doings on the streets at the centre of his perception of the urban; though his attention to poverty and crime is marked by curiosity, he maintains the distancing irony of the adventurous traveller.

Does the street, particularly at night, give us a realistic image of life in the city? Or does it provide each observer with what he has come to see? Did the moralizing metaphor – 'shuddering I let the veil fall over this night-painting of our times'[66] – inspire repulsion or a real curiosity? Was the unveiling intended to enlighten? Was the street really a *meeting place* for the various social groups in the city?

In the years around 1840 night in the city becomes a subject of public debate. Those who speak of the night, however, must know it too: those who dared go 'out' through the nocturnal streets were growing in numbers. It is certainly true that city-dwellers' walks through the urban streets can also be read as *journeys of inspection and reassurance*; they patrolled their (constantly growing) area of the city, perhaps enjoying the thrill of a brief visit to the living areas of the 'elements' they see as 'dangerous', noting with a pleasurable shudder that something is 'seething' – and assured themselves that no explosion threatened yet.

It may also be that on these walks, particularly because they were undertaken with this reassurance in mind, they did not see 'everything', not the whole city, not every dark corner. Because few of them were really looking for danger – only for a hint of it, and salvation from danger was part of the excursion programme from the beginning – their perception of the city (and of the night) remains necessarily incomplete.[67] But also in their inability to see and to recognize 'everything', the night-walkers give the impression that they are witnesses to the creation of a distinct new world: 'At this time', writes Louis Chevalier, 'the night really begins to exist as something particular, no longer simply as a simple darkening of things that otherwise do not change their nature'.[68]

Night is more than simply a darker version of the day. Daytime behaviour cannot (any longer) be taken over into the night, for *nocturnal behaviour in the city* has first to be learnt, this being above all a matter of dealing with fear and danger. To conclude this chapter, here are two texts to illustrate the uncertainty about this 'new' night: Eduard Devrient writes in 1840 in his *Letters from Paris*:

> The party separated after 1 o'clock, and for the first time I found the streets of Paris completely empty of people . . . Where during the day one cannot escape from the deafening noise, I could hear nothing but my own footsteps and the murmur of fountains. Near the Palais Royal I met a patrol. The soldiers were walking in single file, close to the houses on either side of the street, so as not to be attacked at the same time and to be able to give each other assistance. This reminded me that at the very beginning of my stay here I had been advised to walk like that at night, and in any case to take a cab if I had to go home on my own.[69]

The Palais Royal was still central to the night life of Paris, but it was gradually losing its *raison d'être*, as in 1837 the shops and gambling saloons had been closed. Soon it was no longer the centre but only a starting-point for nocturnal walks that led outwards to the boulevards: 'In Paris around 1840 there was a small group of about a dozen night-walkers who met at about midnight almost every night in a café in the Palais Royal. All they shared . . . was a love of the night and of night-time walks through Paris.'[70]

The same place, the same time – and such different pictures of the night. The shackles of the past still weigh heavily on Devrient, who still sees the night as alien, something against which one has to arm and defend oneself. In contrast to this, new and unusual but full of excitement, one has the *vagabondage nocturne* through the city; danger is sought out and challenged, and pleasure in the discovery of this new world and pride in having taken the decisive step out of the shelter indoors and onto the streets are part of the newly forming *urban mentality*: the complete city-dweller has to learn to master the night.

The opportunity to do this only arises because the night is no longer totally dark, but the chance was not taken up as soon as it was available. The first gas lights had been burning in Paris since 1819, in Berlin since 1826, and their number rapidly increased, lights and points of orientation multiplying in street after street. Lighting *characterizes* the topography of the nocturnal city, but it does not create it by itself. Only when the opportunities for nocturnal perambulation provided by the new light meet with the willingness – or the need – to appropriate this side of the city, are the shackles thrown off and a new departure made.

# Digression: In a new light

> In honour of mysterious night
> the police put out
> today, first night of the May moon,
> each faint flame of dawn
> in the lanterns of the city.
> Four moons the dark mysteries will last
> and four moons long no lamp
> shall shine in splendid Berlin,
> in the capital of lights. –
>
> But be not fearful, friend!
> Be reassured! I'll lead the way,
> I know by heart
> the streets of home.
>
> LUDWIG ROBERT, *A Berliner's*
> *Promenade through His Neighbourhood* [71]

Our image of night in the big cities is oddly enough determined by what the historians of lighting say about *light*.[72] Only with artificial light, they tell us, do the contours of the nocturnal city emerge: the city is characterized by light. From this perspective the history of the city is a history of progressive illumination. Night is inevitably expelled into the realm of prehistory and mythology. None of the many histories of lighting, which in their different ways all describe the triumph of light, is able to dispense with a preliminary description of the impenetrable terrain of the nocturnal as an alien region of fear that is conquered and finally subjugated.

For a history of the night it is no easy task to establish a different point of view; and of course one can't contradict the material evidence. But concentration on the light sometimes means that the intrinsic nature or indeed recalcitrance of the night is not perceived.

Only 'in the sixteenth century', according to Wolfgang Schivelbusch, 'do there emerge the first signs of a permanent and properly

When evening comes, the Berlin lamp-lighters go out with the tools of their trade. Woodcut, late 19th century.

installed public lighting system'.[73] At night, it is said, the inhabitants retreated into their houses, and in almost every city there was a permanent ban on venturing out. But where there are 'highway robbers and vagabonds'[74] to threaten, the world outside the locked houses is not dead. Police ordinances certainly prescribed that no one was to be on the streets at night without reason, or without carrying a light. But the non-observation of police ordinances has a history even older than that of lighting: the ordinances were the expression of a long-standing debate, a reaction to the deplorable state of affairs that nocturnal 'activity' represented in the eyes of the police. The authorities used *light as a factor of order*. Compared to the day, night is unstructured, less ordered and therefore potentially threatening. Fear of darkness is stirred up and used by the authorities as an instrument of discipline; but can we conclude from this that the night was essentially avoided from fear?[75]

The authorities' claim to control over the *whole city* through the control of its main arteries is linked to the centrally organized *street* lighting begun in the late seventeenth century. The street lamps stand as signs of this comprehensive claim to power, which is not restricted to the pursuit of criminals (made easier in the light), but intended to make clear to the whole population who it is that owns the street. With each new light that illuminates the street, however, the circle of those who dare go out at night grows. In reality, the streets soon no longer *belong* to the 'night-revellers and the immoral' alone;[76] many workers, both men and women, were about in the city in the late evening and early morning hours, and they were doubtless grateful for each new light.

Wolfgang Schivelbusch has told the story of the introduction of gas lighting in Paris, which happened slowly and against much resistance, and of the destruction of street lamps during the revolutions of 1830 and 1848. The years around 1840 would also see technical advance: while in 1835 there were 203 lights in Paris, by 1839 there were already 12,816 – on 6,273 lamp-standards.

The light of the old oil lanterns, they used to say in Berlin, 'was just enough to make out how dark it really was in Spree-Athen'.[77] On 21 April 1825 the Imperial Gas Association, later the 'Englische Gasgesellschaft', signed a 21-year contract with the Prussian Interior Ministry and the police authority, in which it committed itself, against a payment of 81,000 taler kurant, to set up 1,300 street lamps. The first street illuminated by the new light was the promenade Unter den Linden, and 19 September 1826 saw the first gas flames lit:

Yesterday evening we saw for the first time the prettiest street of the capital, which is also our most pleasurable walk, the Linden, in the bright glow of gas lighting. A great crowd of curious onlookers were attracted by this spectacle, and all of them were surprised: for we have never seen the Linden more brightly lit by the most splendid illuminations. Not in meagre little flames but as broad as a hand the dazzling light shoots forth, so pure that one can perfectly well read a letter at a distance of 20–25 paces . . . Soon the other main streets too will be illuminated in the same way, *and Berlin*, which is famous for the pleasurable impression it makes during the day, *will also agreeably surprise its visitors at night.*[78]

As in the other cities – Pall Mall, Oxford Street, Regent Street and Piccadilly in London; place Vendôme, place du Carrousel, rue de la Paix and Palais Royal in Paris – in Berlin too it was the main streets and squares of the city centre which took advantage of the new light. In the contract of 1825 there was a clause specifying that the company did not commit itself to 'illuminating smaller alleys and less important streets, because the laying of conduits to those places would not be worthwhile'.[79]

The burning times of the lamps was fixed at 1,300 hours, the police authorities laying down the distribution of these hours among the months and days; many lamps burned only until midnight, and at the full moon and during the summer months from May till August they remained altogether unlit. The tables of burning times drawn up by the police read – in Paris as in Berlin – like a *night and light topography* of the big city, and from the bright centre there extend chains of light that get thinner and thinner as they approach the outer areas of the cities, which would remain in the dark for a long time to come.[80]

Only in 1847, after the contract expired and with the growing self-confidence of the Berlin city adminstration, was it possible for them to take over the lighting for themselves – although it remained linked with the night-watch and street cleaning until 1854 – and to extend the lighting in the following years; by 1849 the burning times had also been increased from 1,300 to 2,400 hours per year.

1 BEAUTY OF THE NIGHT IN THE LIGHT

Delays in the spread of the new lighting technique had a considerable effect on perceptions of the nocturnal city: while the gas lights were supposed to bathe the centres of the cities in a magical illumination and while on the boulevards 'luxury lighting' came together with the newly discovered entertainment of the evening walk (an association which the lighting historians in their emphasis on light like to call 'night life'[81]), other parts of the city remained in the dark.

One form of perception of the nocturnal city puts light and the experience of light in the foreground; one of the most beautiful descriptions from this point of view – and, moreover, from high up on the heights of Montmartre – is given by Julius Rodenberg in 1867:

> Right in the middle of the heart of the city there appears a golden dot, another one here, a third there, a fourth – one cannot say how quickly they follow one another, they can no longer be counted. The whole of Paris is studded with golden dots, as closely as a velvet gown with gold glitter. Soon they wink and twinkle everywhere, and you cannot imagine anything more beautiful, and yet the most beautiful is still to come. Out of the dots emerge lines, and from the lines figures, spark lining up with spark, and as far as the eye can see are endless avenues of light.[82]

'Gas light is an important element in our cultural life, and we metropolitans remember the earlier oil lanterns only as faintly as they used to burn . . . Our lamp-lighter is a restless, agile and speedy fellow, a Mercury of illusions.' (Robert Springer, 1869.) Photograph by Bill Brandt: *Gaslighter*, c.1930.

An indispensable figure in stories of the night: the *allumeur de réverbères* in Paris. Anonymous photograph, Paris, *c.*1900.

The beauty of the light and its ability to delineate the city, to let it shine out in contrast to the surrounding darkness, these effects are of course particularly memorable in an *overview* of the whole city; but on the brightly lit streets inside the city they also have an effect which delights the observer. As evidence of this let us quote Gottfried Semper's exclamation: 'How glorious is gas lighting!'[83] The impression of a 'universal' illumination, given expression by many contemporaries, is, however, imprecise; many areas in the cities remained for a long time without the new lighting. But these impressions are not entirely false, for they transmit the atmosphere of the time:

> In this one sees the climactic point of the development of light, the achievement of the final triumph after man left the caves which he knew how to light and heat with an open fire. *The night life of the big cities, the life of evening and night in general gains an impetus and a zest from the new sources of light.* The long northern winter was vanquished, as Paris – *la ville lumière* – shone in the glow of the gas lamps, and in London, Berlin, and the great cities of Northern Europe the city emerged as a *brightly-lit island in the ocean of darkness*.[84]

The extreme expression of this belief in light is the scheme for a lighting tower which – as an alternative to the Eiffel Tower planned for the Paris Exposition of 1889 – would shine 'bright as day' and totally abolish the night over the whole of Paris. Eugène de Mirecourt had already had such visions of the future in 1855. In his flight through the ages the night-devil Asmodeus takes him to the year 1955 when everything is brightly lit, there is no longer any darkness.[85] What is true of the view from above onto the dark landscape with the cities as islands of light, is also true inside the cities themselves: the Parisian boulevard could be experienced as an *inner space*, because it contrasted like an island of light against the surrounding darkness; but even as the pleasures of evening, the visits to restaurants, cafés and theatres, the *flânerie* through the arcades, were the doings of a small minority of the city's inhabitants, so were the brightly lit streets only a small district of the whole city which they claimed to represent; and the 'night life' too that happened there was only a small part of the total nocturnal life of the city.

At the same time, and in the same cities, another form of perception appears; it consciously sets itself off, however, from the centres of light and entertainment and directs its gaze at those districts which have not been touched, or not yet, by street-lighting, and for a totally different motive: that of control. Such texts about the 'night side' confront the blaze of light with its counter-image.

A 'social sketch' from the *Gartenlaube* presents a prototypical account of a journey into the dark regions of the cities; its essential moment is *confrontation*. 'No city in the world is richer than London, but none either has such depths of wretchedness.' Away from the streets 'paved with gold' there are dark regions of poverty; those who do not discern them do not see the whole city: 'So it was my intention, after having over-indulged in her gleaming side, *also to find the reverse side* and to undertake a few expeditions through it.'[86]

The expeditions into the dark regions are made vivid with metaphors of light; the darker the streets the deeper the descent seems to be. The depictions of these 'flip-side images' however are dubious in many ways; 'romanticism' and even 'demonic charm' may exist only for the intruders, not for those who live there. News from the world of darkness nevertheless makes it clear that there exists, alongside the sea of light, another picture of the night – and of social reality.

The news from the darkness seems threatening and challenges the authorities' control. Their agents too undertake 'expeditions' into the dangerous regions, and they bring the light with them. The police goal of control over the whole city remains; they accept, even if hesitantly, the appearance of nocturnal entertainment life in the centres, and they now direct their gaze (reinforced by light) towards the dark zones. It is the function of lighting 'to guarantee security and free circulation during the hours of darkness'.[87]

Now the police have the additional task of protecting the lights (because they are also protected by them) and securing the authorities' monopoly of their deployment. The thought that this monopoly could be put into question appears unbearable, and the fear that the whole city would be sunk in darkness – a state of affairs not at all unusual a few decades earlier – grows with the extension of the street itself. In October 1872 the workers of the London Gas Company threatened to strike, and when it came to nothing the *Deutsches*

After midnight on the Thames Embankment in London: curious onlookers from all walks of life marvel at the brilliance of the new electric lights, which outshone the old gas lamps by far. With this new 'miracle' London was once again years ahead of Paris and Berlin. Woodcut from *The Graphic*, 1879.

*Handelsblatt* commented: 'So . . . the thought of leaving a large city in darkness could in no way be justified.'[88]

In parallel with the development of a lighting system thrown over the city, complaints increased about the 'situation' in the city neighbourhoods still in darkness. More and more, 'nocturnal insecurity' is equated with the absence of light, and the erection of street lamps in dangerous places is seen as an appropriate measure to restore security.[89] So the light brings out the growing contradictions within the city; the brighter it shines in the centres, the more starkly do the outlines of the darker regions stand out.

Light doubtless plays an important role in the 'discovery' of the night side of the city, but it also stamps the view and the perception of the discoverer. To him the nocturnal regions seem to be the left-over remains of a dark past, a region which does *not yet* enjoy the pleasure of illumination. Many come 'out of the light' to visit the dark places, and they all take with them into the darkness their metaphoric lights – of enlightenment, religion, the bright political future.

65

'A light is as good as a policeman',[90] as it was said in London. Light has different functions in different districts of the city. Marc J. Bouman draws a distinction: 'Ornamental or "luxury" lamps lit the boulevards of the elite while police or "control" lamps seemed to protect them from crime.'[91] This 'rearrangement separated rich from poor', and 'also highlighted for the first time the popular contrast between areas both poor and dark and others that were wealthy and bright.' This separation had consequences for aesthetic perceptions in particular, and on the literary representation of the urban. The lights 'illuminated the geometric *City Beautiful* aesthetic', and symbolized progress as distance from nature; for the 'other side' there remains the image of the jungle.

The imagery of light becomes yet more prevalent with the beginnings of electric lighting in the 1880s and the 'definitive conquest of the night'.[92] The facts and myths of electrification are the object of various studies[93] and need not be examined here. Like its predecessor, the new brightness was welcomed enthusiastically: 'Those who turn into one of the . . . squares from a gas-lit side street', reports the *Illustrirte Zeitung*, 'have the impression of entering unexpectedly from a half-dark corridor into a hall as bright as day.'[94] In 1930 the author Bruno H. Bürgel recalls this difference, using a similar image: 'My father, who still came from the days of lighting by oil-lamp, led me proudly through this Berlin, storming forward through the wealth of light in seven league boots. *A step into the side streets, and you felt set back by centuries.*'[95]

More than ever before, light was a big city's mark of modernity, and its absence was felt as a lack. During the preparations for the Universal Exhibition of 1900 the streets of Paris were for a few years only inadequately lit: 'Paris, ville lumière trop obscure.'[96] The Paris *Revue des deux mondes* was even clearer in March 1904; amongst all the necessities of life in modern society artificial light is the one that can least be done without.[97] As a result of a strike by power-station workers in 1907 – there is nothing new even under an electric sun – Paris was thrown back to the age of *clair de lune*, the incident making part of the *ville lumière* a *ville des ténèbres*, a city of darkness.[98] From one minute to the next, according to Jacques Lardy, the varied activities of the city were interrupted, its intellectual life almost 'abolished'.

It was so bright that one could even read the newspapers by the new light. C. Saltzmann: *The First Electric Street-lighting in Berlin, Potsdamer Platz (1882)*, painting, 1884.

A nostalgic farewell to the old gas lamps as they make way for electric light: 'Disparition des anciens becs de gaz à Paris'. Anonymous photograph, Paris, c.1880.

A poem written about the event indulges in even stronger images: light is the most beautiful sun of the city, and when it is extinguished the city is robbed of its radiance.[99]

It is not just light that marks the modernity of the city; the rapid succession of inventions immerses the city in an ever brighter light, generating the sensation of living 'fast' – and the forced fall back into darkness seems all the more frustrating. Real competition develops between the European cities for the honorific title of 'City of Light'; Berlin in particular is at pains to catch up with the French metropolis and if possible to surpass it. Hans Ostwald, of all people, who like no other undertook the exploration of the 'dark corners' of his city from the beginning of the new century, sees a totally new beauty emerging with electric light: 'One thing however forces our admiration: the city's wealth of light in the evening . . . And so perhaps as the *city of light* it will gain more friends out there in the Reich – and perhaps also be loved as the bringer of light.'[100] Berlin's 'light-advertising' seems to have gone down better abroad than in the German Reich, which didn't care very much for its 'city of light'; in 1912, when a group of 'city electrical engineers' from the Australian city of Melbourne visited Europe, the road to Berlin, 'electrically the most important city',[101] was not to be missed.

These brief snapshots show what great significance contemporaries attributed to brightness, and thus to the overcoming of darkness. In both Berlin and Paris the First World War brought the pleasures of light to an end; and when the capitals retained an already much reduced nocturnal entertainment life, they were the target of vehement attacks from the provinces.[102] There are texts from these days too which report on the rediscovery of darkness. The sudden forced *pause in the lighting business* led many an observer to notice again the forgotten beauty of the dark: the colours of the night at the various seasons, the reality of long winter and short summer nights. Patience became (once more) a nocturnal virtue. The inhabitants had to acquaint themselves anew with their cities, move differently within them, rely on a closer contact with them.

Strangely enough, the brightness of the light had obstructed rather than facilitated the view of the nocturnal city, and when the lights were switched on again after the war, brighter than before, there were many who missed their night. Legrand-Chabrier wrote in the newspaper *L'Opinion* that darkness wraps things softly, while electric light makes them up too beautifully and gas light even distorts them; 'Since the War', he continues, 'there is no longer any true night life in Paris, at least not on the streets.'[103]

The question asked repeatedly since the beginning of artificial lighting, whether it is brightness or darkness that marks the true 'nature' of the nocturnal city, seems apparently to have been answered in favour of light. In the 1920s the image of the city more than ever can only be grasped through extremes: on the one hand, the 'cult of light and electricity'[104] was pursued further and further, and on the other, the city's misery could not (any longer) be hidden from the light – the contradictions were making each other clearly perceptible.

In the week of 13–16 October 1928 the German capital celebrated a festival: 'Berlin in the light'. Materially as well as metaphorically everything was once again brought together to prove the inner connection between *light and progress, light and modernity, light and the metropolis*: neon signs, illuminated shop-window displays, floodlit public buildings, vehicle lights – a veritable parade of lights. In all the texts about this event light is conjured up as a technical achievement, as an economic factor, but also as a sign of beauty[105]. In this may reside the official recognition, and at the same time the enslavement, of 'night life', above all through advertising: 'Berlin has become the city of aesthetic neon advertising. It is precisely the neon signs that give the metropolis in the evening its markedly individual note', said the official festival programme, and the *Berliner Tageblatt* wrote, 'light has been put in the service of advertising all along the line'.[106] One did not have to wait long for an answer; the *Welt am Abend* saw in this an attempt 'to whitewash the wretchedness that exists in the capital and get drunk on a futile illusion . . . Are there in Berlin no dark streets and squares which have already been waiting a long time for a humble, dim gas light?'[107] Max Epstein put it even more succinctly:

> They leave war-cripples to freeze on the streets,
> But they illuminate the streets.
> This is its true and terrible face:
> Berlin in the light.[108]

In these years the texts of the nocturnal walkers become markedly more melancholic; they sum up a development of the city night which is only insufficiently reflected in the history of light, which even becomes invisible in the blinding brightness. More reliable than its deceiving glow are the texts of those who know the 'topography of the home streets' in the dark as well.

# iii Night and Security

Darkness frightens. The theme of *nocturnal insecurity* runs like a leitmotif through texts that deal with the city night. Those who dare go out on the streets at night expose themselves to danger. This is an idea that marks the authorities' regulations and other measures regarding nocturnal behaviour, but even today it informs the feelings of nocturnal walkers who defy the warning: 'On rentre en territoire nocturne: c'est le danger.'[1]

Concepts such as 'security' and 'insecurity' gain their significance from the fact that their limits are imprecise and their meaning cannot be clearly determined; this imbues them with the force of threat. The powers of the state authorities are nourished not least by the fact that they alone are competent to define security: in their eyes it is guaranteed by the presence of a power which is as total as can be. When this is not possible, the presence of power has to be symbolically replaced by a refined system of regulation, and disobedience to the rules is punished. Insecurity therefore threatens where there is great opportunity for disobedience and little possibility of control.

However tightly the limits of the regulatory system are drawn, security always has temporal and spatial dimensions: for the forces of law and order the highest degree of security is achieved when nobody challenges their right to organize space and time, when at a given time everyone under their supervision is at the place prescribed and fulfilling the function allotted to them. In this, *public* space and the time spent in the public sphere are more strongly subject to control than private space and time.

The streets of the nocturnal city therefore represent a terrain of potential insecurity from two points of view, and the forces of law and order make a particular effort to keep the night hours under their control. At the moment when the cities 'come out of their shells', the authorities strengthen both their presence on the nocturnal streets and the regulatory system that is to organize this terrain.

With this there begins a public debate about nocturnal security; on the one hand there emerges among various groups of the population a growing need to spend the night outside their private spaces,

Um die Sicherheit wäre es besser bestellt
Würde Straße und Platz durch „OSRAM" erhellt !

'After midnight, every street lamp is as good as a watchman', they used to say in Paris even in 1850. The new electric light made street-lighting yet more effective in policing. *Osram-Lichthaus*, film cartoon, 1925.

which creates on the other hand a pressure on the forces of law and order to justify themselves: of necessity, they discover the propagandist possibilities of the discourse of night-time insecurity. When for very different reasons more and more people are about at night and recognize that it is possible to venture out without encountering danger, then the simple argument that the night is full of perils loses its credibility. The gap that has been created must be filled with *intimidatory propaganda* and the implantation of fear, and this is accompanied by a *propaganda of morality*.

I explore here four different areas in which this debate about 'security' and 'insecurity' is expressed: the night-watch, closing times, the criminal world, and homelessness. In each of these areas, questions of organization and questions of perception, the 'reality' and the 'imagination' of the night, intersect. In each of these areas, in different ways, it is a question of *demarcation*. The history of night is full of debates about limits: what is still permitted, what is now forbidden? What is still possible, what is not? If the rules that have been in force for a long time are now no longer valid, what should replace them?

# 1 The night-watch

How many hundred times have I thought that every judge, every Minister of Justice or Police, every bishop, every doctor of body or soul, should have spent a few years as a night-watchman in different areas of a big city.

*Memoiren eines Berliner Nachtwächters, 1845*[2]

The night-watchman is a figure from the urban past, from the 'good old comfortable days',[3] conjured up without fail in texts which hold the modern, brightly lit city night up against a picture from earlier, darker times. He cannot be absent from this picture:

A dim light flickered only from a few windows of the overhanging attic floors. It was a curious sight, a mediaeval town on a quiet, dark evening, its thousand corners, recesses, turrets and arches strangely illuminated by these escaping beams, wonderful and alarming, secret and sinister. And now one light after another goes out, the walls darken, the black shadows loom out shapelessly . . . *Around the corner sounds the night-watchman's horn,* his night-song competing in its discord with the howling of cats that grows loud on the steep-sloping roofs.

Historical research on the city has paid little attention to the figure of the night-watchman, who in various works is mentioned only in one connection, as a sign of the formation of bourgeois self-confidence in the towns of the Middle Ages. So it is reported that in France in 595 King Chlotar II proclaimed an edict which committed the inhabitants of the cities to set up night-watches, *gardes de nuit;* in 1150 the guilds of merchants and artisans provided 'each night a certain number of men, in order to look after the security of the city'.[4] In Paris the *guets* (watches) were first replaced by *archers royaux* (royal archers), succeeded in 1563 by the *guets royaux,* until finally, at the beginning of the eighteenth century, the civic obligation of the watch was ended and the task taken over by the *police royale.*

The urban historian Lewis Mumford regrets this process, in the case of the English cities, as a loss of civic activity in the service of the city; in 1693 an order of the Corporation of London provided that *from sundown to sunrise* there should always be more than a thousand watchmen posted in the city; for the maintenance of this body of

*73*

men, according to Mumford, 'a high sense of civic duty' was necessary and because this was lacking, the order fell into oblivion in the
eighteenth century.[5]

In Berlin, the first 'attempt at organized protection against
nocturnal evil-doers'[6] was linked temporally and metaphorically
to the 'Wittenberg Enlightenment', that is, the Reformation. Elector
Joachim II ordered the provision of nocturnal watch-fires at various
places, fires which were to be lit by the town militia and kept going
by the night-watch: and after 11 p.m. nobody was to be out on
the streets. There has been a city night-watch in Berlin since 1677,
and it was always at the centre of public attention when nocturnal
'incidents' disturbed the peace of the inhabitants.

In 1808 the administration of the Berlin police was transferred to
the city government, as civic authority; by 1822 it had been transferred to the police authority, in the context of the new police regulations for Berlin as the capital and royal residence. The Berlin city
authorities' records relating to the 'raising of night-watch monies'
start in 1813, and until the end of the 1830s the administration was
concerned above all with matters of cost. The raising of a 'night-
watch rate' – 'one half of one per cent of the amount of the rent'[7] –
was hardly controversial, as it was to go to the establishment of new
night-watch posts, which was precisely what was being demanded
in the growing Berlin of the years after 1830, by the inhabitants of
newly built streets in particular. 'The expansion of the city' is the
main argument put forward for the setting up of new posts and
even new night-watch districts. In 1839 the Berlin city council was
having 'thoughts about the transformation of the local night-watch
service . . . *as the existing system is absolutely inadequate to present
needs'*.[8]

It was no different in Paris. The French Revolution at first led to
the abolition of all the night-watch arangements, but by Year 10 of
the new Republic (1803) the Prefect of Police was already writing to
his superintendents that it was urgently necessary to reintroduce the
*patrouilles grises* of pre-revolutionary days: patrols of twelve men
were to be about the city in the hours between 11 p.m. and 2.30 a.m.[9]
In the years that followed several proposals were made to the
Prefecture of Police for the establishment of an improved *garde de nuit*.
In 1812 the Baron de Gérando presented his project: 24 companies
made up of eight officers and 75 men were to be on patrol every
night in every arrondissement, to guarantee the security of Paris,

74

'théâtre des crimes et des accidents pendant la nuit'.[10] Those who were encountered '*à pied dans les rues*' without justification were not to be immediately arrested but would be able to obtain, for the price of 50 centimes, a *laissez-passer* that would allow them only to go home. However, 'those individuals who misuse their *laissez-passer* by walking about in the streets and not going home (*en se promenant la nuit et en ne pas rentrant chez eux*), are to be taken to the Prefecture of Police'.[11]

Gérando's proposals were rejected politely but quite firmly. In 1826 a new proposal was made; according to the man who made it, a former colonel, the night-watch was to lead the city out of the 'true chaos' of the revolutionary period. But only two years later, on 12 February 1828, the Prefect of Police decreed that 'in view of the insufficiency of the present means for the maintenance of nocturnal security' a special brigade was to be set up 'au service des rondes de nuit'. By a decree of 14 March 1829 the opening times of the police stations in Paris were extended to 10 p.m., and the commissaires themselves placed under the obligation, at least once a week after the closing of their offices, to do rounds of the places seen as the potential catalysts of nocturnal disturbances.

From the documentation one cannot tell exactly what the police understood by 'nocturnal disturbances', what it was they feared and wanted to prevent. The debate on a better organization of the night-watch, however, clearly took place at a sub-political level, because the political changes of the 1830s and even of 1848 had little effect on it. The worries of the police are for the city itself. In 1831 the Prefecture of Police made a new attempt: 'It is one of the first duties of the police and their constant endeavour to watch over the security of persons and property . . . The night that affords security to the wrongdoer also demands a more active surveillance.'[12]

From now on the net of nocturnal surveillance was woven more and more finely. From 12 January 1835 onwards it was the task of five *brigadiers* and 40 *sergents de ville*, 'to go through the streets and squares of their district, often changing direction and maintaining the greatest silence'. Full of pride, the police report for the years 1830 to 1848 quotes a newspaper article in which the work of the night-patrols is lauded and their constant presence on the streets praised for guaranteeing the safety of the newly discovered passion for the nocturnal walk – now hardly any longer the subject of moral condemnation:

If on occasion you used to find yourself alone in the streets of our capital between 1 and 3 o'clock in the morning, looking anxiously at the faces of the few passers-by, always in expectation of one of those attacks of which one hears so much, then you must feel grateful for the night-patrol, which is somewhere nearby, its mere silent presence guaranteeing your safety.[13]

The night-watch very obviously has a double function; by patrolling the streets at night more attentively and more systematically than before, it opens the nocturnal city to a large circle of adventurous people. Conceived as an attempt at maintaining the old nocturnal order, the reorganization of the night-watch effectively contributes to the lifting of limits.

THE TASKS OF THE NIGHT-WATCH

On 15 March 1840 the head of the Berlin police authority asked the city council 'for the convocation of a conference to clarify contentious issues'.[14] The outcome of this and other later conferences was a precise 'service instruction' for the work of the Berlin night-watchmen; an additional 'order' explained their duties in detail: 'Each night-watchman is allocated a night-watch area for special supervision, and these areas are grouped to form the districts of the night-watch masters who oversee the night-watchmen.' Between 10 p.m. and 5 a.m. in winter, and between 11 p. m. and 3 a. m. in the summer, the watchmen have to announce the hours 'with a tin whistle', and 'diligently go about' their area, taking the side streets as well and often changing route; they are to notify concierges of open doors and windows, and report to the police any burglaries they may discover.

> 10. Beggars or lewd persons encountered at night, who remain on the streets, on public squares or under the bridges, are to be arrested by the watchmen and delivered to the nearest station . . .
>
> 11. They are to stop those who foul the streets at night, who obstruct passages or pavement to the hindrance of passers-by, or who walk the street with naked light or coals, and then report them for punishment . . .
>
> 12. What they have discovered about any thieves' dens or resorts of prostitutes they must report to the watch-master the next day.
>
> 13. If during his hours of service a night-watchman is himself found to have entered a beer-house or place of ill repute and to have drunk

76

or to have had dealings of any kind with low and dissolute persons, then he shall not only be dismissed but also be punished accordingly.[15]

For these varied tasks the night-watchmen received a salary of six talers per month. This explains why another form of service, not mentioned in the regulations, had to be provided as a source of income on the side: the night-watchmen had the keys to numerous residential buildings in their area, and for a small remuneration they would open the doors to late home-comers. What is more, in the 1840s and 1850s complaints accumulated against night-watchmen who were collecting fines from landlords whose buildings were not 'properly' locked up; this arrangement was long tolerated by the police authority, and was only forbidden in 1859. The watch-masters had to supervise the night-watchmen and their ways of life, and to do this they had to go through 'the areas assigned to them at undefined and changing hours and inspect the watchmen at their duties'.

With the expiry of the contract between the Ministry of the Interior and the Imperial Gas Association the connection between the night-watch and lighting also slowly came to an end; in the view of the police authority, from 1847 the night-watch should be exclusively its responsibility. And indeed the new service instruction of 1853 shows the increasingly police-like character of the activity: 'The night-watchmen and watch-masters are to ensure the maintenance of order and the security of persons and property', they are to fulfill this task 'in peacable co-operation with the police', they have to wear a full uniform and 'do their rounds without interruption, in all the streets and squares of their area'. Homeless 'vagabonds' and 'females, who by their behaviour on the streets raise the suspicion of being engaged in street prostitution' they now have to take immediately to the police.[16]

THE STRUGGLE OVER THE JURISDICTION OF THE NIGHT-WATCH

In the years after 1850 manufacturers from the neighbourhoods of the Hamburger and the Oranienburger Tor increasingly turned to the police authority with unhappy complaints about the situation at night – 'and now, particularly in the evening, there is a positive bivouac of dissolute persons of both sexes'[17] – and with requests for the establishment of more watch-stations. The growing complaints accompany the emergence of industrial zones in North and East

Berlin; but at the end of 1861 they also led the police authority to take stock of the public safety situation in the whole city. This then provoked a debate about responsibility for the organization of the night.

'The public safety of Berlin at night', says a report of 12 January 1862 by Police Commissioner Ahne, 'has unfortunately recently often been disturbed.' The press had reported nocturnal attacks, burglaries of business premises, 'namely, the almost daily burglaries from shop windows'; these unpleasant events were so numerous 'that one feels, not without reason, that some part of these troubling phenomena has to be put down to the inadequacy of the nocturnal guard on the city'. The fifteen watch-masters, Ahne continues, are simply not in a position to supervise the night-watchmen adequately, the number of watchmen is too small as a whole, and their work is underpaid.[18]

The city council also feels that wrongdoers are growing in 'impudence' and in 'sense of security';[19] but it places the responsibility for this on the police. What is the night-watch? Is it 'nothing but a municipal institution' whose function is now no longer carried out by the municipality itself but by officers specially detailed for this, which of course has to be paid for by the municipality? This was the argument of the police authority, while the city was of the opinion that the 'whole activity in employment of the night-watchmen is related to the maintainance of public peace, order and security . . . and these tasks are the duty of the police' – which meant they should be paid from the funds of the Prussian Interior Ministry.

This debate is not just about money; it marks a growing argument between communal self-administration and the police,[20] between a (left-)liberal-inclined city council and a police authority increasingly militarized since 1848. In these years around 1860, in which the 'developing industrial economy' was making lasting changes to the social and cultural as well as topographical structure of Berlin,[21] the needs of the manufacturers were of great importance; if one of them, especially when speaking in the name of a landowners' association, turned to the city with the threat 'to refuse to pay taxes until the said ills are repaired',[22] then the city could pass this criticism on to the police and challenge their authority. The police had not yet given up on their ideal of the closed city, while the administration was beginning to accept the night as part of urban life. In their rearguard action the police intensified their anti-night propaganda in Berlin, and in Paris as well.

78

'The nocturnal attacks that Paris has been witnessing since some time', writes the newspaper *Le Public* on 4 July 1870, 'make us think about the reintroduction of the old *patrouilles grises'*; and *La Patrie* of 7 February 1872 reports that 'there is talk of the organization of two batallions of night-watchmen,' each made up of 600 men, to patrol 'all the streets of Paris' from 10 p.m. till 6 a.m. Like a 'security cordon', this almost military unit is to be placed between the different regions of the night, between the bright, glittering world of the boulevards and the 'dark' quarters nearby.

But to the city politicians this view of the night promoted by the police no longer seems relevant; the police still want to restrict nocturnal life in general, and in their propaganda they combine political unrest, the social threat of the 'dangerous classes', and nocturnal entertainment into a single image of disorder. On this point the police administrations of Paris and Berlin are largely in agreement. Against this, the Berlin city authorities want to get to a situation where the police deal exclusively with the prosecution of crimes and no longer interfere in the nocturnal life of the city:

> The division of the police into day and night police no longer corresponds to the needs of a modern metropolis; the present night-watchmen are not acquainted with police duties as they are performed during the day . . . And (so) we are in accord with the city council in the conviction that the present evils can only be thoroughly and lastingly overcome by the total *abolition of the institution of the night-watch* and the amalgamation of the hitherto separate day and night police.[23]

This text could be given a key position in the history of the city night: the night is accepted as part of the city, the old measures for its 'security' are no longer sufficient, the new situation is irreversible and demands new methods. But need and recognition alone do not yet create facts, and the discussion has only begun.

FROM THE NIGHT-WATCH TO THE POLICE

To the 'modern' eye the figure of the night-watchman is risible; the night-watch service appears as a pre-modern solution to a modern problem, which is only made worse by this old-fashioned organization. Two texts from Berlin can be given here as examples:

> It will probably have come to your attention, when you visited the capital of the country for the first time, or at least got to know Berlin by

night, with its hustle and bustle on the streets, that the security of the metropolis is essentially in the hands of those friendly-looking men who in the evening after 10 o'clock walk about on the streets of Berlin with a whistle and a big set of keys. You will probably have noticed this all the more as you will have already read many times in the papers about the atrocities and crimes that have taken place, or are said to have taken place, on the streets of Berlin.[24]

These words were spoken in a debate in the Prussian parliament on 7 April 1875. In the meantime, Berlin had become the capital of the Reich, and its industrial development and the massive influx of population had reached new heights. This period also sees the appearance of an *urban irony*, an attitude which fundamentally approves of the big city, which may criticize many bad developments but is in general positively inclined towards the city, defending it against its ignorant (but influential) critics from the provinces.

This argument about the exaggeration of reports of alleged nocturnal incidents was not used only by councillors who were friends of the big city; the Berlin police too defended themselves against overblown depictions of the situation – 'it is part of the business of the garrulous reporters of many local newspapers to write reproachful articles, continuously concocting stories about the worrying insecurity of Berlin'[25] – but of course their motivation is different: they want to maintain the existing organizational form of the night-watch service, and to uphold their view of the nocturnal city. The critics of the old night-watch argue against this:

> If we pick on one thing, the institution of the night-watch, then we have to say that the night-watchman who, for the usual nickel, locks up every house, who only knows his area from the nocturnal side and who therefore does not know it in reality, as day and night are so different, only together giving us a picture of life – we have to say that these night-watchmen, unmodern at the very least, have become an obsolete phenomenon in this monstrous hurly-burly.[26]

So far in this chapter we have talked only of Paris and Berlin. London had gone its own way early on. In 1748 the 'blind judge' John Fielding, brother of the novelist Henry Fielding, was stipendiary magistrate for the Bow Street police district, and there created his own police force, the 'Bow Street Runners'. Their patrols through this area of newspapers and theatres, of markets and taverns, quickly made them famous; around 1825 the force consisted of 150 men, but their pay was so low that they also had to take on private commissions. Four years later, in 1829, the London police was thoroughly reformed, and the Metropolitan Police was created. One of the significant causes for this reorganization was the insufficient security of the nocturnal city, 'the nightly indecorum and danger of the London streets, the incidence of theft, robbery, and burglary, and the precarious situation of a capital whose principal safeguard on occasions of public disorder was the fidelity of three thousand guards'.[27] This was very obviously not enough, the existing 'Establishment of Nightly Watch and Nightly Police' having been found inadequate in the big city.

So it happened that around 6 p.m. on Tuesday, 29 September 1829, 'several parties of police constables' marched through the streets of London, setting off from Scotland Yard and elsewhere, and took up their activities – a sight and a step in 'the making of modern London' that was described by many contemporaries: the night-watch as the task of a modern police organization. There is absolutely no doubt that it was London's excellent economic position in those years that allowed this more modern approach to the problem to be adopted earlier and more decisively than in other cities; but a different understanding of police work also played its part. The administrative report of the Berlin police in 1882 goes into this: 'The London constables have really and fundamentally only street duties, they only have to attend to what happens on the street in front of their eyes.'[28]

In Berlin, on the other hand, the police still saw themselves as the real administrators of life, whose jurisdiction was not restricted to visible public space. Despite its many activities – which in Prussia as in the German Reich always had a political dimension – this report mentions proudly, for example, that the number of beggars, prostitutes and 'homeless vagrants' 'brought in' in Berlin in 1878 was 52,111, while in London it was 54,610 – no significant difference in the absolute numbers but a 'success' for Berlin even if you consider that London had for a long time been a city of over a million inhabitants. The Berlin police want to keep the old forms of organization of the night-watch service (particularly its payment by the city), which is why it can only become half-heartedly involved in the discourse about increasing nocturnal insecurity. The supporters of the reform of the night-watch service, on the other hand, demonstrate a new attitude towards the night, having come to the understanding 'that there is no sharp demarcation between day and night'.[29]

In Paris the Prefect of Police laconically informed his superinten-dents: 'I have decided that the night-watch service (*le service des rondes de nuit*) will cease, with effect from 30 June'.[30] The new strat-egy provided for the erection of alarm posts throughout the whole area of the city. In a report 'on ways of increasing security in Paris' this is justified by the fact that given the growing population it has become urgently necessary to increase the number of 'points of con-tact' between inhabitants and police. But there is also a resignation: the police are no longer capable of overseeing and controlling the whole city during the hours of night. With the alarm posts they pro-vide a substitute, using the new technical possibilities available to them, but the dream of total control is over.

The setting up of the *kiosques avertisseurs*, which are easy to operate, is an occasion for a precise stocktaking of nocturnal Paris. For every point in the city at which such a *kiosque* is erected, the report gives the 'motive': 'deserted at night', 'situated near brothels', 'a dangerous place at night', 'totally deserted and not very safe'.[31] Most of the *kiosques* are situated on the boulevards, usually at 'strate-gic' locations conveniently near the streets of prostitution, like the rue St Denis, or the deserted streets seen as places where pimps and 'apaches' are to be found.

With this deployment of alarm posts the police secured the changed nocturnal topography of the city, and they noticed that the night had in the meantime started to take over various 'diurnal' functions of urban life – in the fields of circulation and the supply of foodstuffs and energy. This area too had to be secured, and for this the old patrols were no longer sufficient.

REMNANTS OF THE OLD NIGHT

At the same time as this modernization was being undertaken, remnants of the 'old' pre-modern city night still existed. The aboli-tion of the patrols had one consequence in particular, which was that 'strollers' and 'revellers' were no longer arrested and no longer had to identify themselves; now everybody was able to walk through the streets as they pleased. In the same year, 1881, the Prefect of Police told his superintendents to be particularly attentive to the *chiffoniers*; the traditional feeling of insecurity with regard to the old figures of the night was still so strong that the Prefect was able to use them to reintroduce the night patrols through the back door.

The old form of night-watch is mocked in many different texts, in Berlin too; hardly any story of 'Berlin Life' does without a caricature of the Berlin night-watchman. Max Ring, for example, begins his story of the 'Rück-Kompanie' – a group which helps families threatened by seizure and forcible eviction to leave their homes secretly (at night) and to take their possessions with them – with a description of the atmosphere: 'Midnight has long gone; the streets are deserted and unpeopled; only here and there does one meet a swaying night-reveller or a suspicious rascal. Nor does the area's watchman want to be seen, and he rests from his rounds in some sheltering doorway or friendly tavern.'[32] It is abundantly clear that this night-watchman is incapable of dealing with the new dangers of the night. A phrase like 'Berlin under the night-watchman' has no longer anything threatening about it, and, on the contrary, may express a nostalgia for the supposedly 'good old days'.

## A MODERN POLICE FORCE

In Britain, after the Glorious Revolution of 1688, central government had largely withdrawn 'from the supervision of local government'; only a few voices, such as Michael Dalton's in 'A Guide for the Early Stuart Justice of the Peace', encouraged them 'to ensure that night-watches were kept in the town from sunset to sunrise'. The watchmen 'were authorized to arrest "persons suspect of being nightwalkers, be they strangers, or others that be of evil fame and behaviour"'. In the 1770s the City Marshal Thomas Gates 'organized his men effectively against some criminal gangs, and in the following decade a small, regular patrol was organized for the city's streets'. From 1791 onwards these watchmen wore uniforms, and an armed patrol 'based at Bow Street, was watching the main roads into the centre of London from evening until midnight'. This is interesting, because it suggests that the authorities felt that the city was threatened by insecurity and danger, above all from outside. In 1812 the Night Watch Regulation Bill was introduced, setting, as Clive Emsley wrote, 'minimum standards for the parish watches of metropolitan Middlesex'; but resistance from the parishes, 'concerned at losing control of their watchmen', led to the with-drawal of the Bill. In 1828 there was a 'Night Foot Patrol' of eighteen officers and 82 men.[33]

The new police force was supposed to end the organizational chaos. 'Sir Robert Peel was the father of the force. He passed an Act through Parliament in 1830, the preamble of which explained that "the Nightly Watch and Nightly Police have been found inadequate to the Prevention and Detection of Crime, by reason of the frequent Unfitness of the individuals employed and the Insufficiency of their Numbers."' The real novelty in this attempt was the subordination of this police force to the Home Office, the police appearing as an 'instrument of government'.

Although the Metropolitan Police of London had already been set up in 1829, the police historian Stefan Petrow dates the phase of its transformation 'into a recognizably modern professional police force' to the years after 1870.[34] Until then the unity of police activity had probably been more formal than real, existing only at the level of laws and regulations. At the beginning, too, the abolition of the division between day and night police had only been partially implemented. In their 'Report from the Day and Night Police Commission' of 23 May 1832, Messrs Wood, Jones, Wilson and Prior recommend the establishment of a committee 'to investigate the whole system of Police of this city by day and night, and to consider and report the best plan in their opinion of uniting the police of this city under one system and one authority', and they address a request to Parliament to pass an 'Act to consolidate the Day Police and the Nightly Watch'.

> Up to 1839 London was protected by the famous watchmen, who took over the duties of watch and ward. When Sir Robert Peel set up the Metropolitan Police he proposed to incorporate the City Watch so as to have the whole of London under one force. But the City offered the most strenuous opposition, and put forward, as usual, the claim of their ancient charters and privileges; they were successful, and a sepa-rate force under their own control was allowed them.[35]

Here we see the reflection of a process which differentiates London from the other cities. Until the end of the eighteenth century we can more or less equate 'London' with what is called the 'City of London'. While there was no increase in the area under the jurisdic-tion of the City, the population grew considerably and suburbs were established into which the population of the City was driven, as City warehouses, banks and other public buildings arose in the course of the nineteenth century. This process lasted a long time. While in 1821 there were 124,000 people living in the area covered by the City, from 1850 there is a process of shrinkage; in 1900 the City's population was no more than 27,000, and in 1931 only 13,000. And the City of London did not care about these suburbs: 'All around London were these new districts with no form of government but the parish with its vestry meeting.' Parish councils covered districts which counted tens of thousands of inhabitants, and 'thousands of people found themselves driven outside the City, and with no form of municipal organization'. The visible representative of the authorities was the constable, whose task it was 'to keep order'. 'Here in 1831 lived some one and a half million people . . . whose local affairs were variously managed or mismanaged by the vestries of over ninety parishes or precincts situated in the three counties of Middlesex, Surrey and Kent.'[36] In the whole country there had been endeavours at reform which had in parts been very sucessful, and in 1835 London was, apart from a small town in the North, 'the only unreformed borough'. In a *London Report* of 1837 the parliamentary commissioners emphasized the 'importance of central administration of paving, sewage, and lighting of streets'.

It is in very great measure the street – in its technical aspects, its function in the flow of traffic and supply of goods, but also its external aspect – which triggered the attempts at modernization. In 1855 the Metropolis Local Management Bill was enacted, its most important consequence being the establishment of the Metropolitan Board of Works, which was able to disregard the old boundaries even before there came into existence a unified political structure for the organization of urban life.

In James Winter's *London's Teeming Streets*, one of the best books on streets that I have seen, the author describes and analyzes the various functions which emerge in the street or have to do with it: Imagining, Straightening, Smoothing and Regulating, Policing, Enjoying, Working, Cleaning, Rescuing, Breathing, Inhabiting and Planning. It is no accident that the word 'imagining' stands in first place. Authorities, interested social researchers, and the inhabitants themselves had all of them first to learn what was the significance of the street in a growing metropolis. Here were expressed – and became outwardly visible – the new, modern forms of social intercourse in the metropolis, the streets becoming the mirror of social contradictions, the meeting point of the different cultures. It is therefore not surprising that concepts for working on or dealing with the streets, originally entirely functional in character, have a highly metaphorical aspect: 'cleaning' and 'rescuing' do not signify only the work of cleaning the street and protection against fire. The second, deeper meaning of the words finds expression in the language of the Christian missions. John MacGregor, founder of the 'Shoe-Black Brigade' and the 'Open Air Mission', drew up programmes with the aim of 'using the streets to save souls'.

Many went 'onto the streets'. The Highways Act of 1835 in fact instructed the police to remove every person 'who shall willfully obstruct the passage of any footpath', and this legislation might also very well hit the well-meaning preacher who blocked the streets with his 'Open Air Meetings' and so obstructed them in their modern function as channels for the flow of traffic.

NIGHT LIFE AND DANGER

In the years after 1880 the debate about the danger, insecurity and immorality of the nocturnal city gained in intensity in all three cities, London, Paris and Berlin. The life of entertainment conquered new areas and (outer) districts of the city: Montmartre in Paris, where in the winter of 1881–2 the Chat Noir opened its doors as the first cabaret, followed in 1889 by the Moulin Rouge; and the Hasenheide in Berlin. There emerged, notably in the revue, new forms of mass entertainment that combined elements from the theatre, the fun-fair and the old café-concerts. The paths between the city centres and the new entertainment areas filled up with nocturnal life and came under the scrutiny of the authorities. The traditional perception saw here only the 'vulgar rabble and its bustle, endangering public security',[37] 'elements . . . which at night set out from here on their dangerous raids, and then blow their loot in the company of common prostitutes'.[38] Organized crime, gangs with fixed 'hiding-places' from which they set out on 'raids' – the 'nocturnal side' of the metropolis was spreading, and the night police were insufficiently prepared for it. Added to this there were struggles over jurisdiction: the area for which the Berlin police was responsible ended at the boundaries with Schöneberg, Wilmersdorf and Charlottenburg. An establishment with female service within

Aristide Bruant sang about the Chat Noir, the most famous establishment on the boulevard de Clichy in Paris: 'Je cherche fortune, autour du Chat Noir, au claire de la lune, à Montmartre le soir.' Anonymous photograph, *c.*1900.

the bounds of Berlin had to close at 11 p.m., but its patrons simply crossed the street 'to an establishment of the same type which has *plein pouvoir* the whole night long'.[39]

Alongside the peripheral areas the Friedrichstrasse, the centre of the city and of entertainment life, also remained at the centre of attention; not only for the police, but also to an increasing extent for the Church – in this case the Friedrichswerder District Synod – who were concerned by 'the outrageously uncivil and immoral hurly-burly which develops every evening and every night in the Friedrichstrasse and the arcades, which has become so extensive that after 6 o'clock in the evening it is almost impossible to pass this area with a decent lady'.[40]

Individual contributions build up the horror-picture: it would 'be enough to damage the reputation of a decent man' if he were to be seen there; it would embarrass any decent person to 'go about among such a gang'.

The night can no longer be easily understood. New themes emerge: the criminal underworld, prostitution, the closing time for taverns, bars and restaurants. In addition, the cities are growing, and Berlin in particular grows fast in this period, and in a mostly uncoordinated manner. The new times demand new forms of organization; the 'side effects' of advancing urbanization call forth different reactions: on the one hand the files of the Berlin police authority filled up with complaints about the disturbance of the nocturnal peace, about the noise of the taverns and the 'hurly-burly' of the night-revellers; while on the other hand some sort of counter-movement was also coming into being. Here it was argued that certain features, such as nocturnal entertainment life, but also homelessness and prostitution, had become indivisible parts of life in the big cities, that one could 'control ' them but in no way could they be 'abolished'.

Struggles about the city itself are sparked off by issues of the night; the defenders of the city and of urban life put up a fight against the reproaches of the critics who overemphasize the negative side and in doing so disparage the city: 'It is well known that the security situation in Berlin is better than its reputation,' writes the *Berliner Neueste Nachrichten* in June 1885; 'in the provinces particularly, utterly fantastic ideas are often circulated about the dangers of our public streets.' Judgement on the security situation is obviously a matter of perception: 'It is years since insecurity in the Berlin area has been as great as it is now,' wrote the *Düsseldorfer Anzeiger* at the beginning of June 1885, while on 13 June of the same year the *Berliner Volkszeitung* countered: 'So it can be said that as regards general security Berlin is better than its reputation.'

The interesting question is not who is right; the question is much more how these shifts in perception come about. Police statistics on crime and prostitution are equally accessible to all the authors. But the critics of the night see in the modern phenomena signs of the decay and dissolution of an old order, while a more pragmatic viewpoint sees the admitted problems as soluble in the context of the development of the city. This battle is not restricted to Berlin; it is a battle about the *metropolis* and its future, which is also waged in London and Paris.

In Paris too complaints about nocturnal security take up a great deal of space in the files of the Prefecture of Police; in 1891 the deputy Georges Berry once again suggested the (re-)'creation of a night-watch service'. 'The police', according to Berry, 'are incapable of guaranteeing security, and the newspapers report endlessly on how unsafe Paris is at night.'[41] On the basis of these journalistic reports and in connection with Berry's proposal, the Conseil Municipal of Paris asked for more detailed information about the number and type of crimes.

The monthly statistics of *'crimes et délits'*[42] then provided by the Prefecture of Police do not support the claim that criminality was constantly increasing, the danger growing always greater. The real danger was the fact that the forces of law and order were losing complete control over the night; but as enemies of nocturnal freedom and the breaking-down of barriers, they use in their propaganda the old scare of the 'danger that lurks in the dark' – even if they know very well that the image is untruthful.

On 1 October 1894 in Berlin too the long-demanded change finally came about. 'The replacement of night-watchmen by policemen is now gradually being implemented,' and the city night-watchmen are dismissed, all the court cases to prevent this having failed. Luc Gersal (Jules-Emile Legras) composed the swan-song for this well-known figure:

> He makes a round of the streets in his care, himself closing the doors that have accidentally been left open, and now his reign begins. Slowly, hands behind his back and ears listening out, he ambles up and down the pavement . . . These poor men have to be at their post from 10 o'clock at night until 5 or 6 o'clock in the morning, without

89

anything to distract them than unlocking doors and looking at the paving stones . . . All the same they keep a good watch, and one is seldom bothered in the streets of Berlin, whose surveillance is not difficult, by the way, as they are almost all straight and long. Night-time Berlin is no den of thieves, as Tissot called it; for myself I have to confess that after midnight I feel more secure there than in Paris.[43]

As the 'officers of the Royal Police Authority took over exclusive responsibility for the nocturnal security services',[44] other tasks, such as the closing of houses and the patrolling of industrial areas, were taken over by private watch and closing services; these services worked together with the police, even if not always without friction. They saw their task primarily as the protection of property, the prevention of robberies. Criticism of the 'business practices of dishonest night-watch organizations' was soon heard;[45] notably, however, the number of newspaper reports of nocturnal attacks and disturbances did not diminish, even in the early years of the next century.

NIGHT WITHOUT WATCHMEN

Inhabitants of the areas of the city touched by the nocturnal 'events' asked for 'up-to-date' measures by a modern police – 'this deplorable state of affairs occurs no less often during the day than during the night' – demanding 'uninterrupted surveillance'[46] and even threatening to take things – their protection – into their own hands: 'The danger exists at night, and of course it is greatest at night, and if we are not to be protected, then the citizens know what they have to do: they will protect themselves.'[47] These citizens and the newspapers that represent them claimed a *right* to nocturnal security; but were they right to do so? Was the security of the city and its inhabitants really more endangered at night than during the day? This is obviously more a question of feeling, of mood and evaluation, than of statistics.

In the years that followed, discussions about the reintroduction of the night-watch came to an end in both Paris and Berlin. The police changed with its changed duties, the two most important fields of activity being the fight against crime and the fight against public immorality. The old night-watch had had its day. In the *Eclair* in 1906 Ernest Laroche shed a small tear:

We were fond of the night-watchman. Our memories of him are mixed with those of innumerable old stories and tales of earlier days, tales which enchanted and sweetened our childhood; and now if we close our eyes we seem to see his silhouette passing by, we believe we hear his nocturnal call and the melancholy rhythms of his song. This brave man, who walked the streets alone with lantern and staff in hand, was like the guardian angel of all the city's inhabitants.[48]

The childhood of the metropolis is over, and this changes the quality of the nocturnal city very considerably. The 1920s in particular, a high point for nocturnal entertainment as it was a low point for nocturnal wretchedness, would have to do without the night-watchman, without the one who best knew the night side of his beat.

A drawing from *UHU* of October 1925 anticipates anonymous surveillance on TV monitors:

'*The night-watchman of the future, who will monitor the nocturnal streets on a wall of televisions*' – modern night has to manage without the person who knew it best. A utopian vision from the Berlin magazine *UHU*, 1925.

## 2 Closing time

*The million-strong city, whose life and bustle streams with-*
*out cease and which seems to find in its own restlessness*
*ever-new forms of entertainment and of unease, can only*
*allow itself a short period of daily rest.*

PAUL LINDENBERG (1895)[49]

With the night-watch the authorities had attempted to organize the
public *space* of the nocturnal city and to keep it tightly under control.
Equally great efforts were made to determine and control the *time*
during which the city 'came out of its shell'. These efforts were
closely connected to the attempt to monitor and control the growing
urban proletariat. Before we take a closer look at *closing time*, the area
in which these attempts found practical application, a few more
general reflections are necessary.

### TEMPORAL STRUCTURES AND PERCEPTIONS OF TIME

The development of a 'rational time', an hourly organization of time
no longer dependent on the course of the sun but on the conditions
of life and work, is one of the most important preconditions for the
emergence of modern society.[50] The hours available to one each day
are divided according to whether one is working or not: every single
individual's day, and so his perception of time,[51] is marked by his
occupation and the conditions of the organization of his work, but
this division of the day very decisively influences his whole way of
life. In general the processes of modernization and urbanization also
transform the forms of association and communication between
people and change the time-perception of the whole society.

The experience of the city and life in the city – composed of many
individual daily activities – also marks the time-perception of the
city-dwellers. The appearance of great variety and the possibilities
it affords for the creation of one's own life show the individual
how the situation in the city is different from life in the village, in
the provinces. It was part of the traditional structure of order in the
provinces that you could not escape it except by flight;[52] life in
the city makes new demands on the perception of time, but also
opens it up to new possibilities.

The need to adopt, to learn a *new attitude towards the night*, was also one of the new demands in the process of industrialization. In this the spread of night work played a significant role. However it cannot be seen unequivocally as a phenomenon of *urbanization*, being rather related to general *industrialization*; it plays a role in the city but it marks the perception of the nocturnal city only marginally.

## THE CITY WORKS AT NIGHT

The first areas, outside agriculture, in which night work was under-taken were navigation, mining and watch-service, and these are not specific to the city.[53] For the period around 1900 Jon. Sternkopf lists the following professions in addition to security and watch-services, in which there was regular night work: transport institutions (navigation, railways, post, telegraphs); water, gas and electricity companies; newspaper printing plants; hotels and restaurants; night cleaning; mining; blast-furnace works, iron and steel works and rolling mills; brick factories and glassworks; sugar factories; chemical plants; paper and cellulose factories; and waterworks. In this inventory, alongside the heavy industry there also can be detected a metropolitan element: traffic, services, communication, and energy supply – these make possible the circulation of urban life and they have to function at night as well.

Among the few authors who dealt with the subject of 'night work' at all, even fundamental questions were controversial. Was night work harmful? Does it represent a 'moral danger' or 'does it prevent sin'? We should note that working and business hours have a decisive influence on the 'temporal activity pattern' of a city.[54] The creation and development of night shift-work plays an important role in the *continuous activity* by which the metropolis is recognized. More and more people were about in the night hours, on their way to work or on their way home, and they needed to be supplied, they needed to be transported. Important for us is the fact that the growing demands of the work process and the confined and to some extent inhuman conditions of housing create the preconditions for a shift of the necessary relaxation from the area of the family and home into the public realm.

The fact that the city itself no longer sleeps plays a decisive role in the picture of the city night; different authors, for example Ulfilas

93

Müller in the journal *Daheim* (1901), contrast the dominant image of a night life marked by pleasure with a picture of work:

> If it is a question of describing 'night life' in the metropolis, then curiously even the writers who are familiar with the true situation think above all of describing the nocturnal *pleasures* of the big city, and give an account of the places where slovenliness and vice celebrate their orgies! And yet this kind of metropolitan night life is not at all the most interesting, which is found much more where *honest night-time work* is done in the big city, work that is as hard as it is necessary, because the whole traffic and business of the day is for the most part made possible by the preparations already being made for it at night, and the defects caused by the traffic of the previous day are remedied.[55]

The description that follows is truly impressive. Here too traffic plays a big role, work in the railway stations, the repair of the track, but also work on the streets, where paviours and tarmac-layers are busy – this is night as the repair of the day; there is work being done in the telephone exchanges and post offices, on the sewers, on cleaning the streets; there is work in market halls, in police stations, in the (private) night-watch services, in the fire service, in the hospitals and in the warehouses, at newspaper printing presses. Those who remain fixated on the entertainment side get no impression of the working city, which is accessible only to 'those who are intent on study and visit night workers at their occupations'.

This picture of Berlin at work is used in various ways; it may serve to illustrate the confrontation of activity and leisure; but it can also stand for the sleeplessness of the big city:

> A few hours, hardly two or three, is the time during which Berlin falls into an unsteady, often disturbed slumber, from which it is often violently aroused, like a feverish person rising from confused dreams, too excited even to take the necessary sleep. When the dying night struggles for power with the waking day, then is the time when the pulse of the capital city beats at its weakest, when its stony limbs are no longer or not yet surrounded by monstrous noise, when in the more distant parts of the city . . . one could believe in the total paralysis of all life in the tremendous sea of houses.[56]

And even there, in the 'more distant parts of the city', the picture of the sleeping city is no longer true; 'Berlin's toilet', the repair of streets, 'is done during the night, only visible to a few night-birds.'[57]

In the proletarian, revolutionary literature of the 1920s this con-

94

frontation from the bourgeois *feuilleton* of the turn of the century is still painted with affection, but drawn with sharper edges: in his novel *Barrikaden am Wedding*, Klaus Neukrantz describes night in the workers' districts as miserable and shorn of entertainment – because the day with its worries and fears 'has long since poisoned the nights'; on the streets there are the police patrols, the homeless and a few drunks, but 'in the apartment-canyons of Wedding, tightly packed with people, night comes early. The workers' nights are short'.[58] In the *Vossische Zeitung* Ehm Welk sets out a similarly unromantic picture of work against the clichés of the 'purveyors of Berlin crime-stories and big-city fairy tales':

> In some bar or other a gramophone or radio is screeching out a charleston or a ballad for its three patrons – sounds from another world, 'for Kurfürstendamm people' they say here. But not many hear the words, for most are asleep, because they are tired and poor.[59]

As well as articulating a complaint – whose validity we do not wish to underestimate here – these images of working Berlin, and the juxtaposition of the Berlin of leisure and the Berlin of work do something else: they illustrate the development of a new temporal structure in the city, in which the hours of the night also gain a new value. They emphasize the impression of the 'continuous activity' of the metropolis, they illustrate the differentiation of nocturnal life in the cities, and above all of their social and socio-topographical dimensions; they give a picture of many contrasts in which the nocturnal city is recognizable as a world of oppositions and confrontation.

IMAGES OF NOCTURNAL PLEASURE

With the process of industrialization the newly created needs for relaxation led to the establishment of a *leisure industry*, and with it a leisure infrastructure in the city, which primarily comes into action in the evening and during the hours of night. In Paris the years around 1840 are decisive in the formation of a *metropolitan* entertainment life. For this period, during which the population of the city grew to an unknown extent through arrivals from outside, the historian François Gasnault also noted a multiplication of *bals publics*. In 1840 Prime Minister Thiers decided on the construction of new fortifications; now the *communes rurales* of Montmartre,

95

La Chapelle, La Villette, Belleville, Charonne, Bercy, Vaugirard, Grenelle, Auteuil, Passy and the Batignolles were included in a second 'inner' belt of the city. The 'intra/extra muros' relationship lost importance, the city no longer stopping at the old barriers, and the half-rural, half-proletarian entertainment establishments of the new *faubourgs*, the suburbs, were integrated into the entertainment topography of the Parisian *noctambules*. The radius of their nocturnal rounds increased significantly, an 'excursion' to the north or the south of the city adding interest to the programme, and there arose the impression that 'à Paris, le plaisir est partout'. Everywhere in the city there were islands of entertainment, still isolated from each other, related only to their close neighbourhoods – but with their rounds and their noisy explorations, the evening and night-time revellers created the network that made of Paris the 'capitale du plaisir'.

It is often not easy to identify why a particular establishment proved attractive, why there follow further developments in its wake, why a particular part of the city suddenly develops into a centre of night life; perhaps the dance halls and little theatres of the *faubourgs* gave an indulged and curious Paris audience the illusion of a fresh, unspoilt performance and a greater sense of adventure than the usual inner-city offerings could provide. The expectations of this public also changed the character of the performances. Night life 'conquers' these districts in waves, and a tendency towards levelling seems inherent in the process, and repeats itself. In his history of entertainment in Montmartre, Louis Chevalier describes how the news of the 'real' entertainment, 'de vieilles traditions et moins vulgaires', reached the boulevards and tempted their public towards the remoter districts, until one day 'à jamais maudit', forever damned, the Chat Noir opened its doors there; and in 1929 Bob Landsberg described in *Querschnitt* the predictable fate of the 'Negro dance hall in the Rue Blomet':

> Perhaps – it is still not decided – soon or a little later, the large mass of onlookers, the addicts of the sensational, the followers and fellow-travellers, will trail in the footsteps of the first discoverers, the true aficionadoes and rare initiates, and will enter the Negro dance hall in the Rue Blomet – the same way as they inevitably penetrate wherever there are people who seem to be interesting, even if the latter have have no ambition to draw their nice neighbours' attention to themselves. This is what happened with the 'apaches'' dives and with the artists' bars.

This could also happen here. Then the brave landlord will surely not fail to make his profit. He will put up his prices, set up tables where champagene is obligatory, put oleander trees in front of his establishment, and issue numbers for the cars which park in the street. But the present customers will not come here any more. They will look for another refuge.[60]

The question of how far the working population can actually 'decide for themselves how to make use of the time that is increasingly available from generation to generation'[61] is also of great interest to research on the night: as the conditions of daytime life in the city varied so greatly among the different groups and classes of the population, so did those of the night. But the variations of evening and night-time entertainment are not infinite, and the differences manifest themselves less in *what* can be undertaken in the hours of leisure, as in *how* – and this perhaps most of all – *where* the 'entertainments' took place. Karl Marx and Friedrich Engels noticed the 'brutal form' which the 'pleasures of the proletariat' had to take on because of their long working hours (i.e. the short time remaining for rest) and the 'qualitative and quantitative restrictions on the pleasures accessible to the proletariat'.[62] On the other hand, among the workers and within workers' cultural movements there appeared early on already institutions which committed themselves to 'meaningful' organization of the hours of evening and night. Here one may note that many theoreticians of workers' culture share with bourgeois social reformers the horror-picture of the night – and the fear of the seductive powers of alcohol, immorality, and disorder. In both we find the conviction that the night presents a particularly good opportunity for the development of *strategies of control* and of regulation of entertainment needs.

The focus of these efforts of control were the *places* of nocturnal entertainment; the police, who did not wish to do anything against the spread of a bourgeois entertainment industry, saw with suspicion how in the districts where the proletariat lived there was emerging a specific infrastructure of proletarian 'entertainment'. The pub[63] became the point of crystallization of the new workers' culture, an intersection of sociability, culture and politics, which also offered the opportunity for political meetings, for political exchange.

97

As night falls, the cleaning of the city begins: '*Nocturnal street-cleaning with rotary-brush machines.*' Woodcut, after a drawing of Berlin by E. Hosang, 1878.

Mediated by a critique of the proletariat, the description of (male) proletarian culture as a 'constant curiosity, an insatiable hunger for information, an addiction to entertainment, an immoderate letting-off of steam, a lust for sensation and . . . a consuming *interest in anything at all*'[64] touches the whole city; the classification of 'brief, rapid and repeatable pleasures' (cigarettes, beer, fast-food places, kiosks, cinemas, newspapers) as a form of mass culture that appeared with the proletariat, also provides bourgeois criticism of the city with new opportunities for its condemnation of urban life. On the street, the place of meeting and communication, those who hunger for experience get new sustenance, and on the corner awaits the pub, as the place of sociability and opportunity for political exchange; 'in the big city the worker lives amongst amenities which seem to him to be unattainable in his life and work',[65] and here the pub exudes a 'fateful attraction'.

The arguments against nocturnal life – feared as a breach of order – are not fundamentally different, whether they are addressed to 'the proletariat', to a bourgeois public or to the 'city-dweller' in general. On the one hand the nocturnal city offers – everybody – a large number of commercial and employment opportunities, 'for which the daytime does not suffice'.[66] On the other hand, the places and offers of the night are focal points for the 'intensified surges of life as they push further out into the late hours', filling-stations where the 'interest in anything at all' can be satisfied.

In many ways the city 'comes out of its shell' at night, breaking the chains of a traditional ordering of time. The forces of law and order, responsible for the maintenance of peace, order and security in the nocturnal city, have to adapt the measures they take for the fulfilment of their tasks to the changed situation. Control of nocturnal movement through the city becomes more and more difficult; the more there is life on the street, and the more various and differentiated this life becomes, the more numerous become the potential areas of conflict.

One attempt to control and to keep a 'firm grasp' on the nocturnal city is the regulation of the closing times of establishments accessible to the public, the *imposition of a unitary time* that is to organize and structure the night.

AFTER HOURS

Before the industrial era 'closing time' played no role in the prescriptions and comments which deal with the regulation of nocturnal life. The general ban on going out after the curfew or *couvre-feu* essentially prohibited 'running about outside', made disturbance of the peace a punishable offence, and saw 'nocturnal revelry' in principle as raising the suspicion of prostitution. The total control of *public* spaces was sufficient; an additional surveillance and regulation of *internal* spaces only became necessary when drinking and immorality, the two main offences against order, became established in permanent premises *and* when these spaces became accessible from the outside, from the street. When they attract such a large public that it generates a certain street life, and public order thus seems threatened, the authorities have to think up rules and regulations for the internal spaces. By an edict of 1 May 1662 the Great Elector Friedrich Wilhelm of Prussia, ordered such regulations for the night life of Berlin:

> As we have forbidden all brawling in the whole country so we cannot allow such things to occur in our royal residences . . . We therefore now order and command brewers and citizens, as soon as the spigot has been closed at the sound of the drum, no longer to serve beer, or allow it to leave the premises, nor to keep drinking customers in their houses or taverns.[67]

With this edict there begins a long history of rules and regulations 'concerning', as it says in the archives of the Berlin Police Authority, 'the establishment of dance halls and tobacco-divans, as also the nightly intemperance within them, and the regulation of closing time'.[68] In this respect too the years around 1840 occupy a key position: with the spread of drinking establishments over the whole city and their increasing variety of form, new measures become necessary. The annual police report for 1839 on order and morality in Berlin weighs the pros and cons of a special order:

> His Majesty would therefore doubtless desire *that the nocturnal intemperance in beerhouses of the uncultivated classes of Berlin be controlled.* As one may suppose that persons who visit wine cellars and restaurants etc. where spirits, beer, or wine are served are amongst the well-off and probably also the cultivated classes, *from these, on the other hand, one need fear no nocturnal disturbance of the peace,* so premises of this kind may be exempted from the regulation of closing time.[69]

Police thinking is particularly marked by the idea that people belonging to the wealthy and 'cultivated' classes have the right to visit establishments where alcohol is served and there pursue their pleasures, because after leaving them they are supposed to walk or drive peacefully home, causing no disturbance on the streets. The 'hubbub' at any particular place only comes to police attention when it leads to disturbances of the peace: 'Singing and the making of noise in these establishments as a rule only starts around 10 o'clock and lasts until 2 or 3 o'clock in the morning, *when the greater part of the company comes out drunk in order to continue the scandal on the street* and insult the night-watchmen.'[70]

On 18 February 1840, von Puttkammer, the Berlin Chief of Police, wrote to the heads of all police districts instructing them that they should intervene only where they observed or feared disturbances. Here the function of closing time is still to exert control over the nocturnal entertainment of the lower classes and – one step short of closure – to put a stop to 'excesses' at establishments with a better class of customer.

A little earlier on the Paris police had faced the same problems and had solved them in very similar ways. On 24 May 1841 the Prefect summarized the closing-time policies of the past 20 years:

It often happens that when leaving an establishment near the Barrières of Paris during the night people disturb the public peace with screams and shouts, that they fight among themselves and insult and mistreat passers-by.

These incidents, which must be brought to an end, take place on Sundays and Mondays, and on holidays when the wine merchants keep their businesses open longer than permitted.

The police regulation of 3 April 1819 provides that all cabarets, cafés, public houses, billiard halls, dance halls and other public amenities in the *communes rurales* in the area of the Prefecture must close at 11 o'clock at night from April to October, at 10 during the other months, after which their owners or employees are not allowed to provide any food, drink or games.[71]

The closing time for inner Paris was on average an hour later, but was more strictly observed; 'un usage qui a acquis une sorte d'autorité', a custom which had taken on the character of a regulation, set the closing time for public establishments 'dans l'intérieur de Paris' at midnight.

The extensive economic changes brought the old regulation of time under attack from two sides. The first *ordonnance* on closing time in the files of the Paris Prefecture of Police dates from 1 November 1780. Recalling the all-night *couvre-feu*, it regulates not only closing times but also opening times, thus establishing a period closed to entertainment, decreeing:

> that in Paris, landlords, café-owners, dealers in wine and spirits and others who serve drinks may not *open* their establishments before 4 o'clock in the morning (from 1 March to 1 November) or 5 o'clock (from 1 November to 1 March), and must close their premises at 10 o'clock in the evening in the winter, and at 11 o'clock in the summer.[72]

Given the increasing traffic in the city, this basic regulation, whose 'exact observation makes possible such a desirable and necessary unity in police measures', could not be upheld for long. The first exemptions concerned particularly establishments in the streets around the market halls: the earlier deliveries of goods begin, the earlier the taverns can open. *Ordonnances* from the Prefecture of Police in the years after 1840 document a constant battle between the police, who demand 'uniform' regulations, and innkeepers and their clients, who for various reasons seek a liberalization of the rules, in this contributing to the further differentiation of nocturnal time.

The enemies of tolerance often take their stand on moral arguments; for them extended opening hours in taverns were seen as a challenge to morality and order – not totally unjustly, because extended hours create the preconditions for the spread of a new nocturnal infrastructure. On the (short-term) re-establishment of the Berlin brothels in 1851, Theodor Bade wrote, 'but we go further now and ask: how long were the brothel doors open to the public? Horribile dictu: until 2 o'clock in the morning!' Before, the brothels had had to close at midnight; now 'the new arrangement added two more night hours – once again a terrible mistake!'[73] Such criticism was aimed not only at the brothels, but also, and above all, at the newly created workers' pubs of the industrializing city. Here a distinct new milieu was developing, which was seen as both politically and culturally threatening, providing rallying places, meeting places, little niches in which there might develop resistant forms of communication and action, reason enough for increased watchfulness on the part of the forces of law and order. The imposition of closing times as an instrument of control played an important role, in addition to surveillance by (mostly plain clothes) police agents.

A Berlin police decree of 9 March 1866 introduces the concept of 'prohibited time': '[it] is decreed *that the "prohibited time" extends from 11 o'clock at night until 4 o'clock in the morning.'*[74] In the cities closing times become versatile instruments, used in the fight against prostitution as well as in initiatives for the improvement of workers' morals; the Berlin police authority reports that 'undoubtedly such dance halls, which are visited exclusively by prostitute women, in which for the most part dancing previously used to continue until 3 o'clock in the morning . . . could only have a harmful effect, whatever one might think of the alleged necessity of such amenities in a large city.'[75] This final clause is interesting as a sign that the restrictive measures of the police were not at all uncontroversial. Their arguments are many:

> One of the greatest influences on the commercial position of innkeepers and on the moral and economic behaviour of the people is . . . always the setting of the so-called closing time . . .
>   The customers, drinking late into the night, not only have cause to spend beyond their means, but after a night's revelling also become incapable of returning the next day to their daily activity with the necessary physical and mental freshness, the later hours not only directly diminishing their wealth, but indirectly at least also their capacity for work.[76]

This view, though, could hardly find implementation in practical measures. The police had to learn that life in the big city had a momentum which became more and more difficult to control: 'The ordained hour for the closure of establishments serving alcohol is 11 o'clock. *The situation in the metropolis, with its continuous restless bustle, day and night, does not however permit strict adherence to these early hours,* and it has thus become customary to regard midnight as the closing time applied in Berlin.' In June 1878, however, as a result of 'abuse of this tolerance', licences for new establishments were awarded on condition that they should close at 11 o'clock, extensions being allowed only after a period of proven orderly management. As the police saw it, the 'demoralizing, harmful influence of drinking establishments' increased as the hands of the clock advanced; in the

103

eyes of the guardians, moral and political 'demoralization' go hand in hand, and over-long opening hours symbolize the 'general loss of cohesion and stability':

> It can certainly not be denied that over the last decades the increased opportunities for gluttony and loose behaviour and their consequences have significantly contributed to the workers becoming accustomed to needs and pleasures which earlier were unknown, wasting their meagre wages every night in taverns and ruining their financial situation. They finally lay the responsibility for their reduced circumstances at the door of the government and its regulations, which they blame for the evil consequences of their own pernicious way of life; as a result they become dissatisfied citizens and fall under the influence of Social Democracy.

So Social Democracy is seen as benefiting from gluttony and 'loose behaviour' – while eminent representatives of the workers' parties were waging a fight against pubs and against alcoholism, which in their view degraded the workers, making them submissive servants of capital and alienating them from political life.

A decree of 22 July 1879 set closing time for drinking establishments with female service at 11 p.m., the police referring in their reasons to similar regulations in Paris and London; but for Paris at least this cannot be confirmed. Here an *ordonnance* of 31 December 1878 provided that closing time was 'à 1 heure précise' for the whole city; an *ordonnance* of 28 June 1879 then set closing time for places of entertainment on the boulevards at '2 heures précises du matin', and at the same time establishments in the neighbourhood of Les Halles were for the first time granted the right to open the whole night through: 'landlords in the neighbourhood of Les Halles, in the area circumscribed by the boulevard Sébastopol and the rues Tiquetonne, Jean-Jacques-Rousseau, Saint-Honoré, du Louvre and de Rivoli, are permitted to keep their establishments open all night during the whole of the year.'[77]

This new measure was the result of a survey ordered by the Paris police in April 1877. In it are listed the establishments which for various reasons enjoy an extension of opening hours: the number of cafés, cabarets and other places which closed only at 1 a.m., 2 a.m. or not at all was so great, and the reasons for the exceptions in their favour so difficult to reconstruct, that it must have seemed more sensible for the Prefecture of Police to introduce a more generally generous regulation. Of the cafés Defert, Lenoble and Vanniez, all situated in the area of Les Halles, it was said: 'These establishments enjoy a tolerance, though it is no longer known why. They are indeed closed at night, but it is enough to knock a certain way to be allowed in for the whole night.'[78]

This survey deepens our knowledge of the topography of nocturnal Paris. Without a doubt the boulevards are the focal points of 'night life' as far as it is characterized by places of pleasure and entertainment – 'establishments there enjoy a tolerance in accordance with long tradition, because they are situated on the boulevards (comme étant situés sur les boulevards)' – particularly the boulevards des Italiens, des Capucines, Poissonière, Montmartre, Saint-Denis and Saint-Martin, the last two already communicating with the neighbourhood of Les Halles, the second centre of night life. Streets and areas neighbouring these centres are also included, like the rue du Faubourg Montmartre off the boulevard Montmartre and rue Drouot in the 9th arrondissement, links to the place Pigalle.

In 1891 the Chief of the Berlin Police made observations which show that closing times were already losing some of their importance as measures of control: 'The police regulation of 9 March 1866, currently in force, no longer takes sufficient account of the changes which have occurred since its promulgation. With Berlin's development into a metropolis since the '70s, not only has traffic increased considerably in intensity, it has also . . . so developed that even during the night there is hardly any slack period.'[79] The most important thing is to prevent pimps and criminals finding a hiding-place in drinking establishments 'after nocturnal activities'. It is no longer the late night but the early morning hours that are at the focus of police attention: 'Given the fact that . . . landlords are permitted to reopen their establishments as early as 4 o'clock in the morning, situations have developed in the life of the streets at night which urgently need drastic change.' 'In the early morning hours, on the street', outside ill-famed night cafés and seedy bars, events are taking place which 'lead to serious disturbances of public peace, security and morality . . . ' The Chief of Police therefore demands that the owners of low dives and low-class coffee houses cease their activities between the hours of 4 and 6 o'clock in the morning. Pimps, prostitutes and other figures of the night should early 'disappear from the public sphere'; this first goal of police activity remains unchanged, and its achievement was intended to reduce the number

105

of annoyances 'to which industrious workers on their way to work are often enough exposed at this hour, and to spare children on their way to school the sight of loose women arm in arm with their drunken companions'.

The regulation proposed was to define the hours between 11 p.m. and 6 a.m. as 'prohibited time', allowing the possibility of exceptions for establishments near factories, building sites and markets. Discussions on the proposals lasted exactly ten years; there was opposition, as might be expected, from the trade, but also from the ranks of the Berlin city council. An order of 27 July 1900 requested all police districts to report on the closing times of bars and night cafés, and on the advantages and disadvantages of the introduction of later opening hours. The reports support the arguments of the Chief of Police, which was also to be expected; they also provide evidence about nocturnal street life in the years around the turn of the century. A significant change, one records, was the new habit of 'only visiting theatres, drinking establishments and other places of entertainment at a late hour, and therefore extending the period spent in them into the morning hours'. The slack period late at night 'has almost totally disappeared, at least in the main streets of the city, the traffic on the streets and the bustle in the drinking establishments continuing without interruption, almost undiminished in intensity, from the previous evening until the following morning'.[80]

In their reports, various police districts stress that it would make sense to keep the 'better' establishments open; they would provide travellers and a large number of workers with a place to stop off before departure or before starting work. But the general tendency is as follows:

> These establishments close at 2 o'clock but at 4 they are already open again. Only then begins the real night life of those elements who only visit places where they can move about as they please without being bothered by the landlord . . . If by the closure of such low-class establishments, a source of moral decay, one were to rob these easy-going night-lovers of their hideaways, then many things in Berlin's night life would improve.

> These night cafés are notoriously the starting-point of numerous noisy scenes, scuffles which move out onto the street, and the main reason for the revolting sight of drunken, well-dressed gentlemen and their easy-going female company on the streets at the start of the day's public life.

. . . so that in particular the appearance of drunken persons of both sexes on the public highway in the morning hours should no longer offend the sensibility of industrious citizens and incite the worker and artisan to hatred of the well-heeled idlers.[81]

When the nocturnal scenes complained of by the police are even discussed in the press, with an undertow of criticism of the forces of law and order, as in the 'metropolitan picture' drawn by the *Deutsche Tageszeitung* of 6 February 1901 – 'in the early morning the area around the Oranienburger Tor is unique. From all sides industrious people stream towards work through this central traffic intersection, and in their midst the stars of the *demi-monde* stride proudly with heads held high . . . Several cafés are already or still open, horse-drawn carriages stop in front of them, and the riff-raff pour in to reckon up and report on the experiences of the previous night' – then the police in turn have to defend themselves, and it is 'self-evident that the police organs have to intervene immediately against excesses of this kind'. From the circle of the city councillors too there is criticism that the police may be carrying out long investigations of the problem and are always making new demands, but that these have little effect on the concrete situation; on 25 March 1901 the council wrote to the police authority to the effect that it could only support a new regulation on closing times if they were fixed from 11 p.m. to 5 rather than 6 a.m., because 'many of the young, unmarried workers are forced to take their first breakfast before work in public establishments'; but when the Chief of Police assured them that he would make wider use of his power to grant special authorizations, the council finally agreed. On 14 May 1901 a new police regulation was published, which laid down 'that closing time extends from 11 o'clock in the evening until 6 o'clock in the morning'.[82]

Now begin the first discussions at council meetings, with members complaining in particular that they have not been informed on time. A particularly negative feature of the new regulation, it is felt, is the fact that an appropriate rule could not be found which gives exceptional authorizations an important place and leaves judgement on the 'respectability' of the establishment in the hands of the police. The associations and organizations of the Berlin food and drink trade and the dance hall operators also opposed the new regulation; their protest meeting on 15 July 1901 noted that the policy of authorizations was applied 'in a rigorous manner'.[83] In reply the police authority was able to muster impressive figures: by August 1901

1,460 catering and drinking establishments (of a total of 10,829) had applied for authorization to open early, and only in 198 cases had it been denied.

The reports of those who visited Berlin in these years rather confirm the police view. Berlin's popularity as a tourist destination seems to have put it into real competition with the other great cities, London and Paris, and it is not only the illumination of the nocturnal city but its 'staying power', the night that never ends, that is used as a yardstick of modernity and progress:

> Berlin's night life is notably lively. Has Paris been overtaken in this regard? And will one not, one day, have to change the geography of Babylon and Nineveh? Unter den Linden, on the Friedrichstrasse, and around the Leipziger and the Potsdamer Strasse, the bustle never stops, all night long. Many establishments do not close at all. When the last customers leave, the clearing up is done and then it is time to open up again.[84]

Jules Huret compared this situation with that of the place Blanche and the place Pigalle in Paris – where, in the meantime, the nocturnal hurly-burly had reached the heights of Montmartre (and long overstepped the frontiers of the 'heures de fermeture'). On his night tour through Berlin 'under the guidance of proven, recognized experts' the traveller from Paris discovered the variety of night life around 1900, seeing pubs 'where life is extinguished around midnight' and others 'which are hardly yet awake by this nocturnal hour'; the walk takes him not only from evening to morning, but also from generally accessible, innocuous taverns to the specialized establishments patronized by the 'connoisseur': for the leisured traveller the effort 'to hold out' *a whole night through* becomes part of the nocturnal folklore of Berlin. The 'guides to the night' also react to this, raising the 'night on the tiles' to a new importance: '*2 o'clock at night*. Couples are leaving the Palais de Danse and the Moulin Rouge. The glowing red letters on Maxim's go out. This is the sign that in the casinos of Under den Linden, at Toni Grünfeld's and at the Montbijou in the Jägerstrasse, at the Neue Buffet in the Französische Strasse etc. the lights go up and the champagne buckets are readied. After the ballrooms and bars have shut the elegant generally look in at the 'Pavillon Mascotte . . . Here the atmosphere is characteristic of the elegant night-spots of Berlin . . . There is much beauty among the cocottes, who are now starting "the day" fresh and lively, dominating the scene.' This tour through the Friedrichstadt ends at Dreher, a simple wine-bar, where in the early morning, around 5 o'clock, the remains of the elegant revellers gather together, 'high on champagne and nervous excitement'. A second tour takes Huret to the north-east of Berlin: 'Identity papers should be taken along, just in case. Stay together and do not join the company of strangers! The tour should be done without one's lady.' The route takes in the Café Lang on the Friedrichstrasse, the Winkel am Tore in the Hanoverschen Strasse, the Café Steuer and the Strammer Hund, finally, around 6 o'clock in the morning, reaching the Erlanger Krug in the Elsässerstrasse: 'New customers are always coming in. Young men, their long hair hanging down over their faces, and prostitutes dominate. Students, night-walkers, and everything the traffic brings in at such an unusual hour sit in between.'[85]

Jules Huret too believes (and writes) that 'in the workers' and industrial areas things happen' in exactly the same way as on Unter den Linden. Faithful to the traditional model, towards the end of his account he describes the street cleaners who clear away the rubbish of the night; the picture of night has already congealed into a cliché: the workers are alien to it. In his study of the proletariat published in 1906, the sociologist Werner Sombart wrote:

> At best we find out how it [the proletariat] starts the day when we get home, tired, at five or six, after a night spent dancing or in an extended game of poker, or when we go to the railway station to catch an early train . . . Then we are amazed to suddenly catch a glimpse of a totally alien world. We didn't know that they were there, these hundreds, these thousands 'going to work' at a brisk walk, in twos and threes, mostly without speaking, working tools or coffee jar in hand, in long columns. They . . . hurry now into the arms of the giant Moloch, the factory whose shrill whistle at 6 o'clock, when we once more turn comfortably round in our beds, announces that its inmates' individual life is now over for eleven or twelve hours.[86]

'Only the evening', Sombart concludes, 'returns him [the worker] to himself', but then there is fatigue, the family and perhaps the pub. The two images of leisure and work cannot be reconciled.

In Berlin, as in Paris, the world of pleasure demands the whole night for itself, and the police battle painfully to maintain a 'prohibited time', however short, 'and when nasty closing time approaches and it strikes 4 o'clock, the nice men and women get upset about the heartlessness of the authorities, who put an end to the fun just when it has started to get going'.[87] Edmund Edel wrote this in 1914, shortly before the First World War put an abrupt end to night life. The *ordonnance* from the Paris Prefecture of Police documents the official end of the night-intoxication of the *belle époque*: 'closing time for restaurants and bars in Paris and in the Département of the Seine has been fixed at 10 o'clock.'[88] In Berlin too, the Police Authority decree of 14 December 1916 imposes a more stringent regulation of closing time and introduces severe restrictions on the external illumination of buildings and on the lighting of shop windows. Of course, night life went on within the tolerated level, as Magnus Hirschfeld was to describe in depth – with critical side-swipes at the nights 'behind the lines' – in his *Moral History of the [First] World War*.[89]

THE REGULATION OF CLOSING TIMES BY LICENSING

The history of London nights is closely linked to the history of the licensing laws. Although they were provided for by legislation, here temporal restrictions did not play a decisive role from the very beginning; much more important was the question of who had the right to sell 'intoxicating drinks' 'on' or 'off' the premises. In 1903, Sidney and Beatrice Webb, who a few years later were to collaborate in the great social inquiry carried out by Richard Booth, published a study of the history of the development of these laws that gets as far as the middle of the nineteenth century.[90] T. R. Gourvish and R. G. Wilson have only recently continued the story with an account of further developments after the Beer Act of 1830.[91] 1830, they say in their introduction, is 'a good date to begin a history of the modern brewing industry'. The establishment of 'beer houses' alongside the existing inns, taverns and ale houses, was revolutionary 'in its immediate social consequences', and decisive for the 'dramatic transformation' (B. Webb) that followed, because a purely democratic institution was created: the 'pub' as we know it to this day, a metropolitan phenomenon.

After a debate lasting more than fifteen years it was decided that 'after 11 October 1830 any rate-payer could apply for a two-guineas-per-annum excise licence to sell beer'. 'Be it therefore enacted . . . that . . . it shall and may be lawful for any and every person under the provision of this Act to sell Beer, Ale, and Porter by Retail in any part of England, in any House or premises specified in such licence.'[92]

This law also had profound effects on the structure of the temporal order: 'The regulations of Parliament as to hours of closing, etc., were simply set at naught.'

The opening hours laid down in the Beer Act comprised the period of 5 a.m. to 10 p.m., except on Sundays because the new public houses had to remain shut during the church service – and there were now many of them: in the first six months after the new law came into force 24,324 licences were issued across the whole country, and a further 45,717 in the following eight years. The beer house became the central focus of a moral critique: 'For forty years, justices, parsons and police would lay the blame for most of the evils of the new industrial society at its door.'[93] The anti-alcohol movement of 'teetotalism' emerged in the 1830s as a reaction to the new developments, and the Temperance Party made its first public appearance in 1834.

The Licensing Act of 7 August 1840 revoked the power to decide opening hours that had been granted to justices of the peace, a universal provision seeming more politically appropriate: 'No person shall have or keep his house open at any time before the hour of Five of the clock in the morning nor after Twelve of the clock at Night of any day in the week in the cities of London or Westminster, or within the boundaries of any of the boroughs of Marylebone, Finsbury, Tower Hamlets, Lambeth, or Southwark.'

In the 1860s closing time for beer houses was first midnight, then 12.30 a.m., and only with the start of the First World War was it brought forward to 10 p.m. The issue of licences had been controlled by the magistrates since 1580, and since 1729 there had been annual 'brewster sessions' for the purpose. The regulation of opening hours was thus closely connected to the question of licensing itself, and was hardly debated outside it, and in this the situation was completely different from that in Paris or Berlin. New Licensing Acts in 1872 and 1874[94] made no decisive changes in the matter of 'closing time', which until the creation of the London County Council was not seen as the responsibility of the city. Only in 1888 did the county justices hand over to the newly created central institution 'the duty of licensing houses or places of music and dancing'. In the same year – significantly for the public image of the London streets – the County Council, exercising powers on the basis of the Disorderly Houses Act 1751 and the Public Entertainment Act 1875, set up a Theatre and Music Halls Committee. But here too the extensive debate about levels of jurisdiction within 'Greater London' prevented the adoption of a unified procedure.

Brian Harrison analyzed two 'drink maps' from 1887 and 1899 in order to determine 'London's pub geography'.[95] His functional description of the pub as 'transport centre, recreation centre and meeting place' is certainly valid, and his comparison of the internal characteristics of the two competing partners – pubs on the one hand, the temperance movement on the other – may lend support to the thesis that the pubs too, deliberately or not, had a function: keeping people, men at least, off the streets.

THE 1920S: A BRIEF PERIOD OF OPENNESS

After the First World War the development of closing times reflects a lack of direction on the part of the administrations, an uncertainty as to whether the tumult was over and something new could begin: in Paris closing time was set at 11.30 p.m. on 15 April 1919, at 1 a.m. on 14 October, and on 5 November 1919, only three weeks later, it was changed again, to midnight. The *ordonnances* of 29 May 1920 and of 3 January 1921 once more set closing time at 1 a.m., and at the same time the regulation setting the earliest opening time at 4 a.m. was suspended.

In Berlin too it took a long time for the restrictions brought about by the war to be lifted. On 3 May 1920 the Association of Hotel, Restaurant and Coffee House Owners presented a petition to the government requesting it once again to recognize a later closing time as a necessity of life. If they were able to keep their coffee houses open the 'pests of metropolitan life that promote immorality' would be left high and dry. By a decree on 19 August 1921 the Minister of the Interior finally revoked the 1916 regulations and set closing time at midnight, and at 1 a.m. in exceptional circumstances; but care had to be taken 'that the new rules correspond to the justifiable needs of the general public, yet not fuel the addiction to pleasure and expenditure of certain circles. It hardly needs to be emphasized that the *seriousness of the times dictates extreme restraint in the area discussed here*'.[96]

The new extension of opening hours was criticized by the temperance and anti-alcohol organizations. When Konrat Weymann, a member of Berlin's Higher Administrative Court addressed the 16th International Congress against Alcoholism in Lausanne, his report

The late-closing bar was the last resort of the night-revellers: the night-time life of the street was channelled into designated places, with alcohol as the main attraction. Photograph by Volker Bittner: *The Big Sleep*, n. d.

went beyond the simple criticism of immoderate drinking to become a criticism of the night:

> One can say that as a mass phenomenon alcoholism is particularly prevalent in the evening hours . . .
> There is no doubt that the early evening hours, let us say until 10 or 11 o'clock, give the great majority of people enough opportunity to satisfy their need for convivial relaxation over a drink in a public house. One could add that in general the later it gets the less does this conviviality correspond to inner need . . .
> The dulling effect of alcohol combines with the consequences of loss of sleep at night, bringing about a decrease of pleasure in work. Late drinking hours do substantial economic harm, but they also have various culturally damaging effects. They are an expression of our distance from nature and from natural conditions, and they increase that distance . . .
> Late drinking also has an adverse effect on family life. . .
> Late opening hours significantly increase the already great danger of sexually transmitted diseases . . .
> Late drinking encourages criminality . . .
> I see no adequate reason why the members of the wealthy classes should be able to claim greater opportunities for conviviality in public houses. *Above all, however, I cannot grant the night life of which Berlin, the city of my birth, was unfortunately so proud some years ago, any claim to a place in the public order.*[97]

It is in the struggle against all this that mandatory closing time is supposed to help; like the police, the judge sees the danger that with a stricter rule (11 o'clock) 'secret drinking places' might spring up to meet the needs of nocturnal revellers. The *circumvention of closing times* is a subject often taken up in the 1920s in news and features about the metropolis. Under the nice title 'Bacchanals, anybody?' Egon Erwin Kisch describes how only a few establishments in the dark East Side of the city dared to stay open after closing time, taking in 'fellows weaned of night-time sleep', and in general he concludes 'that night life is over at 1 o'clock at night. Thousands of people see themselves put out onto the street at that hour and have to go home, although they have absolutely no wish to do so. Now begin the activities of the nomadic night establishments, and a new secret profession, which today already numbers far more than a thousand members, the profession of the tout.' The good tout sits in a night-club, makes contact with company that appears to be solvent, and 'when one reluctantly parts company at closing time, he then intimates smilingly that he does not yet have to go home, he knows a faultless establishment . . .'[98] The tout's activities were also graphically described by Egon Jacobssohn and Carl Zuckmayer.[99] It was not least through such reports that in the eyes of foreigners and provincials Berlin, the newcomer, lost its 'innocence' in both the 'positive' and the 'negative' senses. On 13 January 1923 the Mayor of Frankfurt wrote to the Prussian conference of cities:

> The public interest urgently demands that the impression of permanently frenzied pleasure-seeking on the part of the population that is generated by the places of entertainment in many major cities already opening during the day, be eliminated . . . It is not a role worthy of the cities of Germany, at the hour of its deepest political misery, to become places of amusement for foreigners.[100]

The moral view of things is strong and forcefully put: 'Persons whose need for amusement in these serious times is not satisfied by 12 or 1 o'clock at night really do not deserve that their wishes be taken into consideration by the public authorities.'[101] The argument put by the Restaurant Employers' Federation in a letter of 10 July 1923, that 'Berlin is the only metropolis in Germany, and can therefore be treated differently to other cities with regard to closing times', did however have its effect. If closing times are to be taken as a measure of economic development, it then appears quite logical that in April 1926, 'after the complete stabilization of the German currency over the last two years', the Berlin City Council asks for a further extension of opening times. There are still dissenting voices, for example – not surprisingly – in the *Gastwirtschaftliche Zeitung*, the organ of the Association of Hotel, Restaurant, and Coffee House Employees:

> London, New York and other world cities have a much greater number of tourists than Berlin, and there the nocturnal hurly-burly is unknown. What was it like, the pre-war Berlin night life whose return is so ardently striven for? On the outside, an exaggerated elegance, which however the specialist could not be allowed to approach too closely. In the cafés every piece of stale cake was illuminated by at least six light-bulbs. But what was actually on offer was always a quite awkward and inadequate imitation of the Paris and Brussels night-spots and of the American entertainment of the day. Everything that apparently made Berlin night life so attractive could be seen in the original in these cities, where it was so much better.

The two poles of the city night meet '*Round the back of a restaurant*', as the waiter observes the homeless collector of left-over food. Photograph by Bill Brandt, London, *c*.1930.

If Berlin had been London or Paris it wouldn't have bothered to keep drinking establishments open during the night for the sake of tourism. But Berlin remained, and for a long time unfortunately, so far behind these two world centres that it had to attract international tourism with something the other two world cities did not have, and did not want to have. That was the night life of Berlin before the war.[102]

Of course the employees, like their employers, speak in their own interest. It is still valuable, however, in giving us a totally different perspective on the 1920s in Berlin: here the pre-war years appear as the true high point of night-time Berlin (even if it is held up to ridicule), and here too Berlin night life appears as a performance for foreigners, not as something for the Berliners themselves. Even if the international comparison is put forward as a pretext – of course Paris has its nocturnal life and did want to have it – the tense, laborious, strained side of Berlin's night life becomes apparent in this text.

These protestations did not help, and by a decree of 19 October 1926 'the hours of closure are set between 3 o'clock in the morning and 6 o'clock in the morning'.[103] This rang out like a call to battle, and the central board of the Home Mission and such organizations as, for example, the German Women's League for an Alcohol-free Culture wrote outraged letters of protest to 'sinful Babylon' Berlin, reborn with official benediction.[104]

It was the Prussian Minister of the Interior, Grzesinski, who had to respond to these petitions, and on 31 March 1927 he published a memorandum 'on the extension of opening times in Berlin'. This text is a document of the changing self-image of the police. According to the minister, their task is *only* to see to the 'maintenance of public peace, security and order', and the fight against the misuse of alcohol and more generally the surveillance and regulation of people's ways of life is not their concern. There was a great need for nocturnal relaxation; inadequate housing conditions were not the least of the reasons why many people had to spend their leisure time 'outside'. In addition to this, the new legislation did away with many problems associated with the old: for example the need to supervise drinking establishments, which kept the police from other tasks, and the setting up of illegal night-spots for a public 'that wished to amuse itself for longer than the offical closing time allowed'.

With this the police almost gave up – after the night-watch, whose organization it had already adapted to the changing circumstances –

'One of the greatest influences on the inn-keeper's profits and on the moral and economic conduct of the people is . . . the setting of the so-called closing time.' Three o'clock at night, time for the bill. Photograph by Felix H. Man: *Three in the Morning in the Romanisches Café – the Head-waiter prepares the final bill*, Berlin, 1929.

a further traditional strategy for the control of the night: 'prohibited time'. It was no longer possible to close off the urban space at night, and it was no longer possible, either, to fence in the time conquered by nocturnal life.

## 3 Criminal worlds

> 'Meet me tonight at 10.30 at the Villa Colonna, in the "little box" that you know.' This was a note from a friendly officer in the Berlin criminal investigation department, whom I occasionally used to accompany on his night-time raids on the criminal world of Berlin. 'There are some inquiries I have to make, and I hope to be able to show you a few specialities of our criminal underworld.'
>
> GUSTAV RASCH (1870)[105]

The two preceding sections dealt with two police strategies for maintaining nocturnal order in the city. In the course of the 90 years between 1840 and 1930 the tasks of the police had changed; their ideal, the night-sleeping city, could no longer be reconciled with changed conditions of life and work in the metropolis, and the 'old' measures for the control of urban space and time were no longer effective. The night-watch as an attempt to keep the whole urban space under control had become as anachronistic as closing times had been as an attempt to save the idea of 'prohibited time' for modernity. In both cases there had been public criticism: the police should mind their own business – the fight against crime.

Crime, criminality, the underworld – this a theme, a cluster of ideas that inevitably imposes itself when one talks of the big city. Here too, and perhaps here more than in any other aspect of our story, we are confronted with *images*, with *imaginations* that obstruct our view of the reality of the city night. No other subject takes us so far into the *liminal area between imaginations and realities*,[106] because, as a rule, the confrontation with crime occurs through the media. They offer us such images as this: 'It is night, and rain is falling onto the gleaming tarmac. The black silhouette of the city towers against a sombre starless sky. Every few seconds there is the flicker of neon from a bar. The streets seem dead, but against the wall of a house a shadow is moving.'[107]

As television viewers and readers of crime novels, at this point we expect to see the gangster, hat drawn deep down over his eyes, the detective in his trench coat, or perhaps a beautiful woman, a stranger who the next instant will fall victim to a crime. We expect the 'case', we await the darstardly deed. In real life, nine times out of ten, round the corner will come a harmless drunk, a newspaper boy or a courting couple; but this is uninteresting. Normality is boring, for journalists as well as for the police; only disturbance, only sensation is worthy of a place in the story of the city night. Books and films, newspaper stories and police reports have made night in the big city a setting for the *dangerous situation*.

THE CREATION OF THE UNDERWORLD

The reduction of the nocturnal city to its unusual, mysterious and dangerous sides; the metaphoric coupling of the concept of night with words like danger, fear, horror and threat; the furnishing of the city night with appropriate personnel, with their own language and their own – peculiar – behaviour; the decoration of the 'milieu' with corresponding visual features: streets slippery with rain, flickering lights, dark corners; these are the preconditions and structural elements of a thorough and comprehensive *creation of the underworld* in the city. At the beginning of this story there stand two texts, which are quoted often enough: Eugène Sue's *Les Mystères de Paris* and Edgar Allen Poe's 'The Man in the Crowd'.

The protagonists of both stories, Sue's Rudolf von Gerolstein and Poe's anonymous narrator, undertake *expeditions* into the darkness of the city, both finding there an unknown, terrifying world, the world of the night:

> I shall attempt to present to the reader some episodes from the life of other barbarians as much outside civilization as the savage tribes so well depicted by Cooper. Except that the barbarians of which I speak are in the midst of us; we may rub shoulders with them by venturing into their haunts . . . These men have their own customs, their own women, their own language, a mysterious language, full of deathly images, metaphors dripping with blood . . . On 13 December 1838, on a cold and rainy night, a man of athletic build, dressed in a shabby jacket, crossed the Pont au Change and penetrated into the Cité, the labyrinth of narrow, twisting, ill-lit streets that lies between the Palais de Justice and Notre Dame. That night the wind was blowing violently through

the alleyways of this dismal neighbourhood; the pallid glimmering of the gas lights, agitated by the gusts, flickered in the stream of dark water that ran down the middle of the slimy cobbled lane.[108]

As the night deepened, so the interest of the scene deepened for me; for not only did the general character of the crowd materially alter (its gentler features retiring in the gradual withdrawal of the more orderly portion of the people, and its harsher ones coming out in bolder relief, as the late hour brought forth every species of infamy from its den). . .[109]

The direction of the gaze has been fixed; in both cases the path leads from the light into darkness, from the world in which 'we', the author and reader, belong, into another, an alien world beyond and below the familiar surface, but only a few steps away, still close enough to touch. Eugène Sue in particular gives the familiar idea that everything has its 'flip side', a topographical anchorage in the city. There is, at the edge of the city (as in London), or even at its centre (as in Paris), another city, unknown, of unknown size, and thus all the more threatening. The fact that both 'expeditions' take place at night lends the terrain an even more threatening aspect. Here is 'the criminal's natural element',[110] according to the usual interpretation, drawn larger than life, unreal – but formative of the imaginary world of future generations. In their texts both authors trace a *movement*: both worlds within the city may be unfamiliar to each other, but they are not static, nor are they sharply divided.

RECONNAISSANCE PATROLS

On the one hand there was the danger that this 'underworld' might spread, conquering street after street and finally penetrating the world of safety. On the other hand a growing number of *spies* were sent into the labyrinthine darkness from the world of light. They set out to explore the unknown territories 'on the map of the metropolitan jungle',[111] so as to prepare the terrain and the 'barbarians' who lived there for their final conquest by civilization.

From either point of view, the multiplicity of the 'other' world became increasingly visible; the spy, whether journalist, scientist, missionary or policeman was at first confronted by an impenetrable conglomerate of deviant behaviours and lifestyles that could not be disentangled. The 'barbarians' live, work and communicate, so it

**Statistique des Crimes et Délits**

M.

Rapport de l'Année 1899

Crimes et Délits :  Paris

| | PROCÉDURES CONTRE | | INCULPÉS | | |
|---|---|---|---|---|---|
| | Inconnus | Individus connus | Envoyés au Dépôt | Laissés libres | En fuite |
| Abandon d'enfants | 58 | 302 | 68 | 147 | 53 |
| Abus de confiance | 114 | 1287 | 336 | 507 | 585 |
| Adultères | 1 | 406 | 9 | 888 | 1 |
| Assassinats (Signaler spécialement les parricides) | 5 | 10 | 7 | - | 3 |
| Assassinats (Tentatives d') | 3 | 31 | 34 | - | 5 |
| Attaques nocturnes | 238 | 86 | 74 | 9 | 111 |
| Attentats à la liberté du travail | 2 | 35 | 12 | 24 | 1 |
| Attentats à la pudeur | 9 | 111 | 43 | 63 | 14 |
| Avortements | 35 | 12 | 11 | 2 | 7 |
| Banqueroutes | - | 19 | 4 | 4 | 9 |
| Bigamie | - | 2 | 2 | - | - |
| Blessures par imprudence ou inobservation des règlements | 94 | 1360 | 42 | 1272 | 84 |
| Bris de clôture | 68 | 242 | 91 | 132 | 89 |
| Coups et blessures volontaires | 269 | 1772 | 476 | 1270 | 142 |
| Délits de chasse | 4 | 80 | 5 | 70 | 2 |
| Déserteurs. — Insoumis | 1 | 491 | 515 | - | 1 |
| Destruction de récoltes | 2 | 5 | 2 | 3 | 2 |
| Détournement de mineures | 1 | 22 | 5 | 13 | 5 |
| Empoisonnements | 1 | 12 | 4 | 7 | - |
| Enlèvement d'enfants | 7 | 5 | 2 | 3 | 7 |
| Escroqueries | 182 | 737 | 366 | 255 | 699 |
| Exercice illégal de la médecine et de la pharmacie | - | 17 | - | 16 | 1 |

In Paris around the turn of the century there was much talk of the growth in 'nocturnal attacks'; police statistics contradicted, but could do little to counter, this idea of the danger of the night. *Statistiques des Crimes et Délits* issued by the Prefecture of Police, Paris, 1889.

seems, according to their own rules, according to their own laws, which constitute an unbreachable defensive wall against the first onslaught of civilization.

These defences cannot be overcome in one fell swoop, and new strategies have to be devised to remove individual stones and so render the wall permeable and unstable. Over the years the gradual accumulation of the results of research on the alien culture in the underworld of the big cities, in the East End of London, in the Cité and in the neighbourhood of Les Halles in Paris, and to a lesser extent in Berlin's north-eastern districts, led to new distinctions. If in 1846 a report on the Berlin workhouse could still talk of the 'proletarians and criminals of the residency',[112] 50 years later we see the 'underworld' divided up and recorded under countless different categories. This differentiation allows the authorities to react in different ways to the different forms of 'deviance' and 'disturbance'.

In their practical work the authorities exploited these possibilities, but – and this is the reverse of this development – in their publications they project the image of the closed-off, unified and so threatening *counter-world* of the criminal, leaving all distinctions aside and insisting on the reality of their horror-picture of the underworld.

The main points of police work are the same in each of the great cities; the fundamental task, the maintenance of public peace, order and security, is divided up between two equally general ways of proceeding: on the one hand, it is a matter of keeping the areas and regions thought of as *potentially dangerous* under perpetual surveillance and constantly refining the tools that are used: the 'eyes and ears'[113] of the police. On the other hand, the areas of the city regarded as *potentially endangered* have to be saved and protected from the penetration of 'crime'. In this the police also had to take into account the fact that in the course of the years the passages between the two worlds had become more numerous, and that other measures taken by the authorities – such as the spread of street lighting or structural changes in the city – were always producing changes in the topography of order and danger. Police methods become more and more refined (and here there are local differences of course), with the establishment of increasingly specialized departments covering crime, prostitution or homelessness, and other threats to order, whose work meshes together ever more smoothly. The big change here in the years between 1840 and 1930 is the gradual isolation of the concepts of 'crime' and 'criminal' from the initially almost indissoluble complex of the *classes dangereuses*, from the countless marginal groups of the excluded and rejected. 'Criminals' are now those who still 'remain' after the application of all police, educational and social-hygiene measures for the maintenance of security and order, and after the painful division of marginal groups into smaller units that are easier to govern: they are the inner core of the threat.

This is absolutely not to say that the 'criminal world' really does represent the greatest danger to the order of the city. At any rate, social reporters from Eugène Sue onward, despite all the weaknesses of their descriptions, had drawn attention to the socially explosive force of poverty and misery and with this set in motion the whole institutional apparatus of social reform. Nor did their horrified

contemporaries in any way underestimate the danger of a politicization, or even political organization of the wretched. But these under-
standings could not prevent the images and ideas of the criminal
world becoming the most forceful symbols of the danger to the city.
In all three cities, the police made use of them to justify measures of
surveillance and restriction of public freedom of movement in the
name of the generally accepted fight against crime.

In his study of 'Criminality and Everyday Life', Dirk Blasius has
shown how the everyday life of the lower classes could be seen as
threatening in the eyes of the authorities: 'To the "riches" of everyday life, alongside the traditions that still survived in it, there also
belonged the possibilities of living it up, branded by critics of the
everyday as "addiction to pleasure".' When at the beginning of the
nineteenth century there was a growth in public opportunities for
'entertainment', for example at shooting festivals or fairs, members
of the lower social classes also demanded their right to entertainment and sought to participate in the privileges already enjoyed by
others: 'Here they learnt to draw breath.' Critical observers of this
development recognized 'the social push effect' and denounced the
excessive consumption of alcohol at festivals, and also in the beer
and spirits houses, the blurring of social differences and the readiness for conflict ('propensity for crime', says Blasius) as *promoting
crime*.[114]

Because the 'criminal world' was thought to be so dangerous, the
reporters who dared penetrate it could be celebrated as particularly
courageous. So they too, like the police, had to reinforce and embell-
ish the picture of a dangerous world – even if the reality of this world
largely remained closed to them. Here we arrive at an important
point in the story of the city night: whatever we discover about the
'criminal world', whether from reporters or from the records of the
police, it is marked by such strategies, clothed in imagery, organized
by the objectives of the spy, filtered through the imagination of
what constitutes a 'case', a 'disturbance'. We can learn little about
the reality of metropolitan criminality, but all the more about one
of the elements that forms the image of the night.[115]

SPIES AND POLICEMEN

As a rule the reporters did not dare go into the centre of the 'criminal
world' alone; they would entrust themselves to the guidance of a

connoisseur, a policeman or a detective, accompanying him as he went about his duties. Their descriptions have many things in common, regardless of the place of their creation: the journey into the dangerous zone is extensively described, especially the *path from the bright streets into the dark corners*, from the accessible city to its hidden districts. After that the 'public', the population of the 'dark alleys' and 'sombre houses', is painted with great attention to picturesque detail, before the actions of the guardian of the peace swiftly put an end to the goings on. The model for such 'escort studies' was provided by Charles Dickens: during his visits to the thieves' dens, to the hideouts of 'infamy', he 'deemed it prudent to associate myself with a brace of policemen who were well versed in the ways of the localities I wished to examine'.[116] The first of these reports, 'On Duty with Inspector Field', appeared in *Household Words* on 14 June 1851; it starts on a fanfare with the words: 'How goes the night?' This becomes the motto: reporters see it as their task to communicate a picture of the dark city, to make their readers aware of the existence of the 'other side'. The policemen know the terrain, are 'equally at home wherever we go', and lead the reporters to lodging houses, pubs and dance halls, showing them the different 'criminal types'. They keep track of the picture, they maintain order, and where it is necessary – this is the reporters' message – they strike. Fears are awakened in the reader and at the same time laid to rest, but never completely.

In 1870 Gustav Rasch, 'writer of critical social reports and political columnist',[117] described 'One night in the criminal world of Berlin'; as a prototype, his report deserves citation at some length:

We went up the Königstrasse towards the Kurfürsten Bridge, along the colonnades whose interiors were now hidden in deep, black shadows. The street was almost as lively as during the day, although those walking along it belonged to a totally different class of the population than do those who occupy the main shopping streets of the city during the day. The tower of the Kloster church chimed 11 o'clock. . .

When the night-birds recognized the appearance and uniform coat of my companions they would wander past us shyly, or totally unconcerned, depending on the burden on their conscience or on whether or not they were under police supervision; because in that case they are not permitted to leave their homes after 10 o'clock at night and are subject to immediate arrest if they are recognized. . .

Between the new Friedrichstrasse and the Bischofstrasse there is a

A less familiar illustration by Heinrich Zille: 'Dark Berlin', the Kaiser-Wilhelm-Strasse, not far from the Stadtschloß. Heinrich Zille: *S'dunkle Berlin*, 1898.

long, narrow alley that leads off the Königstrasse, which winds like a stone snake from the Königstrasse, through a tangle of small houses, and climbs up to the Spandauer Bridge. This street is nowadays one of the headquarters and encampments of the lowest criminal life of Berlin. It is the meeting place of the rogues, confidence-tricksters and pickpockets . . . who live in the neighbourhood, and of those unfortunate young women who shun the light.[118]

No cliché of this type of night literature is missing: the gas flames of the 'rare' lanterns 'flickering here and there', 'occasionally sinister figures would scurry along the houses of the street', a night-watchman 'patrolling up and down the street' reported that 'peace and quiet were only an illusion'. The policemen and their companion force their way into a cellar, the 'rogues' present are overpowered and taken into police custody. All of this happens very quickly, the performance is over, the policemen climb up from the cellar and 'the lights of the gas flames flickering in the wind shimmer on their metal insignia and the metal points of their helmets'. The night however isn't over yet, further hideouts are visited, not only in the same infamous neighbourhood, but also in places 'of totally unsuspicious character', where 'after midnight . . . the dangerous rogues of the

A raid on a 'criminal dive' in Berlin – the territories of the underworld were visited on a regular basis, and pictures of such police actions both reassured and worried the public at the same time. Drawing by F. Linder, 1906.

capital meet together'. The evocation of *threat*, of *possible* dangers, and the love of detail in the description of the alarming atmosphere take up much more space than the description of the police action itself. In making a comparison with a similar tour undertaken five years earlier, Rasch unintentionally comments on his own way of proceeding: 'Today the street seems even darker and eerier to me than it was in those days. Perhaps it was the growing darkness of the night sky; *perhaps the darkness may also have been in my imagination.*' An indication of how striking and influential was Rasch's report is the fact that a year later the journalist Victor Tissot copied it shamelessly and published it as 'my report on poverty and crime in Berlin'.[119]

The imagination needs statistical support. Again and again the reporters try to verify, to shore up their descriptions. So an *image* of the city is created in which crime occupies a dominant position:

Big cities are the natural meeting points of the criminal world. Already themselves producing much in the way of questionable character, by the manifold advantages they offer all shady creatures, they attract all that is equivocal and dubious from round about. In the forceful grip of the masses that surge in the big city, driven by interest and passion, the

127

individual disappears. And what is more, what a multitude of hiding places! And what a multitude of opportunities for transgression! Nowhere can the situation be more favourable to those who need to shun the light. The statistics also show us, for example, that in London there live a good fifth of all the criminals in England. In the case of Paris, in relation to France, the fraction is even greater, and now since its entry into the ranks of the great European cities, the capital of our German Reich can no longer avoid the consequence of its massive expansion, the presence within it of a quite numerous guild of criminals.[120]

In the years after 1870, as a result of its massive expansion, the German capital experienced, like London and Paris, a process of modernization of its social policies. This only appears in disguised

*'The peril that lurks in the dark'*– a picture of the dangers on the way home, an indictment both of criminality and of nocturnal revelry. Illustration of London by Gustave Doré, 1863.

fashion in the reports. At first 'police custody' plays a central role in the descriptions, as a collection point for everyone 'picked up at night'. The dissolution of this pre-modern concept, the differentiation introduced among the 'equivocal and dubious' figures of the night and the establishment of special institutions for the different groups – beggars, homeless, 'virtuous poor', prostitutes, and the segregation of the men, women and families picked up – all this creates greater room for manoeuvre for the police and for the fight against crime. Klaus Bergmann has pointed to the fact that in these years the attention of social reporters shifts away from the street and towards the closed spaces of the new 'institutions'; this corresponds to the changing activity of the police and their constant specialization. The reporters' *language*, however, remains tied to the detail of existing traditions. Even an author like Bernhard Hesslein, who strongly condemns the 'social situation' that gives rise to crime, uses the stereotypical 'nocturnal walk through the dens of misery', and he too delights in the 'company of a police officer well known to us'. He does however add certain reservations:

> For the criminologist, it may be an interesting and useful nocturnal walk to visit Berlin's dives, dens of misery and vice, but for the humanist, for the philosopher, it is repulsive, humbling and discouraging to catch a glimpse of this terrible world . . . Only the police are privileged to constantly train their eyes on the pestilential dens of the capital city, but these eyes can neither help nor heal, neither comfort nor counsel, they can only threaten, punish and deter, *and yet all these wretches are in dire need of the gaze of the philosopher*, who sees the need for the relief and healing of such terrible ills of humanity.[121]

Does this gaze of the humane witness, well-meaning, helpful and unbiased by images, actually exist? It is certainly not easy to find evidence of it. Hesslein, however, distinguishes himself from the other authors on two – for us very important – points: he sees the 'principal cause of the steady increase in crime' in the 'isolation of the criminal world brought about by our laws and institutions'; and the contribution of these reports from this threatening world to this 'isolation' should not be underestimated. But above all he does not essentially draw a horror-picture of the night: 'Even if in secret, it is not always under the veil of night that crime goes abroad; it is usually active in the light of day.'

The constant presence of 'crime' – as topic, image, and weapon in debate – in the social discourse of the turn of the century[122] through-out the whole of Europe shows how little the 'philosophers' had been active here. The sensational content of the reports about crime would always weigh more heavily than a nuanced description of urban and nocturnal reality: the existence of night-clubs, for example, is always attacked, while simple reflection would make it clear that they give the police considerably greater possibilities of control than many 'secret', constantly changing 'hideouts'. The undersides of urban life cannot simply be wiped out: he who wants the glamour of the city must live with its wretchedness, and those who praise the temples of entertainment should not rebuke the dens of vice.

MISSIONARIES AND STATISTICIANS

The representatives of church missions are among the experts on the urban night. They must rebuke the 'dens of vice', yet they still develop a different picture than do the spies who only dare to go into the darkness in the company of the police. Their picture of the big city is not marked only by crime, but also by the existence (or the conjuring up) of strong counter-forces for salvation. In his introduc-tion to Volume IV of Henry Mayhew's *London Labour and the London Poor*, the Reverend William Tuckniss wrote that the compilation of criminal statistics could only be the starting-point but not the aim of a serious engagement with crime:

> Nowhere are these hopeful indications more manifest than in this giant metropolis, where the various conditions of ordinary life seem to be intensified by their direct contact with good and evil...
>
> It is here, within the crowded areas and noisome purlieus of this greatest of great cities, that we may gather lessons of life to be gained nowhere else – and of which those can form only an inadequate con-ception, who dwell only in an atmosphere of honied flowers and rural pleasures...
>
> London then may be considered as the grand central focus of opera-tions, at once the emporium of crime and the palladium of Christianity. It is, in fact, the great arena of conflict between the powers of darkness and the ministry of heaven.[113]

So it is necessary on the one hand to describe and analyze the 'oppor-tunities for crime' generated by the big city, but it would be wrong to give them one's entire attention. For this reason Tuckniss prefaces Mayhew's collection of discussions with 'those who do not wish to

The documentary photography of the 1930s takes up and echoes the depictions of fantasy: 'Three men talking' in a dark street, an image of nocturnal danger. Photograph by Bill Brandt.

work, including prostitutes, thieves, swindlers and beggars' with a no less impressive list of 'agencies for the suppression of vice and crime', above all the ecclesiastical welfare institutions for children, young people, the unemployed, the homeless, and for alcoholics and prostitutes, for without this addition there would be conjured up an impression of a helpless city at the mercy of the forces of darkness.

The public reception of Mayhew's study, however, shows that this impression was dominant. All attempts to differentiate between the different categories of the 'criminal classes', to discover the social causes of individuals' descent into crime, even Mayhew's enormous achievement in allowing the people concerned to tell their life stories for themselves – all efforts, then, to proceed scientifically remained largely without effect. What caught on with the public was a horrifying picture of 'London's underworld', a universe of threat.

In the ideological debate about the causes of the alleged increase in crime and the conclusions that should be drawn from this, the *city as the site of modernity* found itself the focus of criticism. Some texts from the Christian missions described life in the cities as the symbol of Man's breaking away from God; the crimes born 'of its womb' were seen as condign punishment for the 'scenes of sexual licence' that took place there. In the publications of politically motivated social reformers the city is on the other hand seen as the symbol of capitalist society, which itself produces the 'rejects', the 'underworld' that will bring about its end: an apocalyptic picture on both sides.

Research that consciously attempted to steer clear of such images did not have an easy time of it. Charles Booth started research for his seventeen-volume work on the *Life and Labour of the People in London* in 1886, in the infamous East End of the city. Even in this district, he estimated the numbers of the 'lowest class' at 11,000 inhabitants, about one and a quarter per cent of the population. The scientist's description is aimed at sounding the all-clear rather than raising the alarm: 'The hordes of barbarians of whom we have heard, who, issuing from their slums, will one day overwhelm modern civilization, do not exist. There are barbarians, but they are a handful, a small and decreasing percentage: a disgrace but not a danger.'[124]

On closer inspection the picture of the 'underworld', the 'criminal world' dissolves into different elements; poverty and neglect are predominant, but crime not at all. The social scientist sees the problems as soluble by a gigantic effort on the part of the state and the public. But Booth's description has almost no effect on the *picture* of the nocturnal city, for the images of threat and insecurity are stronger. Jack London, for example, drew a totally different picture of the *People of the Abyss*:

> It is rather hard to tell a tithe of what I saw. Much of it is untellable. But in a general way I would say that I saw a nightmare, a fearful slime that quickened the pavement with life, a mess of unmentionable obscenity that put into eclipse the 'nightly horror' of Piccadilly and the Strand . . . They are a new species, a breed of city savages. The streets and houses, alleys and courts, are their hunting grounds. As valley and mountain are to natural savages, street and building are valley and mountain to them. *The slum is their jungle*, and they live and prey in the jungle.[125]

In such texts the picture of the criminal world has a curiously static quality; life in the cities may indeed be changing, its economic basis may be constantly shifting, but the idea that 'underneath', beneath the surface of the visible, there exists another world that resists all change, that evades all attempts at reform as well as control, this idea does not lose any of its grip. All the more pragmatic efforts of social scientists such as Booth or of missionaries like Tuckniss remain ineffective against the power of these images.

During these years especially, town planners and statisticians, and also many police officers, welfare workers and doctors, speak and write about the big city as a place whose problems may be great but are susceptible of solution. The tendency towards a *decline in ideology on closer acquaintance*, particularly in the course of long-term activity in 'underworld' locations, can even be seen in highly ideological organizations like the Home Mission of the Evangelical Church. In the years around the turn of the century travellers and journalists whose interests were not exclusively focused on the 'night side' produced many publications on the 'structures and functions'[126] of the *modern* city: measures to overcome building and housing problems, for the improvement of hygiene and of the traffic situation and so on, are presented as triumphs of modern thought, modern technology and modern planning. The 'realm' of crime is reduced to its real dimensions, presented as a side-issue. The Berlin journalist Paul Lindenberg underlines this ambiguity when he says that the 'hustle and bustle of the city' provides cover for many things that elsewhere would not dare emerge in daylight, but that it also gives thousands of people a place and the possibility of advancement, who would be lost elsewhere.[127]

From this point view it also becomes possible to correct popular ideas about crime in the big cities: 'According to a common, widely repeated assertion', writes the Leipzig *Illustrirte Zeitung* on 1 March 1884, 'the number of crimes is constantly increasing. With respect to these morbid inclinations, the results of scientific inquiries recently presented to the House of Representatives by an official of the Prussian Ministry of Justice are reassuring . . . They were first given proof that particularly in recent times the figure for serious crimes and misdemeanours, the decisive factor in each set of statistics, has been decreasing.'

The *discourse of the criminal world*, whose aim it is to throw a 'glaring light on the world of swindlers and criminals, who make trouble in the darkness of the big city',[128] breaks down when faced with the reality of crime; precisely because of this, deliberate use could be made of it as an instrument in the ideological debate on the city. I want to show, with three examples from different times in the three cities, how the discourse of the criminal world marks perceptions of the city (and the city night): in London in 1888, Paris around 1910, and in Berlin around 1925.

CRIME IN THE NIGHT: JACK THE RIPPER

Danger lurks in many forms, and it is everywhere. But in a few areas of the city the threat is particularly serious; in London it was the East End that attracted these projected fears: 'The East End of London is the hell of poverty. Like an enormous black, motionless Kraken, the poverty of London lies there in lurking silence and encircles with its mighty tentacles the life and wealth of the City and of the West End.'[129]

In the eyes of church and police this was the 'City of Dreadful Night', this was where the 'bitter cry of outcast London' would ring out, this was where William Booth, founder of the Salvation Army, found his 'Darkest London'. In 1888 many features of this image came together, and far beyond the confines of Britain the East End of London came to symbolize the criminal element in the city. William J. Fishman has shown how already in earlier years there had been a feeling that the East End was topographically, but also economically and spiritually, distant from the rest of the city. The people who lived in this different world were as alien and unknown as the life they led there, 'until slumming became fashionable in the 1870s and 1880s' –

and even then, or particularly then, descriptions were dominated by clichés and misrepresentations. A demonstration by the poor population of the East, in Trafalgar Square, in the heart of the city, gave this vaguely threatening fear a political dimension. The press called on the police to suppress the feared insurrection mercilessly, and public opinion was on the side of order, reported no less than George Bernard Shaw – until, according to Shaw, 'an independent spirit took things into his own hands': this was Jack the Ripper.

> When George Cross walked through dark and empty Buck's Row on his way to work about 3.40 a.m. on the morning of Friday, 31 August 1888, the only light was a solitary gas lamp at the far end of the street. On one side of the street was a warehouse wall, and on the other some terraced houses which were occupied for the most part by better-class tradesmen. He was opposite these houses when, in a gateway leading to some stables, between the houses and the board school, he saw a bundle that he at first thought was a tarpaulin. It was only when he crossed over for a closer look that he realized that the bundle was a woman.[130]

This nocturnal discovery stands at the beginning of a hitherto un-exampled debate on the insecurity of life in the big city, a debate conducted in shrill tones: 'It seemed as if society as a whole had needed some horror such as this to awaken it to the fact that within cab-hire distance of the palaces and mansions of the West End there were "tens of thousands of fellow creatures begotted and reared in an atmosphere of godless brutality . . .".'[131] The victims of the unknown murderer were prostitutes; their life stories, published in the newspapers in the course of the search for the perpetrator, were descriptions of poverty and wretchedness, of repeated stays in workhouses and hospitals, of escape into drink, of the horrifying brutality of their childhood homes and of their failed marriages, of everything that had led them to the streets. The East End had once again lost all the romance of 'slumming'. The night-story of the Ripper led to an intensive debate about the function of the police, who were unable to solve the crime, symbol of the danger; more generally too about the situation that had been so suddenly illuminated. Here too, however, sensationalist reporting had the effect of hindering understanding. In 1888, of all years, the annual report of the Commissioner of Prisons registered for the whole of London, and for the East End as well, a 'general reduction in crime in the metropolis'. Here too then, statistics could only render *one* historic reality; the other reality is made up of the – no less powerful – fantasies of fear and terror, which made 1888 the 'year of the murders'. Above all, however, this story was to mark the night view of London for many a long year: the combination of different elements – the nocturnal terrain, the poverty-stricken districts, prostitution and perverse crime (and on top of this an incapable police force) – created an ideal setting for detective novels, films and stories, in which the event was elaborated on at such length that it came to stand as a characteristic symbol for *this* nocturnal city.

## THE PARISIAN 'APACHES'

Here one clearly sees the differences between the prevailing images of the different cities at night. In Paris the romanticization of criminal life takes on totally different features. Here it was the 'apaches', the slightly idealized, secretly admired small-time crooks from the area around the place de la Bastille, who were the focus of public attention and journalistic reportage. In the newspapers, stories of nocturnal muggings and knifings were for a long time carried under the heading 'Faits divers', 'miscellaneous news', until in the years between 1900 and 1914 their apparently growing numbers promoted them to the front page. In Paris the discussion about the decay of the whole society – the form taken by the argument about the costs and consequences of Modernism – sparked off for instance by the alleged uncontrollability of the urban underworld, made use of this example:

> Why are our residential neighbourhoods so crowded with these 'apaches', who so quickly progress from lay-about to criminal? One day we will have to find out where this army is recruited from, to understand why it is constantly growing, and why, despite all the arrests and convictions, the number of these miserable dens is not decreasing.[132]

Much of the blame can be laid at the door of the police. During their raids and nightly round-ups they picked up only the poor and the unfortunate – neglected children, elderly beggars, the rejects of society – and the real criminals were not to be found amongst these. For their part the police blamed late closing times, and above all the all-night opening of the 'dens' around Les Halles and the Bastille, for their inability to effectively carry out their task. The constant reorganization of the Paris police was no longer enough. They had to answer

136

Policemen in London's East End find
Chinese smoking opium '*In the Den*'.
(There are always journalists present.)
Illustration from *The Strand Magazine*, 1890.

two questions: how could one guarantee that 'peaceable' citizens
enjoyed nocturnal freedom of movement, and at the same time, how
could one ensure that they did not become the victims of night-time
attack while doing so? Here too the 'students of criminality' had
only an inadequate grasp of nocturnal reality. Their texts are caught
up in a strange mixture of abhorrence and fascination; the authors
tell of a continuous confrontation between the 'dark' city and the
forces of order, but they do not succeed in their real aim, which was
to provide information about what the criminal world was really
like. Images of 'popular' criminality had already been so firmly
established that the pre-war mood of panic seems strangely excited
and exaggerated. In 1907 *Le Matin* published a series of articles
under the title 'Paris aux "apaches" – où on les trouve'; what was
meant as a description of an inescapably lurking danger could also
be read as a guidebook for a visit to the underworld. In the 1st

arrondissement the pont des Saints-Pères and the place de la Concorde were to be regarded as 'dangerous', the Jardin des Tuileries, the garden of the Palais Royal and the rue Saint-Honoré were equally terrifying, and then of course there was the neighbourhood of Les Halles, the rue Saint-Denis, the boulevard Sébastopol, the streets off the *grands boulevards* – all the city's tourist attractions, in fact. The account lends a visit to these places the character of a test of courage. Like it or not, the tourists and natives too had to pass 'à travers les repères du crime et de la débauche', and the 'apaches' were everywhere. 'Now they have become one of the attractions of Paris, like the Eiffel Tower or the Dôme des Invalides.'[133] The accuracy of this observation is demonstrated by a description in a *History of Parisian Manners* published in 1927:

> Already long before the war there was a tour organized for foreigners, and open to anyone, called the 'tour of the grand dukes', which even the police knew about and tolerated. One did the 'tour of the grand dukes' disguised as an 'apache' so as not to arouse too much suspicion, which might have prejudiced the peaceful course of the expedition. You visited all the infamous bars, cellars and dives of Belville, Montmartre and Les Halles, and you could drink a traditional glass of mulled wine with one of the most famous 'apaches'. The 'apaches' themselves did not even mind this tour, because they were proud of the attention they were given. The participants would follow a route planned in advance and were accompanied by civilian minders . . . This is 'Paris by night' as supplied by the travel-agents.[134]

BERLIN IN THE 1920S

Similar operations also existed in 1920s Berlin. Saugmeister, the former head of the Berlin CID, recalled, 'Excited by different accounts, the Berlin public surrounds the *Ringvereine* [the criminal fraternities] with an aura of drama and romance',[135] and 'in those days it was a thrill for men and women of the better classes to move about the underworld in their tail-coats and ball-gowns'. In his book *Heimweh nach dem Kurfürstendamm*, PEM, a well-known Berlin journalist of the 1920s, describes how, after a visit to the Toppkeller in the Schwerinstrasse, 'the cellar bars . . . gave the better class of nocturnal revellers a chance to get a last drink in when the normal establishments had long since shut for the night. They enjoyed rubbing shoulders with the *demi-monde* and the underworld, feeling the thrill of living dangerously.' He met the members of a *Ringverein*: at the opening of his 'Kabarett der Unmöglichen' the men of the 'Faith, Hope and Charity' fraternity stood outside the door demanding money; this was their patch, after all. In Berlin too there were experts on the night, touts usually employed by night-clubs, who would meet travellers even at the railway stations, promising exciting adventures: 'Shady Berlin, Sir? Berlin as she loves and lives? An individual escort through the world of vice?'[136] Even this sad surrogate could awaken the imagination; though the result was predictably disappointing, traces of the attraction could still be found in the trivial remains.

Images of night-time Berlin in the 1920s are highly conflictual; even from an overview of the innumerable memoirs one gets at most a kaleidoscope of different elements. The first thing to note is the multiplication of places of entertainment and their 'quasi-democratization' into mass institutions. This was connected to the emergence of a new 'employee culture', and quite possibly also inspired by the example of the United States.[137] ('Berlin today is a city with a pronounced employee culture', Siegfried Kracauer tells us in 1930, and, 'When one ventures among the employees, [this little expedition] at the same time takes one inside the great modern city.'[138]). The night-watch and closing time have lost their impor-tance as factors of control, and new regulations on working hours and the emergence of service industries have made it possible, if only slowly and with many hindrances, for broader sections of urban society to have their share of 'leisure'. The technical innova-tions of the pre-war period too, such as the cinema, have overcome their teething problems and can be made accessible to a wide public. Many forms of evening and night-time entertainment such as revues and cabarets that until now had been reserved for a privileged circle – or the courageous cross-border adventurers – are both changing and opening up to a wider public, and there appear new forms of enjoyment such as tourist cafés and amusement parks, deliberately tailored to the great yearnings and modest financial means of the employees, Kracauer's 'little shop-girls'. In this respect Berlin certainly looks towards New York; one sees this in the growing number of jazz bars where American artists appeared, and in the revue theatres where 'American chorus-girls became a European sensation', bringing with them a 'culture of technical excellence, a fascination for the formal possibilities of the record performance'.[139]

139

Democratization, mechanization and industrialization moulded the new character of night-time Berlin. 'In the evening, suddenly the whole rhythm stops, collapses into itself as if snapped': this was how Stefan Zweig could still describe nocturnal New York in 1912. He added later: 'Written in 1912, when New York at night was not yet the most magical city of light in the world.'[140] To European eyes New York had the advantage that her 'modern' nights did not have to throw off such a burden of restriction as did those of Paris or Berlin; on the other hand the attraction also worked in the other direction. 'The 1920s in New York', Peter Conrad writes, 'are a belated version of the aesthetic European 1890s',[141] and many American tourists and artists looked to Paris and more and more to Berlin for the true night life of the age. Josephine Baker went into raptures over the latter: 'Berlin. I found it dazzling. The city had a jewel-like sparkle, especially at night, that didn't exist in Paris.'[142] A beautiful evocation – though it was to establish a cliché – of the Americans' life in the metropolitan jungle of Berlin is given by Christopher Isherwood's novels, and the film *Cabaret* that was made from them. It is not only splendour that is visible here, but the poverty and misery are more decorative than accusatory in the way they are represented.

One of the elements of the image of the 1920s is the fascination (and imagery) of the electric light as the mark of Modernism – and here too, incidentally, there is an interesting reference to New York. At the World's Fair in 1939 Consolidated Edison presented the city as the 'City of Light – Where Night Never Comes',[143] a sign of the fear of night overcome. But this too is contradictory: this 'Yippee, we're alive!' syndrome is also characteristic of the sense of standing on shifting ground, and many observers noted the same intense urge to enjoy the adventures of the city after the experience of the war.[144] Furthermore, in republican Berlin there was real political instability; night was often drawn as the theatre of political conflict, and again and again writers and journalists tried to capture the Berlin of domestic inflation or of the world economic crisis by the juxtaposition of bright lights and political danger in the darkness – certainly a disastrous combination. Again and again, too, in such texts the element of nocturnal criminality forms the bridge between these two seemingly unrelated worlds. According to Walter Benjamin, one image in which 'the images of woman and death'[145] and those of the city interpenetrate is the motif of the 'sex murder', a changed, modernized revival of the Jack the Ripper story, fed by new fears, that excited attention in drawings (by George Grosz, Rudolf Schlichter, Otto Dix and many others), in novels, songs and films.[146] But also more generally the image of the criminal becomes a stereotype in the representation of Berlin of those years. In the widely read newspaper reports he appears as a 'shady figure, primitive, rough and violent, and constantly drunk' – a product of the city, a victim of circumstances.

Towards the end of the 1920s, however, the picture changes. The readers of these reports and novels were also products of the city and victims of circumstance, facing the same difficulties in life – inflation, the housing shortage, unemployment, the absence of political direction – that turned a minority into criminals. For many people the gulf that separated the 'half' from the 'whole' world seems to have become narrower, and those who slip downhill are no longer 'wild' strangers, but might be one's own neighbours. In these conditions there is also a change in the tasks of the police, the force that stands between the two worlds and is supposed to keep them apart for the good of the city as a whole. In the 1920s the Berlin police were very visible in the streets, a symbol of the maintenance of *internal* order that had been lost after the war. The 'Streifbeamtenschaft' had a particular role, its members patrolling the whole area of Greater Berlin – 'often in varied disguise, which could be adapted to the environment – so as to drive the professional criminals from their hiding-places'.[147] One of their leaders, Detective Superintendent Ernst Engelbrecht, made valiant efforts to counteract what were in his view over-sympathetic descriptions of the criminal milieu. He reported on the heroic fight against the underworld:

METROPOLITAN NIGHTS

Theatres and cinemas have long since closed, and the public streams out from the wide-open doors of the café-concerts and other establishments. The crowds briskly make their way home through the streets, on foot, by car, by taxi, or by tram. But it takes a long time for the masses to thin out, and for the streets to become empty and lonely again. Now only a few passers-by hurry through the streets, cautiously looking around to see if harm threatens them from anywhere, *because the city night, the night of the criminal*, has begun.[148]

The region described by Engelbrecht in his numerous publications has found a solid place in the mental topography of squalor and crime in Berlin. In the way they are constructed, his descriptions too,

The 1930s brought an end to the all-embracing social responsibilities of the police. A traffic policeman in Piccadilly Circus, London, 1934. Photograph by Felix H. Man.

'a collection of long-vanished curios, amongst which he himself belonged', as Eike Geisel had it, belong to the traditional discourse on the criminal world for which reality is not an issue. He scatters his depiction of the present with traces of the past and outmoded concepts, and in this way exerts a great influence on the image of the city at night: images of night are associated with concern and uncertainty, and images of the forces of order with security. Engelbrecht is aware of everything, he knows every hiding-place, and in raids and other operations he depicts himself as ruler of the night: 'Dead on time, I appeared at the centre of the area of operations and blew my whistle for the start.'[149] According to the expert, a visit to a night-club is dangerous and unsafe, and it is even more dangerous to go out – without protection and company – into the 'dark quarters' in the eastern and the northern areas of the city. The nocturnal *street* is very particularly unsafe, and properly considered, the night itself: 'When in the provincial cities the citizens are already in the arms of

142

Morpheus and streets and squares are deserted and empty, the streets of the metropolis are busy with people' – a deceptive image of pleasure and leisure because: 'The peaceable citizen who has to go through the streets at night hardly notices anything of the many dangers which stalk him, and often thinks the nocturnal life and bustle as harmless as himself. Yet the metropolitan night keeps claiming its victims.'[150]

## THE UNMODERN UNDERWORLD

The results of this way of representing the night are contradictory. On the one hand, the police can commend itself as ruler of the night, and on the other hand it almost encourages fear and public debate in doing so. An imaginary picture of the 'metropolis' emerges that appears anachronistic, even for those days. A text by Robert Heindl in 1928 presents this view of the 'metropolitan world of professional criminality' in an exemplary fashion. This survey of different cities was intended to show that the existence of the 'other side' was part of the basic furniture of every great city, its nocturnal element. Heindl seems to provide local topographical detail, but only repeats the stereotypes introduced to the underworld by Eugène Sue, almost word for word:

> Those who visit a big city as strangers will only reluctantly walk the night-time streets of the outer periphery, imagining them to be the hiding-places of disreputable riff-raff, whereas these are almost all to be found in the centre of the cities. It is in the 'heart of the city', usually immediately next to the main streets for shopping and entertainment, that the professional crooks find their dark hide-aways, the sleeping-quarters, the buildings with two exits, their cellar-bars half sunk in gloom even at midday, and above all their great ally: prostitution. *In the narrow twisting lanes of the old town, where the sun never penetrates and whose cobblestones are eternally wet and stinking*, this is where they are at home; this is where they disappear when they are pursued. In these sinister passages which often give directly onto broad avenues lit by shining shop windows and advertising hoardings bright as daylight, *there lives a people completely outside the law who allow themselves to be governed only by their own perverted instincts . . .*
>
> This contrast between light and shade is most striking in Paris. Those who stroll in the evening through the *grands boulevards*, full of pleasure seekers and tourists . . . will be well advised not to turn right into the side streets after midnight, because many of them belong to

the dark side of Paris ... Its centre ... is the Halles Centrales, the great food-market, during the day a feast for the eyes, at night a place of terror, a refuse heap of physical and moral decay, the meeting place of homeless and shady characters.

In London the picture is similar. The stranger who comes out of the British Museum and travels the short distance through Museum Street to Oxford Street, the great shopping street, usually has no idea that he is a few steps away from Soho, one of the most infamous areas of London...

In New York it is the same. Broadway is all light and glamour. Wall Street is the channel through which flows most of the world's money. And close by is the most disreputable area of the city, the area between the Bowery and Broadway, of which the travel books only say that a night-time visit 'is inadvisable for ladies in any circumstances, and generally so for foreigners'. In Berlin, too, directly behind the commercial palaces of the Alexanderplaz, illuminated by a thousand lights, lies the Scheunenviertel, the wildest area of the million-strong city.[151]

Having said all this, Heindl has to concede, in the case of Berlin, that 'the number of night-time attacks on peaceful passers-by' is not particularly high; those who sway through the streets under the influence of alcohol may well be in danger, but those who walk soberly and with circumspection will as a rule reach their destination unmolested. Much more common than the often-described nocturnal attacks are thefts by pickpockets and other *diurnal* 'activities'. As a 'big-city' phenomenon there remains murder: but here too Heindl fails to establish a conclusive link between the 'dark corners' he describes at the beginning and capital crime: murder happens mostly indoors.

For the best part of a century, descriptions of the big city and debate about its possibilities for 'good and evil' have been accompanied by this discourse on the criminal underworld; it has created a picture of the 'other', the bad side of big-city life, and provided the representatives of anti-city positions with plenty of ammunition. Above all it has painted night in the city as a realm of constantly threatening danger, the street as a space of uncertainty. In doing this it has time and time again preserved 'the old, the unmodern, the early stage that is being superseded' – as H. A. Kober characterized the underworld in the journal *UHU* in 1929.[152] While the real conditions of life in the cities were changing dramatically, the discourse on the underworld remained strangely static and unaffected. It

144

provides no objective insight into the nocturnal city, but stands for the 'unmodern' that must be overcome – and for the shackles that over and over again impede the progress of the new.

## 4 *Homelessness*

*Defenceless in London! Helpless in London! Homeless in London! What stories of pain and sorrow are contained in these words! . . . Where these thousands and thousands of homeless disappear when night comes, who can tell?*

ANONYMOUS (Die Gartenlaube 1866)[153]

*Who are the homeless? The negative answer is: they are no criminals.*

GUSTAV SCHUBERT (1885)[154]

THE FEARS OF THE HOUSED

When night comes, the city's inhabitants are to retire to their homes: this is what the authorities want. But what happens to those who have no home? 'Going about at night' on the streets was not allowed until the middle of the nineteenth century, and those who ignored the prohibition had to reckon on sanctions and endure the accusation that they endangered security and morality. What happened to those who were on the streets neither for pleasure nor with 'dark' intentions, but because of unavoidable necessity?

Homelessness is the most visible expression of destitution, and it becomes visible at night. During the day there is traffic on the streets; in the evening everyone goes back to where they belong, and there remain those whose poverty is so great that they have no place to go. But this visible destitution shows – publicly – that something is not in order; it is a provocation. The threat represented by the pauper population had to be reduced and controlled in the double lock of social policy and police surveillance.[155] The information available to us is stamped by the views of the agents of church and state who investigated the life of the poor: their reports are marked by outrage, fear, pity and contempt, but despite the many similarities, they differ from the reports on the criminal world in one important respect. Here too we find stereotypical, negative characterizations; here too

145

something categorically alien is described; here too real sensory perception is rare. But the images of the criminal world as a rule dealt with a chimera, a product of the imagination, an imaginary counter-world – 'Those who dared go into these dirty alleyways at night were not always sure of being able to leave them safely and unharmed'[156] – while pauperization really did threaten society – and the city! – as a possible fate, as an expression of uncertainty about society's ability to keep its nocturnal aspects under control. Texts and reports on homelessness give only limited and indirect information about real poverty and destitution, but they inform us directly about the housed population's fear of the night.

HOMELESSNESS DEFINED

In nineteenth-century texts a distinction is generally drawn between the 'virtuous' poor, who are settled and willing to work, and the 'wicked' poor who beg or wander the country. In the context of the strategy of 'bettering the poor through work' forced-labour institutions took on an important role, replacing the poorhouses of the eighteenth century and acting at the same time as more rigorous penal institutions. The new workhouses were to mop up the 'dregs' of the poor who could be provided for in no other way, acting as a 'sump' for those who were not reached by any other provision for the poor.[157] Those who were not only poor and without work but who were also homeless, those then who 'prowled about' the streets, were more than a nuisance. The establishment of workhouses in which vagrants were to be disciplined and forcibly adjusted to a life within fixed spaces and boundaries is a side effect of industrialization, and they have a particularly important role in the big cities, the centres of this development. In the Ochsenkopf on Berlin's Alexanderplatz, reported Gustav Rasch, 'the whole mass of Berlin's poor and wretched and its rabble of the most depraved and degenerate classes are penned, or when space permits of no other solution, even cooped up together in wild confusion'.[158] Even by the middle years of the century this 'wild confusion' no longer corresponded to the current ideas and concepts of those responsible for policing the poor, who had noticed that in the cities in particular there were many different reasons why people might have to spend the night on the streets – and that different measures therefore had to be developed in order to take them off the streets.

146

In terms of both practice and definition, the separation of the 'phenomenon' of homelessness from the 'confusion' of poverty, destitution, illness, immorality and crime takes place slowly and in stages. In this process one sees many similarities, but also – particularly in the field of metaphor, of folklore, if you will, in the imagination – interesting differences between the different cities. In many accounts from London, Paris and Berlin, the years around 1870 are rightly at the centre of attention, because it was in these years that most of the city-centre shelters for the homeless were established – but the process had begun even earlier, in the late 1830s and early 1840s, when the cities were 'growing out of themselves' and contemporaries noticed with horror who was being left behind.

NIGHT SHELTERS

With the accession of Queen Victoria there began in England an era of social legislation; in 1838 the Poor Law commissioners issued a directive recommending the accommodation of the 'vagabond poor' in workhouses, but in 1840 already the 'Committee for affording shelter to the Houseless' was running three shelters in London, which were opened during the winter months and had room for about 1,000 people. Those who made use of these soon came to the attention of the police; William Jones, Constable 157D, ordered to 'look to the night asylums at the time the vagrants came out', noted 'that the persons who generally attended at the night refuges were the worst of the vagrants, the lowest of beggars'.[159] The differing perceptions of welfare organizations and of the forces of law and order repeatedly led to disagreements; in the eyes of many a guardian of the peace the night refuges were a real encouragement to 'vagabondage': 'There can be little doubt, that as the certainty of obtaining a night's lodging and food gratuitously has become more generally known amongst this class, coupled with the entire absence of any effectual inquiry into their habits or course of life, their resort to workhouses has greatly increased, and will no doubt continue to do so.'[160]

But it was 'inquiry into their habits or course of life' that would in fact cast doubt on these negative images. The 'London City Mission' had been at work since 1835, with a few hundred missionaries out in the city (389 in 1860), and 'in this way the whole city is surveyed by this effective machine'; their regular reports in *The London City*

*'In front of the homeless shelter'* – waiting to be let in. The bourgeois press portrayed a negative image of rowdy behaviour and drunkenness – which greatly alarmed those who had a roof over their heads. *Illustrirte Zeitung,* Berlin, 1885.

*Mission Magazine* provided detailed information about the living conditions of the poor. It was the Christian missions that first discovered and communicated the great importance of the night; the 'London by Moonlight Mission' and the 'Midnight Meeting Movement' had a nightly presence on the streets of the city and drew attention to the large number of 'houseless poor'. From visiting the poor to holding nightly 'meetings', the path led inevitably to the erection of the 'night shelters'. The image of the 'utterly destitute and friendless of good character', which the missions opposed to the police image of 'idleness and vice', arose from the daily work of the welfare organizations; it wasn't until 1864 that this new image succeeded in imposing itself, at least partly, on state institutions and the Homeless Poor Act was passed. Of course the missionaries' texts are not free of prejudice and reproaches against the poor, against their 'turning away from God', and their immoral way of life, but in effect they direct a vigorous accusation of lack of compassion against society and its authorities: 'Are there no longer any pious people in Oxford Street, in Holborn, and in the other parishes which lie close to the poverty-stricken neighbourhood of St Giles? Are the poor to weep and pray in vain?'[161]

148

In France, too, the decisive pioneering role of private and church-based welfare schemes can be seen in the development of a functioning 'Hospitalité de Nuit'. 'In the middle of our [nineteenth] century the indigent poor once again found themselves on the streets of France'; in 1846, in Gien-sur-Loire, the physician Dr Ballot set up a homeless ward in the local hospital, but 'we have to wait until 1872 to witness the erection of the first night shelter in the modern sense, in France'; this time it was in Paris.[162]

In Berlin too a *municipal* system to combat homelessness developed only slowly. The very titles in the archives illustrate the uncertainty of the responsible institutions: in 1816 the city council opened a file 'Re. people who have become homeless in general',[163] recording without any value judgement a new phenomenon that was creating pressing problems for the city. In 1825 there is the first entry in the 'Records of the Paupers' Directorate concerning measures for the reduction of homeless vagabondage'.[164] In a letter of 5 June 1838 the Paupers' Directorate also instructed the administration of the work-house, 'in all cases where persons are put in the workhouse because of homelessness', to check these persons very carefully: everywhere in the files one notes the suspicion of fraud, the idea of individuals unjustly burdening the public purse, a fundamental suspiciousness with regard to the homeless.

Homeless families are entered separately in the annual statistics of the workhouse. Seventy families 'consisting of 237 persons' were given shelter there over the year in 1837, and 66 of these could be discharged again the same year. In 1838 the figures are lower, with 44 families, but they rise steadily in the years that follow. On 8 October 1853 – that is, one week after the beginning of the new quarter and the changes of accommodation related to it – the *Haude-und Spenersche Zeitung* reported, 'furthermore there have never been so many homeless families as at this time', and draws the conclusion: 'Need has become more pressing.'

NIGHT SHELTERS AS PART OF THE CITY

Such reports are increasingly frequent in the 1850s, and the topic becomes of interest to the public; the shelters and gathering-places of the homeless attract a long line of the curious – reporters, journalists, artists and sociologists – who file their impressions of the places of the night: 'sleeping in an open field is prohibited by law; on the streets, to take the pavement for a pillow is prohibited by law . . . if the police in London were not more magnanimous than the law, the *wretchedness of night* would even be much more wretched than it is.'[165]

The accounts emphasize the role of the shelters in ensuring greater security on the streets – 'many will be put off roving about at dusk or later' because at a late hour they will be denied entry and so not find a bed. The report in the *Gartenlaube*, which takes London for its subject but is equally valid for Berlin, appeared in 1866, and in many respects is typical in the way it presents the shelters. First the gaze glides over the *whole city*, the author juxtaposing splendid façades with the existence of a great number of poor and homeless people; then the reader's attention is drawn to the few charitable institutions – 'it is a long, gloomy building in a gloomy street in gloomy London' – and before entering, the gaze is directed onto the street in front of the building:

> Already long before 6 o'clock in the evening, groups of people, mostly of the female sex, are waiting in front of the entrance, old and young, with children and babes in arms. Those who are 'used to it' press close to the door, but others, who may be taking this step for the first time, stay waiting at a great distance, as if they did not belong here.[166]

The description of the interior which follows would not be complete without its being framed by the scenes of admission at night and discharge in the morning; the authors do not want to show only the wretchedness that can be seen, for example, in the stories told by 'care-worn faces'; the shelter is rather to be described and experienced *as part of the city*. With this the responsibility of the whole city and of society for these events is emphasized: wretchedness is visible, it is not just hidden in the shelters but in the evening and early mornings it is present on the streets. For our purposes the description of the interior of the house is less significant, but let us quote an impressive picture of the 'vagrant poor':

> The shoes are stored until the next morning. In rows, as if on book-shelves, the shoes stand pointing towards the wall; heavy ones and light ones, big ones and very little ones, what wretched journeys have they not made! These seamen's shoes come perhaps from the storm-tossed deck of an East-Indiaman; these women's shoes in the next room may have tramped from one end of Britain to the other; these shoes

belonging to a beggar child have stood a thousand times on the pavement of London Bridge, the little feet within them numb with cold, and the body above swaying with exhaustion. Nor does the elegant patent-leather boot fail to make an appearance, if only as a ruin...

The *Gartenlaube* later claimed that it was this article which gave the 'actual impetus' for the founding of the Berlin shelter for the homeless; in fact there had already been discussions about the establishment of such an institution in the Paupers' Directorate, in church circles and at the city council.[167] The businessman Neumann had raised the matter at the Friedrich-Werder District Association, Police Commissioner von Wurmb called the idea 'so exceptionally humane and timely that he urgently desired its realization'; a committee of merchants, factory owners, public officials and intellectuals was formed, and 'a humane society whose goal is to establish shelters for the homeless', as it was described in the administrative report of the police authority, 'came to life'.[168] The 'procurement of appropriate premises' was a big difficulty; after a long search a former artillery workshop on the corner of Dorotheenstrasse and Wilhelmstrasse was rented, and on 3 January 1869 the shelter was opened. In the course of this first year the shelter took in more than 13,000 women, girls and children, but the administration of the workhouse complained that there too the number of homeless was increasing, and so in 1870 a men's shelter was erected on the same plot of land. In 1871 the women's shelter was transfered to 3, Füsilierstrasse, later No.5. In 1873, a city shelter was finally established, particularly for the relief of the totally overstretched police cells; it stood in the Pallisadenstrasse in 1877, and from 1878 in the Friedenstrasse at Nos. 55/56. Here, as in the private establishment, only short-term accommodation was available: 'Those who repeatedly visit the shelter for the night will be brought before the police officers present and receive a caution, which is formally recorded. If within five days they have not found themselves accommodation, they are handed over to police custody in due form.'[169]

TASKS OF THE SHELTERS

The arguments between care and control continued. The police authority had to deal above all with the 'doss-houses', the 'night hostels which against the payment of a few pfennig give the most wretched and most dissolute a place to stay for a night or two'; it also criticized the 'weak control' in the shelters. The same argument took place in Paris at the end of the 1870s, and the administration of the shelters saw sufficient cause to justify its work to the police:

> Paris has often been designated the modern Babylon; those who so reproach it see nothing more than its luxury and its pleasures . . . In Paris . . . both public and private charity have until now disregarded those *whose wretchedness is seen as a crime or at least misconduct*. Would you like to know what becomes of these luckless people? Some, so as not to fall into the hands of the police, walk the streets the whole night through, often plagued by tiredness and hunger, until a church door opens to them . . . Others who still have a few sous look for shelter in doss-houses, where they must try and sleep surrounded by offensive and blasphemous language. Yet others cannot resist the temptations of poverty and are driven to fornication, crime or suicide.[170]

The accommodation of the homeless was a significant step in the organization of the whole city. Now there was – not yet sufficiently, but more than before – an opportunity to find shelter the police could act more severely against illegal doss-houses. In 1880 in Berlin a police regulation 'Re. night shelters' came into force, whose goal was to drive the 'existing population of the doss-houses' into the shelters, imposing strict hygienic and sanitary measures and prohibiting the accommodation of persons of different sexes in the same building. The number of doss-houses fell from 21 in January to eight in December 1880, another step towards total control of the night.

The shelters grew in importance, and this was reflected in the increasing number of reports from such places. Lucius Mummius explains the reason for these visits in the following way: 'The idea of greater familiarity with the fate of the unfortunate in modern society is so utterly contemporary' that one can rely on public interest in taking a look at places which offer the poor 'what thousands of its affluent citizens can easily acquire for money: a shelter, a hospitable roof, a home for the night'.[171] Compassion for the fate of the unfortunate becomes largely acceptable, but the tradition of improvement through work has not all been lost; in August 1878 one Herr Zeitler, a 'householder', published an announcement in the *Vossische Zeitung* attacking the policies of the Berliner Asyl-Verein:

> The mediaeval shelters in churches and poverty guilds were abolished when society recognized that they had become a *public danger through*

*abuse*. The same fate seems to await the night shelter run by the Association for Homeless Men, if the association's committee believe that when taking people in they need not make any distinction between those who are homeless through no fault of their own and the work-shy rabble...

The connivance of the police authority, in *exempting from registration all those who spend the night in shelters* – even now after it has been made compulsory to carry identity-cards – is applauded by all those who fear to register with the police.

The committee's idea that 'if the criminals spend the night in shelters, they cannot sin against society' was not shared by those who only saw the shelters as new criminal hideouts; in their view the shelters could be used to take 'anti-social elements' off the streets, but only as a preliminary form of police custody; when compassion rules, when everybody is taken in, when all are 'equal' for the hours of the night, then the shelter has failed in its purpose. For them the shelters had to be part of a police strategy for the maintenance of power over the night; against this, the majority of members of the shelter associations were of the view that the night should be maintained as an area of freedom, as a period of 'cease-fire' between the forces of law and order and the homeless. According to the Social Democrat committee member Paul Singer, the Association did not set itself up as a 'judge of guilt and innocence', but 'releases the needy in the morning as unidentified and unknown as when it opened its doors to them the previous evening'.[172]

REPORTS FROM THE NIGHT SHELTERS

Reports from the shelters seem strangely torn between these two ways of seeing. On the one hand many artists and writers collected their material 'by obtaining information about social misery from policemen or shelter employees'.[173] In his analysis of drawings from English workhouses and shelters Peter Schmandt has shown how strongly reporters' descriptions were influenced by the fact that they were walking in the *footsteps of the police*, consciously or unconsciously propagating clichés about the criminality prevalent in the homeless milieu; descriptions of the queues in front of the shelters too often illustrate only ideas of the homeless as 'work-shy' or 'vagrant'. On the other hand, many reporters, whether working with pen or brush, were unable to close their eyes to the reality of misery.

Often interweaving them into tendentially negative or moralistic texts and images, they told true tales of woe.

The reports came from nocturnal voyages of discovery into the alien milieu of the homeless; many reporters spent only one night in a shelter. Today's interpreters are quick to condemn such excursions as a form of 'slumming', as undertakings 'of a voyeuristic nature', and indeed many descriptions of the confrontation of misery and charitable wealth can hardly be surpassed in their cynicism (and unintentional comic effect) – but they are nonetheless descriptions of this confrontation. In his biography of Dr Thomas John Barnardo, 'the man with the lantern' , E. E. Ronner tells of an episode that illustrates this conflict. After one of his passionate public lectures about the miserable life of London's street children Barnardo was invited to dinner at Lord Shaftesbury's, and after dinner the following conversation took place:

> Could you to take us to one of these dens where such wretched children spend the night?
> – I'd be glad to do that at any time.
> Well . . . as I may suppose that all the gentlemen present would be interested in getting to know your nobody's children, I suggest we seize on the opportunity and start out immediately.
> – I'm afraid that won't do . . . For the simple reason that it is still too early. But if the gentlemen will bide their time till after midnight, they may convince themselves that I have not exaggerated.
> – Wonderful . . . Gentlemen, you will all join in this excursion, will you not?
> There were shouts of agreement from all sides. Shortly after midnight the news arrived that the carriage that had been ordered was standing before the house, and Shaftesbury was able to signal the departure that everyone had been waiting for. Probably none of the late passers-by who witnessed the respectable top-hatted gentlemen climb into the carriage would have suspected that their destination was the miserable alleys of East London.[174]

The 'top-hatted gentlemen' cannot believe that anyone could sleep on the street 'on such a night', 'let alone one of these children'. But Barnardo finds a hideout in a back court, from which finally 73 children crawl out. At Dick Fisher's coffee house, which 'is open all night', they are provided with coffee and bread, and each is given a penny. Barnardo can offer shelter to a few children, and the others have to go back again. A sentimental story, of course, a touching

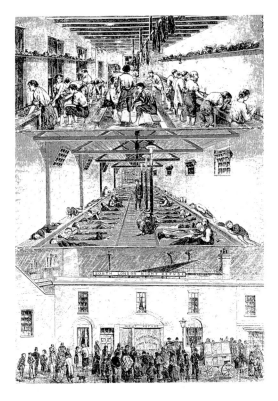

Inside the shelter there is military order. Outer cleanliness was part of the programme of improvement.
*A London night shelter,* drawn from life by Dammann.

scene, welfare as 'a kind of entertainment', a thrill, an adventure, 'pleasure in one's own splendidness' – this may well all be true,[175] but this judgement itself seems no more than cynicism, if at the same time Barnardo's role as propagandist, as reporter and as provider of desperately needed help is not acknowledged. If they wish to inform the public, for those who want to help there often remains no other way than to appeal to their feelings, to their pity; they need the 'top-hatted gentlemen', for they cannot do without a certain measure of pathos. A poem read on the occasion of the hundredth anniversary of the Société Philanthropique in Paris made this appeal: 'The misery is great, and Paris is so vast; and despite the many donations this body has only a small hostel, far out in the suburbs. Misfortune travels there from far away. Help to shorten its way: found a further shelter. You fortunate ones of this world, for whom it is so simple to do good: give.'[176]

Homelessness was already part of the city, even if some did not want to admit it: 'Paris, this fantastic city, of which such wonderful things are said, which shines in our imagination like a miracle! Here live happiness and pleasure! Paris! Here the small merchant can do good business . . . And then comes the day, when he can no longer pay for his hotel: *there he stands in the middle of the street, at the moment when the city is so brightly illuminated that it simply insults him in his nakedness.* Now come the corrupting thoughts and the guilty temptations.'[177] Those who want to avoid the 'pensées corruptrices' and the 'tentations coupables', who believe that homelessness is not a crime, must find *urban* solutions to the problem, but the going is never too easy for them:

> – Why do we build shelters? First of all to give those families who through ill luck have fallen on hard times a roof over their heads, and secondly, *to render the work-shy of no fixed abode harmless at night by giving them a roof over their heads* . . .
> – If we want to do the thing properly we have either to build a big shelter in the centre of the city –
> [lively disagreement]
> – Yes, gentlemen, this is the only way, or if you do not want that, then we have to build several small shelters all over the city.[178]

The Christian missions provided for the 'inner cleanliness' of the homeless – at night practical welfare and ideology went hand in hand. Gustave Doré: *Bible-reading at the night shelter*, c.1870.

156

An illustration from the *Berliner Illustrirte Zeitung* of March 1885 shows a picture which by then had become familiar: people waiting in front of the shelter, with men on the street, drunk, waving wine bottles, aggressive, fighting – exposed to the police intervention provoked by the scene. But when the unhappy side of social misery is to be shown, it is women's faces that one sees, women's stories that one hears. The 'immeasurable and ever-growing' destitution was a problem that increasingly affected women. Ruth Köppen has dealt with this in detail, and she concludes that women made up the majority of the permanently homeless, while temporary homelessness on the other hand was mostly a problem for men.[179] In both Paris and London, in fact, the first night shelters established by private associations were intended for women (and children). Many women who were genuinely homeless were picked up not on account of this but on suspicion of prostitution. Women are regularly mentioned in the reports: the images of the 'helpless' young woman with children put out on the street and of the work-worn, impoverished old woman were guaranteed to arouse pity. But only a few journalists could refrain from mentioning the allegedly high number of 'loose prostitutes' in the shelters. In the eyes of the vice police too the shelters were 'dens of prostitution', while for the managers of the shelters the line was still that nocturnal need should be met, regardless of who it was required assistance.

To the question posed by the social reporter Hans R. Fischer (who on his expeditions through the wretchedness of Berlin visited the women's shelter once again in 1890), as to how a woman had ended up here – 'Was it her own or someone else's fault?' – the woman running the shelter answered him: 'I think that every woman visiting the shelter deserves forgiveness and compassion . . . not one deserves to be thrown out.'[180] And in one report from 1894, faithful to the model, 'In the Homeless Women's Shelter in Berlin' describes first the environment around the shelter and the way there, before attention is directed at the inmates:

> Lothringer Strasse, wide, with boulevards in the middle, but still no competition for the streets in the West. Schönhauser Allee, Linienstrasse, Dragoner- and Grenadierstrasse – finally a small, quiet cul-de-sac. It seems that none of the noise of the big city gets through to it.

157

[Füsilierstrasse] No. 5, a three-storey house. Friendly light shines from the glazing of the middle door, from the ground floor on the left and from the first floor. How comforting a sign to so many poor abandoned women, as they stand on this spot and stretch out their hand towards the bell . . . The police do not have access to the shelter, and those who entrust themselves to it are safe for the night they spend there.[181]

The shelter is an island of light in the big-city night, a haven for the shipwrecked, who are not asked where they come from nor where they are going. Such descriptions are questionable. They tell of a longing, seemingly shared by reporters and readers: a longing for safety, protection, warmth. In the city night the danger of 'being thrown out' is particularly great, and the fate of those who are thrown out is particularly hard – in this world the shelters symbolize *the hope for a place to belong*, and the shelters of the Home Mission of the Evangelical Church were called 'Herberge zur Heimat' [Hostels at the Sign of Home].

There is another side to this. Many literary texts describe the fascination – stronger in the Paris of the *clochards* than in Berlin – of 'radical homelessness' for those settled in their sedentary ways.[182] Here the condition of vagabondage stands for a fundamental refusal of all ties, for the *choice of freedom*; in this the desire for security is turned 'outwards, to the street'. The real vagrant, according to the cliché, does not want a home in the city, and stays in places which signal departure at any moment, railway stations in particular, only visiting the shelter in situations of extreme emergency, during intense cold. Both these cases tell us a great deal about the hopes and the fears of the housed, about the fear of loss of the familiar, and about the hope for a new freedom through the loss of ties.

HOMELAND BIG CITY?

In the stony sea of the great city the homeless are shipwrecked, but the shelter cannot save them: 'for a while it holds out a lifeline to the drowning man and then quickly pulls it back again, abandoning him once more to distress and the danger of going under.'[183] In 1901 Constantin Liebich described the nocturnal odyssey of a man who cannot go to the shelter because he would be handed over to the police; he tries to find shelter anywhere, but is flushed out every time by the night-watchmen or the inhabitants:

158

After this experience Wilhelm decided to spend the night walking around. Rain was still pouring down in buckets. *Oh, the inhabitants of the houses,* who had robbed him so cruelly of his little place, where in his view he could have rested without bothering anybody, they did not know how bad the weather was, how fiercely the wind whistled. Wet to the skin, trembling with cold, Wilhelm now turned southwards. He came to the Oranienburger Tor; the clock only showed 11.30. He walked down the Friedrichstrasse, endlessly long. The lamp-lighters were turning off the bright flames of gas. Wilhelm saw the brightly lit cafés and the cheerful people within. The horse-drawn trams still rolled through the streets with their happy and contented passengers. He met thousands of people who were almost all in a hurry, all of whom had a destination, every one a home, every one a roof over his head.[184]

This juxtaposition of dark and miserable night on the one hand, and bright and cheerful night on the other, is reinforced by another scene, when the lonely wanderer comes upon three night-revellers 'in their cups', boasting about the money they have spent – 'not worth mentioning for such a fantastic night!'– and when he approaches them to beg for money they call for the policeman who is meant to keep the nocturnal rabble off their backs. The city is no longer felt to be a homeland, it is no longer a space of freedom; it is hostile.

Paul Grulich had a similar experience, of which he published an account in his book *Demon Berlin* of 1907. For four weeks he played the role of a homeless person: 'As I love the night, for the secrets masked behind its foggy veils, midnight made me think of starting out . . . My path led me from Steglitz right into the heart of the gigantic city, in whose deepest darkness I now wanted to disappear.'[185] Grulich knows, and emphasizes again and again, how artificial his situation is; he can break off the experiment whenever he wants. In time, however, an overwhelming paralysis gains the upper hand over all the exotic, romantic or secret solicitations of the night. His conclusion is sobering: 'I will not set out a second time to take up the fight with "Demon Berlin".'

Such experiences cannot stop others from trying it themselves, though generally only for the one night, so as 'really to get to know Berlin', 'not from unhealthy curiosity', 'not to have an "interesting adventure"'. Hermann Heijermann very vividly describes the road into darkness from the brightly lit centre of the city – 'the lamps

A life on the edge of death: homeless people spend the night with the Salvation Army in coffin-like boxes. Salvation Army, London, 1888.

stormed towards us in a wearying frenzy of bright flames and shadows like whirling bats' – through an intermediate stage in the outer districts of the city – 'the at first so dazzling, opulently ardent illumination began to wane' – and on into the dark alley in which the shelter lies.[186]

While reports from the criminal world do not so much describe as conjure up the *potential danger* it represents to bourgeois life, accounts from the life of the homeless indicate the fragility of urban life: homelessness appears as a threatening possibility, as an occurrence which can shake the not-so-secure foundations of life and of the city. As the sign of a deeper conflict – how can the city master the threatening tendencies that it generates? – the topic of homelessness becomes a political instrument.

REFORM AND POLITICIZATION OF THE CARE OF
THE HOMELESS

In 1907 there was an outbreak of food-poisoning in Berlin's municipal night shelter, caused by the consumption of spoilt fish (some claimed it was caused by alcohol). The authorities' apparent neglect of the homeless gave Rosa Luxemburg the pretext for a report, 'In the Shelter', in which she not only attacked the police authorities, but also the tendency in her own party to see the homeless not as victims but as miscreants, and therefore to deny them the solidarity of the workers.[187] The fact that the victims 'were already far advanced on the road of despair', as it was put in an anti-alcohol pamphlet by R. Burckhardt,[188] would not have had a reassuring, but rather a threatening effect.

In Berlin, the years after the First World War in particular were 'marked by the reform of provision for the homeless'; its aim, even more clearly than before, was to separate the various functions of the shelters, breaking the connection as much as possible between welfare and policing. It also brought improved sanitation to the building in the Fröbelstrasse, a greater focus on care and help with finding employment. This Social Democratic concept met with considerable difficulties; the Berlin Shelter Association in particular, which had for a long time proclaimed such a policy, had found itself in great financial need after the end of the war. It was hardly possible to collect donations during the period of inflation, and the association had to sublet rooms in the Wiesenstrasse. On 1 October 1926 it signed a contract with the city in which it was provided 'that controls upon admission shall be carried out according to the rules of the municipal shelter in the Fröbelstrasse, and by city employees . . ., and from that moment on the police had access to the building'.[189] This modernization seems to have been successful, both in the positive sense of the provision of more effective care, and in the negative sense of increasing control. The welfare organizations, and particularly journalists from newspapers belonging to the Communist, Social Democratic and later the National Socialist parties continued to express criticism: 'I thought the shelter was there to help the homeless. Do people have any idea of the bottomless despair that reigns there? Not so much the unutterable misery and sorrow, as the spirit, or rather the deadly spiritlessness of the institution.'[190] The shelter itself was repulsive: 'I would have liked to turn round, but I was terrified of the night', wrote an anonymous reporter in the newspaper *Der Deutsche*, and another journalist gives a similar impression in the *Rote Fahne* in May 1926:

> The 'Palm' in the Fröbelstrasse brings a shudder even to the unemployed who live in the most miserable holes. . .
>
> For the bourgeois the down-and-outs who come there evening after evening in search of a roof over their heads are the 'scum of the earth', 'crime itself'. . . The few gas lamps, in perfect tune with this

atmosphere of despair, lit my way, when, shivering, one cold spring evening, I walked up the Fröbelstrasse. So I stood in front of the dark entrance. Individually or in groups, limping and hobbling, on crutches and sticks, the endless queue of misery crawled along and into the greedily open mouth of the archway, gaping black in the night. Tomorrow morning it will spit them out again, onto the street which is their home. Berlin is a big city, and misery creeps away into its corners . . . Finally, around half past six, we are let out. And whilst I breath deep gulps of the fresh morning air, wretchedness wraps itself more tightly in its rags. They will be back here tomorrow, and the day after, and again, and again, and again.[191]

On their nocturnal wanderings in eastern Berlin the reporters discovered 'a whole army' of people who had been rejected by civilization, 'the wrecks of life' who had lost work and home, who could resort to the shelter for six weeks, but then, hopeless, had 'to wander through the nocturnal streets of Berlin, nervously avoided by the citizens'.[192] The growing criticism led the city administration to invite selected representatives of the press to the Fröbelstrasse, and indeed at the end of 1926 and the beginning of 1927 there appeared a few articles in the *Deutsche Allgemeine Zeitung* and in the *Tägliche Rundschau* which gave a positive assessment of the shelters' work for the homeless. The *Kleine Journal*, cynically enough, identified the waiting-rooms of the big Berlin railway stations as the 'Eldorado of the homeless'.

Homelessness is a touchstone of the city's viability – and of attitudes towards the city. In March 1929, two newspapers, the Social Democratic *Vorwärts* and the Nationalist *Germania*, published the same article in rapid succession, both giving it the same subtitle – 'Shelter inmates, vagabonds and unemployed in the capital' – but in one the title was 'Alluring Berlin' and in the other, 'Demon Berlin'.[193] Perceptions of homelessness swung between the two extremes, together with perceptions of the whole city. Towards the end of the Weimar Republic, pragmatic efforts towards a solution to the problem were overtaken and shouted down by more visionary conceptions of city which politicize the discourse about the loss of the sense of the city as a home. In 1932 the Berlin city councillor and welfare-administrator Hermann Drechsler developed a socialist utopia from the description of the many sad fates encountered in his work:

Over there, above the woods, a haze of light rises up, a wash like the Milky Way, but brighter and more intense.
    It is the reflection of the city. Down there, where the light comes

from, life is being created, born, abused; over there a thousand-fold life is making its din in the streets and the shops, in the department stores with their illuminated advertisements, in the hotels, in the clip-joints and dives with their smells of beer and sweltering flesh, where vice and crime thrive as if in huge greenhouses, where the poison of alcoholism and every disgusting disease are spread from body to body. . .

And from deep in the background there rises up the gigantic fist of the awakening proletariat, higher and higher, terrible in its power, swelling into the ink-black sky like the smoke plume of a volcano . . . And the rumbling from the sky and from the earth below heralds the time when this fist will rain down its blows.[194]

Very soon, other fists were to rain down their blows, and the National Socialist measures for 'cleansing' the city of its nocturnal elements would put a brutal end to this phase of socio-political experiment and humanitarian aspiration.

163

# iv  Night and Morality

*A young man offers his company to a young girl*
*unknown to him, to whom he is attracted, and although at*
*first she rejects him, by his modestly persistent advances he*
*succeeds in the end in gaining her agreement.*

    *The young man says: Dear miss, aren't you frightened*
*to walk all alone as twilight falls?*

    *The young girl: What should I have to fear in a civilized*
*country and a populous city?*

    *The young man: You are too inexperienced to guess the*
*dangers which with increasing darkness may attend your*
*every step. Allow me then to offer you my company as*
*protection.*

    *The young girl: I thank you, though I can make no*
*use of it; I shall courageously defy the dangers, in which*
*however I cannot believe.*

LEOPOLD VON RIESBECK (1863)[1]

In this story, intended 'as instruction . . . in starting a conversation in a suitable, attractive and interesting manner, and continuing it with elegance and tact',[2] Leopold von Riesbeck has the young man tell the young woman horror stories about a 'gang of fiends' who 'are abroad' in the city. To this she replies that the best defence against such dangers is to reject *any* company, even that of her modestly insistent adviser with his probably sinister intentions. But could 'the young girl' do without an escort? Was the nocturnal street a place in which a woman could go as she pleased?

At first glance the source material on the nocturnal metropolis seems abundant and varied enough to describe a whole world. In the course of working through it, however, one quickly realizes that certain elements, certain themes that belong to this world are under-represented in the multitude of texts and archives. In this respect too research on the night can easily be compared to a nocturnal walk through the city: one has to find pathways in the darkness, not taking the merely obvious for the real, discovering the 'traces' of the invisible and following them on detours away from the well-illuminated

The city's toilet takes place at night. 'Only those who are intent on study and visit night workers at their occupations' can gain a picture of the whole city (U. Müller, 1911). Photograph by André Kertész.

Members of the public watch the laying and smoothing of tarmac. Photograph by Friedrich Seidenstücker, 1927.

main streets. But if the search for such traces is to be more than the collection of rare curiosities, one has to ask the reasons for the absence of these themes.

The representation of the nocturnal city has been, with very few exceptions, the business of men, as it still is today; women do appear in texts, but as a rule as objects, elements of an ensemble perceived and described by men. Is the nocturnal city then a man's world, built and arranged by men and for their own needs, a world then that can only be properly made use of by men, and in accordance with the rules laid down by them? Or is (and was) it a space, which in practice can and could be properly made use of by both sexes, and is it perhaps only the records, the state of the sources, that are an expression of male dominance? The two alternatives imply different strategies of research. In the first case the city night would have to be described as a man's world, with all the characteristics that make it available to men but inaccessible to women. The other case would dictate an intensive search for new sources, and for hidden clues in the existing sources, which depict the nocturnal city from women's point of view and represent it as a *space of action for women*. Neither of these two ways of proceeding does justice to the dilemma, however; and I will therefore attempt to describe the city night as space of confrontation, a space of encounter between men and women, as a place where their wishes, needs and desires, fears and hopes meet, and contradict or – seldom enough – complement each other.

The German language, like the French, has at its disposal a concept that well expresses the difficulty which arises with this strategy: the words *Sitten* and *mœurs* each denote a certain customary social behaviour, and at the same time attribute a certain moral value to it. *Sittengeschichten* and *histoires des mœurs* tell of the relationship between the sexes and through this attempt to characterize the socio-moral values of a period or of a city. Those who report on *mores* tell us about ways of behaviour that are customary, widespread, 'established'; at the same time there is in such descriptions also a 'subterranean' connotation of morality and decency, which offers an interpretation of behaviour in terms of morals.

In this respect *mores* – like the concept of 'security', which attempts to grasp the relationships in the city between order and disorder, between 'top' and 'bottom' – become the measure for judging the relationship between the sexes, and the public expression of the latter the gauge of what morality is supposed to mean. In his *History*

166

*of Public Morals in Germany* (1897) Wilhelm Rudeck ventures some definitions which I would like to adopt here: 'By morals I understand the sum of all the customs of a period, by which the relationships to sexual life are contained' and 'It is their setting in the *public sphere* which is the feature that separates documents of public morality from amorous tales'.[3] Nevertheless, 'morality', like 'security', is not a neutral category, but an expression of dominant ways of thinking, and so something changeable. Debates about the 'moral' situation in a city are so interesting because they do not just report on what ways of behaviour were usual in a particular period, but also on which groups in the city were challenging these values, and in what way.

Here too it is the case that the state, and, let us emphasize this, also the clerical authorities, attempt to secure their own power through the right to define what is morality; and here too they create institutions which replace a directly dominating presence, ensuring adherence to the rules and punishing violations. These institutions are the first to register any changes in social behaviour and social relations. In 1926 Berlin Police Chief Albert Moll tried to describe the relationship between 'police and morals':

> It is the task of the police to protect morals, to the extent that the interests of the state demand it. The fact that at times custom and morals coincide cannot be doubted; but that they are not to be equated is shown by the example of Diogenes, whom the modern police would probably not have allowed to live in a barrel, as it was not within a dwelling. Today he would be arrested by the police as a homeless person...
>
> If everyone were free to transgress moral rules then truly *morality* itself would be endangered . . . Morals protect us from rapid, arbitrary change, they guarantee the stability of society and the state. And the police, the body charged with their enforcement, have a duty to fight the dangers that threaten the state.[4]

Manners and morals may change, like the standards by which what is 'moral' and what is 'immoral' are measured; but as long as they are valid, the police have to ensure they are observed, and their violation – or, even more tellingly in our context, transgression, or overstepping the limit – is seen as a danger. The nocturnal street in the big city is one arena where persistence and change in 'morals' can be observed: it attracts with promises of freedom, of independence, of the possibility of over-stepping limits, while at the same time, and to a greater extent than almost anywhere else, it is caught in a fine-spun net of surveillance: this net is visible in part in the figures of the policeman and the many other 'moral guardians', but in part it is invisible, represented by the behavioural rules and moral ideas in force. The restrictions on nocturnal freedom hit women far more than men, and their possibilities of movement are much more radically obstructed by the visible and invisible controlling authorities of the night.

## 1 *Women in the city night*

This double barrier formed by the dominant ideas of morality and men's conceptions of freedom is still powerful, and bars women's autonomous access to the nocturnal city: Ulrike Scholvin has described the big cities as 'spaces of imagination closed off to me', as places which tempt one towards adventure, but erect an almost insurmountable obstacle in front of it. Of course cities today are no longer 'prohibited' spaces, and an infrastructure of niches has been created which is accessible to women without any problems.

> But on the streets between, which have not been built for us or by us, we still have to move strategically, always prepared to have to justify our presence . . . Because the cities onto which we cast our projections, so as to lose ourselves in them, are blocked with images which our wishes have not produced, and which are not images of the women whom we would like to be.[5]

The restrictions on freedom concern the reality of the nocturnal city as much they do its imaginary content; women's needs and wishes are not fundamentally different from men's; for both it is a question of being able to enter the nocturnal city freely and independently, without 'exposing themselves to senseless hurt and discrimination', and of being able to move in it – through the *whole* city, during the *whole* night, not just in certain spatial and temporal reserves. But men's freedom of movement has a real restrictive effect on that of women.

The projections that Ulrike Scholvin describes – to be able to lose oneself, to let oneself drift, to live tempting adventures, and also to be allowed to be alone and be able to resurface unhurt – do not differ in content or in language from those expressed by men; but men's projections often concern women, and injure their aspirations.

One of the reasons for this may be that in the literature the topos of 'the night as woman' is described and conjured up again and again, in different variations:

> After the fall of darkness other powers rule than during the day. In the symbolism and myth of most peoples the night is chaos, the scene of dreams, it teems with ghosts and demons, like the sea with fish and sea-monsters. *It is female*, as the day is male, and like everything female it brings quiet and terror at the same time.[6]

Unlike Klaus Theweleit, for example, with his 'metaphor of the flood',[7] Wolfgang Schivelbusch does not analyze this male image of the 'night as woman' but takes it endlessly further, like an anthropological constant factor. What does it mean, that 'the night is female'? In this image too, in the end, one only finds 'woman as landscape of desire', a terrible, fascinating, and above all alien terrain, which inspires fear and has to be conquered.

The street abolishes boundaries: in the manifold possibility of the street, walking, seeing and searching are one and the same. Undine Gruenter, who describes a man's nocturnal expeditions through Paris, makes the connection between city night and male-dominated sexuality apparent: 'Into the anonymity of the nocturnal street, through which already the sharp gusts of morning are blowing, *I slip as if into a cave'*, and, elsewhere: *'One should be able to penetrate into a city as into a human body.'*[8]

In recent years, women researchers on the city have started to pursue the traces of the female element in urban reality and imagination; they have taken up subjects which male-dominated research has always left disregarded.[9] At the same time, women's groups have campaigned to 'reclaim the night'. In this formula there is as great a whisper of mysticism as in the undifferentiated notion that 'the night is female', vague memories of witchcraft and Walpurgis Night. It nevertheless provides a clue to the decisive failing of the nocturnal city: as long as it is not as accessible to women as it is to men there can be no talk of freedom: 'Night belongs to man, he can afford it. A woman at night moves differently through the streets: she walks as if down the middle of the road, equidistant from dark entrances and the din from pub doors.'[10]

In a conversation about the beauty of the Parisian nights of the past, the historian Louis Chevalier remembered: 'C'était la chasse'.[11] It was a hunt – for pleasure, for a glance, for a meeting, for a woman.

Without being asked, and against their will, women who were about the city at night – for whatever reason, and who asks about men's reasons? – became potential quarry, potential victims. The discourse of the always seducible seducer quickly turns out to be a male fantasy, because when women really go hunting, of their free will and for their own pleasure, then fear makes its appearance in the men's texts, a tendency 'to connect the dangers of the big city with the threat emanating from female sexuality'.[12]

In men's texts, both belong together: yearning for the city and yearning for 'woman', fear of the city and fear of woman. The linking element which unites the 'desirable'[13] and repellent characteristics of the city, of the night and of woman, is the theme of prostitution. The suspicion of prostitution fell upon women who were about at night unaccompanied and without justification, and not only in the cities: 'The freedom of the streets was not unlimited; young, single women were considerably restricted in their freedom of movement. *The decisive boundary here is set by the darkness and the moral dangers associated with it* . . . Those who were about at night in order to amuse themselves or even to meet friends, were suspected of "night-revelry", and this was punishable,' writes Carola Lipp.[14] She traces the history of these prohibitions, in the case of Würtemberg, back to 1536, when a land ordinance decreed that 'no one shall go onto the street at night in summer after nine o'clock'. 'No one' – in principle this covered both sexes; but as a rule men were only apprehended if they were infringing other prohibitions apart from that on 'going about by night'. In the police statistics for the 1840s night-revelry appears always as a female offence.

In the big cities, in the period of their escape from the bonds of tradition, social control was weaker than in the villages, but still strong enough to identify female transgressors of the moral law. 'Public life as the sphere of immorality', wrote Richard Sennett, 'the public as an immoral domain meant rather different things to women and men . . . *The public and the idea of disgrace were closely linked.*'[15] As we have seen, in the years around 1840 bourgeois men little by little conquered the evening and night streets as a space of movement; in this a significant role was played by the development of street-lighting and the furnishing of the streets with halting-points which followed it: cafés, shop windows and theatres. From here, from the illuminated centres, there set off the expeditions into the darkness, into the nocturnal quarters of the cities. The ability to find one's way in the dark, the opportunity to get to know and to master it becomes a fundamental precondition for the ability to meet the demands of modern urban life. Women were for a long time denied this opportunity, and men's and women's pathways through the city did not develop at all at an equal rate.[16]

The more men's ascendancy was expressed in their participation in public life, the more women were restricted to the domestic sphere. The only way out was 'female' involvement 'in the service of poor and suffering humanity',[17] in activities caring for the sick, in the charitable field. This could involve visiting poor families, which of course meant visiting the poor neighbourhoods. So, while men tended to experience the 'dark corners' of the big cities as regions of adventure, of challenging danger, of self-affirmation – and as 'hunting grounds' – women found themselves confronted by wretchedness and poverty, the 'night sides' of the city which arouse pity.

IN MEN'S EYES

In the years of the onset of intense industrialization, which led many young women to move to the cities, there were women about in public – and at night – 'women who saw no other possibility than to earn a living by prostitution'.[18] The growth of street prostitution, with the presence of prostitutes on the public streets and squares, may have increased the attraction and adventure of the city night for men, but narrowed women's room for movement even further. In their effort to differentiate themselves from prostitutes, many bourgeois women employed in charitable works distanced themselves particularly strongly – and in a particularly moralizing manner – from public 'immorality', 'looking down reproachfully on those women who had transgressed the norms of bourgeois sexuality'.[19]

The attraction of the forbidden, for men one of the significant attractions of the night – Alfred Delveau writes of the *lorettes* of Montmartre: 'Ce ne sont pas de femmes, ce sont des nuits'[20] – also touches women; while men can allow themselves to be drawn by the attractions, women must develop a reinforced protective shield against these powers of seduction, and perhaps the moralizing language of the moral movement can also be ascribed to this. A more understanding attitude, as expressed by Willy Hellpach in 1907, was rare:

171

During the day the girls are busy. When evening comes, and the shops close at long last, they can look forward to going home to impoverished circumstances, often enough to witness cheerless family scenes, to go to bed and then back to the shop the next day. Day in, day out. This is not an attractive weekly calendar, when the path from shop to the home passes beer-palaces and cafés beaming bright. And all this in the years of sexual development, when the heat of sensual desire tingles for the first time in every nerve. Was it therefore surprising, that there developed a burning desire, after all the daily toil, for once also to enjoy in the evening a little of the wonders of the big city which display themselves so insistently?[21]

Here it is clear what opportunities the night would have been able to offer for the fashioning of one's own leisure, and if possible, one's own freedom; but it is these young women precisely who moved in a dense net of rules and prejudices that did not allow them a right to venture out independently: 'As a young girl, do not allow your eyes too much freedom', a contemporary manual enjoined, under the heading 'How should I walk on the street?'.[22] In the eyes of men and of many women, women in the night landscape were either whores or angels; between these alternatives, women were left with very little space for self-definition. So, for example, Friedrich Naumann writes of Henriette Arendt, the first female police auxiliary in Stuttgart in 1903: 'The policewoman is as such the *representative of human care in the female underworld.'*[23] The counter-image is given by Ernst von Salomon, from the point of view of the Freikorps fighter in Weimar Berlin; horrified, he reports on the 'whores' who 'prowled behind the front established by our combat groups', who, as if it were the most natural thing in the word, 'laid hands on our bodies, which had just been exposed to the flashing fire of the machine guns'.[24]

Women who ventured into the city night had to expect to be identified with one of these images – or with a strange amalgam of both. It was only in the 1920s, with the attempt at a general democratization of life, that the space of the nocturnal city opened up for women. The 'new' women of the republic – 'in general they have the speed of their Berlin, which makes people like us so breathless', wrote Franz Hessel[25] – stepped beyond existing boundaries, even that of the morality to which they were supposed to be subject. The level of women's participation in public life was doubtless higher than before, but many restrictions were still in force: if women wanted to

The policemen provide security – but they also make sure that the city does not
become 'woman's own'. Photograph by Bill Brandt, London, c.1935.

hold their own in the city, they had to find their way in an environment made by men. In the texts of the enemies of nocturnal life the presence of women on the streets appears as a strong sign of decay and of the threatening fall. But in the texts of lovers of urban life as well, women are often only present as window-dressing, as decorative elements: dancers like Anita Berber, playmates like Kiki de Montparnasse,[26] actresses and singers are the 'flowers' of metropolitan night culture: they are companions, women who 'belong', but not to themselves.

In January 1927 the *Vossische Zeitung* published an interesting discussion in which these ideas were taken up and tied in to the (nocturnal) everyday life of women in the city. The following extracts tell us about the state of 'morality' in big-city Berlin and women's attempts at 'walking unaccompanied'.

UNACCOMPANIED WOMEN

In Neuköln a waiter shot dead a drunk who had importuned his mother on the street . . .

This tragic event once again draws attention to the situation in which women and girls find themselves when unaccompanied in public. There are many who claim that harassment by men has in recent times become unbearable.

The newspaper gave three women the opportunity to express themselves on the subject, and it also asked Dr Bernhard Weiss, the head of the criminal investigation department of the Berlin police, for a response. Mady Christians wrote:

When I came back to Berlin at the end of the war and worked in Germany for the first time as a young adult, the impression I got of women's place in Berlin's public life was as surprising as for our women the comparison with other countries is embarrassing . . .

My walk home from the theatre took me through very busy streets, through the Linden and the Friedrichstrasse to the S-bahn and from [Bahnhof] Zoo through the Joachimsthaler to the Kurfurstendamm. If they used the lock-up here as they do in America, there would have been a fair crowd of men in the cells every night.

Of course you can defend yourself. I even had a brilliant trick: if I noticed that someone behind was about to catch up with me, so as to walk alongside me and have a word, I would let my handbag dangle carelessly on my arm, and the very moment the man came right up to me and wanted to talk, I would briskly switch the handbag to the other arm, looking at the wrongdoer with a frightened and outraged expression on my face. Without exception, their words stuck in their throats from shame. No man is happy to be taken for a pickpocket by the object of his tender attentions.

You have to do things like that, because just walking faster, yelling at them or treating them with disdain no longer puts them off. It is quite shameful that women in Berlin have to protect themselves like this, and I think it would be a very good idea to adopt the American way of having the police come to the rescue of women in such trouble.

This was the cue for the police. Bernhard Weiss responded to the complaints with a description of police work on the streets, at the same time giving an interesting insight into the way the police see the street, and women 'walking unaccompanied':

At the beginning of September 1903, [the Berlin chief of police] set up, on an experimental basis, a special plain-clothes patrol covering Friedrichstrasse, Leipzigerstrasse, Potsdamerstrasse and Unter den Linden. Its duties were to be . . . 'mainly surveillance and prevention'. It is interesting, not just from a policing point of view but also psychologically, that the instructions on how they were to carry out their duties specified that 'If the detectives see that a man is pursuing a respectable lady in an obvious and persistent manner, approaching her or accompanying her against her will, they should step protectively to the lady's side, identifying themselves as detectives. That the man's attentions are unwanted will be evident from the woman's behaviour, that she quickens her pace, attempts to avoid him, makes gestures of dismissal or looks around for help.'

There is, however, an obvious problem for the police. What, for example, are their criteria for judging a woman to be 'decent' and 'respectable ' in 1903, when unaccompanied women fell even more strongly under suspicion of prostitution than in 1927? Was the benevolent attention of the detectives also available to women of the lower classes? Weiss goes into this further:

This experimental 'ladies' protection service' proved to be worthwhile, and in January 1904 it was therefore considerably extended. Detectives protected unaccompanied women not only on the main streets of the centre, but also in more distant areas of the city, in order, as the new police instructions explained, 'to provide the necessary protection also to women and girls of the working class'. In January 1911 there was a reorganization, the special ladies' protection service being closed down and its duties assigned to the detectives of the vice police. This new arrangement, which lasted until after the war, was certainly not an ideal solution to the problem of ladies' protection. Given the nature of their policing activities, which are part of the battle against female immorality, the vice-squad detectives do not appear to be the appropriate guardians for decent ladies.

For Weiss the problems were the low number of police officers on the streets and the difficulty in proving 'harassment'; many men turned the tables, representing 'themselves as the victims of solicitation' – just as the vice squad focused on prostitutes, and not on men, as a threat to order. Two other women, Dr Gertrud Haupt and Annemarie Horschitz, got a chance to speak in the same issue of the *Vossische Zeitung*:

> Although men have for decades recognized women as equal collaborators and companions, they still seem to find it difficult to rid themselves of the *idea that every woman unaccompanied in public is in search of adventure*. In Berlin in particular, harassment has reached such a level that the authorities must do something.
>
> German women look with envy at their more favoured sisters in London, New York and (here the American influence has worked miracles) even in the Paris of such ill-fame.
>
> Given this strong police support, the women of Berlin must now take up with renewed courage the hitherto hidden struggle for equality with unaccompanied men.

> The police want to look after us, and look after public morality. It's a nice, chivalrous plan, and applause is guaranteed. Just one piece of advice and one request: don't lag behind America, don't just protect us women from being accosted and harassed by your personal intervention and the force of authority; no, threaten the 'criminals' with heavy fines, prison and – compulsory marriage. In New York the resourceful 'bobbies' dress up in women's clothing to look for foolish men who allow themselves to be led astray into murmuring unseemly requests.[27]

In this letter a slightly ironic tone can already be detected; this is particularly noticeable in the international comparison (so popular in the discussion of night life) – 'In Paris? Well, Paris lives on the charm of its gestures. And this importuning is one of them.' On 29 January 1927 the discussion in the *Vossische Zeitung* was continued with two further contributions, one from Lotte Spitz:

Hand on heart, you women who often have to go somewhere alone: on the countless occasions that professional or social engagements have led you to walk unaccompanied in the Berlin streets at any hour of day or night, how often have you been seriously harassed? From the darting glance, the casual exploratory remark, to continuous harassment from a persistent man? Where are the men who let you go your way without batting an eyelid, without a word forming on their lips, without speeding up their pace?

And another thing: the uniformity of female attire requires of strolling gentlemen – particularly at night – the exercise of heightened and sophisticated powers of differentiation. In nine out of ten cases, when the lady walks faster, and pays no attention, the gentleman will see the hopelessness of the enterprise and let her go.

Admittedly, on certain streets, at certain corners, a cheerful expression or the smile that comes to one's face at some idle thought, can on occasions be misinterpreted and taken for an invitation. But even then the uninvited suitor will recognize his error in the clearly unfeigned and spontaneous horror of the accosted lady.

Lotte Spitz argues that police officers should be called on for help only when there is absolutely no alternative; because otherwise it would be 'left to the watching police to draw the line at which an innocuous flirtation in the street, in the course of which an at first not at all unwilling lady might have been suddenly scandalized, turns into real harassment'. The police should keep a better watch on dark side-alleys, but in principle women can 'stand up to their man'. In her contribution, Margarete Caemmerer also speaks in favour of greater self-confidence:

Is 'pursuing' someone itself going to be a crime? We should not be so hidebound as to condemn out of hand one of the nicest nuances in the game of love. Whether the pursuit ends in the unaccompanied woman being accosted depends solely on her behaviour ... We women should show a little bit more self-confidence and not immediately call on the police.[28]

But such attitudes cannot simply be adopted at will; under the prevailing conditions it wasn't easy to abandon the victim perspective, finding strategies for making one's own way through the (nocturnal) city rather than giving up one's newly discovered independence and calling for the policeman.

The nocturnal city is a place of risk, of potential danger, and it is charged with sexuality. 'Pleasure and danger'[29] are counterbalanced, and any description would be false were it to foreground only one of the two aspects. In many of the more recent feminist texts we find elements of a new 'enclosure', a tendency to withdraw into forms of thought dominated by concerns for security and public morality, and too rarely is there any interrogation of the value and the significance of such self-imposed limitations. So we too often have to rely on texts by men that describe 'women of the night', texts in which the traces of an emancipated life may emerge when they are read against the grain, as for example in Philippe Soupault's *The Last Nights of Paris* (1928):

> She loved only the night, which every evening she made her own, and her arts became effective only when she left behind the light to enter the dark. If you looked at her carefully, you couldn't imagine she lived during the day. She was night personified, and her beauty was nocturnal. Just as one says, quite automatically, 'As bright as day', so one could say of Georgette only that she was as beautiful as night.[30]

The myths, however, are tenacious and long-lived. Perhaps a closer look at the history of the 'whores' and 'angels' will help us to understand them better.


## 2 Prostitution

Men and women meet on the streets of the nocturnal city; they are both more aware and made more aware of their sex than they are in daytime. Their meeting has an unequal character: all men and all women, regardless of what they are doing in the city night, move within it under the conditions of general social relationships they have not created themselves, but which stamp their attitudes and behaviours.

Prostitution is an extreme expression of the unequal relations between the sexes. Historically, as also today, it stands as a symbol for different motivations, different gazes and different views, different ideas about walking in the nocturnal city. Even if individual women or men walk the night with other motives, with other demands, they are followed by suspicion and reproach. Prostitution weighs down on the image of the city night borne by all who venture out in it.

It marks – or rather, perhaps, used to mark – the nocturnal topography of the city, its presence shaping the scene on the street. The reality and, even more so, the imagination of the nocturnal city is populated by a cast of prostitutes and their clients, vice police, voyeurs and missionary nuns. Prostitution not only concerns different sectors of social organization, impinging on various types of social relations; the control and regulation of 'public immorality' are also seen as tasks of the *state*. The existence of prostitution represents a comprehensive challenge to the authorities' jurisdiction over the nocturnal city and to their powers of definition: what is 'moral' and what is 'immoral', what is to be allowed and what is to be forbidden, how much freedom is possible (and for whom), how many restrictions are necessary; these questions are discussed again and again using prostitution as an example.

CONTACT WITH THE STREET

Accounts of prostitution in the Middle Ages and in the early modern period describe it as a *phenomenon of enclosed spaces*. In those days too the authorities would always act when 'sexual misconduct' drew public attention, when for example 'shameless' scenes took place in the neighbourhood of bawdy-houses and similar establishments. Nonetheless, as Regina Schulte says, 'prostitution was incorporated into the system of urban social relations and subject to its forms of commerce'.[31] An integral element of this policy, however, was the prosecution of unofficial 'street-corner prostitution', which was less easy to control. The discourse on the danger of *prostitution clandestine* runs through the debate like a leitmotif; more even than brothel prostitution it becomes the very embodiment of immorality, particularly requiring the protection of the night. 'Lurking' in unexpected places, escaping control, it is closely connected to the phenomenon of homelessness, allying itself, as experience shows,[32] with the criminal world, threatening the city with sexually transmitted disease.

The Berlin 'Ordinance against the seduction of young girls into brothels and for preventing the spread of venereal disease' of 2 February 1792 is the first document in the 'Records of the Council of the Royal City of Berlin, concerning local brothels and prostitution', whose first volume covers the years between 1792 and 1849.[33] Most attention is devoted to problems relating to the brothels. From 1810 onwards the topographical centre of brothel prostitution was the alley An der Königsmauer. This allegedly isolated quarter gained its notoriety from travel writing: 'We would not advise anyone who wishes to escape the fate of Orpheus to go by daylight through this lane', wrote Adolf von Schaden in 1822.[34]

What went for daylight was even more the case for the dark. 'For the most part of the evening and night a prostitute stood in front of the brothel door as bait', writes Hans Ostwald, and: 'with the arrival of midnight the brothels were apparently shut, the entrance door being locked and the shutters closed, but inside the bustle went on till 3 or 4 o'clock in the morning. To maintain communication with the outside until that time, little flaps were built into the shutters, at which a girl stood watch. If a night-reveller approached, she would call out and invite him to enter.'[35]

In the eyes of the public guardians of morality, the streets and alleys in the brothels' vicinity became an increasingly dangerous terrain. What happened inside the houses was hidden from public view, but now sexual immorality entered into 'communication' with the outside world. The closure of the brothels was more and more loudly demanded by neighbours, church representatives, and concerned parents whose children had to walk past them on the street. Within the Prussian government too a process of rethinking was going on. On 25 June 1839 the Minister of the Interior wrote in a circular to the government of the Rhine Provinces: 'I have been unable to approve the repeated requests made to the Royal Government for the licensing of brothels, as in my opinion the advantage one hopes for from such a course of action is illusory . . . The police should never abandon the repression of vice.'[36] The discussion of the question in Prussia and the rest of the German Reich over the next decade would be marked by this opposition between a strategy of reducing 'vice' through control and demands that it should be thoroughly repressed rather than tolerated. In France too, in the late 1830s, there began a debate about prostitution, but this was conducted in slightly different terms.

ENCLOSED MILIEUS

The trigger for this discussion was a book by Alexandre Parent-Duchâtelet, *De la Prostitution dans la Ville de Paris*, published in 1836.[37] He was the first to attempt a comprehensive account of the phenomenon, and did not content himself with examining the reports of the police and administration; he was above all 'a field investigator, an ethnologist of the cesspool': 'I have been to all the places I have described . . . I was able to visit the houses in question at any time of day or night; and I was there able to make a considerable number of important observations; during the day I accompanied the physician, and at night I was taken round by a police officer from the bureau [the vice police].'[38]

These precise observations in the field, and in Paris this also meant in the brothels, showed him a *contrésocieté souterraine*, an underground society which brought with it moral, social, sanitary and political dangers. The consequences he drew from this (as described by Alain Corbin) made him a pioneer of the state regulation of prostitution as part of the overall organization of the city:

1. It is necessary to create an *enclosed milieu*, invisible to children, honest women and even prostitutes outside the system; enclosure makes it possible to carry marginalization to the limit and to contain extramarital sexual activity; it constitutes a dike to prevent any spillover.
2. This enclosed milieu must remain constantly under the *supervision of the authorities*. Invisible to the rest of society, it is perfectly transparent for those who supervise it.[39]

'Tolerance' of the brothels includes keeping them under constant control; once this has been dealt with, the *Police des Moeurs* are left to fight against clandestine prostitution and pimping, and to ensure a separation from public life. This is why the creation of specific *milieus* is matched on the other hand by an attempt to define 'des lieux interdits', prohibited places. At the centre of discussion is the 'prohibition of the public highway to prostitutes (interdiction de la voie publique aux filles publiques),' which first comes up in connection with the Palais Royal. This was the starting-point for the nocturnal excursions of the Parisian *noctambules*, the streets between the Palais Royal and the Halles Centrales being the principal resort of street prostitutes, a terrain under the surveillance of a brigade from the 'Service des Moeurs', which prescribed precise rules of behaviour to the prostitutes:

They are only allowed to take part in the public circulation half an hour after the time set for the lighting of the lamps, but in no case before 7 o'clock in the evening, and they are not allowed to stay there longer than 11 o'clock in the evening.

[They are forbidden] to stand about on the public highway, to congregate there, to walk around in groups, to walk back and forth along too short a distance, or to allow themselves be followed or accompanied by men.[40]

According to this decree of February 1841, the gardens and the area around the Palais Royal are prohibited places, as are the royal gardens, the covered arcades, and the banks of the Seine, and also 'les rues, les places et lieux obscurs et déserts', the dark and deserted streets and squares: their nocturnal appearance is to be brought under the control of light and is not to be allowed to escape it. In addition to the regular provision for police custody sixteen police stations were designated as 'dépôt provisoire des filles publiques', collecting points regularly visited by the *Sergents de Ville* before midnight. These stations, distributed across the whole city, attest to the inefficacy of the establishment of the enclosed milieus.

The unspeakable is expressed statistically: this tabulated list of 'tolerated' brothels produced by the Paris police gives details of amenities – 'rooms, for the purpose of orgies'. Police tolerance of the brothels brought the morality movement onto the scene.
List of *tolérances* from the Prefecture of Police, Paris, 1864.

182

'On the pavements of the rue Notre-Dame-de-Lorette two lines of women were hurrying towards the boulevards, sticking close to the shops, petticoats raised and noses to the ground, with intent faces and never a glance at the window-displays. This was the famished descent from the Bréda quarter as the gas lights came on' (Emile Zola, *Nana*). Anonymous illustration, Paris.

H. A. Frégier's work, *Des classes dangereuses de la population dans les grandes villes*, was published in Brussels in 1840. His account of an inseparable conglomerate of crime, prostitution and other elements of the 'dangerous classes' made a more decisive impression on the work of the police than did that of Alexandre Parent-Duchâtelet, which was both better informed and more discerning. The police repression of prostitution also hit many other women from the lower classes: 'The night-time expeditions generally took place between midnight and 1 a.m. on the boulevards, and consisted of barring the thoroughfare and then, by an immense casting of the net, of driving into the arms of the agents all the unfortunate women found within the perimeter. . .'[41] The officers of the vice squad saw prostitutes everywhere; in their eyes all who were about on the streets at night were already essentially suspect, and women were particularly hard hit by this suspicion and its consequences. This approach also had another consequence, undreamt of by the police: more and more people became aware of 'public immorality' as the streets were opened up to a wider public, and they also witnessed the police's inability to bring it under control.

As Hans Ostwald wrote, the police had 'to convince themselves that not everything can be regulated in a great city with the rank and growth-rate of Berlin'. On 15 November 1843 the Ministry of the Interior requested the abolition of the brothels, and at the end of 1844 the royal cabinet issued an order to this effect. In the annual report of the Berlin vice police for 1853 it is laconically stated that the closure 'took place [though only in 1846!] without noticeable disturbance', but this is not the whole truth. There was a public debate:

### THE LESSER OF TWO EVILS

Who did not read with joy in the newspapers that on 1 January 1846 all the dens of prostitution in the capital are to disappear? How human, how Christian, how noble is this decree! But will the final aim be achieved by this? Will the closure and sealing-off of these sinks of iniquity prevent their overflowing their banks, flooding healthy land and causing unspeakable disaster? – Would it not be more advisable, in populous cities, from which coarse lechers are rarely absent, to allow these cesspools to exist and to control them stringently?[42]

Against this, police chief Wilhelm J. Stieber[43] puts an interesting argument for the abolition of the brothels: it is necessary 'to explore the deepest and most secret folds of our social relations', and one should 'penetrate' these relations 'in accordance with the principles of science and humanity, and drag them into daylight'. Superficially, this view corresponds to the democratic mood of Berlin in early 1848. But Stieber uses these formulae as instruments in the struggle against the dangerous classes of the city: 'There are three terrible enemies with which our age has to struggle almost everywhere . . . namely, *the proletariat, crime and prostitution.*'[44] The purpose of investigative penetration is exclusively to control, to secure, and to prepare for drastic measures of 'cleansing'. Although the respectable public in Berlin did not show much tendency towards public social life, indeed because of this, places of entertainment, particularly

184

during the hours of the evening and the night, 'are abandoned to the powers of prostitution'. The enemy had a tendency to spread everywhere: Behrenstrasse, Schützenstrasse, Münzstrasse, Jägerstrasse, Schlossplatz, Alexanderplatz, Kastanienwäldchen, the square by the Catholic church, Rosenthaler Platz, Lustgarten, Louisenstrasse – all contaminated terrain, 'but the Königstrasse too teems every night with street prostitutes along its entire length, and the part of the Friedrichstrasse between the Leipzigerstrasse and the Dorotheenstrasse, the stretch of the Leipzigerstrasse which lies between Mauerstrasse and the Dönhoffplatz, both sides of the Linden and the Landsberger Strasse'.[45]

The contradiction is obvious: the spread of street prostitution was a result of the war against the brothels, and it grew even more after their abolition, 'for the very natural reason', as Carl Röhrmann commented, 'that the income of the brothels has gone over to the street prostitutes'.[46] In his condemnation of the social situation which forced women into prostitution, Röhrmann stood on the same political ground as Friedrich Sass and Ernst Dronke, the journalists already quoted, who both gave the topic of prostitution considerable space in their descriptions of Berlin, though they had focused on the 'traffic' in coffee houses, dance halls, and ballrooms. In their treatment of the topic, however, they spoke in the same unobjective tone as the enemies of the big city: for Sass 'vice', 'depravity', 'foolishness', 'hedonism' and 'idleness' are the grades of the 'whole scale of Berlin's conditions of life'; the 'thirst for piquancy' and the 'thorough frivolity of the capital' are evidence of the illusory life of an emergent metropolis that is outwardly prosperous but inwardly already decayed, and even the 'lower classes of Berlin exhibit all the sins and failings that derive from the character of our big cities'.[47]

> Hopefully, however, no stranger who spends some time in Berlin will miss a visit to Kroll's establishment on one of its glittering evenings or nights. Here many a veil can be lifted, and one may gain profound insights into the state of Berlin life. But strangers usually miss the main things, and they may be content not to have had a bad experience. Above all they should not believe they are seeing 'decent' Berlin. What whirls and flutters around them is irresponsible Berlin, brought there either by wealth, extravagance, lasciviousness, or boredom, by need, employment, juvenile foolishness, or for swindling or prostitution.[48]

Only the first three balls at Kroll's, Sass continues, were attended by the 'respectable public'; after that came prostitutes, and also pickpockets and gamblers, 'with their dark following', and 'by the eleventh or twelfth [ball], prostitutes already formed the greater part of the female company'. Had Herr Kroll tried to ban them from his establishment he would have run the risk of bankruptcy, because prostitution 'in Berlin has become the mainstay of the whole of public life and amusement'. Here the discourse about the criminal world, the growing threat to the security of the city finds a parallel in the discourse on prostitution, as the threat to the morals of the city.

NIGHT AS CREATOR OF OPPORTUNITY

In 1846 there began a phase of intensive reflection on the problem on the part of the Berlin police and other bodies concerned with prostitution. 'A well-known local police officer has been sent on a journey abroad', writes the *Vossische Zeitung* of 15 January 1850, 'in order to report on the institution of licensed brothels.' The brothels were to be reinstated, and their supervision assigned to a newly created commission, among whose members were Hofrichter, the head of the vice police, and the physician F. J. Behrend, author of the memorandum 'Prostitution in Berlin and the measures to be taken against it and against syphilis'.[49] Behrend was adamant on the reintroduction of the brothels:

> Those who have yielded to vice and crime never feel at home among people of regular life, but seek their refuge in the havens of vice. Their instincts drive them always to the resorts of vice, of sexual impropriety and shame, and here in Berlin it was to the Königsmauer that the criminal riff-raff were most attracted . . . [The problem today], the consequence of the closure of the brothels, is that it led to the establishment of many secret, quite secure establishments . . . and robbed the police of an extremely effective and usually successful means of tracking down and locating these riff-raff.[50]

If it is not possible to drain a 'marsh' or even make it disappear altogether, then the authorities must circumscribe it, keep it under surveillance, 'and create ditches and channels into which the pestilential agents can be diverted. Is prostitution not such a marsh?' The forces of law and order were forced to try out new methods, and the nocturnal city became a field of experimentation for modern strategies for securing power. 'We live in an exceptional period of social

186

experiment,' said Julius Beer in 'The closing of the brothels and the moral consequences for the city of Berlin', a lecture published in 1856. A similar view was also expressed by Theodor Bade. In his text 'On the decay of morals in the big great cities, with particular reference to the last ten years',[51] published in 1857 after the final closure of the brothels, he remarks on the penetration of society by prostitution and ascribes the chief responsibility for this to the police. The old brothels, according to Bade, were so repellent that many a man would crawl 'home in shame' after one visit and never return; afterwards the secret houses not only spread over the whole city, but were so tempting that they were a great attraction, providing a 'plausible pretext: to have a closer look at the secret so mysteriously veiled. Whenever acquaintances met there they had the most exquisite excuses: just "once out of curiosity" or "to get to know the area."' The fact that the new brothels, which were no longer even called that, were open 'horribile dictu, till 2 o'clock in the morning!' rather than until midnight, came in for particular criticism: 'Though it might be that the hours around and after midnight yield richer booty, it is just as certain that it was not proper to mention it. It is sufficiently well known that this made the brothels nocturnal gathering places. . .'[52]

Bade's writing created quite a stir at police headquarters and led to the establishment of a file 'Concerning local moral conditions'.[53] The Prussian Minister of the Interior demanded a report from the Chief of Police and required, as did Bade, that öffentliche Dirnen be forbidden to frequent places of amusement. Police Chief Hofrichter saw in this a 'too great severity against the one (female) sex', for as it says in another report, it would be 'a great punishment' for other young women 'no longer to have this pleasure'. Obviously the police had no great confidence its own capacity to differentiate between the 'dangerous sirens' and other women. Hofrichter suggested as an alternative that no public event should go on later than midnight, drawing an impressive picture of the night from the perspective of the police:

Such a rule would foster morality and order, and also thrift, particularly among the working classes. Until 12 o'clock in the evening at the latest there are sensible fathers, mothers and older people present in the public establishments; the frivolous and less respectable, more particularly the younger people, usually control themselves, restrain themselves and try to retain a certain outward propriety.

187

After 12 o'clock, however, when the consumption of strong drinks makes itself felt, *they let themselves go*, as they call it, and independence and frivolity take the place of the restraint previously forced upon them. More money is squandered and more mischief is made after midnight than before. *A night of revelry is followed by a lost day.*[54]

The increase in street prostitution was not the only consequence of the abolition of the brothels; it contributed to a further diversification of night life in general. Of necessity there appeared new institutions (or new forms of existing establishments), which 'secretly' – at least in the eyes of the guardians of morality – were used for prostitution. According to the administrative report of the Berlin police headquarters, the *Tingel-Tangel* developed between the 1840s and the 1860s from the harp orchestras which used to play mainly in wheat-beer establishments (some as residents, others itinerant) . . . In part these *Tingel-Tangel* were but houses of pleasure under a different name.'[55] Establishments with 'female service' had to close at 11 p.m., and 'at 11 o'clock precisely the door is locked and the windows are veiled by thick curtains. But behind them the entertainment is only just beginning, and lasts until around 3 or even 4 o'clock in the morning, by which time things are not too respectable.'[56] As in Paris, various establishments in Berlin set up *séparées*, or private rooms, or presented 'veil-dances' on a stage which was used earlier in the evening for 'respectable' performances, particularly during the hours of night when the entrances were officially closed. Other establishments too, which could not be counted among the secret brothels, were seen by critics as possible places of encounter and assignation, and this all the more the later business went on after midnight.

The night itself appears as the real 'provider of opportunity',[57] and when the establishments close the bustle continues on the streets, until finally the 'abominable scene ends only with the light of the morning sun'. Even if the regulation of prostitution differed from city to city, the rhetoric was everywhere almost identical. In the archives of the Paris vice police for these years we find numerous complaints by citizens about disturbances of the nocturnal peace,[58] and from London William Acton reports: 'As the night advances, the number of disorderly characters present in the streets increases; this is especially the case in those nearest to the places of amusement frequented by prostitutes and their companions . . . Although I have admitted that the liberty of using the streets should not be denied to

*Zum strammen Hund.*

'No entry to women after 11 p.m.' Closing time serves to regulate 'morality and decency' – and to maintain a night life whose attractions are available above all to men. Illustration by Heinrich Zille: *The Zum strammen Hund Restaurant*, 1929.

women merely on account of their being prostitutes, there would, I think, be no harshness or undue interference with the liberty of the subject in requiring such persons to withdraw from them within half an hour after the time at which the Argyll Rooms and similar places of amusement are usually closed.' [59] The discussion in London however differs from those in Paris and Berlin. Here the fourth volume of Henry Mayhew's *London Labour and the London Poor* caused a stir because Mayhew and his assistant Bracebridge Hemyng published the transcripts of their discussions with poor prostitutes in the London parks and gardens relatively uncensored; social causes and motives were foregrounded much earlier on. The Metropolitan Police Act of 1839 forbade prostitutes ('night-walkers') loitering in public places, and obstruction of the public footpath was to be dealt with immediately by the ubiquitous policemen.

It is interesting to see how international comparisons with other capitals are used by both authorities and their critics in all three cities. 'City councillor Schäffer explained', the *Vossische Zeitung* reported on

22 March 1861, 'that the problem of prostitution has reached an unprecedented level on almost all the the city's streets, and that in this Berlin by far outstrips such other cities as Paris, London, etc.', while William Acton would in turn praise Paris, where in his view the police 'keep the streets passable for respectable women at all hours of the evening' – an assessment the Paris newspapers did not share at all. These international comparisons give little insight into the reality of the other cities, but they vividly express observers' sense of the shortcomings of the night in their own cities and what they would like to change.

FREEDOM OF THE STREET

From the 1850s onward there appeared, particularly in London, a new kind of night literature, *Hints to Men about Town*,[60] guides to well-known and secret brothels, 'accommodation houses' and clubs, often with precise details of the names and 'specialities' of individual prostitutes: beneath the surface of Victorian prudishness there existed a secret culture, a nocturnal life of sexuality,[61] whose most famous protagonist could be said to be the author of the autobiographical *My Secret Life*. His memoirs, which tell of the world of prostitution in parks, gardens and hidden courtyards, the sailors' pubs near the London docks, the preference of men of the upper classes for 'contact with poor girls, cheap whores and maids' and the particularly English passion for flagellation, give an 'authentic glimpse of nocturnal London from the pornographer's point of view' for the period from 1840 to 1880. His immediate interest in the events of the night made him an expert, his fantasies themselves testimony to a subjective authenticity – but also testimony to a *masculine* authenticity: the nocturnal city appears exclusively as a hunting ground for men's sexual desire, where women are meant to be 'available'; like the vice police the pornographer also thinks of women who are about at night, in badly lit streets or in the region of the docks, as prostitutes.

At the end of the 1860s the question of 'how closely the world of men is connected to the great evil that weighs on the shoulders of our people'[62] becomes the subject of public discussion in both Berlin and London. In Berlin in 1868 the Central Board of the Home Mission published a memorandum on immorality and gave a copy to every member of the Prussian Landtag. In the debate that followed the theme of the street played a significant role: according to the deputy Brauchitsch it was a matter of stopping 'a certain traffic on the streets'. With this the vice police was brought into the centre of debate; it is 'always after the people who have once fallen into its hands', remarked the deputy Dr Löwe, thereby cutting off the possibility of a return to a life outside prostitution from those who 'in the inexperience of youth [and] the swiftness of the blood which flows through their easily swayed hearts, have found themselves on the wrong path through ignorance of the situation'. Deputy Künzer drew the conclusion that 'morality can never be instilled in the heart of a people by the police'.[63] The discussion covered fundamental issues. Could morality be constructed? To what extent might the state intervene in the lives of the people? The big city was where the debate about the risks and opportunities of modern life was held, the screen onto which were projected both the striving towards freedom and the yearning for security, and it was in this context that the question of *women's freedom and security* was broached for the first time.

In England in 1869 the Contagious Diseases Act of 1864 was amended and tightened. The law allowed the police to detain any woman they found 'suspicious' and take her for compulsory medical examination. In the autumn of 1869 two groups were formed to protest against the law, the 'National Association for Repeal of Contagious Diseases Acts', and the 'Ladies' National Association', which had the same aim. The women's voices, especially that of their spokeswoman Josephine Butler, found an echo among the public. Butler's criticism of the double standards manifested in the law – prostitution 'under police surveillance' was allowed, while freedom of access to the street was made more difficult for all women – was supported by other groups in the emergent women's movement and workers' organizations, but also by church groups, doctors and lawyers. A central argument was that 'so far as women are concerned, [these provisions] remove every guarantee of personal security . . . and put their reputation, their freedom and their persons absolutely in the power of the police'.[64] The battle against the law was also a women's struggle for their right to move freely on the streets of the city. This was threatened not only by arbitrary police power but also by the negative image that many men had of women walking unaccompanied: 'Even decent men deny them protection. The young men strolling on the streets think only that a

191

woman of good reputation does not allow herself to be seen in the evening.'[65]

From Berlin too there were reports that 'decent women and girls are attacked in the evening by officers of the vice police and exposed to shameful and dishonourable treatment';[66] the police attempted to justify their behaviour, and their response confirmed the reproach:

> The uninterrupted surveillance of prostitutes on the streets is carried out by patrols of two or three men who walk the streets of their district at any hour of day or night. During the day their appearance is often enough to drive away the prostitutes; in the evening, however, and during the night, the latter behave more brazenly, often causing a nuisance to the public, and the officers are then forced to intervene against them.
>
> Women who are *not yet* known to the officers as prostitutes, but attempt to gain the attention of men through very conspicuous behaviour, are first admonished by the officers to preserve public decency.[67]

Paragraph 361,6 of the Criminal Code, which made unsupervised prostitution punishable by imprisonment, brought with it tighter controls which mostly related to behaviour on the streets: 'On the streets and squares their [prostitutes'] behaviour must be such as not in any way to draw attention to itself'; it was forbidden in particular 'to stand on the street, to walk back and forth a short distance, to generally roam about'. Walking on certain streets and squares in Berlin was completely forbidden: Tiergarten, Königsplatz, Friedrichshain and Humboldthain, Unter den Linden, Behrenstrasse, Mauerstrasse, Rosmarienstrasse, Wilhelmstrasse and Neue Wilhelmstrasse, Friedrichstrasse and Charlottenstrasse, Kleine Kirchgasse, the Universitätsstrasse up to the Dorotheenstrasse, Kaisergallerie, Opernplatz, Pariser Platz, Zeughaus and Kastanienwäldchen. Precisely here, in the Friedrichstrasse for example, were the centres of street prostitution, and women who walked there unaccompanied were in principle under surveillance. It was no different in Paris, and there too, as F. Carlier wrote, '*prostitution clandestine* was no longer at all secret'.[68] Of Berlin the anonymous 'Dr X' wrote: 'The whole centre of gravity of prostitution is today situated on the street. Everyone can see it, everyone gets used to it, points of contact with all classes of the population are everywhere being established.' Prostitution, however, is no 'light-loving plant, *its essence is darkness*'.[69] By the time it was formulated, this notion no longer corresponded to reality, and it seemed all the more important to the police to push immorality out of the public limelight. Writing about London, Robert D. Storch says that 'The constant position of the Metropolitan Police all through the nineteenth century was that the streets of central London should be made an illegal market for the vending of sexual services.'[70] From 1883 to 1887 the London police conducted a regular crusade against street prostitution, but by 1886 the Contagious Diseases Act had to be repealed, and the police saw themselves exposed to serious allegations – of false arrests, corruption and blackmail. The attempt in London to introduce vice police on the model of Paris and Berlin had failed, but in these two cities too the institution came under increasing pressure. Friedrich C. B. Avé-Lallement speaks of their 'terribly euphemistic name' and asks the policeman, who is supposed to know what is really going on in the street, 'why he lets the seducer walk off *in flagrante*, while binding his pleading victim like an animal, and throwing her into prison and proclaiming her a trollop before the whole world?'[71]

Women and girls who moved to the big cities had a difficult time finding home and work; unemployment and homelessness were close and constantly threatening. Large sections of the morality movement did not acknowledge this; as it was put in a *Natural History of Berlin Women* published in 1885, they didn't want to think about 'how one could do away with the shameful stain on Berlin society by improving women's conditions of employment'.[72] Those who denounced young working-class women's 'craving for pleasure' and offered them the cosy, happy family circle or worthy, boring entertainment 'in good company' as an alternative to the dance hall, the pub or the street did not do justice to their demands and needs (including the sexual). In his paper on 'Fallen girls and the vice police from the standpoint of practical life', Detective Superintendent von Baumer addressed the morality associations directly:

> The morality associations always shout at the police that they belong in the street, watching to see whether the law is broken; but even this is too much for them, as in an article in the first issue of the *Korrespondent* of 1881 a woman exclaims indignantly:
> 'Do you wish to tolerate the direct personal humiliation represented by the police surveillance to which all are subjected?'
> Even the awareness of being watched is already too much for this woman, but the police are here to watch the public without exception, for those who are not criminal could yet become so. Is it any wonder

that on hearing such cries of indignation someone should say to me, 'The whole thing gives me the impression that the ladies are afraid of coming under moral control.'?[73]

For the internal logic of the police role – to keep the whole city under control at all times, and at night in particular – the argument is conclusive: the police (still) believe that the nocturnal city is fundamentally a *terrain interdit*, and those who nevertheless want to be there are fundamentally suspect. With his anonymous quote the superintendent confirmed the reproaches of the feminists: he declared that those who demanded unhindered access to the streets were potential prostitutes who feared control; those who hindered the work of the police – which was intended to protect society, against venereal diseases for example – made themselves the accomplices of public sexual misconduct. The police saw the prostitutes as possible carriers of venereal disease; in effect the policy of regulation and control acted as the protecting hand of the state administration, accompanying men to their immoral assignations, as Josephine Butler argued.

But the morality movement too, even its feminist wing, underestimated the appeal of the nocturnal city as a theatre in which men *and* – if in a very restricted measure – women could experiment with themselves and the possibilities open to them. None of those who subscribed to the idea that morality could be generated wanted to improve conditions on the nocturnal street in such a way that access, that is freedom of movement and security, was also guaranteed to women. In their publications they depicted the nocturnal city as a swamp in which those who dare venture are irredeemably lost, and they take the big city itself as a focus of attack.

THE GUILT OF THE CITY

In Prussia in 1870, after the debates in the Chamber of Deputies, which in its own view had been a disappointment, the Central Board of the Home Mission tried to promote the establishment of an association which was to 'provide a platform for all those interests of importance to the protection and improvement of public morality among the population of Berlin'.[74] Their memorandum on the subject draws a picture of an immorality that lurks everywhere in Berlin, threatening the whole city, even its 'better' parts: streets, pavements, shop windows, poster sites and newspaper kiosks are *media of sexual impropriety*, as are the small ads in the newspapers;

194

families are breaking down and no longer provide any support; the world of work affords no protection, particularly for women, even intensifying the 'unhealthy stimuli'. The imagery of such texts was international; of the cities of Great Britain, the *Edinburgh Medical Journal* wrote: 'Let anyone walk the streets of London, Glasgow, or Edinburgh, of a night, and, without troubling his head with statistics, his eyes and ears will tell him what a multitudinous amazonian army the devil keeps in constant field service, for advancing his own ends. The stones seem alive with lust, and the very atmosphere is tainted.'[75] And on 5 November 1871 the Berlin *National Zeitung* wrote in an article much noticed and much discussed:

> When a foreigner, a Spaniard or a Russian, comes to Berlin to find out about the 'Prussian discipline' about which there is so much to be read in our pious newspapers, he first discovers Berlin's sexual indiscipline. It isn't necessary to wait for May Day and to visit the region of . . . wretchedness in the Harz mountains: in the Friedrichstrasse and elsewhere in Berlin it is Walpurgis Night day after day. In the most frequented streets of the German capital: what a witches festival from the Blocksberg! Here the whole crowd of witches romp about as they please; here they swarm in wild and jubilant abandon, joyful in victory; in speech and word, in glance and gesture, in screams and whispers, in gait and dance, in act and behaviour, they make it known *that the field is theirs*. They have long since reduced the great city of Paris to subservience, and the emulation of Copenhagen does not satisfy their pride; to take possession of Berlin, not to sit in some den but to rule in public and in the heart of this city, to have dominion over it, to brand the witches' mark on it and make it famous for its servility, this is a goal worthwhile.

The statistician S. E. Huppé too, who in principle ascribed the existence of prostitution to social causes, noted an 'opportunity for demoralization'[76] and in general an increasingly sexual atmosphere in the city; requiring strategies for moralizing the city and urban life. Reacting to the witches article, Superintendent Hofrichter, still in office, demanded stronger laws against procurement and better possibilities of intervention against the proprietors of public establishments which promoted prostitution. Neither did the spokespeople of the Home Mission allow themselves to be diverted, and at the end of 1871 they sent a new memorandum, 'Public immorality, with special regard to Berlin', which was discussed at a meeting of the city council at the beginning of 1872. In this discussion it became abundantly clear that the councillors were not prepared to accept measures that might restrict the (newly acquired) 'metropolitan character' of Berlin. This attitude, marked by the new metropolitan consciousness, predictably met with virulent criticism. In his article on 'Berlin's moral and social situation' Johannes Janssen summed up the press coverage of the years 1870 and 1871, which amounted to an accusation that the authorities were allowing the city, including the 'dark' sides emerging within it and breaking out of it, to develop without control:

> In this great social centre opportunities for earning spring up from the ground mysteriously and tempt with siren voices; *but pleasurable consumption everywhere creeps furtively behind*, and softly and unnoticed, like a thief, it snatches from one's pockets the whole income so dearly bought! . . . The life of the big city is a sham – sham – sham! Glitter on the outside, emptiness within, and poverty without end.[77]

In this situation of general dissolution, of lack of ties and unbridled do-as-you-please, immorality has an easy run of it. It offers its services to those who have lost direction, as compensation for their daily burdens; a promise of joy, of pleasure, of relaxation. Criticism is again directed at the city which allows this:

> Berlin is big, Berlin is a metropolis, but is Berlin happy? Take a closer look, you foreigners, who think when you walk along Unter den Linden that happiness is at home here . . . Every day one hears people shout that Berlin has become a metropolis, puffing themselves up in their smug megalomania. We too say that Berlin is becoming a metropolis – unfortunately, we have to add, *a metropolis of poverty and metropolis of fraud.*[78]

The task of redefining and re-establishing morality under these circumstances is, as F. Oldenburg wrote in the *Fliegende Blätter*, both the most important and the most difficult 'for the big cities'; they are the centres of life, sucking in what comes from the outside, and in turn they have an effect on the provinces; their social life is 'of the most complicated, and beneath its surface, itself almost impossible to grasp in its entirety, it contains hidden worlds that can only be discovered with difficulty and then only in fragmentary fashion'.[79] This feeling wasn't limited to Berlin. In Paris the spread of street prostitution was met by an increase in the number of *maisons de tolérance* to be established in certain areas which could be supervised, but there was disagreement on this. F. Carlier wrote, 'such an area would be uninhabitable for the decent population, because it would be very difficult to maintain public order.' What's more, the police tactics of supervised tolerance were no longer effective: '... tastes had changed, causing clients to prefer the apparently more impromptu encounters of the street.'[80] To look, to follow someone with one's eyes, and to make contact on the nocturnal street were among the newly acquired patterns of behaviour that made the street attractive – first of all only for men. For the representatives of morality, the 'guilt' of the city lay in the fact that it could not curb its powers of seduction. The range of texts dealing with prostitution now grew wider; as 'opportunities' became more varied, those who did not allow themselves to be impressed by the warnings increased in number, and at the same time the voice of its enemies became more shrill.

## CURIOSITY AND SPEECHLESSNESS

> Dear reader, have you ever gone around the Friedrichstrasse and its side streets around midnight? Then you may also have seen a young man standing innocuously in front of one of the doors, smoking a cigar and gazing at the stars. If you see such a star-gazing cigar-smoker again, go up to him and give him a certain look. He will then look carefully left and right, to see that there is no night-watchman or some such nearby, and then you will find him a most obliging gentleman. He will open the door for you...[81]

Nocturnal life escapes control; if it is restricted in one place it will find an outlet somewhere else. J. Werner commented ironically on the laborious and unsuccessful efforts of the morality movement, conjecturing that 'in part it is the fault of the devil himself, who cannot be that easily chased away'. With this he struck a new note: metropolitan self-consciousness took account of the existence of prostitution, and refused to utter screams of horror.

Curiosity was the mark of a small group of sexual researchers who were unembarrassed by the phenomena and reported more or less unconcernedly on the rich ethnological treasure of the human 'night side': on the erotic vocabulary of the city dwellers; on changes in the ideal of beauty; on rites of clothing and dressing up; on dirty jokes, funny stories, street ballads and poems; on the adoption of new techniques such as photography or the newspaper small ads by the sex business, making no attempt to marginalize these realms of experience by reference to some imagined 'normality'. Hugo E. Lüdecke,

197

for example, reports relatively openly on 'German brothel streets' and remarks proudly that it is 'not everybody's thing, to feel at home in places where today's highly sophisticated love games present their *animal* side in a so often disgusting fashion'.[82]

Animal perhaps, possibly disgusting – but still of this world, not the work of the devil. Lüdecke describes the 'Schlamm' (the 'mire'), the red-light district in Halle, and reports that 'a patrolling police-man or two stationary officers are quite sufficient to keep watch and to maintain order by themselves'. Policemen maintain the 'order' of 'disorderliness', protecting the Schlamm – this is truly a provocative picture, and an argument for the opponents of the localization of controlled prostitution. At the same time there is an obvious criti-cism to be made, which Lüdecke substantiates with examples, that the police were condemning the prostitutes to remain in the Schlamm.

In 1895 the realization that it would be necessary to speak 'about certain things', even as a woman, indeed particularly as a woman, moved the Social Democrat Johanna Loewenherz to 'visit a night café'; as Vera Konieczka put it in somewhat restrained fashion, she was 'not entirely free of moral revulsion '. This is how it reads:

> I had visited one of the most famous of Berlin's night cafés. For the first time in my life I entered such a place, and I felt as if its horrors sur-passed all description. What had been possible for me to endure in the imagination – the moment I saw it before me in reality, I was overcome by the evidence of my senses. I suffered. My feelings and thoughts raged about me confused and tormenting. My brain was overcome by a kind of numbness, and I was grateful for it, for it was kind. With this at least I only saw these hideous things as if through a foggy veil, and sometimes I felt as if they were, as if *they could not be real* – as if a mas-querade were taking place before me, with crazed spirits risen from Hades – satyrs, fauns and their ladies performing in front of me . . . Unreal! Unliving! A madness, the monstrous product of a fevered imagination.[83]

Such publications caused as great a sensation as the pseudo-documentary pornographic literature widely disseminated in the years around the turn of the century, which recounted the life of prostitutes or the goings-on in brothels, massage-parlours, baths or the back rooms of night establishments, such as, to mention only one example, the *Novel from Berlin W.* by Hans v. B . . . r, which described real places in the city:

I used to wander about at the zoo, this breeding ground of exotic beasts and of immorality on a Berlin scale . . . These people, corrupted to the very core, were celebrating orgies of shamelessness . . . From the dance halls in the Halensee and Südende, where shop-girls, seamstresses and ladies of similar position amuse themselves, I used to drag four or five girls home with me at at the same time. Here I would get them drunk and let them dance the Matchiche naked in front of me.[84]

Both forms of 'reportage' made their contribution, against their will, to the police image of the 'sluts' and thus to the formulation of the aims of police action: 'The goal of the vice police', wrote Alfred Blaschko in 1902, 'is above all to *render prostitution invisible*, to restrict it to brothels or to dark and out-of-the-way streets, the inner court-yards of tenements, to the hours of evening and night, to remove it from public streets and hence enforce its stringent separation from good society.'[85] Despite the growing criticism, the police did not wish to give up their task. In 1907, the understanding – imposed by public pressure, but intrinsically questionable – 'that for a decent female person there is nothing more humiliating than to be sus-pected of engaging in professional prostitution' – led to new orders for the vice police: uniformed officers were only to intervene when they were absolutely sure of their 'case', but as a rule officers in civil-ian clothes should do the work, proceeding cautiously and avoiding attention.[86] It was the same in Paris, where officers dressed in civilian clothing (*en bourgeois*) could easily be mistaken for passers-by and *flâneurs*, and were thus able, without any problem, to keep watch on the women whose behaviour they found suspicious.[87]

At the beginning of the twentieth century, texts in which women too spoke more openly and militantly about prostitution became more numerous. Criticism of police actions led to reflection on a new organization of the nocturnal city; the exercise of police authority should not only be restricted but brought under the jurisdiction of the city authorities, and (also) be transferred to women. A first step in this direction was taken not in Berlin but in Stuttgart, where in 1903 Henriette Arendt was hired as a police auxiliary. In his preface to her account of her experience, Friedrich Naumann tries to play down this unheard-of occurrence with much praise, equating her work with the activities of the Christian associations; much more important however is the fact that it was the first time a woman dealt with prostitution in an official capacity. Henriette Arendt called for the transformation of the workhouses into educational institutions, and proved that the system of police surveillance 'in an over-whelming number of cases causes only damage which can never be repaired'.[88] For her it was fundamental that there can only be one morality, equally binding on men and women. In this she was in disagreement with the majority in the 'German Society for the Prevention of Venereal Diseases', whose congress in March 1903 still supported the thesis that women had no sexual needs, 'only the yearning for a child'. Saying nothing about what was clearly in front of one's eyes was a habit in this society. It was Anna Pappritz and Katharina Scheven in particular who fought against this silence, for a realistic enlightenment; in her book *The World of Which Nobody Speaks* Anna Pappritz deals explicitly with the ways of talking about prostitution:

> The veil which decent bourgeois society attempts to draw over the world of which nobody speaks, is not thick enough to hide it, but is transparent enough to spur on the imagination, to stimulate curiosity; the veil hides the darkest, most ugly depths and only lets shimmer through what tempts and tickles the senses.[89]

In contemporary discussions, at the congress of the Society for the Prevention of Venereal Diseases for example, prostitution appears on the one hand as an expression of general social conditions – a sign of decadence and decay – on the other as a vestige of the pre-modern, one of the last obstacles on the way to a modern organiza-tion of the city. The contradiction can hardly be resolved without renouncing a clear distinction between the 'old' and the 'modern' city: the big city at the end of the nineteenth and the beginning of the twentieth century carries with it, made visible in its 'night sides', the inheritance of the past, and it is still unclear about the appropriate forms for dealing with this inheritance. Both the vice police and the morality movement had to face this contradiction; both felt that the strategies of the past – silence, hiding, controlling, sanctioning – no longer worked, but neither was capable of finding new strategies. The police hung on to their procedures, although – as Abraham Flexner noted in a comparison between London, Paris and Berlin – the existence of a specific 'morality police' in Paris and Berlin, compared with its absence in London, had no effect 'in terms of public order and morality'.[90] The representatives of the morality movement were stuck with their reproaches against 'foolish women' or 'extramarital sexual intercourse [as a form] of non-professional prostitution'.[91] There was still agreement on both sides on criticism of the city: 'The real seducer is not the individual man, but the big city', and, 'first of all it is the street, and just strolling about'. The seductive power of the nocturnal city drew young men and women under its spell, awakening sexual desire in some and a yearning for an easy life in others.

Graphic material illustrating this attitude – and its curious consequences – is presented by Else Spiller in her book *Slums, Experiences in the Slum Neighbourhoods of Modern Cities*, published in 1911. A young lady, the foreword announces, had travelled to the big cities, where, under the guidance of the 'slum pioneers' of the Salvation Army, she visited their nocturnal regions. Again and again in her urban descriptions from Holland, France, England and Germany she is confronted by 'Light ' – 'brightly lit streets, well-turned-out people, pleasure and gaiety' – and 'Dark' – 'how much misery is contained by the grey walls of a city'[92] – and again and again it is the night in which the glaring misery of the homeless, the poor and the prostitutes becomes visible. She was, she writes, 'forced to walk through a living hell', and describes the 'bright reflections' of the centres of amusement, seeing the 'open doors' of the bars and ballrooms which promise the knowledgeable the 'discovery of questionable pleasures', and she realizes, startled: 'When I went back out onto the street again, I saw that night life had taken on even greater proportions, though the time was already well past midnight.'

In all her examples there is a strange relationship between perception and judgement; in many cases the tone of disappointment seems dutiful; fascination shimmers through again and again. It's not that the outrage is faked – but it has to fight hard against a feeling of being thrilled. Curiosity and sheer pleasure cannot be overlooked, but the author is unable to admit this to us or to herself, covering the secret pleasure in a torrent of words.

FALLEN SISTERS

When the London theatre district developed, two night-worlds separated from each other in public perception: 'Gradually the centre of nocturnal pleasures shifted to the quarter near the Haymarket, the streets of that neighbourhood abounding with night houses which were not empty till dawn.' Only increasing control drove people into the streets and from there further and further away. Closures resulted in 'flood[ing] a number of small streets of the West End with a crowd of wretched women who, hunted from place to place by the police, wander about throughout the night'. Bohemian clubs, restaurants and gaming houses were opened, and men of pleasure strolled from place to place – a network of streets was created, which itself took on the character of a large *pleasure haunt*, denying the area its nature as street. The idea of *night side* becomes metaphorical, as the 'other' side, what is outside, beyond the permissible – and controlled – world. *The Night Side of London* is then the title of a book which deals with the 'white slave trade', what's more in an extraordinarily unpleasant and anti-Semitic way.[93]

Both are supposed to be alien – the night side to the city, prostitution to English society. The nocturnal view of the city is more strongly separated into two worlds – pleasure and light on the one hand, danger and darkness on the other – in London than in Berlin or even in Paris. The bright side is represented by the theatre and the music halls. In their vicinity, an infrastructure of pleasure life is created: 'at the back of theatre-world one finds the Bohemian resorts of London: the night clubs, the cosy little supper restaurants, and the café bars', writes Stephen Graham contentedly. 'More or less asleep during the daylight hours, they are thronged at midnight.'[94] The names of the 'resorts' promise much exoticism, perhaps even erotic entertainment, but this is far removed from the 'abyss' of the other night: Chat Noir, Caiffa, Roma, Venice, Round the Clock. 'Great Windmill Street is one of the capitals of all-night pleasure, and if one wanders up the narrow Soho lane just after the theatres empty, to the corner where the clock of the Red Lion public house shows the witching hour of night, one is in the midst of foreign Bohemian life.'

The slight distance in this 'foreign' can be found in many reports from the 1920s. 'London by night has become much more Parisian since the war. And under cover of this gaiety there has been an increase in vice.' Graham supports the intention of a deputation to the Home Secretary, asking him 'to define just exactly what night clubs are'. Is vice – which again comes from the 'outside' – making use of the British institution of the club to bring 'immorality' and an 'evil influence on youth' to London? The bars and brothels, the jazz music and the shrill laughter which escapes into the street from the haunts of pleasure appears here first and foremost as a complex of foreignness.

202

The world of the *bals musettes* near the place de la Bastille – nocturnal thrills on guided tours through 'Paris by night'. Photograph by André Kertész, Paris, 1926.

Robert Murphy is somewhat more relaxed in his dealings with the subject. 'The English underworld in the early twentieth century performed a number of illegal but indispensable social services, supplying prostitutes, drugs, gambling and out-of-hours drinking facilities to the public.' The Defence of the Realm Act forbade the serving of alcohol after 10 p.m. in the evening, though the night-clubs mushroomed anyhow – or because of it. Chez Victor, the Night Light and the Kit Kat Club bloomed and burned out again. Kate Meyrick was 'London's Night Club Queen' in the 1920s, even if she had to close her clubs time and time again: the Dalton Club next to the Alhambra in Leicester Square, the even more famous 43 in Gerrard Street, the Little Club and the Manhattan. The Silver Slipper in Regent Street 'became the centre of London's night life' and, according to Murphy, a place where one could observe 'the cream of Britain's aristocracy rubbing shoulders with . . . the roughest and toughest of the underworld'.[95]

Prostitution was a topic of discussion in London. This might surprise at first, as all observers start from the premise that 'as a result of their puritan beliefs the Victorians were in a neurotic state about sex, a word they tended to equate with sin'.[96] This text, which introduces Gustave Doré's pictures of London, continues: 'It is therefore surprising how much soliciting in the streets was tolerated in Victorian days', and surprising too, one might add, is the vastness of the London literature on the subject. It wasn't only Henry Mayhew who described the 'fallen sisters', the poor women of the East End and their more fortunate female colleagues, the 'Cyprians of the better sort', in the West End. For visitors to the city, too, the view of nocturnal streets meant a new experience. This is Dostoyevsky:

> Anyone who has ever visited London must have been at least once in the Haymarket at night. It is a district in certain streets of which prostitutes swarm by night in their thousands. Streets are lit by jets of gas – something completely unknown in our own country. At every step you come across magnificent public houses, all mirrors and lit. They serve as meeting places as well as shelters. It is a terrifying experience to find oneself in that crowd.

Even if Dostoyevsky adds a 'jolly scenes, altogether', his unease on the street is unmistakable. It is a good thing that there are places into which one can withdraw, and no city cultivated the separation of street and place of retreat as much as London.

Judith R. Walkowitz took the nocturnal street – in its later reflection in Madame Tussauds' Waxworks – as the introductory setting of her study of the 'City of Dreadful Delight'. The 'Jack the Ripper Street' brings together all the elements of dangerous night: 'cobbles, green slime-covered walls, [the] way barely illuminated by flickering gas lamps, mean streets, menacing obscurity, and drunken raucous laughter.'[97] The perception of London as 'dark, powerful and seductive' goes for the 1880s in general, but of course it reached its apogee with the events of 1888. At this point the stories of the night find a real topographical location in the picture of the city.

Steve Jones has drawn a 'Sin Map of London in Victorian Times'. It starts with 'one of the capital's leading flagellation establishments' in Circus Road, leading to the brothels and the flats of prominent *demi-mondaines*, to 'striptease or *tableaux vivants*' in New Road, passing in front of the theatres in Haymarket and Piccadilly Circus, seen as a 'notorious promenade', to the secret brothels for parliamentarians in Lupus Street, and on to Holywell Street, the centre of the trade in pornography. This map shows only four points in the East End – sailors' brothels, and also 'child brothels'. Everything else, with few exceptions, is concentrated between Soho and the City – not 'outside' but in the very centre of the city. The presence of 'sin' and temptation in the middle of public space was for many the biggest attraction.

'Walter' for example recounts a visit to a prostitute. 'Going one Saturday night up Granby Street, Waterloo Road,' he noticed the half-naked women in the front windows of the houses in one street: 'I often walked for the pleasure of looking at the women'. As one woman drags him inside, he feels repelled, the brief sexual act horrifies him, and the experience keeps him away from the street for a while – 'which was a great loss to me, for I often used to go through it to gloat on the charms of the women as they lolled out of the windows'.[98]

In his *Mysteries of London* George Reynolds makes a character-study of the men about town:

> London abounds with such precocious specimens of thorough heart-lessness and worldliness. The universities and great public schools let loose upon society every half-year a cloud of young men, who think only how soon they can spend their own property in order to prey upon that of others. These are your 'young men *about* town'; as they grow older they become 'men *upon* the town'. In their former capacity they graduate in all the degrees of vice, dissipation, extravagance, and debauchery; and in the latter they become the tutors of the novices who are entering in their turn upon the road to ruin . . . These men upon the town constitute as pestilential a section of male society as the women of the town do of the female portion of the community. They are like the reptiles produced by the great moral dung-heap.[99]

In his study *The Worm in the Bud* Ronald Pearsall writes, 'whoring was their favourite pastime'. And he adds, 'they did not have to mill around London in an aimless way, wondering whom to accost and which was the best way to find a whore; there were handbooks for them'. These did indeed exist and it is certainly not too bold to see them as sewer-guides to the the urban night which would lead the *men about town* to 'vice', by preserving them from accidents and from too close an acquaintance with the nocturnal streets. Such books might be called *Hints to Men About Town* or *The Man of Pleasure's Pocket Book*.

The arguments of the moral movement had changed little since the 1840s; for every new development in nocturnal life (which always reflects the development of the whole city) they regularly reacted with the same incantation of imminent doom, the end of all morality – when the brothels were abolished and when they were opened again for a brief period, when the dance halls came along, when female service was allowed, and when women were once again forbidden such employment opportunities, when opening times were extended and when they were restricted again. But the world had not gone under, nor had the city, that 'whore of Babylon' – on the contrary, in the eyes of many observers the metropolis had proved its capacity for survival and its right to exist in the way it dealt with the challenge of the night. The preachers of morality lost their credibility.

In this context it seems sensible to me to look more closely at whether the atmosphere of the period between the turn of the century and the First World War really can be characterized as a 'dance on the edge of the volcano'. This is to go beyond the frontiers of research on the night, but 'night life' is part of that complex of decadence which is seen by many not only as the expression of a blindness to the pressing social problems of the period, a deafening, exaggerated 'hurly-burly of amusement', but also widely held to be one of the causes of the downfall of the old world, contributing to the coming of the catastrophe of a war that was to bring civilization to an end. Often cited as evidence for this view is the Expressionist poetry and painting of the pre-war years, in which, as Jost Hermand summed up, 'the world of the big cities [is] evoked as a world of the "abyss", "putrefaction", "urban mire", "ulceration", and "decay", in which a life worthy of humanity is near impossible'.[100] Hermand cites many of the concepts and metaphors we have already met in the course of our perambulation through the texts of the city night: decadence, decay, degeneration, disease and death; apocalypse, last judgement, Sodom and Gomorrah, Moloch and Baal. Night images and night visions play a significant role in this complex, 'the whole aggressive plenitude of the metropolitan night'[101] constituting a context within which individuals can experience only alienation, rejection and psychological homelessness. Disease and death lurk in the streets, symbolized by the whore under whose sensual mask decay has already set in. There is, for example, a common interpretation of the work of Georg Heym: 'The cities are characterized by night; 'city night' . . . is a shorthand characterization of the ever-recurring typical situation. It is of decisive symbolic significance that Heym always describes evening and night in the cities; in the inescapable gloom there emerges an *oppressive premonition of imminent catastrophe.*'[102]

Here, I think, the mistake in interpretation becomes evident. In retrospect, seen from today, in the awareness of the catastrophe that really did occur in 1914, these texts may give such an impression. They do indeed express a conflict in the metropolitan experience of these years, and to this belongs not only the feeling of being overwhelmed, but also the experience of being 'at the same time drunk on all the possibilities' offered by the city.[103] Many poets, writers and painters were part of this urban life, and in their desire to shock and provoke they wished to be as thought of as 'urban vagrants at least'; the places of the nocturnal Berlin and Paris which they depicted as so terrible and frightening thus became their real and only home: cafés, variety theatres, dance halls, night-clubs, brothels, and the streets of prostitution.

'Berlin lives in an eternal whirl of dance', Edmund Edel wrote in 1914. 'On Saturday night the whirlpool turns at its fiercest. In the earliest hours of Sunday morning the dance halls are so packed you can hardly breathe in them . . . This place [the Lunapark ballroom] is frequented by members of high society and by many artists, who cultivate dancing above all as a sport. The ladies are not exclusively cocottes, but women painters, actresses, wives with their husbands, and girlfriends with their boyfriends create a piquant mix.'[104] Indeed Berlin danced, Berlin visited music cafés - 'everywhere violins and craning necks, and the purest joy and pleasure as the elegant conductor on the rostrum, baton in hand, flicks the merry airs straight into the coffee cups' – night restaurants – 'A proper night restaurant only opens its doors at 2 o'clock at night. When the great ballrooms close the night restaurants continue the orgy of champagne. A wise police has forbidden dancing after 2 o'clock at night. Nobody knows the reasons for such timing . . . because after dancing and boozing for a couple of hours, there's no way the idlers are ready to go home immediately' – and bars – Edmund Edel tells of 'those joyous nights' when at daybreak 'one crawled into another low dive, where one appreciated the honour of being able to keep company with dubious characters'.[105] But all these descriptions make for tame reading, compared to what the critics of night life will make of it.

Already in the first year of the First World War there appeared in the *Zeitschrift für Bekämpfung der Geschlechtskrankheiten* an essay by J. Flemming, 'Night life in the great German cities', a key text for an understanding of the enemies of the night at that time:

> The great national enthusiasm and gigantic expression of power inspired in the German people by the present war has filled every German heart with such proud joy, and shown us that there is still a huge measure of healthy strength in our people. Nevertheless, we cannot ignore the fact that in the last decades before the outbreak of war there were forces at work in the body of our people which had begun to undermine the health and competitiveness of the nation...
>
> Should a peace agreement force us have to resort to the sword again in some years' time, so as to complete the work now begun to secure our world position, then it will be decisively important to maintain the strength of the people at as high a level as possible for this renewed battle; should the present war itself afford us the full wage of our work, all the more will it be a sacred duty to protect our people from the degeneracy and debilitation that unhappily come all too easily with the winner's enjoyment of a secure and honourable freedom.
>
> The principal fault in this area is our young people's great and unmistakable *lack of restraint in the enjoyment of life* . . . In no other country was there in so many cities such ample opportunity for 'amusement', i.e. for slumming. Berlin has the sad fame of marching at the front in this field. In Berlin every night, in innumerable bars, clip-joints, night cafés and dance halls frequented by the *demi-monde*, and even on the street, there blooms a night life that has no equal in any other great city . . . [Here] *every night a portion of our people's health is brought to its grave...*
>
> The whole process takes a certain time, because the majority of visitors do not come with the already formed intention of indulging in nocturnal dissipation; visitors first have to be brought gradually into the mood by the milieu surrounding them; the establishment therefore has to be open for long hours, because business as a rule only starts around midnight, as the early evening hours, for the Germans, are used differently and better...
>
> One can argue whether the extraordinarily extensive welfare system provided here for the sick and the weak truly benefits the health of the people, and whether the system of the old Spartans, in which the inferior were banished and abandoned, would not be more suitable . . . If the state continues to look on quietly while *our young men are ruined morally and physically by a wild night life* then in a few generations our people's strength will have gone![106]

Flemming demands that licences be withdrawn from night establishments and that closing time be legally fixed at an hour 'not later
than midnight'. More interesting, however, than this concrete
demand is the spirit which gave rise to it: the direct link between the
maintenance of readiness for war and the fight against 'slumming',
and between contempt for the 'inferior ' and contempt for nocturnal
life, has seldom been so starkly expressed:

> The squalid holes to be prohibited generally serve as a refuge for
> uninhibited lechers, *who are in any case no great loss,* as regular, exclusive
> frequentation of private clubs is in the long term too expensive for the
> majority of our young men and women and probably also too monoto-
> nous. Club life, however, presents fewer dangers to the physical and
> moral health of young people than just wandering about the streets. . .
>
> I dispute the fact that a considerable part of the German people,
> once having left their 'wild years' behind, extend their everyday enter-
> tainment . . . long after midnight. For the very great majority of the
> customers of public houses midnight is time to leave . . . One surely
> cannot begrudge the beer-drinking petty bourgeois or the harmless
> young man taking his girl out for the evening their pleasure. One
> would think, however, that for them too there is entertainment enough
> to be had before midnight.

Dancing Berlin: after defeat in the First World War, under the suspicious gaze of
the provinces and fiercely criticized for its 'constant stimulation of erotic pleasure', the
capital plunged into the brief nocturnal frenzy of the 1920s. *Im Sauseschritt, c.*1924.

The advantage of the confinement and supervision of irregular sexual activity would be that once it had been removed from the public sphere it would lose its attraction, the 'gloss' lent to it by the nocturnal street. This argument found no support among the majority of members of the Society for the Prevention of Venereal Diseases, Alfred Blaschko for example, who fundamentally agreed with Flemming in seeing night life as unnecessary to the inhabitants of the big city and to the essence of the metropolis, but turned even more vehemently against the reintroduction of the brothels, these 'schools of perversion'.

THE 1920S: A NEW PICTURE OF THE STREET

This pre-war debate continued through the First World War and into the years after 1918; but it then encountered a different public, in all three cities. I think it is best to follow the debate in Berlin, where it found the strongest expression. In 1919, the twelfth edition of Ivan Bloch's book *The Sexual Life of Our Times*, first published in 1907, ran to 70,000 copies. His text and the numerous quotations from the beginning of the century had survived the war and the warlike mood, but they too met with a different reception from a public marked by the experiences of war. In this way many of his formulations acquired a new meaning: 'The drudgery imposed on the great majority of people by the fierce struggle for survival no longer leaves any time for the pure, undisturbed enjoyment of life, for a profoundly deep experience of reality and quiet joy in it. No, our leisure life today carries the sting of pain within it, because the will to live . . . has today degenerated into a desperate addiction to the most violent possible sensations.'[107] Given the poverty of the first years after 1919, and the changed, that is democratic, circumstances, this comment took on a new significance.

It is again the night, the maker of opportunities, which offers sensual pleasures. Willy Hellpach wrote:

Urban life brings with it the means to a much more extensive stimula tion of the senses than life in the countryside, and the sensually thrilling and overpowering character of the city has been developed to an unprecedented degree in the metropolis of today. The city is the typical agent of that state of sensual and nervous stimulation which characterizes our generation historically, and the city-dweller is the typical representative of nervous tension in its modern guise. The word sense already points to sensuality . . . When the senses are more strongly solicited, then erotic desire increases, losing its periodic structure in favour of a constant awakening or an apparent slumber from which it may be awakened by the slightest touch. . .

*And city life is night life!* The more urban it becomes, the more one-sided is the big city – and this is driven to an extreme in the metropolis. This is not without its consequences in the arrangements for amusement. Only night life brings together the wealth of stimuli, the ever-changing thrill, which lead to increasing sensuality; and once the life of pleasure has become habitually nocturnal, then this in turn tends to lead to all enjoyment being inevitably tied to the city.[108]

The night has more and more taken on the status of a counter-world, a world which not only has its own laws, but which also tends to overturn the rules valid during the day; 'the artificial sun of our metropolitan lighting' is no enemy of sensuality. The standards of the old order and of the old morality are flouted at night. With the war lost, however – and this can be seen in Paris without a doubt, even with the war won – the old order had broken down. To the enemies of the big city it looked as if the counter-world had won a victory with the establishment of the democratic system, with its centre in the big city. From the beginning of the 1920s the journalistic struggle against the night belongs among the traces of the past but not overtaken social order, which makes life difficult for the young democracy. The most varied authors use the traditional image of the night – addiction to pleasure, intoxication and dizziness of the senses – to express their fear of the future and their criticism of the present. Many again depict the city night as the symbol of threatening decline, as the herald of approaching decay, a sign of the instability of the new, unloved 'order'. More than before, the critique of the night now becomes an instrument of propaganda, precisely because disorder and immorality can be ascribed to the new democratic 'system'.

There are few opposing voices. In her article of 1919, 'The Social and Economic Bases of Prostitution', Katharina Scheven considers whether this new system is not more capable of remedying the disgraceful state of affairs, and considers the possibility – greater under democratic conditions – of bringing about a change in the relationship between the sexes. Her theme is 'prostitution as a problem of men',[109] and her conclusion is that the great social tasks need 'everywhere the collaboration of women'. The problems are concrete: it is a

211

question of housing reform, of women's access to professional life, of better training opportunities for young women workers, and also of the provision of better sexual information to the young, a reform of the whole school system; in general it is a question of creating the conditions in which women will be able to express themselves, meet and circulate in public space as the equals of men. Only social equality can create the conditions in which men no longer see women as the (purchasable) objects of their desire, as goods; only greater freedom and rights for women in all social matters – and this involves the lifting of the taboo on sexuality – can put an end to the scandal, that the promise of freedom held out by the city and the night applies only to men.

But this road, adumbrated only hesitantly by Katharina Scheven herself, could not be taken by the morality movement as a whole. The majority of its representatives continued to fight loudly against all forms of sexual permissiveness, remaining closely attached to the attitude of its founders, which was non-urban and critical of culture and modernism, while only a small minority, mainly women, turned to practical efforts to organize welfare provision for prostitutes in a manner appropriate to the times, and to protect inexperienced women coming to the city from the danger of prostitution 'during the night which is so full of dangers for them'.[110] Alongside the development of communal provision for the welfare of prosti-tutes,[111] that is, the establishment of municipal institutions to pro-vide care and counselling, women's activity was the second element of the strategy by which the vice police were to be deprived of their powers to decide on women's fate. In publications on this subject emphasis is generally put on the significance of preventive care, a task which does not interest the police; but 'it has happened more than once that a single homeless night in Berlin was enough to do a girl irremediable physical and spiritual harm'.[112]

Some of the initiatives were successful. On 1 October 1927 a new law on the prevention of venereal disease came into force, the regu-lation of prostitution was suspended and the 'vice police' as such was abolished. The police could now however act against a 'man or woman' who, 'in a manner violating decency or morality or other-wise unlawful shall publicly incite or offer themselves for sexual misconduct'. This law had far-reaching consequences. It may have put an end to a bad situation long criticized, the state's 'complicity' with public 'sexual misconduct', but it allowed the police a great deal of latitude in deciding what constituted 'behaviour contrary to morals'. All the greater now, for Anna Pappritz, was the need for *women police*.

The law didn't really have any effect on the existence of prostitution. This is pointed out in various publications, very objectively and without malice, for example in the 'Newsletter of the Berlin City Council ', which in August 1929 published the results of the census of 1925, but also dealt with the new legal development in detail. According to this the number of registered prostitutes in Berlin 'on the day of our inquiry [was] 6,191'. The authors also discussed the 'local distribution of prostitutes and prostitution', supplying, as it were, an official topography of the Berlin night, from which it becomes clear that the incidence of public prostitution 'in no way corresponds to the prohibitions against it, prostitutes indeed particularly frequenting a certain number of streets etc. forbidden to them at least at certain times of day or night'.[113]

In his 'reports from the depth of Berlin's underworld' WEKA (Willy Pröger) writes that the prostitutes' social situation may rather have been made worse by the new regulations: 'Sexual intercourse under bridges, in passageways and dark courtyards, in contaminated cellars and on floors strewn with filth, behind shacks made out of planks, in open cubicles such as one sees at the barber's . . . On the street or in the bars during the day, when night comes they're at work.'[114]

In the archives of the 'Project for the Care of the Endangered' at the Central Committee of the Home Mission we find numerous reports from different cities, in which one can read almost identical statements about the 'state of the streets' after the new law had come into force. 'There [in Stuttgart and Nuremberg] it was generally felt that prostitution was much more noticeable on the streets than before.'[115] The representatives of the morality movement gained a picture of the extent of the horror on their 'nocturnal excursions', and at their 'morality rallies' they demanded a renewed tightening of the law: 'And it is – horribly! – true that [in Frankfurt] there are groups of girls on the pavement, in a way that one used not to see before. Although only at the late hour appropriate to their business, when one shouldn't any longer really see any young people who could be corrupted by them.'[116]

The 'state of the streets' is an ambiguous concept, denoting both the real appearance and the metaphoric aspect of the street. While the representatives of the morality movement were concerned with the superficial appearance of the street, Willy Pröger published a new collection of reports, a walk through the 'sites of Berlin prostitution'; but what here, in the collage, almost looks like a dialogue, a shared wrestling for an appropriate representation of the problem, is in reality rather more a critique of the increasing polarization of forms of perception at the end of the 1920s. In the crisis situation which encompassed and threatened all areas of life after 1929, 'night life' was once again caught between two ideological millstones. WEKA saw the morality-preachers with their attitude of 'one doesn't talk about it' as a 'plague on public welfare', while his public representation of the situation is criticized as too unvarnished (and possibly tempting). Things are much more often called 'by their proper name', but an adequate language does not seem to have been found for them: on both sides, the description of the nocturnal world is marked by outrage, abhorrence, even contempt – elements of a strategy of *distancing*. WEKA wrote:

> We begin our *truly not very easy walk* through the sites of Berlin prostitution at the Schlesische Bahnhof. One of the most ugly – if not the ugliest – quarters of Greater Berlin. Ancient tenement houses, grey on grey, decayed, badly lived in. The very busy streets see few happy people. They all have their burdens to bear. Unemployment, hunger, misery. Only the very numerous pubs do brisk business. Alcohol, the great 'consoler'. Yes, it is unemployment and hunger that leave only one way open to the women and girls here: prostitution. . .
>
> It's 3 o'clock in the morning. A wonderful, clear night in early spring. It's closing time. Almost at the same moment hundreds of pubs send their customers, not always completely sober, out onto the street. Life comes into the darkness. The great army of prostitutes takes its opportunity to find a last 'client', to earn two or three Marks. With nervous haste a few dozen women rush from one corner to the next. . .
>
> In the evening, shortly before the shops close. All the streets around the Schlesischer Bahnhof are busy and crowded. Neon signs: Hotel, Hotel, Hotel. Ground floor, first floor, second floor. Everything is 'Hotel'. A very large proportion of them lives almost exclusively from prostitution. . .
>
> Krautstrasse, Berlin's proletarian native quarter. Dark, sinister. The houses, cellars and courtyards are decaying, falling to pieces. No window panes. The windows are nailed shut with planks or covered with cardboard. The type of prostitute matches the milieu. Old, impoverished, in rags, infected.[117]

WEKA's wanderings through the whole of Berlin give an impression of the nocturnal topography, but they much more communicate the picture of a city diseased through and through and destined for death. This becomes even clearer in the description of the interior spaces, the cheap hotels, back rooms and cellar hovels: 'If one penetrates into the cellar, descending the neck-breaking, worn-down stairs, the nose and eyes are assaulted by a truly devilish foul-smelling vapour: cigarette smoke, alcoholic fumes, the emanations of hot, dirty bodies and wet clothing hung up to dry are mixed together in a concoction that provokes a sudden nausea . . . A few couples are waiting by a sad gas lamp until they can "go into the back".'[118] The city is sick from within, rotten, and the metaphor of the 'cancerous ulcer' is often used; the city has produced the ulcer from out of itself, it has not fought it in time – or with the right means – and is now being eaten up by it.

On 15 April 1931 Anna Pappritz chaired a conference of experts on 'The state of the streets after the implementation of the law for the prevention of venereal disease', held at the Welfare Ministry in Berlin. It had been organized by the Alliance for the Protection of Women, and the question it was asked to answer was: 'Since the implementation of the law, has the state of the streets become worse, and if this is the case, what is the cause, and what measures might be proposed to control the evil?' The contributors inevitably disagreed; in his conference report in the *Abolitionist* Wolfgang Mittermaier drew the conclusion: 'It obviously depends completely on the attitude of the observer, whether or not he sees the conduct of prostitutes on the streets as worse than before.'[119]

This view is confirmed by a reading of the conference minutes. The pragmatists, policemen and doctors for example, usually claim that that no concrete 'worsening' in the state of the streets can be observed, while local government speakers claim the contrary. Frieda Rothing from the social work department in Hanover also arrives at a rather pragmatic assessment: 'If we are clear about the fact that we will be unable to eradicate prostitution, then we must realize that it has to appear somehow on the big city scene.' What might appear to have been a defeat, a capitulation in the face of the enemy, prostitution, could perhaps be the starting-point for many more far-reaching measures: the understanding that 'a freer attitude to life is trying to emerge' could lead to a more differentiated way of seeing. Many speakers, both men and women, pointed out that a

215

period of economic crisis was not the right time to come to an overall assessment of the problem, and that with economic recovery many things would take a turn 'for the better'. It was Hagemann, the former head of the Berlin criminal investigation department, who formulated the most vigorous criticism of the representatives of the morality movement, at the same time providing an interpretation of the secret motives of the night critics:

> The courts do not at all not overlook the fact that on the street it is particularly those who are importuned who communicate by signs, unmistakable to the observant and knowledgeable connoisseur of metropolitan life, though often unknown to themselves – that they expect this to occur. When then these people are morally outraged, this implies a *psychological contradiction*, which forces one to a thorough assessment of their statements, very much as in the case of those spectators of immorality, now hopefully extinct, who used to take righteous offence after managing to spy something outrageous with their binoculars.[120]

This means that there could really be no question of importuning – it lies solely in the eye of the beholder; those who walk the nocturnal metropolis with a wandering and searching eye (even those who think they are doing this only in the service of a higher cause) are all liable to be accosted. This pragmatic view could provide an opportunity to find a solution – or, better, to develop one – which emerged from the city itself, a solution which questioned the risks of urban living, but would also have been prepared to recognize its opportunities; a solution in whose achievement all those with an interest in the city could participate: local politicians, liberal police forces, health and social work departments. In fact the right moment to enquire about the effects of the new law and to remedy possible faults would only arrive after the economic crisis was overcome. This attitude had no chance of success.

The folklore of the radiant city night, by which our image of the period around the turn of the century and of the 1920s is still predominantly determined, needs, I believe, to be supplemented. This would not be a matter of unmasking the romantic representation of prostitution as false:

> Every night in the private room
> Supper with some gentlemen
> There I eat sweets until my girdle splits –
> Can you imagine what fun this is!

I go round to the races
And I have an account at the bank!
I flew into the light as a grey moth,
But now I am a *grande cocotte*![121]

It would make more sense to establish stronger links between the individual facets of the spectrum of perception than has hitherto been the case. What stands out, not just in the example of Berlin, but in Paris, too, where the folklore of prostitution grew even stranger blooms,[122] is the apparent irreconcilability of the various attitudes towards prostitution. While the revellers of 'night life' exclusively look for pleasure in the city, blind to the social misery and to the exploitation of women, its critics tend towards the other extreme: after the demands of the day, after its 'metallic marching step', 'life cries out for satisfaction'.

Nocturnal life is seductive particularly because it opens up uncontrollable spaces and times outside the law, with the promise that the desire for freedom will be satisfied. The morality movement did not recognize the urgency of these needs – or rejected them. Its view, that prostitution represented a 'social evil', prevented it from seeing that alongside prostitution – and partly even against it – there had developed a lively and multi-layered network of nocturnal activities, nocturnal encounters in the cities; it conducted its fight against prostitution as a fight against this nocturnal life, against theatre performances and cabaret programmes, against the extension of opening hours, against the carefree night life that had become the property of the metropolitans – and above all against women, who were fighting for unhindered access to the life of the street. Those who wanted to 'abolish' or 'prohibit' prostitution, and were not at the same time prepared to hear 'life crying out for satisfaction', had to intervene very deeply into this network of nocturnal relationships and destroy more than just public 'sexual immorality'.

## 3 *Midnight mission*

*Walking at night, with no light of home!*
*On paths through the mire and the shame of the world,*
*And there a little bridge to heaven is built:*
*O joy, when one trusts this narrow span*
*To find his way back and to find his way out!*
*Even at night God's stars don't go out.*[123]

The fight against night life and its sins was not waged only in the press. 'Active compassion', mission in the sense of religious renewal and of *social work among one's own people*, demanded an exact knowledge of the living conditions of the 'endangered' souls. In England in the 1830s the big cities increasingly became fields of missionary activity, as the emerging urban underclass became a clientèle for welfare. Reports on the work of the missions are reports from the 'inside' of the cities,[124] reports about their 'night side', albeit refracted through the particular approach of the missionaries.

From the visiting of the poor there soon developed a planned and systematic investigation of the poor areas of the cities; besides reconnaissance, its major concern was the 'salvation' of the endangered. The hopeless and fallen state of the poor could be exemplified by specific phenomena: the consumption of alcohol, sexual promiscuity, prostitution – all elements of the nocturnal, symptoms of threatening decay. Following the example of London – where the London City Mission had existed since 1835 – at the end of the 1840s Johann Heinrich Wichern proposed the establishment of a city mission in Germany too; here too such phenomena as homelessness and prostitution were seen as belonging to the nocturnal streets, and new paths for missionary work became necessary: pathways into the night.

PRIVATE RESCUE MISSIONS

The British politician and later Liberal Prime Minister William Gladstone married in 1840, and settled with his wife in Carlton House Terrace, not far from Piccadilly. After plans for the creation of a 'lay brotherhood' had come to nothing, he took his concern, the salvation of 'fallen' women and girls, into his own hands: 'Gladstone's method was to walk the streets by night, alone, at least one evening a week, armed with a stout stick for protection when he wandered in unfrequented districts. At first he liked to wait for prostitutes to accost him, and he would then reply with courtesy, simplicity and charm. But often he would accost women himself, and suggest that they should accompany him home, where he told them they would be treated with respect by his wife and by himself, and that they would be given food and shelter.'[125] Neither the suspicions of the public nor various attempts at blackmail prevented him from continuing this work of salvation to an advanced age. In London, in the

218

1880s, the Reverend Frederick Charrington developed more radical measures: 'At night, accompanied by a friend, Charrington prowled through the most dangerous streets, on the hunt for the "foulest sinks of iniquity"; his weapon – the famous "black book", in which he entered the name or descriptions of every person (and none was excepted) he saw entering or leaving a brothel.'[126] The missionary morality-detectives knew that the danger lay on the street, and this was their field of work. Some, like 'Prostitutes' Padre' Reverend Davidson, overstepped their own boundaries: 'He would constantly be found walking in Piccadilly'; he too accosted young girls and took them home with him – until one day, after repeated reproaches, he was removed from his post for 'immoral behaviour'.[127] This was not the only reason why private rescue missions remained an exception, but 'saviours' like Gladstone did pave the way for other projects.

1835 was the year of the foundation of the London City Mission. From its daily work – 'house-to-house and common lodging house visitations'[128] – the mission developed an exact knowledge of social conditions in the poor areas of the city. 'Seething in the very centre of our great cities, concealed by the thinnest crust of civilization and decency, is a vast mass of moral corruption, of heart-breaking misery and absolute godlessness.' At the centre of their complaint, partly as a result of the missionaries' form of work, but also because of the particular place it held in England, is the question of housing. 'Bad housing conditions' and 'overcrowding' were the central themes and the essential causes of other problems: 'Immorality is but the natural outcome of conditions like these.'

The outbreak of cholera in 1832 had also mobilized social reformers in London and forced them to deal with the functions of urban life: the paving and cleaning of the streets, the relief of the poor and maintenance of the peace – these different tasks of the (central) administration had to be seen in context together. In 1837–8 typhoid fever had broken out in East London. In 1838 Edwin Chadwick published the first report 'on the sanitary conditions of the labouring classes in the metropolis', and ten years later some of the demands raised here and in another inquiry of 1842 (Inquiry into the Sanitary Condition of the Labouring Population of Great Britain) were met by the first Public Health Act, of 1848. Connected to this too were the first attempts at urban planning, as Chadwick's report had already included suggestions for the sensible location (even demolition if necessary) of 'cattle markets, slaughterhouses, cowhouses, tripe shops, gas manufactories, burying grounds, etc.'[129] – the discovery of the reverse side of the industrialization process led to reflection on the structure and order of the whole city.

In *The Examiner*, and also in his own *Household Words*, Charles Dickens published a series of articles about the 'sanitary movement'. At the same time he supported the home for the rehabilitation of 'fallen women' proposed by Angela Burdett-Coutts, which was to make possible their reintegration into society – even if this was mostly in far Australia. 'Urania Cottage' was the name of this house in which women were looked after and prepared for a different way of gaining a living. 'Why had they been on the street in the first place? The uncomfortable answer was, they had no alternative.'[130] Those who came to this realization would soon try to make it public. The essential incentive for the writing of *Bleak House* was to arouse interest in social problems through art: 'Fog everywhere. Fog up the river, where it flows among green aits and meadows; fog down the river, where it rolls defiled among the tiers of shipping, and the waterside pollution of a great (and dirty) city.' The great and dirty city, an anxiety-provoking portrayal of darkness and concealment. Dickens tries 'to force his audience to see and understand the hidden, problematic nature of their familiar environment'. London had changed. The images of filth and darkness had to have an effect so strong that the reading public turned and looked about, and became conscious of the changes within their own lives, and in the London familiar to them. The housing situation appears as a central problem – here too the perception of the city in London follows different paths from Paris or Berlin. 'Dickens was coming to believe that the housing issue was crucial, for above all it was poor housing which directly caused the illness – physical and mental   that crippled the poor.' So *Bleak House* becomes a novel of belonging and home-lessness, telling, as it does, of a house and the loss of it.

The arousal of public interest led to the establishment of welfare organizations. One of the most important was the Society for Organizing Charitable Relief and Repressing Mendicity (Charity Organization Society, COS), founded in 1869. According to Gareth Stedman Jones it can be seen as 'a product of the fears expressed by a particular sector of wealthy London in the 1860s';[131] at the same time its concrete activity is the precursor of a modern understanding of social and welfare policy. What is decisive, as for almost all these organizations, is the close relationship to religious ideas, which not only sought the 'salvation' of the individual but also countenanced the organization of 'crusades' against social evils. In the autumn of 1883 the Reverend Andrew Mearns (at least scholarship seems to agree on the author) published an urgent pamphlet whose sensational and therefore effective title was 'The Bitter Cry of Outcast London.'[132] Here too homelessness was the root of all evil, and the 'outcast' are the poor, because they have no home in society.

REFUGES

Friedrich von Bodelschwingh came to Paris as a young priest, in order to prepare for missionary work abroad. Many of the Germans he met in Paris worked as *chiffoniers*, or rag merchants. They were necessarily out and about in the city at night and thus, for the missionaries, exposed to numerous dangers and temptations. Bodelschwingh founded a school for the rag merchants' children and worked in hospitals and shelters. His idea was to convert the 'public institutions of illness and poverty' into refuges for the victims of the nocturnal city. It became apparent, however, not only in Paris, that these institutions were often avoided, and that they were too far removed from the centres of nocturnal life, and could therefore only inadequately meet the requirements of their role.

The next step on this road into the night was therefore necessary: the organizers of the 'Midnight Meetings' in London rented rooms in the inner city entertainment areas, and by leaflets or word of mouth they invited prostitutes and 'night-revellers' to join them for fiery preaching and public penitence:

> Another remarkable movement in our city during the past year has been what is known by the name of Midnight Meetings, at which late hour the fallen have been congregated for a social meal, and then for exhortation and prayer . . . Upwards of 100 women, some of which were of a superior class, have been thereby rescued from a life of sin. . .[133]

The missionaries knew that such meetings would reach 'only a few', so the secondary effect of this work was almost more important: to establish a presence in the life of the night, to penetrate the 'hunting grounds' of vice and not allow oneself be driven out again.

The common thing in all these endeavours is their view of the street; 'the guilt of Berlin' is conjured up as wordily as in London: 'The great cities of the world have become terrible centres of indecency and immorality – the smoke of their sins rises to the heavens like that of smitten Sodom, and it soils the bodies and souls of the whole population.'[134] The missionaries created a city after their own image, and they played the role of minor deities, who – as representatives – pronounced judgement on the big city.

CAMPAIGNS

One of these minor deities was able to make his initial experience in the big city the starting-point of a gigantic empire, the Salvation Army:

> One fine evening of June 1865 a tall, strong-featured man in ministerial garb strode along the northern side of Whitechapel Road, East London. Though a stranger to the district, and not going anywhere in particular, he nonetheless moved purposefully . . . He had eyes only for the people. He saw them crowding into beer shops and gin palaces, multitudes of them; he saw them besotted, poverty-stricken and perishing. Yearning pity and deep concern filled his heart to overflowing. Could he not do something for these lost sheep? [135]

William Booth, 'for the passing stranger was none other', joined the missionaries, 'who were bringing the gospel to the heathens in the jungle of the East End'. He preached at the Midnight Meetings, and he himself convoked the midnight assemblies in the 'tents' near the Mile End Road that marked the beginning of the Salvation Army. If the London City Mission admitted to taking the offensive in its efforts, Booth went one step further: the campaigns he led into the night were planned and organized like campaigns of war. Catherine Booth took on the role of the 'angel of salvation', while her husband the General saw himself as the 'avenging messenger', the 'sword of God'.

It is easy to dismiss the language and behaviour of the Salvation Army and of other missions as unmodern, overwrought, unworldly and ridiculous. But examples of their concrete work, the activities of the 'Slum Sisters' for example, show that one shouldn't make it to easy for oneself in this regard. Wherever state measures against poverty and misery were not effective, or insufficiently so, the

'Moral street sweepers.' Food and shelter were offered by the Salvation Army, which was founded in London's East End in the 1860s by William Booth and conducted its expeditions into the city night from here. Headquarters of the Salvation Army, Whitechapel Road, London, 1890.

missions started their work; the 'moral street sweepers' indeed took over many tasks that had been neglected by state institutions. I therefore think it a mistake to denounce the Salvation Army as an arm of the authorities: the evils they took on were as real as the victims of whom they took care. The characterization of the Salvation Army soldier, the missionary in the inner city, merely as an 'agent of the ruling class' is inadequate. Because the explorers of the city night 'discovered what was hidden in the familiar, the sinister, the publicly repressed',[136] they reported on it, and at times they lived amidst it. Their texts offer one answer to the sweeping challenges of city life, one possibility of grappling with what was in their view the thorough mystification of the night. They are – conscientiously – one-sided documents of uncertainty and of the search for a foothold, a solid orientation. They are witnesses to the contradictory nature of 'inner' urbanization, in the process of which forces are set free which generate fear, and against the threatening darkness they hold up their version of a bright life.

In the case of the Berliner Stadtmission (Berlin City Mission), founded in 1877, work also started with house visits and became more sophisticated in the course of the years. Here too practical work provided a counterweight to the ideological tirades of the spokesmen. Missionaries did collaborate with the police on various occasions, but their attitude to the vice police was essentially somewhat sceptical. Unlike the police, the missions worked essentially in the field of prevention, a good example of this being the early establishment of missions at railway stations in particular, as reception points for girls who came to the city from the country.[137]

The 'knowledge of social disparities, which many of so-called noble nature pass by disapprovingly,'[138] certainly could lead to curious projects. It was thus the aim of the Berlin Männerbund (men's association), 'given the great number of excesses that here endanger morality, with the help of our members to organize *a comprehensive watch over the whole city*', to take note of indecent exhibitions, the advances of prostitutes or excesses in drinking establishments, and to report them to the police. More difficult to interpret – and so much more interesting – is the work of the Mitternachtsmission (Midnight Mission), which in 1906 brought a new strategy to the city night.

STOP! WHERE ARE YOU GOING?

The unpublished documents of the Mitternachtsmission, from which the following citations are drawn, have a way of speaking about the night that cannot simply be dismissed as moralizing propaganda:

> Those who walk at night through the brilliant streets of our capital will clearly recognize that the honour of the Lord is being sullied in the most outrageous manner. Public morality has sunk to a terrifyingly low level. By public morality I mean the moral views of the men of today, not primarily those of women, though they also must protect a people's treasure of morality. But man makes woman. And the position of women amongst a people is a measure of the morals of the men.[139]

The night-mission's women workers followed the 'lost daughters', and their male colleagues were now to start 'to work on the fallen men'. In the early days Pastor Gensichen reported:

> The night mission has now been working for almost a year, distributing leaflets, and delivering oral and printed warnings. Its work is well illustrated by an example that encouraged us greatly in the early days.

One night in October one of us was standing at a tram stop and saw a young man who was in danger of falling. 'I warn you in the name of Jesus,' he said to him, 'go home.' 'I am a Jew,' replied the man so addressed. 'So I warn you in God's name,' was the answer. The young man thanked him politely and went home . . . Encouraged in this way we continued our work – every Friday there were about eight volunteers from the city missionaries – happily, regardless of all the insults on the streets, the work went on . . . At the suggestion of Pastor Le Seur we visited the bars with female service, in which so many of our young men waste their honour and their money. We even visited the pubs frequented by the unfortunate homosexuals. To preserve our own good reputation we were obliged to acquire a modest uniform, which rendered us recognizable at night as workers from the city mission. Two brothers and inspectors go out almost every night, visiting the bad pubs in their area until 11 o'clock (closing time) and then they go to the crossing of Friedrichstrasse and Unter den Linden. There they hand out to young men night-mission leaflets written by us, which very briefly warn of the dangers of sexual licence, direct their attention to Jesus our Saviour, and invite them to visit the city mission inspectors during their hours of consultation. A certain amount of pastoral discussion happens automatically in the course of this activity, so that we have often had to engage in fierce struggle with poor lost souls on the central promenade of the Linden.[140]

Soon the work had to be professionalized. In Hamburg in 1911 the Association of German Midnight Missions was established, the constitution declaring its objects to be 'to organize missions among those in moral danger and fallen men and women, to promote morality among our people through the strength of the gospel, yet to struggle energetically against immorality by every means'. It worked in many different ways, through publications, lectures, the monitoring of the press, the creation of welfare institutions, and itself providing care, but in the foreground stood 'a properly planned night mission in the public streets . . . regular evangelization in the vicinity of the public streets and places of amusement, and the gathering of the saved into congregations established there'.[141]

This last idea was obviously taken from the London Midnight Meeting Movement, but was never very energetically pursued; compared to London, the Midnight Mission in the German cities took a decisive step outside onto the streets. The street with its temptations and dangers is at the centre of all accounts of their work, as in this report from Dresden:

Before going out in the evening with our helpers, to do our missionary work in the streets and alleys of the city, we gather together to pray and hear God's word. Every evening we ask God for a pure heart in the midst of the filth we must see and hear, and we ask our gentle Saviour for gentleness in the midst of ridicule and scorn. . .

First of all in the streets of ill-repute: at nightfall we enter a usually poorly illuminated alley. The windows are heavily draped, the houses closed up. But the doors are alive. As we pass by, the door opens, and through the crack, careless of the police prohibition, a woman gives a quiet, enticing call. . .

As what goes on in the street is an open secret, and for young people an all too interesting secret, whole hordes of the curious pass through these alleys during the hours of evening. They stand around, a few here, a few there, 'We're only looking'. So the imagination is inflamed. The next time they are bolder, they drink for courage and. . .[142]

Description is followed by reproach. One can no longer remain silent from false shame and false decency: 'Shine a spotlight into these dark corners! And then let us go there, to warn, to help and to save!'

In these ladies dressed in the latest fashions the uninitiated do not immediately recognize the *demi-monde*, but to the trained eye it isn't difficult. To it, the night-time street quite soon presents itself in another light . . . Because the business of the street is an open secret among a wide circle of young women, these inexperienced, curious young things copy the behaviour of the prostitutes, just so as once to experience an adventure. . .

Our visible weapons are our leaflets . . . To hand one out in the narrow alleyways is to goad the conscience: 'Think of your mother', 'Think of your sister', 'Think of your God', printed in bold letters on red paper . . . A yellow leaflet, intended for those whose destination seems uncertain, contains a short warning with the question: 'Where are you going this evening?' . . . We go out provided with these. We always work in pairs in the alleyways, standing on corners and getting in the way of the young men coming round them, and we also patrol back and forth. . .

On the street, the work is somewhat different. Here one has to keep a sharp eye on the prostitutes. First we follow them surreptitiously; but we observe the men who come close to them. And whoever approaches the prostitutes with a glance or word or gesture, we confront with a leaflet and a word of warning. . .

And when someone shouts to the helper: 'With this leaflet you have ruined the whole evening for me!', is that not also a success?

It wasn't easy to dissent in the face of this moral offensive. In the missionaries' reports there is often mention of men who refuse to be diverted from carrying out their intentions, who even heap the leaflet distributors with 'scorn and ridicule', but public criticism was rare. The *Berliner Morgenpost* at least reported an interesting case: a man who was going home alone from the Friedrichstättische Theatre at 11 o'clock in the evening had been given a piece of paper, on which serious reproaches were addressed to him:

TO THE YOUNG MEN!

Why are you on the street tonight? Please answer yourself honestly!

You will recognize that you are spinelessly following the voice of sin. You heap guilt on guilt upon yourself. For this you will have to bear the punishment all your life and in eternity. You will be lost forever, you poor, dear friend! What would your mother say if she saw you arm in arm with a prostitute, defiled, fallen?

The newspaper comments: 'It's a bit strong, addressing someone walking through the Friedrichstrasse at 11 o'clock in the evening as if he were some kind of depraved character. And Herr Fritz W. was lucky to be walking through the streets *alone*. If he had been to the theatre with his sister or his wife for example, or, a terrible thing to imagine, his fiancée, then in his knowledge of human nature it might have pleased the leaflet distributor to hand him the paper and so insult the woman at his side as a "prostitute."'[143] But criticism did not challenge the champions of cleansing. Pastor H. Flemming presents the missionary view of the night in a manuscript text of 1913 entitled 'What is night mission?':

What do they want here at night on the streets of Berlin, the uniformed men and women with the white cross on their lapel? To warn, to save, to help, that is what they want!

But whom? We see no one drowning, no one run over, no one attacked. We only see happy people, the joy of life laughing in their eyes. *You* may see laughing faces. *We* see exactly what you cannot see: *people run over, drowning, lost!* How do we know this? Do you see this man with the vacant look, coming out of the pub there? That is a drowning man. Does he not need a sure handhold, salvation?

And there, an attack, a robbery!

Where? I see nothing! There are only two people joking together. Laughing lips, sparkling youth! The joy of love! The joy of love? This is *enslavement to sensuality! The passionate lust for forbidden fruit!* The poor girl! She has been robbed of her honour![144]

227

**Was führt Sie hierher?**

Suchen Sie eine Befriedigung Ihres Geschlechtstriebes?

Folgen Sie einer sinnlichen Erregung?

Wissen Sie auch, was die Folge sein wird, wenn Sie hier einkehren?

Leaflet of the Berlin Midnight Mission, 1910. The language is powerful: 'At night thousands of moths perish in the arc lights of our streets. So does it distress us if you too follow the deceiving urge towards the flickering pleasures of the night.' – 'The lamps of our metropolis light the nights as bright as day. Yet you know that night is dark and that all that glitters is but deceptive appearance.'

The scale of the task is indicated by the mission's tone, its choice of words and its manner of proceeding. It is Jesus himself who sets the task, he 'sends them at night into the bustle of the big city'. The mission has to act, because all other institutions have failed to do so. Flemming emphasizes that although the organization at first also visited drinking establishments, it became 'exclusively a mission to the street'. It consciously wanted to disturb 'the joking and pleasure', 'the effervescent life which manifests itself here on the streets, under the bright electric light'. It wants to ask: 'Where are you going this evening? Is your poor wife worried about you, while out here you seek the nocturnal joys of the big city?' The language of the mission, a continuous appeal to bad conscience, sometimes became brutal: those who turn night into day could quickly come to be seen as 'drones and parasites on society'. Those who were constantly confronted with its forbidden joys had to think about the night. In his 'Sketches from the moral and social misery of the metropolis', E. Heine wrote:

But if man never allows the night to whisper something in his ear, if he never deals with the night side of life, he is in danger of becoming one-sided – the heart remaining dulled to the suffering of the world. Light and shadow belong together in life too.

In what follows I want to try and sketch a moral picture of the metropolitan street. If unhappily in this picture the light is not pre-dominant . . ., the lights will shine out all the more effectively against the dark background.

Light and shadow dart and flicker over the cobbles of the street when at night the gaping maw of the metropolis opens and spits out all the vermin which – frightened of daylight – had lain hidden in the walls or slept through the day after being up all night.

Dark creatures come into the twilight of the streets, flitting past the men; slowly and carefully like octopuses they stretch their tentacles towards them, enticing them, touching them, seducing them – with rouged cheeks, overpowering perfume, laughter, cooing and vulgar talk . . .

What will the NIGHT do to these honest countrymen in their naïveté? . . .

Yes, to this quarter of the city one may apply Dante's famous line: 'Here dies the light!'; yet here too it is as if the light begins to struggle with the dark.[145]

An important aim of missionary work is to protect children, young people and women from the 'vile sights of the night-time streets'. In the case-studies collected by Heine, night-life stories of the saved and of the damned are counterbalanced. Pimps, procurers and 'well-heeled' clients are described as aggressive and hostile; the 'girls' on the other hand are depicted as 'flowers trodden down', who raised anew may bloom again. The missionaries' Christian conception of mankind leads them to a conflict: they would also like to condemn the prostitutes, declare them guilty, but they find it hard to do so. On the one hand Pastor Gensichen calls them the 'most unfortunate among the lost', but then claims that 'the state-licensed prostitutes regard themselves as the mistresses of the nocturnal streets of Berlin'. There the rhetorical question, 'What would Jesus say, if he were to walk one night along the Friedrichstrasse?', becomes a diffi-cult test: his walk through the nocturnal streets forces the Pastor to reflect on the causes of indecency 'at home' and even on the 'hidden part' in himself.

The First World War brought the struggle of conscience to an end; now, 'soldiers of all kinds are involved in Berlin's night life'. Their worst enemy is alcohol: 'Until around midnight they are mindful of their uniform, and as long as they are still sober they keep away from prostitutes, [but] after midnight, throughout the whole city, one may see drunken soldiers in the most repulsive scenes.' There was a second front within the city, and during the war the night mission finally received the public sanction that it had often been denied, and in the fight against venereal diseases it was now doing war-work of the greatest importance:

> A man from the provinces is looking to explore his freedom in nocturnal Berlin. He is handed a leaflet by a night missionary, with the title: *Be warned!* 'You are right,' he says approvingly, 'that is appropriate here.' But how amazed is the night missionary when in the next street he sees the same gentleman climbing into a cab with a prostitute. Resolutely he leaps towards the cab, throws the door open and shouts: 'Sir, for your wife and children's sake, climb down.' After a short struggle, reason and goodness win through. He takes the brother's hand and climbs down, while the prostitute goes off, swearing and shouting.[146]

When the war was over, a new enemy was soon found: Pastor Ludwig Hoppe, Director of the National Society for the Preservation of Decency and Morality,[147] wrote on 'Sexual Bolshevism and how to defend against it', and a leading figure in the Salvation Army saw the fight for the workers' souls like this:

> They are on the streets, and at present this is the only way you can meet them...
>
> The present time particularly calls for this. In Germany we are now at a great turning-point in the history of the proletariat. Indeed, the big city is a terrible swamp. Thousands and thousands struggle to get out of the swamp, in order to regain their selves, to save their bodily, spiritual and eternal life. But with every attempt to work their way out, they are threatened with sinking deeper. The swamp is too muddy, too tenacious, too deep: it will not let go of its victims.[148]

Control of the streets was a significant factor in political debate. The fear 'of the street', of the possibility of those who live and agitate on the streets getting out of control, could only be overcome if the forces of law and order and of morality itself went out and – singing, if necessary – showed their presence on the street. On 23 September 1920 there was a debate in the Prussian Constituent Assembly on 'Nude pictures and immoral writings'. Mentzel, the Nationalist deputy for

Stettin, quoted a 'friend of the people' who had said that 'the streets of the big cities stank of eroticism'. Against this the SPD and USPD representatives of the Left argued that Berlin still appeared to be a city of peaceable industriousness. The USPD deputy Kilian asked his colleagues to tell him 'where such things can be seen . . . We would like to go there too sometime, not to enthuse at the performance, but to work ourselves up into moral indignation.'[149]

A sober, unbiased view of the city, however, had no easy time against the powerfully worded sermons of the missionaries. In his *Metropolitan Reflections*, Carl Sonnenschein quotes his own Easter Saturday sermon, broadcast by the Berlin Funkhaus on the evening of 16 April 1922. In it he warns against the illusion of freedom that draws so many people to the cities. The crude mix of post-Expressionist metaphor, apocalyptic night visions, the promise of salvation, and anti-urban utopianism makes for a doomsday mood, conjuring up the 'German midnight':[150]

> So they travel to the metropolis. Travel! Drive! Hurry! Stumble! Fall! Bleed! Until they have embraced the asphalt and they have kissed Mother Earth, oh so hard here, in the greyness of these streets . . .
>
> Away to the vast city, whose darkness shrouds us! Here no inhibitions disturb us. Here no human countenance will recognize us . . .
>
> O city now revealed! You have strangled a thousand jubilant blooms in the night-frost of spring. You have lowered a thousand gently upraised hands . . . Nothing remains of the games of our youth, of our mothers' songs. We have become grey! Cold to behold! Before the reason of our critics! This is how you lie before me, city unveiled! A sunken, sleeping field of destroyed souls.
>
> You are like a furnace, o city! They tip a thousand little carts into your gullet. They stoke up a hundred fires within your breast. They force a thousand storms among these embers. You eat them all! You swallow them all! You destroy them all![151]

At times the missions' practice and propaganda seem to come from two different worlds. Against this fanfare, one may read descriptions of the concrete work, such as that given by Hans Hyan in his article 'Die Menschen-Mühle Berlin'. Hyan tells how at 12 o'clock at night a train arrived from the East at the Schlesische Bahnhof, and how two girls, probably from Upper Silesia, were accosted by a 'well-dressed person with a brutal face'. He had promised them cheap lodgings, offered himself as guide, and had already placed his arm around one of them when the mission sister arrived and threatened him with the police; he quickly disappeared, 'cheated of his victim, he was swallowed up in the darkness of the train-shed'.[152]

At the great police exhibition in Berlin in 1927, all aspects of work for the welfare of those at risk were presented; 'rescue work' was to give firm bearings to those 'who wander about in the big city; their random and aimless lifestyle, their rush to the haunts of pleasure, their over-loud laughter and wild movements are all merely external *symptoms of a deep inner need*'. This diagnosis simply cannot be true. The sought-after confrontation with the dark, the search for the night-worlds on the streets, corresponds to an inner yearning which is difficult to put into words. In his *Berlin Childhood around 1900* Walter Benjamin attempted to provide an interpretation of the search involved in walking: 'How much I owed this dreamy resistance during the joint walks [with his mother] through the city, I found out later *when its labyrinth opened itself to the sexual drive*.' Benjamin tells of the 'unprecedented urge' to accost a prostitute, and of his many vain attempts before he finally did it, of the endless walks on which he found himself 'hopelessly embroiled in the asphalt toils of the street'.[153] The street was a testing-ground for the inexpressible, the undeveloped, the inexperienced – and at its gates stood guardians who wanted to bar the entrance to this world. Only a few reports venture forth into such dimensions. The far-right author Heinrich Berl, who was dedicated to the struggle against 'red Berlin', polemicized against sensational reports because they rendered 'only reality' and did not seek after 'truth'; but this world of the cities was 'false and decadent'.[154] The missionaries saw and uncovered the urban world as false appearance, but they did not recognize the meaning inherent in the hunt after illusion:

> Trains come and go. People come, people go. Day after day, evening after evening, night after night. Misfortune and want recognize no borders, they have no particular domicile. Young people, still half children, leave the family home; to them the big city seems to be deliverance. The ideal saviour of their storming, impetuous youth. Everything in them shouts for experience, adventure and yearning, these are the watchwords. . .
>
> Berlin, cinema, different work, freedom, this is the dream of young eyes and hearts. Then they give themselves over to reality and they climb aboard the train that brings them to unhappiness, slaves without will of this wild, beguiling metropolitan machine. They avoid the 'Railway Station Mission' sign, as if they fear, unconsciously perhaps,

'Night life'comes to the provinces from the big cities. 'Out so late, Miss?' 'Well, yes . . . I am the night life in Gross-Plaguritz!' Illustration by Jeanne Mammen from *Der Junggeselle*, Berlin, 1925.

that it might rob them of their illusions and set them straight. Then one day they come of their own accord, tired and faded, through the door beneath the sign, knocking on it at their hour of need, and then they are saved from the metropolitan streets.[155]

Some theoreticians of the Midnight Mission saw the contradiction and demanded that it be ended; at the organization's educational week on sexual ethics in Hamburg in April 1928, the expert Dr Harmsen-Berlin soberly noted the loosening of family ties and the earlier start of working life as reasons why for many young people there was no longer any 'undisturbed period of maturation' between youth and adulthood. From this he drew the surprising conclusion: 'Metropolitan life has to be welcomed' as a testing-ground for a new way of life, as a life within the contradictions that exist. This, though, was a programme whose content was still to be determined, publicly discussed and put into practice. But there was no democratic public capable of taking unfamiliar yearnings (and their own unadmitted desires) seriously. In practice, the missionaries' work remains directed to a partial goal; where need is visible, they intervene, 'and for one night, a person is snatched from the street, from the metropolis with its pain and darkness'.[156]

# v Night-walking

Since the years around 1840 the *street* has been at the centre of debate about the nocturnal city. For all the themes we have dealt with already – the night-watch, closing time, the criminal world, homelessness, prostitution and mission – the street has been the *theatre* in which conflicts between order and disorder, between security and insecurity, morality and immorality have been played out. In all these debates it was also the metaphorical place to which the images and ideas of freedom and control, the dissolution and demarcation of boundaries referred. The question of *accessibility* turned out to be decisive for the representation and interpretation of what goes on at night: to whom does the nocturnal street belong, who has the opportunity to make use of the street and the many things it offers? Who is about at night on the streets of the big city? How did the kinds and styles of walking the night change in the years between 1840 and 1930? It is with questions such as these that this chapter will concern itself.[1]

## 1 *Insight while walking*

Though he was himself not speaking of the nocturnal city, Wilhelm Heinrich Riehl, the founder of scientific folklore studies, provided a clear formulation of the idea that underlies the reflections which follow: 'Above all, the explorer of the life of the people has to go on a journey. That is obvious. But I mean *go* in the literal sense of the word, and there are many to whom this is not obvious . . . those who wish to research and to learn on their travels must go *alone*.'[2] Behind this lies the thought that a landscape cannot just be understood from the desk, that its nature opens up completely only to those who walk through it on foot, gaining a sensuous impression of its many aspects.

Can the idea easily be transferred to the city, that complicated mechanism? There is no simple answer to the question. An unqualified 'yes' would obviously be naive – the structure of the city cannot be taken in while walking, just walking past; the functioning of its different individual parts demands thorough, systematic examination. It could be, however, that there are aspects of urban life that evade the penetrating gaze of systematic research, while disclosing themselves for an instant to the person who walks past by chance, particularly at night. The idea can indeed, under certain conditions, be transferred to the (nocturnal) city – if the passer-by is himself receptive, capable of 'seeing with his own eyes and hearing with his own ears'.[3] Seen like this, one passes by not at all 'by accident', but in the certain knowledge that the accident will happen, sometime, somewhere, again and again. Pedestrian investigation of the city demands an understanding of all the possibilities offered by going astray, and above all it demands patience. This is also true, to a certain extent, of the account that follows: it would have been wrong to adopt a systematic approach, because this would not do justice to the uncertainties of the night. The sources here come from patient, searching, straying 'pedestrian investigators', and they tell of many different ways of walking a city by night. In so doing, they supplement the knowledge we have already gained of the city night, relativizing it sometimes in one point or another, but above all they set this knowledge *in movement*.

## 2  *The nocturnal terrain*

As the journal *Le Monde moderne* put it in 1895, streets change their character 'suivant les heures de la journée'; their appearance – and 'reputation' – change with the changing hours. The image of the street changes with its functions. In recent years, research on the street, on street life and street culture, has considerably enriched our understanding of how cities function; two areas are of particular interest from the nocturnal point of view.

In the course of work on the milieus and lifestyles of the lower classes in the eighteenth and nineteenth centuries, attention necessarily turned to the street as living and working space, as the 'home of the collective', as Walter Benjamin called it.[4] At that time, urban culture was mostly street culture; not only did many forms of work and commerce, the exchange of goods and news, and relationships between neighbours, colleagues and partners in love or strife, take place on the street, but they took on a particular character as a result

236

The solitary wanderer in the darkness of the streets becomes a literary figure: 'Often in the second or third hour after midnight he would close the door of his flat behind him and walk down the dark stairs into the street. The city he had roamed all over during the day or evening gained a new and uncertain power over him' (Paul Leppin, 1914). Photograph by André Kertész.

of it. Street life in the areas where the underclasses lived occupied the attention of the authorities not only because it represented a potential 'riotous assembly', but also because life on and through the street developed its own talents and 'virtues' (or 'vices'), which were alien to those who lived differently.[5]

Even those who have observed the city 'from above', from the point of view of power and organization, have also had to concern themselves with the street. In this different context, streets are important as elements that structure the image of the city, as traffic-arteries, as links between the individual centres of ruling presence, and not least as a terrain of military deployment affording access to the living areas of the underclasses in a crisis situation.[6]

From these two points of view there necessarily emerges a third: the streets constitute a field in which conflicts between 'authority' and 'subject' are played out. Based on the respective interests of either side, strategies for the defence of one's own living area or for the conquest of alien territories have to maintain or alter conditions on the street in their own favour. Even if these conflicts do not find violent expression, between the various groups of the city's population, between 'bottom' and 'top', there exists a constant tension which manifests itself in the claim to unimpeded access to the street. The streets of the large European cities of the seventeenth and eighteenth centuries, that is before the establishment of a regular city police force, were marked in a particular way by this contradiction: the upper classes made their streets into a stage on which they could display their power and wealth; while the 'lower classes' were obliged to make use of the streets to extend the restricted living space available to them.[7] For the middle classes, however, the streets were not much more than routes to go to work and back, remaining in fact *terra incognita*; Gloria Levitas has shown how class differences can be seen not only in attitudes to 'the street', but also in the different ways the streets were used. At night, the streets remained the preserve of the 'upper and lower classes'.

In the years that followed, the nocturnal street was opened up to a broader public, but memories of this binary division persisted for a long time: wealth and poverty, splendour and misery, light and darkness also stand metaphorically for the two views of the street at night. This fact itself, I believe, is enough to destroy any hope that the streets might provide a direct, visual expression of the structures of relationship within urban culture. From the appearance of the

238

street only indirect conclusions can be drawn about the structure of urban society, and these conclusions become more questionable the more complex the social organization becomes.

The street is external and internal space at the same time; seen from the enclosed spaces that line it, it is part of the external world, and in the course of the privatization of certain needs and tasks various functions are withdrawn from it step by step. Looking over the city as a whole, however, the street appears as part of an 'inner' structure, which gains new functions in the process of crystallization of a modern urban way of life: 'The Parisians make interiors of the streets.'[8] This process too has contradictory, non-simultaneous aspects. The change in function of the street does not take place from one day to the next, nor in all parts of the city at the same time. Processes that open up access to the street – like lighting, but not just lighting – first reach the streets of the upper classes, which also become points of attraction for the members of other social groups. But for a long time it was the case for everybody that with the fall of darkness, retreat into private spaces, or at least a narrower milieu, was unavoidable.

## 3 *Nocturnal public life*

While towards the end of the eighteenth century the city street by day became the space of encounter between the various social groups, night-time limitations on its public and generally accessible character lasted longer. This also meant that the processes of the 'destruction' of public life, described by Richard Sennett in his book *The Fall of Public Man*, were also delayed in reaching the nocturnal street.[9] Long before the advent of gas lighting the street had been laden with its own history of threatening darkness, and it does not easily throw off this history (and the stories around it) when it becomes artificially lit. Rather, the old darkness and the new brightness combine to produce their own, special atmosphere, in which light does not necessarily triumph. However aggressively the 'glow of light' may flaunt itself, it gains its effect only through darkness, which it fights but never conquers.

Various authors report on the urban population's new relationship to its own public life – which it constructed itself, in which it lived – around the middle of the nineteenth century. Richard Sennett, for example, says 'Public behaviour was a matter of observation, of passive participation, of a certain kind of voyeurism',[10] and he quotes Balzac's phrase from the *Gastronomie des yeux*. What is foregrounded is no longer the possibility of encounter but a self-contained observation of the scene from a distance by those who know and respect the ever more restrictive rules of behaviour. In similar fashion, François Gasnault describes the 'hermetic boundary between the world of the street and the world of the home' that emerges during this period,[11] identifying 'vices privés, vertues publiques' as the slogan of the day: vice and deviance were lived out privately at home, while on the street one's virtues, one's public side, were paraded for all to see.

I do not know whether these claims can really be sustained. The argument that the late nineteenth-century bourgeois were less open and more inclined to display a superficial façade than their ancestors in an idealized eighteenth century is too moralizingly psychological. Given the growing complexity of the city, and also the volume of traffic on the street, the development of a capacity to endure anonymity and even to make positive use of it became a necessity. The development of greater mobility as well, the ability to cope with different demands in different places, is very significant as a mental reaction to the material processes of urbanization – those who in 1840 or 1850 still wanted to use the street in the same way as did their ancestors in the eighteenth century would soon have been 'left behind'.

The diagnosis of public life in the *nocturnal* city should even be turned on its head: it is just around the middle of the century that nocturnal life in London and Paris, and in its beginnings in Berlin as well, begins to push 'outwards' into the streets. And it is precisely the public presentation of vice that becomes the dominant theme of debate about the city. While Haussmann's transformation of the traditional city scene of Paris perhaps really does signify an 'end', as Sennett claims, at the same time there appears on the nocturnal streets an old-new world of experience, which is at least equal to the traditional – the narrow streets of the old town, now in the process of being destroyed – in terms of attraction, even endowing them (as many do remain intact) with a new attraction. It may be that here in the night the yearning for public life finds an outlet that is more and more denied it during the day.

# 4 Streets as stages

Only the street makes the city walkable, makes it available to inhabitants and visitors. Many authors describe the city streets as a 'stage', as a 'theatre stage' even, 'on which, in uninterrupted succession and ever-changing forms, characters appear and disappear, events develop and come to pass, which taken together form something like an orrery of the social world'.[12] The intention of this image is not merely to caricature or denounce the artificiality, the façade-like character of metropolitan life, but much more to express amazement at the multiplicity of the simultaneous, and this impression is even stronger in the nocturnal city:

> Those who enter a great foreign city for the first time are besieged by a multitude of impressions, which are not individually present to consciousness, but which taken together determine the *degree of gaiety* with which one henceforth contemplates one's new life. . .
>
> And when evening comes, when the long double row of blinking lights, past which the carriage lanterns scurry hastily, like glow-worms, seemingly multiplies the length of the streets, then the liking awakened by the daylight view is further reinforced. Paris lives on the street. A walk through the boulevards, or a glance at the stream of people winding past the innumerable cafés with which this gigantic ring of streets is well supplied, makes one aware that one is in a metropolis, in a metropolis which knows how to adorn itself, knows how to encourage and embellish the life of street, and knows this like no other.[13]

Both observation and self-representation are part of metropolitan public life: what may look like a loss of authenticity is much more the possibility of widening one's own horizons, of transgressing boundaries. Only the street produces the feeling that the *whole city* is at 'my disposal' (as city-walker Julius Rodenberg put it); but it is precisely in this that it awakens needs. It offers a network of relations, contacts and encounters, and the ability to find one's way through this network is one of the significant gains of 'inner' urbanization.

Complementary to this, the street is also a factor for *uncertainty*, shaking up rigid ideas, particularly at night, inviting one to step out: though it promises fear and danger, it offers knowledge as reward. As Peter Sloterdijk has his young Viennese physician Van Leyden say, visiting Paris in the late eighteenth century: 'So I notice in myself an inclination for expeditions in the twilight areas and the darkest areas of the city. *I feel that only from there will one understand the way the whole works.*[14] This text has an important function in Sloterdijk's description of the beginnings of a modern psychology; considered outside this context, though, it feels surprisingly timeless. It could equally well come from the middle of the nineteenth century or the beginning of our own (or, more likely, be transferred there). Independent, to a certain extent, of the real, material changes of society, the cities and the streets, there seems to exist an underground form of metropolitan perception which escapes chronology.

Existing studies dealing with the topic of the street and of passage through the city disappoint when they attempt to tie the 'walking ego's experience of the metropolis' too closely to the historical, socio-economic background. In these works the associational, metaphoric power of the street is always evoked, but never truly realized: for if the street is tamed and pressed into a pre-formed concept, it loses this power, becoming one of many elements that help hold the theoretical enterprise together. There are many possible ways of dealing with the 'street': 'The story of the street could be told from every perspective, and still it would not be the myth, which is always more than the sum of its parts',[15] writes Karl Schlögel about the Nevsky Prospekt in Leningrad, but this is equally true of the street as such. Only when the mythical quality of the street – and particularly at night – is accepted and presupposed, can differences – the social, economic and political conditions that mark the appearance of the street and the behaviour of those who use it – be meaningfully considered.

## 5 *Styles of nocturnal walking*

There are two things then: firstly, the night tells one how the city really is, how 'the whole' functions; and secondly, night, and only night, represents the presence of the past, of myth, in the city of the present. There is a risk that both these characteristics may be lost if attempts to make night a second day are successful. When we follow in the footsteps of past night-walkers, this is a theme we find again and again: to record what possibly may go and never return.

Bernd Jürgen Warneken has pointed out that the bourgeois habit of 'taking the air' was not just an idle occupation but also a 'field for the exercise of physical culture and both *sensuous perception* and the spirit of observation'.[16] Grasping the nocturnal city represents an even greater challenge: 'The man who either disdains or fears to walk up a dark entry may be an excellent good man, and fit for a hundred things; but he will not do to make a good sentimental traveller', wrote Laurence Sterne in 1768,[17] adding, 'I count little of the things I see pass at broad noon day, in large and open streets.'

What is frightening can at the same time be tempting and attractive; he who refuses to recognize the attraction of the dark *reacts so violently against it, because he has in him elements which are drawn to it*.[18] Walking in the nocturnal city affords opportunities – within the limits of the walkable, of course – for an ever-renewed understanding of these dimensions of life. The *affinity of revulsion and desire* is rarely as clearly seen as here: 'The true Paris is of course the black, noisy, foul-smelling city hiding in its narrow alleys';[19] '. . .nocturnal Paris is abominable. This is when the population that lives underground comes out. Darkness reigns everywhere.'[20]

Doubtless the observation of the city as dirty, decayed and foul-smelling, which already by the eighteenth century brings with it a sense of its social topography, was also a necessary precondition of strategies to cleanse it;[21] but this still does not explain the great number of journeys into the 'underground'. More importantly, they broadened the image of the world. The view 'from below', which required the penetration of the world of night and the successful overcoming of its dangers, was meant to serve an understanding of the whole. The cities' inhabitants and visitors were frightened by the realization that they had hitherto lived in an incomplete world (of the imagination). Horror at the existence of the nocturnal sides of the city – the city one thought one knew so well – is transferred onto the inner life of the observer; this becomes particularly clear in those who do not wish to recognize the discovery and quickly rationalize it. In the *Gartenlaube* in 1872 A. Ragotzky, minister at the Stadtvogtei Berlin, wrote:

> It is a difficult task to write about criminality in Berlin. A picture is unfurled in which the great city, resplendent in the lustrous glow of its newly acquired imperial splendour, is represented from the point of view of one of its darkest night sides . . .
> If such a state of affairs [as in Paris] is less imaginable here, because we have a strong and authoritarian regime so intimately grown together with our people through a glorious centuries-long history, and because the character of our German people is different from that of the

243

French, we still should not take comfort from this, but rather pay heed to the warning voice of that terrible judgement of God [the Paris Commune]...[22]

Defences are useless, the existence of the city's night sides must be acknowledged. The question is what form of observation best serves this recognition.

FLÂNERIE

When walking in the city is discussed, there is an association, a concept which springs up almost of its own accord: that of the *flâneur*. *Flânerie*, today generally understood as the fine art of walking through a city slowly and attentively, one's appreciation bolstered by learning, has become a self-evident code word among lovers of big cities. With the 'urbanization' of the city and the formation of the city centre, in the midst of the activity of the street (and the reflection of this activity in literature) there emerges a character, the *flâneur*, the stroller, who has the time and leisure to go everywhere that the urban finds full expression 'and nature makes itself scarce '.[23] That is, on the boulevards and under the glass-roofed arcades built at the beginning of the nineteenth century, which, in combining the world of goods (exhibited in shop windows) and the opportunity to stroll, became the symbol of metropolitan life in the 1820s and 1830s; there the stroller with his many aliases – the *flâneur*, the *badaud*, the *promeneur solitaire* – was at home, a conscious urbanite.

Different authors, following Walter Benjamin, have tried to capture the 'socio-historical profile'[24] of this figure, its behaviour and its 'reasons for movement', to link it to a specific historical background, and to trace the changes in the 'type' in the succeeding period. I do not always find the results of such studies convincing, and I believe one of the reasons for this is the fact that the concept is too broad: far too much is to be read into the *flâneur*, is attributed to him. Let us read Benjamin:

> An intoxication comes over the one who walks aimlessly through the streets for a long time. With every step the walking itself gains greater power; the temptations of shops, bistros and smiling women grow less and less, while more and more irresistible becomes the magnetism of the next street corner, a distant mass of greenery, or the name of a street. Then comes hunger. He wants to know nothing of the hundred ways of satisfying it. Like an ascetic animal, he prowls through unknown

244

neighbourhoods until, in deepest exhaustion, he collapses in his cold, displeasing room.[25]

This passage from the notes and materials for the *Arcades Project* is indeed of central importance for any consideration of walking in the city. But does this have anything at all to do with the *flâneur* as we speak of him now? In another text, 'On Some Motifs in Baudelaire', Benjamin writes about the 'man of the crowd' discussed earlier: 'Baudelaire was content to equate the man of the crowd, in whose footsteps Poe's reporter roams this way and that through nocturnal London, with the type of the *flâneur*. We will not be able to follow him in this. The man of the crowd is no *flâneur*. In him composure has produced a manic space.'[26]

This in itself is plausible; but could we say that the one who prowls through unknown quarters 'like an ascetic animal' has a 'composed attitude'? All attempts to find a single structural or chronological order in metropolitan styles of walking are, in my view, destined to failure through self-contradiction. The problem with most descriptions is the fact that 'real' images are mixed up with 'imaginary', literary images. Poe's 'man of the crowd' is clearly a literary figure, but Benjamin's *flâneur* too is a construct, constructed of elements from both observation and literature. The idea that the 'composed' walker is followed by a 'manic' successor cannot be sustained; it seems to me rather that the one joins the other, and that both can be sometimes found in the same person. All the sources allow us to conclude that alongside the 'pure' type described by Benjamin there have been a multitude of other types of urban walkers: the more varied the city and the streets themselves, the more different walkers (and in time women walkers too) they have engendered. It makes no sense to try and bring all these forms together under the concept of the *flâneur*, and it is worth putting the question more precisely. Who walks, when, where, why, and how? The *functions* of walking in the city are as varied as its forms. For us, one characteristic is particularly important: some – certainly not all – walkers distinguished themselves as *good observers of the urban scene*, and it is this, not the name we give them, that makes their texts interesting. What Victor Fournel calls 'the art of *flânerie*' could also be given a different name:

> For those who can understand it and practise it this life is the most active and fruitful. An intelligent and conscious stroller [*badaud*], who

fulfils his duties with painstaking exactitude, that is, *who observes everything and remembers everything*, can play the most important role in the republic of the arts. This man is an ambulant daguerreotype, passionately preserving the slightest traces, and in him the course of events and the movement of the city are reproduced.[27]

Here *flânerie* and observation belong together: 'He who possesses a mind and a gift for observation, and who understands how to stroll, will learn more from the street life of Paris than from many fat books', wrote Ludwig Kalisch in 1872.[28] This is the programme, to learn from street life. This means learning how one should behave on the street in certain circumstances so as to be able to continue on one's way unharmed. It also means learning to form a general picture, as unified and as coherent as possible, from the multiplicity of views and events; this is a difficult task, precisely because the city is constantly changing. So the strollers are forced to go out repeatedly, to make sure again of their surroundings. It is this that leads to the 'topographical excesses'[29] and to the 'intoxication of the street'[30] described by Benjamin.

At night the enterprise becomes both easier and more difficult at the same time. The hectic pace of the day-time traffic slackens off, the atmosphere of the city calms down, and the streets become easier to walk again. But new restrictions limit the capacity for observation; in the interplay of light and shadow many outlines become more clear; others, however, disappear. Perception is as marked by the attraction of the forbidden as by the fear of it; and in the eyes of authority aimless drifting around, at least at night, is still suspicious:

> We do not know the art of taking a stroll, the art of the *flâneur* . . . But that young lady over there, she really seems to be strolling along at the greatest leisure. She is very pretty, too pretty, walking slowly and completely alone, swinging her handbag. Aha, aha! The policemen inspect her suspiciously. *In the busy city of Berlin leisurely perambulation and vice are more or less the same.*[31]

Even if it has its precursors, nocturnal *flânerie* is a child of the new illumination. But the walkers who went out onto the boulevards in the glow of the gas lamps, the *noctambules* of the 1830s and 1840s, took with them a pattern of thought and a type of behaviour from a time of greater darkness: certain texts, for example *Paris la nuit. Silhouettes* by Edouard Gourdon (1842), and *Paris la nuit* by Eugène de Mirecourt (1855), make use of the literary figure of the nocturnal

'Creepy tales': the cinema conserves past images of the night and itself becomes the new nocturnal attraction (Kurfürstendamm, Berlin, 1932).

demon Asmodeus, who shows the hero the city as *his* dominion, that is, as a mysterious realm, but at the same time the attempt is made to represent the (often imaginary) expedition through the city night as an expression of a real, novel creation of this nocturnal world. In many of these descriptions one finds an insight into the *new* beauty of the nocturnal city. Julius Rodenberg's view over night-time Paris has already been quoted; the chains of light are more to him, however, than a simple spectacle; they create the image of the city:

> In our field of vision there emerges a web of flames with countless fine threads: *the map of Paris*, drawn in shimmering strokes, the boulevards powerful skeins of light where they meet; the big and the small streets, filaments of light; the open squares, powerful nodes of flame, which shoot their shining rays in all directions – and all around, like a reddish belt of flames, the suburbs.
>
> This is what Paris looks like when its 40,000 gas flames burn – Paris by lamp-light, when the shimmering tide makes her beauty and every one of her temptations more tempting yet.[32]

### NIGHT-REVELLERS

> . . . [are what] one calls the people who wander the streets and alleys at night, making all kinds of unnecessary noise.[33]

This was the categorical definition still offered by a German dictionary at the end of the eighteenth century. In the decades that followed the concept of 'night-reveller' underwent changes: it was used – and still is today – mostly for people who visit places of nocturnal entertainment – bars, pubs, cabarets and revues – for their own amusement, and has not for a long time had any connection with disturbance of the nocturnal peace. In spite of this transformation from noisiness to conviviality, in the eyes of critics of the night the term retains a negative connotation. Thomas Burke sings the praises of the nocturnal pleasure-round:

> NIGHT LIFE . . . Night-club . . . Night-bird. There is something about the word Night, as about the word Paris, that sends through some Englishmen a shiver of misgiving, and through another type a current of undue delight. The latter never get over the excitement of Sitting Up Late. The others see any happening after midnight – even a game of snakes-and-ladders – as something verging on the unholy; as though Satan were never abroad in the sunlight. . .
>
> But despite restrictions, the spirit of the anthem of Night life, the

Won't-Go-Home-Till-The-Morning spirit, was never extinguished ... It might be called A Song Against All Parents, Guardians And Town Councillors.[34]

This – finally – is 'night life' as it is understood by most people: staying up late and not going home, so as to enjoy the goods offered by the leisure industry. The night-walkers, however, *aimant la nuit pour elle-même*, loving the night for its own sake, go to such establishments only briefly, in order to refresh themselves for their long journey; their goal is the street and direct, unhindered access to the night. Of course these places, the cafés, restaurants, *cafés-concerts*, honky-tonks, variety theatres and bars are part of the furniture of the nocturnal street, without which it would lose a great deal of its power of attraction. A large part of the public is on its way to one of these places, moving on from one to the next, or returning home directly; only a minority finds greater pleasure in a solitary walk. But for them, too, part of the pleasure of the night is their knowledge of the existence of these places, knowledge of their accessibility – and of the possibility of escaping them again.

'In a Music Hall': proletarian forms of entertainment at the moment of their *embourgeoisement*. Lithograph after a drawing by Alfred Concanen, London, c.1870.

As the evening and night-time streets become increasingly lively, establishments of nocturnal entertainment change their character, opening up onto the street, offering the chance to come in for a brief moment, and to leave again at will; they already advertise their services on the street, visible and attractive to passers-by; they open, or begin their programme, at a certain time, sometimes causing queues on the pavement; they must respect closing times and they discharge their customers *en masse* onto the street. The characters of the street and its 'establishments' condition each other, and together they make for an area's 'good' or 'bad' reputation. Yet the idea has gained acceptance that the attraction of a city at night can be judged by the number, variety and the quality of its entertainment establishments. Theodor Fontane has told of a pretty scene from London which brings this out:

> 'Do you know London?'
> 'Well, what do you mean by know? Perhaps I could say "Yes", because I walk about a lot. But really I think I should have to say "No".'
> 'Well, let's put the question more precisely, then. Do you know the seamen's pubs in Wapping?'
> 'No.'
> 'Or Punch and Judy?'
> 'No.'
> 'Well then, so I know what's what, and you are still an innocent.'[35]

In all the great cities, mid-nineteenth-century travellers describe the newly appearing places of entertainment, and as in the example of London above, these establishments are often seen as 'typical' of the cities in which they are to be found, even if many similarities emerge when cities are compared. In this they represent a doubly important articulation, between older and newer forms of entertainment, and between the particular characteristics of the individual cities and the model image of the metropolis.

There exist numerous studies of individual establishments, or on the development of entertainment in specific areas of the cities,[36] but a comprehensive history of leisure and entertainment, an overall view of its forms and functions, has still to be written. Such a history would give a more detailed insight into what was going on indoors, and could significantly supplement this account which concentrates on the street. In this way the links – and the differences – between 'inner' and 'outer' night life, the mutual influence of *lieux publics* and *voie publique* would become visible.

The authorities paid equal attention to both areas, because in their eyes the danger of the night was not just that 'criminals' about on the streets would find in them 'dens' and unsupervisable retreats. Immorality, too, found a new field of activity in these enclosed spaces: dance halls, ballrooms and clip-joints 'with female service' were always the subject of (vice) police control. This was even more the case for the big music halls and variety theatres.

In his *History of Variety* Ernst Günther has filled in the stages of its development: created in late eighteenth-century England, the 'pub and saloon theatres' provided a generally (petit)-bourgeois public with drama, dance, circus and burlesque in indiscriminate succession, 'in association with gastronomic consumption (and disguised prostitution)'. Compared to the more genteel music hall, their programme, says Günther, was vulgar. In France during the 1840s, from the *cafés chantants* where everyday songs of the street and the city were performed, there emerged the *cafés-concerts*, café theatres 'with a marked tendency towards coarse or lascivious eroticism', whose golden age was to be the Second Empire (1852–70). From all these roots there developed the big variety theatres: the Folies Bergères opened in Paris in 1869, followed by the Moulin Rouge in 1889. Already in 1876 the Folies were announcing the appearance of the 'most naked women in the world' (in flesh-toned costumes), but it was only in February 1892 that the first undressing scene appeared in a music-hall programme: 'Mado goes to bed' was banned by the vice police, as was the somewhat more daring 'Yvette goes to bed' of 1894, but a year later 'undressing scenes were the order of the day',[37] although the variety theatres, a fundamental part of the city night, remained under constant police surveillance.

In enclosed spaces night life can more easily be controlled, domesticated, civilized, reduced to a manageable scale. This is a contradictory process: in the authorities' eyes the street represents a fundamentally dangerous terrain, and so there are attempts to 'cleanse' it, to drive out the elements of disorder and immorality. As the Paris boulevards were ever more lavishly provided with cafés, with panoramas and theatres, shopping arcades and display windows, their increased accessibility to larger groups, to a 'decent' public, also brought with it a 'cleansing': the less respectable establishments had to move to different areas, and the amateurs of 'dissolute' night life had to follow them there. In the eyes of other guardians of morality than the police the institutions established in this way were far more monstrous, very likely more than anything else because they were withdrawn from the public view and attempted to imitate the mysterious atmosphere of the street itself. Enclosed spaces excited the imagination of those who were about on the streets. Behind their curtains the moralists suspected 'excesses of all kind', 'indescribable scenes' and 'requests which human shame simply refuses to describe'.

In the course of time these establishments took over some functions of the street, toning them down, institutionalizing them, so to speak, at the same time. Yet the outrage they inspired was even more wordily expressed. This becomes clear in two descriptions of Paris: the first from Siegfried Kracauer, describing the street entertainment to which the young Jacques Offenbach would have been exposed in the years around 1850, the second from Maurice Talmeyr, about the *café-concerts* and music halls of the years around 1900:

> The Paris streets of those days offered a spectacle that might have been designed for a young man who had performed in pub gardens and felt at home in a crowd. On the Boulevard du Temple . . . there was constant festivity . . . In conjunction with the constant noise of the fairground the whirlpool of cruelty, monstrosity, and acts of skill produced a gaiety as variegated as the coloured sticks of rock, and which encompassed all the original motions of the mind from voluptuous horror to childish amazement . . . The whole street was dedicated to pleasure.[38]

> People smoke and drink, they come in and go out as they please, and their eyes and ears are exposed to sights and sounds of the most suggestive and unbelievably equivocal nature. The *café-concert* is the paradise of libertinism and of the most obdurate mindlessness. On top of this are the low prices and the excitation of all the senses that one can have for almost nothing.[39]

Whatever one thought of them, establishments and the street together constituted 'night life'; the linking elements were the 'stroller'and the 'night-reveller', who moved from place to place in search of pleasure and according to their whims. These establishments also provided, as Johannes Willms has noted, an 'experience of freedom' which was rooted in the fact that the programme 'could be attended to in a discontinuous manner',[40] visitors being able to enter and leave at any time. They could also move on from one establishment to another, and in this way make up their own programme for the night – though the commercialization of entertainment and the uniformity that this brought with it at the same time contributed

252

Electric light produces new forms in the nocturnal city: façades on the place Pigalle
in Paris, in the middle the Moulin Rouge, c.1930.

Light as advertising medium: for the Gare du Nord in Paris, Paz and Silva designed a
glowing locomotive which advertised the trains for the 1930 Exposition de Liège.
Photograph by Léon Gimpel, 1930.

In the alternating play of light and shadow the 'top' and 'bottom' of the city also become an aesthetic experience. Photograph by Seeberger: *Rue Rollin, Paris,* before 1939.

The Surrealists drifted in the 'wind of chance', which wafted them to the sites of the old night life. Photograph by Seeberger: *The Boulevard de Clichy at night*, before 1939.

The nocturnal walk through the whole of Paris belongs to the past; pleasure seekers use the Metro at place Blanche. Photograph by Seeberger, 1935.

'Dans les rues' is now just a film title. Night life has withdrawn into enclosed spaces again: the Moulin Rouge in Paris.

to a growing expropriation of enjoyment. This commercialization found particular expression in the banality of what was on offer: like the increasingly numerous 'guides' to places of entertainment, the events play on the strollers' pleasure in the forbidden, moving on the borderline of the permissible (and making a living from it); they have the flavour of notoriety, of the twilight, of the (somewhat) dangerous.

When foreigners come to Paris they want to discover the much praised bustle, and professional 'chaperones' lead them for money to selected night-spots. Often enough they appear there as idiots from the provinces; but even when the visitors follow the *Guides de la vie nocturne*, they often enough end up where the chaperone would also have taken them. There is no real threat of danger. In the guides and the night literature of the years after 1880, during the *belle époque*, another image of the night develops: it is not any longer described in its contradictions, as it had been earlier; the nights of pleasure are abstracted from the context of the multiplicity and contradiction of the whole night, and are represented as a world of their own, which apparently has nothing to do with the other world of poverty and misery. Where the wretchedness is ever mentioned, the guide suggests a quick walk past it: 'You forget these problems at Maxim's and the Café Américain.'[41] From this irony there soon emerges a method: the visiting of places of entertainment appears more and more often as a way of escaping contact with the dark street, avoiding acquaintance with the unhappy parts of the night. So is created the impression recorded by Hans Ostwald, that 'All these dark spots in the picture of Berlin have taken on forms which remain absolutely within the circle of our civilization'.[42] This might mean various things, for instance that 'civilization' has now learned to accept the existence of its own shadow side. But one glance at the texts of contemporary reporters on the night will quickly disabuse one: 'Berlin now wakes up, in a way, for the second time: in the morning for work, in the evening for pleasure!'; 'A night time for sleeping no longer exists!'; 'The sight of the unbelievable motion of people, lights and vehicles that now presents itself to the eye, that is Berlin!'; 'Berlin nights are so colourful, so strongly pulsating, so hot and so very filled with the constant hunt for pleasure and entertainment'; 'For the Berliner, the safety valve for the noisy day is the turbulent night'; 'In the Friedrichstrasse life does not stop at all, and in the early morning the chords of a powerful symphony of almost Bacchanalian lust for life are still roaring out'.[43]

257

Unsurprisingly, the descriptions of actual night life cannot compete with this din. In *Berlin for Connoisseurs, A Tourist Guide to Day and Night in the German Imperial Capital* (1912) or the earlier *Berlin by Night, A Comprehensive Guide to Nocturnal Berlin from Early Morning till the Late Evening* (c.1900) there is a great deal of talk of the night – 'Its veils often bring greater poetry than the day'; 'in its arms the coldest day person . . . finds more lasting impressions'; the hours of night have a 'sweeter, more blissful meaning than those of the day', breathing a 'poetic perfume, a poetry of passion, love and freedom'– going on and on in a saccharine tone so distant from the reality of the night. But when it is a question of describing what is actually going on, one finds moralizing discourse in the guides, outrage about vice on the street, weak images written up in a weak language. The walkers long for the bustle, entertainment and attraction of the night, but they fear its threatening sides, whose existence they nevertheless suspect: pure entertainment is stale. In March 1930 the Berlin magazine *UHU* poked fun at 'what our fathers loved':

> While the acrobats struggled in tremendously tall double stand-up collars until they almost exploded, and the clowns in top hats and tails paraded as if at a funeral, the feminine muse remained scantily dressed. The dancers would rustle their undergarments, the soubrettes were as much about their legs as their voices, their costume a little bit too short at the top or at the bottom . . . In the hall one could comfortably sip one's pint of beer and smoke one's cigar, whilst lending an eye and an ear to the performers on the stage; to sup on the terrace with wine and champagne while at the same time admiring a pretty variety programme, this was seen as chic, as ultra-sophisticated, the pinnacle of the joys of life.[44]

Occasionally, in the midst of the entertainment, one might feel a certain melancholy. In his *Montmartre Nights* Joseph Kessel describes how visiting bars and other establishments, 'd'abord par plaisir, puis par besoin, enfin par habitude',[45] loses its attraction. From repetition grows sadness, yet hope as well: sometime, the dreams have to become reality, and when they do, it will be at night.

PLEASURE IN THE FORBIDDEN

Where the revellers fail, other night-walkers succeed almost against their will: on their excursions, really intended for reassurance, they experience the fascination of the night. Already in the seventeenth

Nachtzauber in Berlin
Der Potsdamer Platz

Berlin promoted itself with a series of postcards promising a '*magic of the night*' that in these pictures always seems very orderly. The Potsdamer Platz, Europe's busiest intersection, tempts the visitor with the Haus Vaterland. Postcard, 1920s.

Berlin bei Nacht:
Friedrichstrasse-Lindenpassage.

And even the famous corner of Friedrichstraße/Unter den Linden seems deserted. Postcard, 1920s.

century, in John Gay's *Trivia, or The Art of Walking the Streets of London*,[46] there are passages whose outward respectability – 'O! may thy Virtue guard thee through the Roads' – cannot conceal a secret pleasure in the forbidden. Clearly there are night-walkers who seek an encounter with the sins of the night, with prostitution for example – but not, or at least not only to use it, but also in order to have a look around the world of virtue endangered, and possibly to endure risky experiences. The night offers opportunities to undergo risk, to overcome dangers – and the walk through the night offers solitude and conviviality at the same time. The possibility of succeeding in finding such a mixture overcomes fear. Pleasure in the forbidden is also the pleasure of observing one's own fear and dealing with it whilst walking. Here too the opportunity can lead to obsession: 'J'ai besoin de tout voir, de tout étudier, de tout connaître,' says Eugène de Mirecourt:[47] 'I have to see everything, to study everything, to know everything.'

There are a few examples of how such passions develop. *The Night-Walker: Or, Evening Rambles in Search of Lewd Women, with the Conferences Held with Them &c.* is the title of John Dunton's very peculiar publication of 1696, in which he describes in detail how he went about night after night, following women 'walking alone', how he spoke to them, inviting them to join him, and once he had them indoors addressing them with stern moral sermons. On the street he would behave like a potential customer. Similar endeavours have already been described in the section on 'Midnight mission'. Many moralizing night-walkers were unable to resist the 'provocation of the senses', the 'sensual excitement' and the 'alarming of the senses by the city'.[48]

It could very well be that the missionaries – and it would be easy to find further examples – experienced a repressed, denied or resisted erotic pleasure in their activities. They too 'penetrate' into the nocturnal city, they too seek the extraordinary experience, they too participate in the cycle of chance encounters, they too see how far they can go. Where the extraordinary can occur, where fear is mixed with pleasure, where the senses are addressed and nobody knows this better than the hunters of immorality – the erotic is at play:

> The gentlemen of the general synod sometimes also make a pilgrimage to the Friedrichstrasse, where it is at its most lively and interesting. There they can find so many things in its repulsive malignity against which they then can warn across the land. Oh, yes, Babel gives them

great cause for concern . . . Babel on the Spree, where sin, the people's downfall, walks abroad in sunlit day as well as in the bright electric night.[49]

Probably the 'frisson of curiosity', as Leopold von Sacher-Masoch put it, strikes as it will; but it is not too much to assume that the minds of those who ceaselessly concern themselves with sin are particularly receptive to it. In the greedy search for vice that is also shared by the authors of the popular 'Histories of morals' there is more than the simple love of adventure, more than just the pride in being able to withstand these challenges. Indeed, authors such as Eduard Fuchs, for example, who sees death symbolized in 'temptation, which lies in wait for man, standing enticingly in his path',[50] or Hans Erasmus Fischer, who in his *Manners and Morals of the Docks* strings one terrible description of 'horrible events' after another, are reporting on something else: they testify to a fear-laden *erotic relationship to the city*, a relationship which engages all their senses. With every visit to the nocturnal city they oscillate between recruitment and courtship, lust for conquest and yearning for submission. They would like to 'plunge into' the city night, to be recognized there as

The morality commission too fell prey to 'the frisson of sexual curiosity' (Sacher-Masoch): 'Your productions seem to be most reprehensible from the moral point of view. Could you please repeat the same.' Drawing by Ferdinand von Rezniczek, 1899.

initiates, to master the rules which apply there. As lovers they are always shocked, less by the unreasonable demands of the city than by the fact that they are capable of meeting them. From this fearful shock – which is the obverse of their great fascination – there develops a hate-filled language with which they punish the street for revealing their weakness.

The stage of being in love, the state of suspense, cannot be sustained for long, even at a level less extreme than this. The most important disruptive factor in this, here too, is the unequal relationship between the sexes: women and men do not enter the nocturnal city as equals. Even if their desires seem the same, they do not have the same opportunities available to them to give them life. 'Erotic expeditions' remain, as a rule, the preserve of men. Here too the entertainment industry offers itself as a substitute; it creates the illusion of satisfaction, and it domesticates the feelings. On 15 September 1928 the *Weltbühne* quoted from the matchless advertisement for a new venue:

> Newly opened,
> the most beautiful and largest place of entertainment in the world.
> Variety from 9 till 3 o'clock.

> The press writes:
> . . .An establishment such as Berlin has never known, which is revue, variety, theatre, cabaret, dance hall and restaurant all in one . . .
> *The chaotic bustle all about one produces a bourgeois feeling of cosiness.*

There are a number of revealing studies on the emergence of sociology from the 'spirit', from the tradition of social reportage.[51] There is a long tradition of visiting poor neighbourhoods, the slums of the big cities, 'penetrating' into miserable districts, in which the themes of social research overlap with those of social work and charitable activity. With night-walks intended to serve the purposes of security too, one observes with the passage of time how an initial experience of shock at the transgression of limits gives way to a sense of banality, how the aimless wandering becomes a targeted, well-prepared and deliberately planned reconnaissance. Normative filters and ideological moments come into play, and as a rule the confines of preconceived ideas – how the city is meant to be – narrows the spectrum of images of the city. The results of such reconnaissance walks are made use of in strategies for the establishment of order and security; related to this is the fact that the motives and method of reconnaissance remain obscure to those who are visited and observed. In the texts which report on such walks for social reconnaissance, one obviously finds fewer signs of pleasure in the forbidden: the erotic components of the night seem to touch more, and also to demand more, than the criminological or the social. But these reporters too take their moral standards for a walk; they are, let us emphasize this, no *flâneurs*. When a city walker becomes a researcher, because he wants to tell his newspaper or his university what he sees, he has abandoned the ideal of *flânerie* – that is, its carefreeness, its irresponsibility. He can no longer walk aimlessly.

## 'NIGHT SENDS EACH TO HIS OWN PLACE'

Outside the doors of the pubs waits the nocturnal city, the subject in the nineteenth century of a beautiful hymn of praise by Richard Le Gallienne: 'London, London, our delight/Great flower that opens but at night/Great City of the Midnight sun/Whose day begins when day is done.'[52]

There may be many correspondences, but in the end it does seem that London is being defined by another form of perception of the night than the other two cities. H. V. Morton sums up: 'When night falls over London ancient and primitive things come to our streets; for night is sinister, dramatic; it brings with it something of the jungle. Beasts of prey and great cities alone in nature remain awake when darkness comes; the one in search of death, the other in search of an extra hour of life.'[53]

Only a few turn their attention to the street; Robert Machray in his *Night Side of London* makes a small exception at the beginning of his study which takes as its subject 'the first two years of the twentieth century'. This is Piccadilly Circus by night:

> For a few minutes the Circus is rather quiet. A bus now and again rumbles up, and interposes itself between you and the Fountain, hiding that mocking image. A girl of the night, on her prowl for prey, casts a keen glance at you, and flits silently past like a bat. Behind you – you can see her with the tail of your eye – pauses a Painted Lady, picture-hatted, black-haired, belladonna'd, rouged, overdressed, but not more so than many a Great Lady. She makes a true picture of the town, of one aspect of the Night Side of London, as she stands with her back to the down-drawn, dull-red blinds of the shop window in the rear. A blind beggar now breaks in upon you with a hoarse, indistinct cry, that sounds like many curses compressed into one . . .[54]

263

*'Ever-Ready*: the car gave a new mobility, and an elegant way of avoiding direct contact with the street. Postcard, London, 1920s.

'Crime without passion': in the gaze of the elegant gentleman one sees a remnant of the yearning that once drove the night-revellers onto the streets. Photograph by Bill Brandt, London, c.1935.

This is the scene shortly before the theatre and the music halls empty out onto the street. 'And then a few more minutes pass, and the Circus suddenly buzzes with life; it hums like a giant hive. Here are movement, colour, and a babel of sounds! Till you get used to it, the effect is somewhat stunning.' Thomas Burke communicates a fascination that does not last long: 'And for ten minutes, or a quarter of an hour, it is as if all the world and his wife and his daughters, his sisters and his cousins and his aunts, drove past you.'[55] The curtain quickly falls on this slice of life, and the 'sylph-like forms' and 'pink-flushed happy faces' are gone as quickly as they appeared. Back into the lounges, the cafés and the beer-gardens, and half an hour later it is 'comparatively quiet' outside. The observer encounters individual pleasure seekers: 'you see, however, these daring fellows disappear into the interior' of the next establishment. Burke at least stays outside: 'now you take time to classify these night-walkers of the Circus into types.' Let us follow him: There is the 'picker-up of unconsidered trifles', an old man who walks up and down the street, his head bowed, living from what he finds; there is the match-seller with the piercing eyes; there are girls, 'wandering wisps of painted humanity that dye the London night with rouge'. There are stories in every face, and only the night brings them to light, yet for Burke even this brightly illuminated night is not the end, or the expression of its true nature: 'It may be questioned if London by night, for sheer, downright impressiveness, does not seize upon, grip and hold you, as even London by day does not. From midnight till about two o'clock in the morning the streets gradually show fewer and fewer signs of life and movement. From two o'clock to four there is a lull, a quiet, a hush, a vast enfolding, mysterious, awe-inspiring silence.' As if the flood had retreated and had left the shore, 'The city sleeps!'

Not everyone sleeps. The newspaper offices and the printing houses work, the train stations are still alive, a few clubs are still open. And the prostitutes are at work. But on the streets it is quiet, it seems. Only those who look more closely will spot 'the waifs and strays of London', the muffled figures trying to sleep on park benches. There are the coffee-stall keepers and other 'providers for the children of the night'. Burke suggests a nocturnal educational tour, which should ideally not be undertaken on foot but by bicycle: From Hyde Park Corner 'you run along Piccadilly to the Circus', Regent Street, Oxford Circus, Tottenham Court Road, New Oxford Street, 'say as far as the corner where is Mudie's well-known library'.

Pedestrians, however, are closer to it. There are still nocturnal characters who know about everything that happens on the street. Photograph by Felix H. Man: *Night-seller of walnuts and peanuts*, London, 1934.

A coffee-stall on this corner supplies at least 20 night-walkers – types like the 'young graduates in the school of crime' or the quarrelling couple. Back to Tottenham Court Road, in the direction of Euston Street, 'a street which has about as malodorous a reputation as any in London, particularly with regard to its night side'. Another coffee-stall where the 'bad men and bad women of the lowest types' can only be made out from a distance. We continue 'across Holborn, and by Cheapside, into the City proper which is now hushed and quiet, even as some forgotten city of the dead'. It is precisely that part of the city which is liveliest during the day that now seems dead. 'You pass through it, and at Aldgate you are on the edge of the other London, the East End – cut off from the West by the City. You reach Whitechapel, and halt in the spacious Whitechapel Road; you behold more cab-stands, more coffee-stalls.'

The popularity of this strange tour, which hardly notices more of the night than a slight breeze from the bicycle ride – why is it so interesting? This too is a tour of reconnaissance and reassurance, whose results – it's not as bad as all that, everything is under control – seem to have been certain even in advance. There was a time, says

267

The fashionable world leaves the theatres. The night awaits. Photograph by Felix. H. Man: *Shaftesbury Avenue, London, as the theatres empty*, 1934.

Outside East End children 'admire the nocturnal elegance of the West End public'. Photograph by Felix H. Man, London, 1934.

Burke, when the Radcliffe Highway, for example, 'presented in low life what the Haymarket and Piccadilly showed in high, or at least better-dressed life'. But this time is over; 'vice of the old historic, full-flavoured, fire-ship sort has been relegated to the side streets.' And these are not gone into. What is there, then, for the 'student of human nature' to discover? The fact that the often evoked 'contra-dictions' are in equilibrium, that things are not so terrible here and are not so wonderful there, is reassuring to a public for whom the city is dissolving in front of their eyes into something more and more confusing. The night reduces the chaos and brings clear outlines back.

In a later book, *Nights in Town*, published in 1915, Thomas Burke's hymn of praise is even more forceful. 'London by Night is the loveliest thing in the world,' he says, and, 'there is no night in all the world so rich in delicate delights as the London night.' And again he invites us on a tour: 'We will have a bloodthirsty night in the athletic saloons of Bethnal Green. We will have a bitter night in the dockside saloons. We will have a sickening night in sinister places of no name and no locality, where the proper people do not venture. We will have a glittering night in the Hoxton bars.' And it never stops, being intended simply to show that 'night life', as Marc J. Bouman claims it was called in London earlier than in the other cities, 'seems a natural component of city life'.

Only in the mid-1920s does there appear literature in which the London night is celebrated. Donald Maxwell's *The New Lights o' London* contains drawings and texts by the author, 'impressions of the glamour and magic of London at night'.[56] Romance is the key-word to the collection: 'Night time is the time to prowl round the city and study.' But what is being studied here is innocuous: the old churches, the bridges, the parks – a 'fairy land' in the nocturnal city. These nocturnal scenes are beautiful – and still. Stephen Graham in his *London Nights* found a phrase which also expresses the approach of Maxwell and of a whole series of other authors: night stands for 'the mystery, the beauty and the suffering of London'.[57]

Graham is still more of a reporter than Maxwell. His picture of the night is marked by social differences. 'Our days are democratic; our nights are feudal. For if there is a seeming equality by day, there is an evident disparity by night . . . The past has a stronger hold on the night than it has on the day. Equality and fraternity come with the sun, lightening and warming us on our way – but they go down with

269

the same. Night sends each to his home, to his own place.'[58] Only he who sets out on a walk through the streets will discover that 'At the same time, London is more beautiful by night; there is a poetry in it which is missed by day', and that 'a feeling of exaltation creeps into the minds of those who watch while London sleeps . . . London at night speaks to the heart, telling its dreams of humanity that has passed.' London is essentially a dark city. 'Our walls are dark. Fog dims our far-off lights; our street lamps have haloes.' The sober, the working city discovers its counterpart in 'romantic and fantastic effects, as if our London were an unreal world'. There is another picture that should not be left out, made unforgettable by Jack London: nobody is meant to sleep in these half-public places, and 'A constable on night duty makes his round and taps the sleepers, bidding them wake up and put their feet down.'[59]

This prohibition on sleep means that many of those who have no home are about all night in the city: 'Many frankly walk all night and get a good sleep somewhere during the day', and 'One commonly meets the night-walkers near the coffee-stalls. You can tell them by the state of their boots. They walk to keep warm . . . The coffee-stalls are a great institution of the London night. Their red-painted panels glow in the darkness.' Here are the meeting places of the few nocturnal passers-by: 'Thither resort the night-watchmen, or pressmen who have put the morning paper ready, or MPs from a late sitting, or men and women from dances, or heavily-muffled workmen on night jobs . . . Upon occasion duke meets drab, and prince meets pauper.'

The geographical divide is vast: entertainment can be found in the West End, but even if it is a night place the East End is no place of entertainment: 'It is a strange, eerie experience to spend a night walking the streets of the East End. You are alone, as it were, with the dead, until the alarm clocks begin to go off. To walk [there] at three, with no other soul in view . . . is an experience not to be forgotten. You might be exploring the tombs of buried London thousands of years hence; you are out of time and the hour; you have entered the grand mystery of life.'

It was in the mid-1920s too that Ralph Nevill published a comparative study of night life in London and Paris: 'The "night life" of great European capitals as it exists today is a social development of a purely modern kind.' In his view the nineteenth century appears as a period of increasing control over a time that had hitherto remained

A little romance in the modern city? The horse-drawn carriage travels more slowly and takes on a new charm. Photograph by Felix H. Man: *A hansom cab in Regent Street, London,* 1934.

free; the story he has to tell is the 'story of the gradual decay of freedom as regards public amusements in modern London'. The eighteenth century saw 'little attempt at interference', and 'a good many resorts remained open all night'.[60] For his own days, the 1920s, Nevill wishes the return of such a freedom, but circumstances have changed irrevocably.

WALKING AIMLESSLY

The expeditions so far have presented many different *noctambules* with their varying characteristics and passions; now, as we approach the end of our journey and already have *plus d'habitude* in walking the nocturnal streets, we meet a night-walker who has already been mentioned several times. Different ingredients of the night-walk come together in this figure, their faded traces reassembled, subordinated to another aim: 'La marche nocturne comme quête de soi dans la ville', the nocturnal walk as search for oneself in the city. Here again one finds the motifs of the investigative walk, as described by Wilhelm Heinrich Riehl but without the folklorization of the metropolis; here we find love of the city and a deep yearning which goes beyond the limits of the search for sexual satisfaction. It goes without saying that these night-walkers are less talkative than their pleasure-seeking colleagues, and that the traces of their solitary walks cannot be found in the police archives; as a rule they are supplied with work and home, so that the registers of visitors to the night shelters are hardly likely to give us any information about them. It isn't easy then to find out about them, but when nothing else helps then there are always stories:

> There once was a Hofrat [privy counsellor] from Leipzig, whose face had been completely disfigured by a cancer (his former friends thought it was syphilis). After the death of his wife he left his home town, where he had until then been a respected citizen, and went to Dresden. There he lived in a hotel, but he was unhappy, because he dared not go out onto the street with his ravaged face. But one day a doctor suggested to him: 'You must become a night person!' The Hofrat followed his suggestion, and from then on went out into the streets only at night. Soon he knew the night and the nocturnal city well, and he loved them, because they were not as hostile to him as the day. Every now and then on his walks he would encounter people 'whom some fate had flushed out into the night': late drinkers, lovers, 'bad women', night-watchmen, police officers, 'even a hurrying doctor or men on their thieving way'.

And he realized that there was still one task left for him: he led groups of blind people through the night, and taught them how to find their way about on the streets.

This story of 'God's night-watchman'[61] is very charming and very serious, and perhaps it is not even an invention. It touches the solitary night-walkers on the nerve. In the eyes of their respectable neighbours, those who for no obvious reason spend hours walking through the night are behaving strangely, abnormally. As a rule one works during the day, going about town on one's business, and night is a time for rest, for relaxation. The rule allows – as we have seen, in the course of time more and more generously – the night hours to be dedicated to 'pleasure', but here too certain behavioural rules must be observed. It is permissible to go window-shopping, to visit restaurants, bars, theatres or cinemas, it is even possible for men to visit brothels, if they exercise the necessary discretion. All these evening enterprises are *purposeful*, they follow unwritten but effective laws, which have been laid down not by the night, but, as can easily be seen on closer inspection, by the day.

If someone goes against this – diurnal – efficiency and simply walks, *without being able to say where he is going*, observers suspect that something is 'not in order' – perhaps not even unjustly; for again and again in the biographies of lonely night-walkers we find moments of shock, motifs of a rupture with the ordinary. The ravaged face of the Leipzig Hofrat is a successful metaphor for the experience of suddenly finding oneself outside society, outside the daily routine for any reason. Once one has left the regular life of the majority behind, it can be rejoined only with difficulty, not only because society is suspicious of the one who has become an outsider, but also because from his new point of view he finds this whirl from which he has been ejected alien and almost comical.

There is a nice illustration of this is in the memoirs of the con-man Harry Domela; from a professional point of view, he understood the artificiality of normality very well. Thrown out on the street, he developed a new relationship to the world in which he had resided for a short while; 'with the distance of an awakening mind' he observed the once familiar and now suddenly 'totally unknown world: a vast city like Berlin brings those who walk through her with open eyes an endless wealth of opportunities to widen their horizons . . . We do not have a goal, and still suddenly all tiredness has vanished.'[62]

At the beginning there is despair and envy of those who 'belong', a yearning for 'life' and shame at being an outcast. Domela avoids the streets of the rich, because he is ashamed of his appearance. But little by little curiosity grows, and with his increasing connoisseurship he grows fonder of the night, in the end going out every night, entering wealthy neighbourhoods without embarrassment, a walking provocation. Admittedly one cannot develop a pattern from this. The 'false prince' was homeless, he had to stay on the streets and he does not romanticize the experience. But still he presents a path which – under less extreme conditions – has also been walked by others: the night offers a refuge, although an uncomfortable one, and the possibility (no less uncomfortable) of finding out something about oneself.

Only when there are no more socially acceptable justifications for their presence on the street can the solitary night-walkers' dialogue with the city begin. Then they themselves become more open, '*disponible*', to the city's vital signs – they come to trust her.[63] The nocturnal walk through the city can appeal to *memory*; it can revive feelings once thought lost, which find no expression in the day; it can awaken a new sense of beauty; diving in, the night-wanderer discovers 'the whole fauna of human fantasies' which, as Louis Aragon says, lives 'in the dimly lit zones of human activity';[64] he discovers the parts of fear and courage living within him, and he finds possibilities hidden in himself which he had not once had to realize: 'It seemed as if I knew nothing of the night,' wrote Philippe Soupault, 'and suddenly I remembered the long walks during which I could have committed the most forbidden acts without being noticed.'[65] Obviously the night really reaches – at least for those who have been wounded, outcast, pushed to the margins in some way – certain sensors in the consciousness, which are not available to the day. The solitary night-walkers suffer under the light which follows them everywhere, and against their will they become scouts for the 'night life' they mistrust. With their search for darkness they keep alive the traces of the past in the nights of today.

# vi An End: Big City Nights Around 1930

*One has to point out a change that has come about only recently, and which may have escaped the attention even of those who witnessed the process . . . It concerns the organization of Parisian life, or more precisely, the manifestation of nocturnal life in Paris.*

L'Illustration, March 1933[1]

One of the most impressive books about night in the big cities is *Paris de nuit*, a collection of photographs by Brassaï, who was a Hungarian, accompanied by a text by the French journalist Paul Morand. The pictures show the *whole* of nocturnal Paris from above, from the tower of the church of Notre Dame, and also from below, from the world of narrow alleyways and cheap entertainment. In a second book, *Paris secret*, Brassaï told how these night pictures came to be published:

> During my early years in Paris, from 1924 onwards, I led the life of a night bird, going to sleep at sunrise and getting up at sunset, and I criss-crossed the city from Montmartre to Montparnasse. I became a photographer so as to be able to capture in pictures everything that fascinated and even enchanted me in this nocturnal Paris, even though I had until then taken no particular notice of photography, had even mistrusted it. This was the genesis of the book *Paris de nuit*, which appeared in 1933.[2]

It was the experience of the night that made Brassaï a photographer; this need to capture what so quickly escapes the eye and the memory is characteristic of many night-walkers, and one finds it expressed again and again in different texts. Brassaï was one of the first to exploit the new technical possibilities of night photography, but what is more important is that the book expressed a certain feeling of the times, that something was coming to an end: a long history of the Parisian night, whose forms had just begun to change decisively, yet whose last traces were still just visible.

The idea that the years around 1930 had seen the 'end of the night' in its familiar form can also be found in texts from Berlin, where it could easily be dismissed as particular to that city if it had been suggested only by reflection on the National Socialists' seizure of power. Parisian authors, however, were even more emphatic on the 'transformation du décor de la vie nocturne' observed in their own city: 'The external appearance of Paris in 1930', Brassaï goes on to say, 'was no longer at all the same as it had been in 1928 . . . In these two years the atmosphere in Paris had changed.'[3] He refers to the worldwide economic crisis, which had also affected France and ended the period of 'affluence and carefreeness'. It was not only the external appearance but also the imagery of the Parisian night that had changed. It was in 1930 as well that H. von Wedderkop wrote in *Der Querschnitt* that Berlin film audiences' enthusiasm for René Clair's film *Sous les toits de Paris* would be touching, did it not also reveal 'something that is very sad, probably because there is nothing that can be done about it': the film has a somewhat ghostlike quality, because it 'conjures up a world that no longer exists'.[4]

Nothing could be done, not so much about the fact that there were no 'apaches' left, that the romance of the underworld had outlived itself, but rather about the realization of this loss. Paris was now only a picture book from the past, and it seemed as though the pictures had all been done, as if the possibility of making new, exciting, adventurous discoveries in the city – and with this the necessity of 'going out' oneself – were no longer there. Those who were still interested in the night could (and had to) content themselves with surrogates, with things already lived. Even if he intended it differently, Klaus Mann's judgement in his autobiography is devastating: 'Parisian night life is a *natural and integral part of Parisian life.*'[5] The stage has been set, the parts cast, night can be entered no differently than the day. In this way the idea that one can 'turn night into day' in the city acquires a totally different meaning: not only can one live the night 'as well', but night is now much more subjected to the laws of day; its threatening parts have been exorcized.

Similar references to Berlin can also be found without difficulty: in 1930 Jean Giraudoux described the much-praised nocturnal revelry of Berlin as 'a daytime growth, like a brothel or a cheap club';[6] Ivan Goll described Berlin night life to his French readers as a cheap imitation of Paris, a 'pseudo-Montparnasse',[7] and in 1929 the *Weltbühne* sneered at 'the few provincials who still allow themselves to be disappointed by Berlin's night life in this area [by the Friedrichstrasse railway station]'.[8] In a report on a trial in 1930 the *Vossische Zeitung*

The police ideal: the patrol can see into the glass houses, and everyone is asleep. But they are wrong: 'Do not believe that it is only want or uncertainty, or the lack of a home or a key, that drives people to wander in the night: oh no, there are also people who do this from passion, from an inborn distaste for bedtime, honourable people too, by the way' (Julius Rodenberg, 1867). Undated illustration by Ch. Girod.

poked fun at the concept of the 'Lebewelt', which had been the accused waiter's answer to the question of what kind of customers frequented his establishment. The newspaper expressed the hope that one might finally find out who the 'Lebewelt' were: 'The places where they take their pleasure and live their joyful life can be identified by name, certain great cities in certain countries . . . But if we go

277

there in the hope of seeing the famous Lebewelt with our own eyes, to hear them speak and to take in their bustle with all five senses . . . always and everywhere we discover an old acquaintance, namely our good old harmless philistine, who goes to work and goes out after to relax, someone who does nobody any harm and will simply be glad that nothing bad happens to him.'9 It was in this period too that Curt Moreck's *Guide to Depraved Berlin* appeared, an attempt to continue the tradition of the night guides of the turn of the century. The attempted lightness fails, and sadness obtrudes between the lines:

> The temperature of everything has fallen a few degrees, everything is a little uncontemporary, everything has somehow become past . . . A little dust has settled over everything, the melancholy of the transitory has percolated everywhere . . . One still visits [the Friedrichstrasse] for polite-ness' sake. One certainly doesn't expect much of it, one has no great illusions about it, but one still comes to it with a certain curiosity.[10]

Above all, the old centre of the Berlin night retains only a museum-like attraction; the new night is in the western part of the city, around Kurfürstendamm and Tauentzien, and this new and 'modern' night life is no longer marked by love of the night but by a yearning for light. Not everybody feels, or regrets this loss. Curt Moreck sings the praises of brightness, while Siegfried Kracauer unmasks its illusory nature:

> The moment the electric current shoots into millions of light bulbs, lighting them up and illuminating the big streets as if by a sudden fire-works display, the real metropolitan feels it in his veins and nerves. It will not allow him to remain at his desk. It calls him out to bathe in the light, and something of the electric power radiates through his limbs. Just a walk beneath the illuminated adverts is like a reviving shower, bringing tone and zest for life, the expectation and hope of experience and adventure, or at least of sensation.[11]

> In the main areas of night life the light is so shrill that one has to stop one's ears. The lights are gathered together for their own pleasure, rather than shining for the people. The glowing signs are supposed to brighten up the night, but only chase it away. The advertisements impress, but do not allow themselves to be deciphered. The reddish glow that remains settles like a veil over thought.[12]

Moreck's text indeed is clearly stamped by the language of adver-tising: 'tone' and 'zest for life' are the domesticated, everyday forms

278

of the old promises of the night. In this luminous environment the solitary walker who seeks the darkness is lost, and, as Franz Hessel remarks, suspect, for he also excludes himself from a second trend that characterizes the years around 1930, in London and Paris as well as Berlin: night-revellers no longer seek the pleasures of the street but – once again – the 'amusement' of enclosed spaces. Joseph Roth interprets the function of 'industrialized cheerfulness': 'It is as if this coarse and uniform amusement industry in all the big cities of the world is creating a uniform type of night-walker, with simplified, stereotypical needs that can be satisfied in accordance with the simplest rules.'[13] The city night seems to be closing itself off again.

With the retreat from the street the night-walk loses one of its fundamental functions: the possibility of self-encounter – 'self-seeking, self-finding, self-losing', as the folklorist Wilhelm Heinrich Riehl called it – is no longer given in the pre-formed, standardized amusements. With this there also disappears the link between the different poles of the night: 'splendour' and 'misery' again stand next to each other without connection, as if they had nothing in common. Either the city of light, the city in the light, is portrayed, *or* the city of darkness. An overall view in which the contradictions are related to each other no longer seems possible.

## 1 *National Socialist nights*

At this point an opportunity is seductively presented for a political interpretation of the night. Its metaphoric vocabulary is fundamentally open to such an attempt to characterize ideological positions; the contradictory nature of 'day' and 'night', of 'light' and 'shadow' has been and still is often used to counterpoise one's own good to the alien bad. As a rule, positive evaluations are attached to the concept of day, while the night often stands for the negative and the threatening. There is a great temptation to interpret a certain form of perception of the nocturnal – fear would be part of it, insecurity, danger, but also yearning and love – as part and parcel of an 'anthropological structure of the imagination, indifferent to the passage of time',[14] as Alain Corbin has done for the perception of landscape. The relationship to the night would then act as a gauge of popular behaviour and the state of society.

I believe that in the main the material speaks against this view. There are individual motifs that appear again and again in all the cities during the period investigated, forms and contents of a social discourse on the nocturnal; but the attempt to construct an anthropological theory from this, with 'the night' as the only constant, is bound to fail in the same way as the attempt to explain a certain political development 'by the night'. This becomes obvious when – as here – the chronological organization of the chapters brings one to the end of the 1920s: until then one can observe in each case a constant, even if occasionally interrupted, modernization of nocturnal life in the big cities, from the perfecting of lighting technique and the adaptation of the night-watch service to the requirements of industrial life, through the democratization of welfare services and the commercialization of the entertainment industry. But what follows, from 1930 and 1933? The 'night' of National Socialism? This would be too simple; here the metaphor of the nocturnal leads to uncertain ground. This seductive formulation does not do justice to the reality of Nazism, and also obstructs an understanding of the 1920s, which in this view appear only as the 'years before'.

It would be extremely interesting to interrogate the period of National Socialist domination on its attitudes to the night. This is a matter for a specific, self-contained study, but a few of these questions may be raised here. It might be that the unmediated juxtaposition of extremes in the Berlin night of the late 1920s made a not negligible contribution to the success of National Socialist propaganda. It made the city more easy to attack, and anti-metropolitan attitudes critical of modernity found starting-points for their arguments on both sides, in the glaring light of the 'city of pleasure' as much as in the darkness of the poor neighbourhoods.

National Socialist propaganda about Berlin was necessarily ambiguous. On the one hand, for the sake of the anti-urban potential voters of the provinces, it had to join in the campaigns 'against Berlin's depraved night life';[15] on the other, it could not present itself in Berlin as anti-metropolitan and provincial. 'Berlin needs its sensations', wrote Joseph Goebbels, 'like a fish needs water. The city lives off them and all political propaganda will miss its target if it does not recognize this.'[16] For Nazi militants the nocturnal city was a place of danger – 'not one evening would go by without our party comrades being attacked by red street mobs on their way home' – and was also alien and incomprehensible:

I still remember today, with deep inner emotion, an evening when, completely unrecognized, I was sitting on the open top deck of a bus with a number of comrades from the early days of the struggle, riding through Berlin to a meeting. On the streets and squares the ant-like swarming of the metropolis. Thousands and thousands of people in movement, seemingly without aim or purpose. Everywhere there flickered the lights of this urban monster. It was then that one of them anxiously asked if it would ever be possible to impose ourselves on this city, to stamp it with the name of our party, whether it wanted it or not.[17]

This strategy necessitated a conquest of the night. The question as to whether this was completely successful or whether the night and nocturnal life were able to put up a certain resistance to the pressures of political power is extremely interesting and cannot be answered simply in passing. There are suggestive clues and evidence to support both possibilities.

1. The National Socialists showed an impressive facility and variety in their handling of fire and light.[18] In the politics of illumination lighting's manipulability proved its worth, allowing itself to be used for the 'propagation of darkness' (Siegfried Kracauer) in both moral and political realms. The Berlin of the years up to 1939 was not itself a dark city. What function did public lighting have in the dictatorship's structure of control? How far could it be brought into the service of power? These questions lead us into the wider field of the National Socialist culture of representation and the politics of aesthetic creation, an area in which studies already exist,[19] but which undoubtedly requires further work.

2. The establishment of nocturnal security was part of the pro-gramme of control which promised to free the streets of crime and itself invented new nocturnal terrors. This seems to be easy to interpret but is probably more complicated, if one takes into account the positive memories of many contemporaries, in which the years between 1933 and 1939 are presented as a period in which 'one could still walk on the streets at night'. Which images of the 'criminal world' did the National Socialists use, which new images did they develop? How did they use existing instruments, how did they transform them for their own purposes? Were nights in the big cities, in Berlin, but also in occupied cities such as Paris or Amsterdam, spaces and times of resistance? The German

281

National Socialist nights: light can be brought into the service of power, its brightness blinding. Photograph by André Kertész: *Berlin, Unter den Linden*, 1936.

edition of Hervé le Boterf's book *La vie parisienne sous l'occupation allemande* is subtitled *Paris bei nacht*. This suggests the generalized terror, perhaps the deliberate policy of curfew, but also hints at the possibility of escaping terror – using the darkness and being grateful for it.

3. The fight against homelessness, too, played a significant role in the propaganda of the early years. On 12 May 1934, Görlitzer, the Deputy Gauleiter of Berlin, visited the shelter in the Fröbelstrasse, and in October of the same year Goebbels himself came: he did 'what no other minister ever did and visited the homeless shelter, that is, he went to see the poorest of the poor, and even there he found, as everywhere else, trust, love, enthusiasm and boundless devotion to the National Socialist regime,' reported the *Völkischer Beobachter*.[20] The number of those admitted to the shelter fell, as the regime had prisons and concentration camps for 'anti-social elements', the 'work-shy' and the 'vagrant'. In what way did the new government use strategies and programmes that were already available to it from the years of the defeated democracy? What did it mean to become homeless in those years?

4. Propaganda texts against 'places of amusement on the Kurfürstendamm' where 'Negro bands played dance tunes' correspond to the idea we have about the relationship of the National Socialists to the city night, and without doubt they represent one side of their policies. As recent investigations have clearly shown, however, the aim of these policies was control of the night, but in no case the abolition of night life. The 'worldly big business of the entertainment centres' remained, as Marko Paysan noted, 'suspect to the official party mentality' but 'tolerance of night life as an unpoliticized sphere helped in the maintenance of power'.[21] The Berlin Nazi leadership had to keep the nocturnal business of the city going, to the horror of many clerical representatives of morality, so as not to provoke the urban population and foreign public opinion. The function of 'night life' under conditions of dictatorship is very clearly ambivalent. On the one hand it offered the inhabitants of the city a 'link to world civilization', a phrase from the letter of a French publisher printed by the National Socialist newspaper *Der Angriff* in November 1934: 'Monsieur Dupont' had been wondering 'what effect the new state had had on the life of the elegant world around the Gedächniskirche':

283

But now in an illustrated magazine I saw a picture of West Berlin, which aroused my amazement and, I will admit, my admiration, to the highest degree. This picture showed the glittering life of a great boulevard still bearing the Hohenzollern name of 'Kurfürstendamm'. Here I recognized the *élan vital* which also fills the nights on our Paris boulevards, and here I think I have found the solution to the puzzle: despite the terrible situation that is reported to exist in your country there must be a surviving vitality which can be seen shining here in West Berlin – *avec illumination . . .*[22]

In reaction to this letter, *Der Angriff* for a few weeks published page-long letters about the attractiveness of Berlin life – and in its endeavours for international renown National Socialist propaganda could not renounce the comparison with Paris. Such articles also had an effect at home, and even the illusion of moving in a free space could encourage a desire for further freedom. On the other hand, the provision of controllable 'free space' was certainly an integral element of a strategy of pacification and distraction. This strategy was precisely strengthened in its effect by nocturnal life retreating to a greater degree than before into closed establishments, away from the street. The bars and clubs became doubly protected refuges for those who did not want to be totally integrated (and also those who, even if their position cannot simply be qualified as 'resistance', still occasionally, like parts of the 'swing youth', found forms of resisting). But here they (no longer) represented any disturbance to public order, but remained in the places provided for them.

Here finally the metaphor of day and night fails. With its specific promises of re-enchantment, which were undoubtedly counter-enlightening, and equally undoubtedly welcome to a majority of the population, was National Socialism a product of 'the night'? Or was it a product of 'the day', the result of the modernization of the everyday and every night life of the cities, which left no room for the creative imagination or the melancholy of solitude? We cannot answer this question, but once again it sums up the contradictory nature of the history of night and presents an opportunity for further research.

# 2 *Morning in the big city*

*You would like to know how best to end a Berlin night?*

CURT MORECK[23]

Night ends with the break of dawn, and with the first light of the morning the new day begins. In between there is a short period of ambiguity: the gloaming. The unclear relationship between night and day in these early morning hours creates a unique atmosphere, which has already occupied many authors. The memory of the events of the night is still alive, but the demands of the day begin to make themselves felt.

There is hardly an image used as often in texts on the city night as that of the *dawn encounter*: the 'night-walkers' go home, stealing ashamedly through the streets, often incoherent, marked by the strain of their nocturnal existence, exhausted by play, befogged with drink – and they meet the road-sweepers and the street-cleaning vehicles which are cleansing the city of the dirt of the night and preparing it for the day; they meet workers on their way to the factory and farmers coming into the city from the country to supply it with fresh groceries and gleaming fruit. Artificial life meets real life, the strong, healthy, lively life of the day.

The champions of the early morning declare it, and themselves, to be innocent; dirt and shame are attributed to the night, as if life began anew each day, as if there were no circle in which day and night follow each upon other. Pierre Sansot compared walking the city at night and in the morning, and concluded: 'At dawn the city has to start to live again . . . In the city one has to cleanse oneself, of the night and its dreams, its unspoken desires. The man who gets up early must wash this bad night from his face if he wishes to escape an indefinite, inexplicable fear.'[24]

The morning walk, according to Sansot, stands under the sign of the 'good mood' – a phrase from the vocabulary of the early riser, which can hardly be applied to solitary night-wandering, to the *déambulation nocturne*. But if the image of the circle is accurate, then the interdependency of day and night is greater than the critics of the night would have us believe; the themes of the night reach far into the day and mark it, even as the night itself is influenced and changed by the structures and rhythms of the day. For there is also another

285

The two faces of the night offer a popular starting-point for the critique of the big city; 'night-revellers' are discovered in the young, innocent morning. Drawing by George Grosz: *Five o'clock in the morning!*, 1921.

side to the encounter at dawn: not ashamed, but proud – and sad, because they have to leave their place of refuge again – the night-walkers go home; if the day were that wonderful they would not repeatedly flee from it.

In all the preceding chapters this second development, the 'day-ing' of the night, could stand as the result of historical change. But what is so clear when 'night' and 'day' confront each other presents itself with less clarity at dawn: without the recognition of nocturnal elements in the life of the daytime city, the day itself remains incomprehensible. The day is defined by a constant clash with the night, often in the form of a rejection, a negation: what has to be 'shaken off' and 'cleansed' is powerful in itself. The conflictual nature of the relationship with the night is particularly noticeable in those who try to distance themselves from it:

> When the time of artificial light arrives, a new world appears: the realm of deceptions, of fleeting reality. To this realm unfortunately there also belong the joys of our metropolitan life. While the seriousness of work is clothed in the free light of day, our rest is associated with the deceptive glow of lamps and candle-flames, uncertain light and deep shadow which favour deception, intoxication, make-believe and lies . . . Our lamp-lighter is a restless, agile and speedy fellow, a Mercury of illusions.

In his text *Berlin Becomes a Metropolis* (1868), Robert Springer does not remain with this critical position, but goes on immediately to describe the importance of the development of the night in the process of Berlin's transformation into a metropolis:

> Gas light is an important element in our cultural life, and we metropolitans remember the earlier oil lanterns only as faintly as they used to burn. . .
> As a result of the invention of gas lighting our life has gained in speed, as it did with the discovery of steam. Since the invention of gas light, our evening life has experienced an *indescribable intensification, our pulse has accelerated, nervous excitation has been heightened; we have had to change our appearance, our behaviour and our customs*, because they had to be accommodated to a different light.[25]

As Springer impressively illustrates, the changes in the night have a particular influence on the processes of 'internal' urbanization, on the communication, perceptions and behaviour of city-dwellers. In this respect, the night itself is not only a world of experience, but also in a very broad sense a *place of learning*. The hypocrisy of the critique of the metropolis does not least lie in the fact that it wants to deny the night what it gives the day. Willy Hellpach, too, who recognized the 'gains' made possible by the new urban sensations, spoke contemptuously of the 'night life of our metropolis . . . as the sum of these kinds of so-called relaxation'.[26] But while 'breathlessness as a solution' – 'on and on!' – appears as productive, exciting and necessary in the life of the day, it is seen as harmful for the life of the night.

Admittedly, various authors have rightly pointed out that the experiences of street life in the big cities and the forms of behaviour developed from these also made an important contribution to the disciplining of the metropolitans, to their 'preparation and adaptation'[27] for and to the process of industrialization. The gains – for example the capacity to overcome moments of insecurity and to acquire confidence from this – can be made useful in the process of production. The modern city was constructed with these qualities, and this development had its dark sides, frictional losses which express themselves in different ways; in parts they could be seen in the appearance of the city – as for example in the Scheunenviertel district in Berlin, in London's East End or in Les Halles in Paris. In these cases the existence of the 'night sides' drew attention to failures of modernization: *Nox revelatrix* here too, the night as revealer – and accuser – of the day. What happens at night is also a product of the day. The critique of the big city was able for years to argue only the opposite; it did not want to recognize that in the 'lust and passion' of the cities, which is so easy to condemn,[28] many requirements of life become recognizable. Many authors demanded the abolition of the night. According to the physician Magnus Hirschfeld: 'The Berliner is often proud of his night life; it is certainly metropolitan, but one should also remember that those who give themselves over to night *life* cannot take part in the necessary night's rest.'[29] The Society for Social Reform too spoke of night work as a 'crime against natural law', when workers against their will and 'under the spur of want are pressed into night work and night life'.[30]

Writers of various backgrounds demand that the night should once again become the refuge of the natural state. The historian Alexander von Gleichen-Rußwurm wanted to go 'back to sleep', suffering with the 'human clockwork' that was constantly being rewound, without a pause, while what was being offered, 'sensations, negro dances, cinema and radio', was not worth staying alert for: 'If the night brings no sleep the morning brings no awakening.'[31] There was however hope for the innocent day threatened by the nocturnal life; and this was formulated even more forcefully – and politically – in 1919 by the Socialist theoretician Karl Kautsky:

288

'The day promises no more than day to me . . . If I observe myself observing the city,
I recognize that I can only hope that this day may end like all other days' (Fernando
Pessoa). Photograph by Pierre Vals, Paris, 1939.

And even the hours of consumption are being poisoned by capitalism, and the time for refreshment and the gaining of new strength becomes the time of a more rapid draining of force. Capitalism extends the working day over the whole day, and for enjoyment there remains only the night; the life of enjoyment means night life, and means not the restoration but the destruction of nervous composure. . .

A Socialist regime would reduce working hours to such an extent that the people would gain the possibility of devoting a considerable part of the day to artistic or scientific enjoyment, to cheerful conviviality, to play and to sport. But it is not merely that they will be able to, but that they will have to find time for this during the day, because in a Socialist society night life will no longer find its servants. Only the spur of poverty can force people to regularly sacrifice their sleep to do night work. And without the night work of some, there is no nocturnal enjoyment for the others.[32]

Under the prevailing conditions real life, life outside work, cannot find proper realization, so goes Kautsky's thesis: what the night offers is a poor substitute, a façade; it is, as *Die Weltbühne* had it, a 'continuation of the day by the same means'.[33] The critics agree with the defenders of the city night on the fact that the night reflects the various stages and aspects of the process of urbanization and modernization. In positive terms: in the 'mentally vigorous atmosphere' of the cities a nocturnal life *must* emerge; only the functions and effects ascribed to it depend on the observer's point of view. It only remains to be noted that the night, unlike the early morning, does not want to hold itself out as innocent. 'Berlin bei Nacht', 'Paris la nuit', 'London by night' – nobody is untouched by these words; for the student of human nature, says H. V. Morton, they have the effect of a whiplash on the imagination, because they promise a short period 'of infinite possibility'.[34]

Admittedly, disappointment and the experience of loss are constant companions on walks through the nocturnal city. This emerges in the historical documents, and it is also the every night experience in our cities today. The history of night hands down stories that seem unfinished: arguments about security, morality and the accessibility of the cities still condition social discourse today. The learning processes offered by the night are far from finished. Nineteenth-century writers' dreams – or were they nightmares? – of the radiant, nightless city of the future have in a strange way come true, yet not come true, at the same time. The night is still dark and sets a limit to the day; but the undecided balance between light and shade, between multitude and solitude, between fear and freedom, which has characterized the city night since the middle of the nineteenth century, is endangered: commercialized 'night life' has made many streets so bright that they can hardly be distinguished from the day, while others are left to emptiness – and so to real danger. Both developments are linked to the fatal tendency to shift much of what made the nocturnal street attractive back into enclosed spaces. With this the diversity of appearance is lost, and many people, many women in particular, shy away, for good reasons, from walking through the nocturnal city; but they may also feel that in their withdrawal they are missing something that only the street can give, and will perhaps succeed in rediscovering the trail of what has been lost, opening up anew the world and the experience of the big city night.

# Photographic Acknowledgements

The author and publishers wish to express their thanks to the following sources of illustrative material and/or permission to reproduce it:

Archiv des Diakonischens Werkes der EKD, Berlin: p. 228; Archives de la Préfecture de Police, Paris, pp. 101, 122, 182; Bildarchiv Preußischer Kulturbesitz, Berlin: pp. 34, 65, 67, 87, 98, 118, 126, 127, 142, 165 (bottom), 249, 253 (top), 267, 268, 271; © Bill Brandt Archive Ltd: pp. 61, 116, 131, 173, 265; © DACS 1997: p. 286; Courtesy of Jane Corkin Gallery, Toronto: pp. 12, 165 (top), 203, 237; Roger-Viollet, © Harlingue-Viollet: pp. 62, 68; Roger-Viollet, © Roger-Viollet: p. 256; and Salvation Army, London: p. 223.

# References

I CONTRADICTORY REPORTS FROM NIGHT IN THE BIG CITY

1 Günter Kunert, 'Nachtblick', in Michael Engler and G. Kunert, *Berliner Nächte. Laternenbilder* (Hamburg, 1986), p. 9.
2 Ibid.
3 Paul Nizon, *Das Jahr der Liebe* (Frankfurt a. M., 1984), pp. 115ff.
4 Joachim Riedl, 'Großstadtratte. Manhattan in Hamburg: Peter Patzaks Film, "Der Joker"', *Die Zeit* (23 October 1987).
5 On this see the study by Dieter Keim, *Stadtstruktur und alltägliche Gewalt. Fallstudie Wolfsburg-Westhagen*, in the series *Wolfsburger Beiträge zur Stadtgeschichte und Stadtentwicklung* (Frankfurt a. M. and New York, 1981); Wolf-Dieter Narr, 'Im Dickicht städtischer Gewalt', in Rolf-Richard Grauhan, ed., *Großstadt-Politik* (Gütersloh, 1972); and also from a folklore perspective, Utz Jeggle, 'Tödliche Gefahren. Ängste und ihre Bewältigung in der Sage', in *Zeitschrift für Volkskunde* 86 (1990/91), pp. 53–66.
6 See Katharina Steffen, *Übergangsrituale einer auto-mobilen Gesellschaft. Eine kultur-anthropologische Skizze* (Frankfurt a. M., 1990), with transcripts and interpretations of discussions with women night taxi-drivers; Hartwig Tegeler, 'Der Schock, wenn die Sonne aufgeht', a night-time programme broadcast by the Hessische Rundfunk on 29 September 1990 – in the tradition of the literature of the metropolis, Tegeler uses a 'night-shadow' as a guide.
7 Brigitte Gensch and Veronika Zimmer, *Gewalt gegen Frauen. Stadtplanerische und bauliche Komponenten der nächtlichen Unsicherheit* (Gesamthochschule Kassel, 1981); see also Maria Spitthövel, 'Frauen und Freiraum. Zur Beanspruchung öffentlich städtischen Freiraums durch Frauen', habilitation thesis, University of Oldenburg, 1988.
8 In Anne Cauquelin, *La ville la nuit* (Paris, 1977), p. 95.
9 Klaus Bergmann, *Agrarromantik und Großstadtfeindschaft* (Meisenheim am Glan, 1970).
10 Gottfried Korff, 'Mentalität und Kommunikation in der Großstadt, Berliner Notizen zur "inneren" Urbanisierung', in *Großstadt. Aspekte empirischer Kulturforschung*, ed. on behalf of the Deutsche Gesellschaft für Volkskunde by Theodor Kohlmann and Hermann Bausinger (Berlin, 1985), pp. 343–61.
11 Johannes Willms, *Paris. Hauptstadt Europas 1789–1914* (Munich, 1988), p. 341.
12 Lothar Müller, 'Die Großstadt als Ort der Moderne. Über Georg Simmel', in Klaus R. Scherpe, ed., *Die Unwirklichkeit der Städte. Großstadtdarstellungen zwischen Moderne und Postmoderne* (Reinbek, 1988), pp. 14–33.
13 Ibid., p. 15.
14 Pierre Sansot, *Poétique de la ville* (Paris, 1988), p. 153.
15 Cameralistics covered the study of economics, finance and police; it was established as a field of study in Germany in the first third of the eighteenth century and represented a first attempt at understanding and organizing the

'whole of the inner life of the state: from the police of religion and morality to sumptuary regulations; from the still half-existing guild system to the first beginnings of a more liberal organization of economic life; from the simple police of security and the prevention of danger to positive state intervention in matters of population, trade and and the civil welfare of its subjects': Hans Maier, *Die ältere deutsche Staats- und Verwaltungslehre (Polizeiwissenschaft). Ein Beitrag zur Geschichte der politischen Wissenschaft in Deutschland*, Politica XIII (Neuwied and Berlin, 1966), pp. 19ff.

16 Kai-Detlev Sievers, 'Volkskunde und moderne Stadtgeschichte', in *Informationen zur modernen Stadtgeschichte* 82/2, pub. Deutsches Institut für Urbanistik (Berlin, 1982), pp. 3ff.

17 Wilhelm Heinrich Riehl, *Land und Leute* (1854) (Stuttgart, 1869), p. 82.

18 Theodor Bade, *Über den Verfall der Sitten in den großen Städten. Mit besonderer Berücksichtigung der Zustände in Berlin* (Berlin, 1857). After the publication of this book the Berlin police authority opened its own file, 'Acta des Königlichen Polizei-Präsidii betr. Die hiesigen sittlichen Zustände', Staatsarchiv Potsdam, today Bundesarchiv (hereafter SAP), Rep. 30, Berlin C, Nr. 16927.

19 See Helge Gerndt, 'Großstadtvolkskunde – Möglichkeiten und Probleme' in *Großstadt* (as n. 10), pp. 11–19. This book arose from the work of a folklore studies institute and so deals with this specific area of history. There are other – historical, sociological, art-historical, literary and scientific – perspectives on the city (night), but here I want to retain the folklore studies methods of collection, reflection and assemblage and contrast them with the theme of the 'modern'.

20 Heinz Brüggemann, *'Aber schickt keinen Poeten nach London'. Großstadt und literarische Wahrnehmung im 18. und 19. Jahrhundert. Texte und Interpretationen* (Reinbek, 1985), p. 20.

21 Hugo Flemming, *Nachtmission. Bilder aus der Stadtmission 14* (Berlin, 1913), p. 3.

22 'Das verleumdete Nachtleben', *Berliner Tageblatt* (29 November 1911), a report on Edison's visit to Berlin.

23 See also Reinhart Koselleck, 'Moderne Sozialgeschichte und historische Zeiten', in Pietro Rossi, ed., *Theorie der modernen Geschichtsschreibung* (Frankfurt a. M., 1987), pp. 173–90.

24 Gottfried Diener, *Die Nacht in der deutschen Dichtung von Herder bis zur Romantik* (Bamberg, 1931), p. 5.

25 Henri Lefèbvre, *La Révolution Urbaine* (Paris, 1970).

26 Gottfried Korff, 'Berliner Nächte. Zum Selbstbild urbaner Eigenschaften und Leidenschaften', in Gerhard Brunn and Jürgen Reulecke, eds, *Berlin. Blicke auf die deutsche Metropole* (Essen, 1989), pp. 71–103, here p. 75.

27 Gotthold Lehnerdt, 'Die Prostitution. Beobachtungen eines Kriminalisten', in Ludwig Levy-Lenz, ed., *Sexualkatastrophen. Bilder aus dem modernen Geschlechts- und Eheleben* (Leipzig, 1926), pp. 171–257, here p. 179.

28 Joachim Fischer and Claudia Wagner, 'Sprachen der Nacht', in *Nachtcafé* 26 (Autumn/Winter 1986/87), pp. 22–31.

29 *Deutsches Wörterbuch. Von Jacob Grimm und Wilhelm Grimm*, Vol. VII, ed. Dr Matthias von Lexer (Leipzig, 1869), cols 145–226; *Handwörterbuch des deutschen Aberglaubens*, ed. Hans Bächtold-Stäubli with the assistance of Eduard Hoffmann-Krayer (1935). With a foreword by Christoph Daxelmüller. Vol.VI: Mauer Pflugbrot (Berlin, New York, 1987), cols 768–811.

30 Ernst Bloch, 'Technik und Geistererscheinungen', in *Verfremdungen I* (Frankfurt a. M., 1962), pp. 177–85, here p. 179.

31 *Kölnische Zeitung* (1819), cited in *Bei Licht besehen. Kleines ABC der Beleuchtung*, pub. Landschaftsverband Rheinland (Pulheim, 1987), my emphasis.

32 *The night the lights went out. By the staff of the 'New York Times'*, eds A. M. Rosenthal and Arthur Gelb (New York, 1965), p. 15.

33 Wolf Jobst Siedler, Elisabeth Niggemeyer and Gina Andreß, *Die ermordete Stadt. Abgesang auf Putte und Straße, Platz und Baum* (Berlin, Munich and Vienna, 1964), p. 11.

34 Ibid., p. 79.

35 I wrote to 26 big cities in the Federal Republic and asked them for information about night-time activities organized by the city. The city adminstration of Mainz wrote back: 'We are not so keen on nocturnal entertainment, which is why we have never had guided tours or such things . . . Every now and again, however, Mainz has proved itself to be a big city in terms of night life, and the police will certainly be able to tell you more about that' (letter from the tourist office, 26 August 1988). The night is properly a 'big city' affair, as opposed to 'nice', when the police have to intervene.

36 Pierre Garot, a Parisian night-bird and student of the nocturnal. Interview in Paris, 14 April 1989.

37 Walter Benjamin, 'Paris, Hauptstadt des 19. Jahrhunderts', in Ralph Tiedemann, ed., *Das Passagen-Werk* (Frankfurt a. M., 1983), pp. 45–59.

38 György Konrad, 'Der verbale Kontinent. Europa – eine Metaphor, die Gestalt annimmt', *Frankfurter Allgemeine Zeitung* (2 July 1988).

39 Alexander von Gleichen-Rußwurm, *Die geistige Entwicklung des modernen Europas. Die gesellschaftliche Struktur*, Vol. XXIII/XXIV of *Das Kulturbild des neunzehnten Jahrhunderts* (Hamburg, n. d.), p. 431.

40 Victor Champier and Roger Sandoz, *Le Palais-Royal d'après des documents inédits*, 2 vols (Paris, 1900); *Le Palais-Royal*, exh. cat., Musée Carnavalet, Paris, 1988.

41 *Les Grands Boulevards*, exh. cat., Musée Carnavalet, Paris, 1985; Paul de Ariste, *La vie et le monde du boulevard* (Paris, 1930).

42 See also Louis Huart, *Physiologie du flâneur* (Paris, 1841), and Victor Fournel, *L'Odyssée d'un flâneur ou ce qu'on voit dans les rues de Paris* (Paris, 1858).

43 Heinz Steinert, 'Nachtleben oder: Fragmente über die allgemeinste Erniedrigung des Liebeslebens (2)', in *Kriminalsoziologische Bibliographie* 38/39 (Vienna, 1983), pp. 81–92, here p. 84.

44 'Were we really romantic fools, those of us who signed petitions just because we found onion soup at dawn more tasty than fast-food or steak and chips? . . . There was a piece of authentic popular culture linked with Les Halles: the market. The fact that the market halls could have been intelligently put to use is also shown by the wonderful last period.' Anna Mohal, 'Herz von Paris oder Schrittmacher? Die Sanierung des Hallenviertels', *Süddeutsche Zeitung*, 29/30 (December 1984).

45 A balanced account of the aims and consequences of the 'Haussmannization' of Paris is given by Johannes Willms (as n. 11), pp. 362–71. The military-strategic element is elsewhere often overemphasized, doing less than justice to the fact that, as Willms puts it, 'Haussmann's transformation of Paris created the preconditions for the great myth in which Modernism comes true, the myth of the metropolis' (p. 371).

46  The Paris historian Louis Chevalier published his *Histoires de la nuit parisienne*
    (Paris, 1982) after years of listening and collecting. Most of the stories come
    from the 1950s, and are set in the area around Les Halles; Chevalier summed
    up his own criticism of the development of Paris in *L'assassinat de Paris* (1977).
47  In Ronald Pearsall, *The Worm in the Bud. The World of Victorian Sexuality*
    (Harmondsworth, 1972), pp. 10ff.
48  Robert Machray, *The Night Side of London* (London, 1902), pp. 9ff.
49  Peter Nonnenmacher, 'Ein wunderlicher, steinerner Traum. Wenn es Nacht
    wird im West End: Streifzug durch Londons Lichter- und Schattenseite',
    *Frankfurter Rundschau* (30 December 1989).
50  Henry Mayhew, *London Labour and the London Poor*, 4 vols (London, 1861–).
    Mayhew worked as 'metropolitan correspondent' of the *Morning Chronicle* and
    began his series of articles in 1849; see also Anne Humphreys, *Travels into the
    Poor Man's Country. The Work of Henry Mayhew* (London, 1977), and *Henry
    Mayhew* (Boston, 1984); E. P. Thompson and Eileen Yeo, *The Unknown Mayhew.
    Selections from the Morning Chronicle 1849–50* (Harmondsworth, 1971); *The
    Morning Chronicle Survey of Labour and the Poor: The Metropolitan Districts*, ed.
    and with an introduction by Peter Razzell, 6 vols (London, 1980).
51  Charles Booth, *Life and Labour of the People in London*, 17 vols (London, 1902–4).
52  Beatrice Webb, *My Apprenticeship* (London, 1926).
53  *Die Friedrichstraße. Geschichte und Geschichten*, text by Peter Mugay, pub. Berlin-
    Information (Berlin/GDR, 1987).
54  Eike Geisel, *Im Scheunenviertel. Bilder, Texte und Dokumente*, with foreword by
    Günter Kunert (Berlin, 1981), p. 12.
55  WEKA, *Stätten der Berliner Prostitution. Von den Elends-Absteigequartieren am
    Schlesischen Bahnhof und Alexanderplatz zur Luxus-Prostitution der Friedrichstraße
    und des Kurfürstendamms* (Berlin, 1930), p. 7.


II  A BEGINNING: BIG CITY NIGHTS AROUND 1840

1  Arlette Farge, *Vivre dans la rue à Paris au XVIII siecle* (Paris, 1979), p. 21.
2  Henri Lefèbvre, *La Révolution urbaine* (Paris, 1970), pp. 29–33.
3  'The street protects the delinquent, for the street pattern is so multiple in its
   possibilities that the policeman is powerless against them. And the mobile and
   constantly changing crowd essentially escapes his control.' Arlette Farge, *Vivre
   dans la rue* (as n. 1), p. 194.
4  James Morier on city development in ancient Persia, cited in R. Murray
   Schafer, *Klang und Krach. Eine Kulturgeschichte des Hörens* (Frankfurt a. M.,
   1988), p. 84.
5  Schafer, *Klang und Krach* (as n. 4), p. 84.
6  'When night came, the citizens themselves recognized the necessity of retiring
   to the safety of their homes.' Yi-Fu Tuan, *Landscapes of Fear* (Oxford, 1980), p. 160.
7  Archives de la Préfecture de Police (hereafter APP), Série DB 1, carton 30:
   Circulation la nuit des Inspecteurs et des Sergents de Ville.
8  Julius von Soden, cited in Friedrich Christian Ben. Avé-Lallement, *Physiologie
   der deutschen Polizei* (Leipzig, 1882), p. 182.
9  *London und Paris, Jg. 1810*, p. 64, cited in Karl Riha, *Die Beschreibung der 'Großen
   Stadt'. Zur Entstehung des Großstadtmotivs in der deutschen Literatur* (Bad
   Homburg, Berlin and Zurich, 1970), p. 64.

10  See also Yi-Fu Tuan, *Landscapes of Fear* (as n. 6), and for the metaphor of the market, Peter Langer, 'Sociology. Four images of Organised Diversity: Bazaar, Jungle, Organism and Machine', in Lloyd Rodwin and Robert M. Hollister, eds, *Cities of the Mind. Images and Themes of the City in the Social Sciences* (New York and London, 1984), pp. 97–117.

11  Werner Sombart, *Luxury and Capitalism* (1922), trans. W. R. Dittmar with an introduction by Philip Siegelmann (Ann Arbor, 1967).

12  List of establishments serving alcohol, with justification for extensions, APP, Série DB, carton 194: Débits de Boisson.

13  François-Auguste Fauveau, Baron de Frénilly, *Souvenirs* (1768–1828) (Paris, 1908), p. 24.

14  Karl Riha, *Die Beschreibung der 'Großen Stadt'* (as n. 9), p. 32.

15  Joachim Christoph Nemeitz, *Séjour de Paris*, chap. 14, cited in Karl Riha (as n. 9), p. 43.

16  See also Wolfgang Schivelbusch, *Lichtblicke. Zur Geschichte der künstlichen Helligkeit im 19. Jahrhundert* (Munich and Vienna, 1983). The differing degrees of darkness are also referred to in Anne Henri de Dampmartin, *Un provincial à Paris pendant une partie de l'année 1789* (Strasbourg, 1789), and Ernst Moritz Arndt, *Pariser Sommer 1799*, new edn by Wolfang Gerlach (Munich, 1982), pp. 173ff.

17  Werner Sombart, *Luxury and Capitalism* (as n. 11), pp. 107–8.

18  Ernst Günther, *Geschichte des Varietés* (Berlin/GDR, 1978), pp. 43ff.

19  Johannes Willms, *Paris. Hauptstadt Europas 1789–1914* (Munich, 1988), p. 217, my emphasis.

20  APP, Série DB 1, carton 194: Chiffoniers.

21  See also Louis Chevalier, *Classes laborieuses et classes dangereuses à Paris, pendant la première moitié du XIXe siècle*.

22  'Denkwürdigkeiten und Tagesgeschichten aus der Mark Brandenburg und Herzogtümern Magdeburg und Pommern, April 1800', pp. 455–7, here p. 456, Landesarchiv Berlin (hereafter LAB), ST, B 4097b: 'Schliessen der Häuser am Abend'.

23  Alain Corbin, *Les Filles de Noce. Misère sexuelle et Prostitution (XIX siècle)* (Paris, 1982), p. 21, in English *Women For Hire*, trans. Alan Sheridan (Cambridge, MA, and London, 1990).

24  APP, Série DB 1, carton 194: Débits de Boisson, No. 269, circular of 25 July 1818.

25  APP, Série DB 1, carton 195: Débits de Boisson, heures de fermeture, No. 46: Préfecture de Police. Ordonnance concernant les Cabarets, Cafés et autres lieux publics situés dans la ville de Paris et dans les Communes rurales du ressort de la Préfecture de Police, Paris le 3.4.1819.

26  Eugène Briffault, 'La Nuit de Paris', in *Le Livre de Cent-et-Un* (Paris, 1831), Vol. III, pp. 127–50, here p. 133.

27  Joseph Alois Mercy, *Berlinische Nächte* (Leipzig and Züllichau, 1803), pp. 1ff.

28  C. von Kertbeny, *Berlin wie es ist. Ein Gemälde des Lebens dieser Residenz und ihrer Bewohner, dargestellt in genauer Verbindung mit Geschichte und Topographie* (Berlin, 1831), p. 321.

29  Ibid., p. 323.

30  Adalbert Stifter, 'Aussicht und Betrachtungen von der Spitze des St. Stephansturmes', in *Die Mappe meines Urgroßvaters. Schilderungen. Briefe,* with an epilogue by F. Krökel and annotations by K. Pörnbacher (Munich, 1986), p. 297.

31  Ibid., p. 298.

32  Ernst Heilborn, *Zwischen zwei Revolutionen. Der Geist der Schinkelzeit (1789–1848)* (Berlin, 1927), p. 85.

33  *Johann Daniel Fr. Rumpf's neuester Fremdenführer in Berlin. Eine Beschreibung nebst einem Wanderungsplan durch Berlin* (Berlin, 1839), pp. 220ff.

34  Adolf Glassbrenner, 'Straßenbilder', in *Berlin, wie es ist – und trinkt, von Ad. Brennglas*, Vol. II (Leipzig, 1842).

35  Max Kretzer, *Meister Timpe* (1888) (Stuttgart, 1976), p. 3.

36  Dr B. Hesslein, 'Berlin um Mitternacht', *Berliner Stadtklatsch. Heitere Lebensbilder aus Berlin's Gegenwart* 5 (Berlin, n. d.), p. 3.

37  *Johann Daniel Fr. Rumpf's neuester Fremdenführer* (as n. 33).

38  Karl Gutzkow, 'Eine Woche in Berlin', in *Der Berliner zweifelt immer. Seine Stadt in Feuilletons von damals*, with an introduction by Heinz Knobloch (Berlin/GDR, 1977), pp. 88–95, here p.88.

39  Ernst Dronke, *Berlin* (1846) (Berlin, 1953), p. 61. (repr. Darmstadt and Neuwied, 1987).

40  See also Wolfgang Jansen, *Glanzrevuen der zwanziger Jahre* (Berlin, 1987).

41  *Illustrirte Zeitung* III (Leipzig, 1844), pp. 188–90.

42  Peter Joseph Lenné, *Erläuterungsbericht zum Project 'Schmuck- und Grenzzüge Berlins'*, Lenné papers, SAP 159, fols 1ff. (Cited in 'Bestandskatalog der Lenné-Pläne in der Plankammer', Part II, catalogue, Staatliche Schlösser und Garten Potsdam-Sanssouci, Berlin [Potsdam, 1989].)

43  Richard Sennett, *The Fall of Public Man* (London, 1977).

44  Asa Briggs, *Victorian Cities* (Harmondsworth, 1968), p. 12.

45  Louis Chevalier, *Montmartre du plaisir et du crime* (Paris, 1980), p. 22.

46  *Verwaltungsbericht des Königlichen Polizei-Präsidiums zu Berlin für die Jahre 1871–1880* (Berlin, 1882), p. 5.

47  Dr H. Wollheim, *Versuch einer medicinischen Topographie und Statistik von Berlin*, (Berlin, 1844).

48  Karl Rosenkranz, *Die Topographie des heutigen Berlin. Vortrag vor der Kgl. Dt. Gesellschaft zum Preussischen Krönungsfest am 18. Januar 1850*, p. 71.

49  Bettine von Arnim, *Dies Buch gehört dem König* (1844), ed. Ilse Staff (Frankfurt a. M., 1982), p. 405.

50  *Die Prostituierten in Berlin, deren Helfershelfer als Louis, Kupplerinnen, Lehnefrauen und ihr schädlicher Einfluß auf die Sittenzustände der Gegenwart* (Berlin, n. d. [c.1850]), p. 6.

51  Marie-Louise Plessen, 'Kommunale Selbstverwaltung und Polizei', in *Berlin, Berlin. Die Ausstellung zur Geschichte der Stadt*, exh. cat. by Gottfried Korff and Reinhard Rürup (Berlin, 1987), pp. 171–3, here p. 172.

52  *Das Urteil des Herrn Appert über das hiesige Arbeitshaus in seinem Buche: Voyage en Prusse. Beleuchtet von Andrae, Prediger an dieser Anstalt* (Berlin, 1845), pp. 5ff.

53  *Haude- und Spenersche Zeitung* (28 December 1846).

54  H. A. Frégier, *Des classes dangereuses dans la population des grandes villes et des moyens de les rendre méilleures* (Brussels, 1840).

55  Jean-Louis Bory, *Eugène Sue: Dandy mais Socialiste* (Paris, 1962).

56  'Norddeutsche Blätter: Berliner Nouvellen, Geheimnisse und Romane', *Beiträge zum Feldzuge der Kritik* I (Berlin, 1846), pp. 16ff.

57  August Brass, *Mysterien von Berlin*, 5 vols (Berlin, 1844–5), Vol. I, p. 1.

58  F. Gustav Kühne, *Mein Carneval in Berlin 1843* (Berlin, 1843), p. 19.

59  Friedrich Saß, *Berlin in seiner neuesten Zeit und Entwicklung* (1846), ed. and with an afterword by Detlef Heikamp (Berlin, 1983), p. 14.

60  George A. W. Reynolds, *The Mysteries of London*, 2 vols (London, 1846–8), p. 1.

61  On this see Peter Drexler, *Literatur, Nacht, Kriminalität. Untersuchungen zur Vorgeschichte des englischen Detektivromans 1830–1890* (Frankfurt a. M., 1991), pp. 157–66.

62  Ibid., p. 24.

63  F. S. Schwartzbach, *Dickens and the City* (London, 1979), p.117.

64  C. J. Ribton-Turner, *A History of Vagrants and Vagrancy, Beggars and Begging* (Montclair, NJ, 1972), p. 243.

65  George Reynolds (as n. 60), p. 2.

66  Franz Josef Buss, member of the Baden Landtag, in a debate on factory legislation in 1837; cited by Jürgen Kuczynski as 'the first essay at social policy in a German parliament' in *Bürgerliche und halbfeudale Literatur aus den Jahren 1840 bis 1847 zur Lage der Arbeiter. Eine Chrestomathie*, Vol. IX of *Die Geschichte der Lage der Arbeiter unter dem Kapitalismus* (Berlin/GDR, 1960), p. 243.

67  Jacques Rancière makes a significant point in his study *La Nuit des Proletaires. Archives du rêve ouvrier* (Paris, 1981): the workers whose texts, poems, notes on dreams, and chronicles of daily 'servitude' to others are analyzed by Rancière do not experience night in the city simply as a short time of 'sommeil réparateur entre les jours de salaires'; they themselves break out of the monotonous circle, meeting secretly at night and reappropriating their time by sacrificing it.

68  Louis Chevalier, *Histoires de la nuit parisienne* (Paris, 1983), p. 17ff.

69  Eduard Devrient, *Briefe aus Paris* (Berlin, 1840), p. 51.

70  Julien Lemer, *Paris au gaz* (Paris, 1861), p. 74.

71  Ludwig Robert, *Promenade eines Berliners in seiner Heimat*, cited in Hans Ostwald, *Kultur- und Sittengeschichte Berlins* (Leipzig, n. d. [1925]), p. 526.

72  'What most strongly evokes the urban? The swarm of lights, especially as one sees it from an aeroplane – the blinding brightness, the neon signs, the illuminated adverts and invitations of every kind . . .' Lefèbvre, *La Révolution urbaine* (as n. 2), p. 159. The counter-images of village and countryside are set 'where the night is still dark'. Karl Schlögel, 'Ein Sommer auf dem Lande', *Frankfurter Allgemeine Zeitung* (27 August 1988).

73  Wolfgang Schivelbusch, *Lichtblicke* (as n. 16), p. 84.

74  'Les rues bouées et mal pavées appartenaient à partir de ce moment aux détrousseurs et aux gens sans aveu qui guettaient dans l'ombre le bourgeois assez audacieux pour oser s'attarder.' Pierre Léon, 'Du Monopole de l'Eclairage et de Chauffage par le gaz à Paris', doctoral thesis, Paris, 1901, p. 1.

75  'Fear of darkness and strangers, often cited as reasons for lights that "control" nocturnal disorder, were once reasons to avoid the night altogether.' Mark J. Bouman, 'Luxury and Control. The Urbanity of Street Lighting in Nineteenth-Century Cities', in *Journal of Urban History* XIV/1 (November 1987), pp. 7–37, here p. 8.

76  'Ce n'était pas seulement aux noctambules et aux débauchés qui couraient la nuit les rues de la ville, qu'il importait que ces rues fussent éclairées, c'était également à ceux que les fatigues du jour empêchent de profiter des commodités de la nuit, à la population laborieuse et probe, qui voyait dans la lueur répandue par les lanternes sa sauvegarde contre un péril qui lui

apparaissait d'autant plus redoutable qu'il restait imaginaire.' Colonel Herlaut, *L'éclairage de Paris à l'époque révolutionnaire* (Paris, 1932), p. 8.

77 'Ein Jahrhundert Berliner Gaslaternen', *Berliner Morgenpost* (19 April 1925).

78 *Vossische Zeitung* (21 September 1826).

79 SAP, Rep. 30, Berlin C, Nr. 18969: Straßenbeleuchtungs-Sachen; Die Auflösung der Straßenbeleuchtungskommission bei Einführung der Gasbeleuchtung.

80 Ibid., Nr. 18998–19000: Die Verlängerung der Brenndauer der Straßenbeleuchtung nach 1 Uhr und die Anfertigung von Plänen für die Straßenbeleuchtung während der ganzen Nacht; APP, Série DA 1, carton 121: Eclairage des Rues à Paris: Tableau de l'Eclairage de la Ville de Paris pour l'année 1840.

81 Wolfgang Schivelbusch, *Lichtblicke* (as n. 16), p. 138.

82 Julius Rodenberg, *Paris. Bei Sonnenschein und Lampenlicht. Ein Skizzenbuch zur Weltausstellung* (Leipzig, 1867), p. 40.

83 Gottfried Semper, *Wissenschaft, Industrie und Kunst. Vorschläge zur Anregung nationalen Kunstgefühls. Bei dem Schlusse der Londoner Industrieausstellung* (Braunschweig, 1852), p. 12. Dolf Sternberger comments, 'Thanks to the general illumination the city night becomes a kind of permanently excited party'. *Panorama oder Ansichten vom 19. Jahrhundert* (Frankfurt a. M., 1974), p. 188.

84 Alexander von Gleichen-Rußwurm, *Die Geistige Entwicklung des modernen Europa. Die gesellschaftliche Entwicklung*, Vol. XXIII/XXIV of *Das Kulturbild des 19 Jahrhunderts* (Hamburg, n. d.), pp. 197ff.

85 'Paris dans l'avenir, n'aura plus de nuits': Eugène de Mirecourt, 'Paris la nuit', in Mirecourt, *Paris Historique, Pittoresque et Anecdotique* (Paris, 1855), p. 78; on the light tower see also Jules Bourdais, *Colonne-Soleil. Projet de phare électrique pour la ville de Paris* (Paris, 1885).

86 'Nachtseiten von London. Sociale Skizze von J. H. Teil 1', *Gartenlaube* XIII (1869), pp. 200–3, here p. 200.

87 Henri de Pontich, *Administration de la Ville de Paris et du Département de la Seine* (Paris, 1884), chap. XXVIII: 'L'Eclairage public et privé'.

88 'Der Streik der Londoner Gasarbeiter', *Deutsches Handelsblatt* (29 January 1873), p. 40. (Thanks to Thomas Krischer for bringing this to my attention.)

89 '"More light!" is the cry of anyone who has ever been obliged late at night to pass the ruins of the former Kleine Burgstrasse and the part of the future Kaiser-Wilhelm-Strasse between the new Friedrichstrasse and the Stadtbahn. Here and there the road is lit with an oil lamp, which only spreads its dim light over a distance of a few paces and leaves the rest of the surroundings in the dark, although the journey is by no means without danger'. *Deutsches Tageblatt* (5 October 1885).

90 Corcoran, 'The City Light and Beautiful', *American City* 7 (1912), p. 7.

91 Marc J. Bouman, 'Luxury and Control' (as n. 75), here p. 8.

92 *Das Kulturbild* (as n. 84), p. 199.

93 Beate Binder, '"Alles elektrisch!", Zur Metaphorik des Fortschritts: Der gesellschaftliche Diskurs um die Elektrizität im Deutschen Kaisereich Ende des 19. Jahrhunderts', master's thesis, University of Tübingen, 1988. Work is also being done on Hamburg, Vienna and Göttingen.

94 *Illustrirte Zeitung*, Leipzig 300 (1882).

95 Bruno H. Bürgel, 'Berliner Sensationen 1882', *Berliner Morgenpost* (6 July 1930).

96  Comtesse des Sesmaisons, 'Ce qui se dit à Paris', *La Nouvelle Revue*, CXV (November/December 1898), p. 715.

97  Gaston Ladoux (Chef de service de la Préfecture de la Seine), 'L'Eclairage à Paris, à Londres et à Berlin', *Revue des deux mondes* (15 March 1904).

98  Jacques Lardy, 'Paris sans lumière', in *Les Annales politiques et littéraires*, No. 1238 (17 March 1907).

99  Ibid.

100  Hans Ostwald, *Die Berlinerin. Kultur- und Sittengeschichte Berlins* (Berlin, n. d.), p. 8.

101  City of Melbourne: City Electrical Engineers' Notes on Tour Abroad, 1912, cited in Thomas P. Hughes, *Networks of Power. Electrification in Western Society 1880–1930* (Baltimore and London, 1983), p. 182.

102  Stadtarchiv Berlin (Ost), today integrated into the Landesarchiv (hereafter SBO), Rep. 01 HV, Nr. 2302: Acta des Magistrats zu Berlin betr. Die Polizeiverordnung betr. Die Festlegung der Polizeistunde.

103  Legrand-Chabrier, 'Paris éclairé', *L'Opinion* (23 October 1923).

104  Gottfried Korff, 'Die Stadt aber ist der Mensch...' in *Berlin, Berlin* (as n. 51), here p. 658.

105  *Berlin im Licht*, festival programme with an introduction by Oberbürgermeister Böß, Berlin, 1928; *AEG Mitteilungen* 10 (October 1928); 'Berlin im Licht', *Berliner Illustrirte Zeitung* (28 October 1928).

106  *Berlin im Licht* (as above), p. 21; *Berliner Tageblatt – Monatsausgabe für Ausland und Übersee* (September 1928), p. 24.

107  *Die Welt am Abend* (26 April 1928), cited in Bärbel Schrader and Jürgen Schebera, *Kunstmetropole Berlin 1918–1933. Die Kunststadt in der Novemberrevolution. Die 'Goldenen' Zwanziger. Die Kunststadt in der Krise* (Berlin/GDR and Weimar, 1987), p. 140.

108  Max Epstein, 'Berlin im Licht', *Weltbrille* 7 (1928). Gert Selle gives us an interpretation of 'form around 1930': 'For the first time the *dark side* of industrial society becomes visible, precisely in the radiant brightness of things, in the perfect aesthetic excess . . . In this brightness is celebrated a subjugation to the myth of technology, a technology which National Socialism will be able to make use of without any trouble for its own ends as a means of domination, and will stylize in its outward appearance as a *blinding beauty.*' Gert Selle, *Design-Geschichte in Deutschland. Produktkultur als Entwurf und Erfahrung* (Cologne, 1987), p. 217.

III NIGHT AND SECURITY

1  Anne Cauquelin, *La Ville la Nuit* (Paris, 1977), p. 5. See also for this concept Werner Conze, 'Sicherheit, Schutz' , in *Geschichtliche Grundbegriffe. Historisches Lexikon zur politisch-sozialen Sprache in Deutschland*, Vol. V: Pro–Soz, eds Otto Brunner, Werner Conze and Reinhart Koselleck (Stuttgart, 1984), pp. 831–62.

2  Dr Morvell, *Memoiren eines Berliner Nachtwächters* (Danzig, 1845), p. 4.

3  M. Rapsilber, 'Das Ende des Laternenzünders', *Der Roland von Berlin* X/40 (1910), pp. 1304–8, here p. 1304.

4  George Fourny, 'Les Veilleurs de Nuit Parisiens', *La Nouvelle Revue*, 3rd ser., XIV (May–June 1910), Paris, pp. 448–58, here p. 448.

5  Lewis Mumford, *The City in History* (London, 1961), p. 316.

6   M. Rapsilber (as n. 3), p. 1305.

7   SBO, Rep. 01 HV, Nr. 2160: Aufbringung der Nachtwachtgelder, Vol. I: 1813–25; Erhebung einer Nachtwacht-Cassen-Gebühr.

8   Ibid., Nr. 2163: Aufbringung der Nachtwachtgelder, Vol. IV: 1837–45; undated minutes.

9   APP, Série DB 1, carton 40: Gardes de Nuit.

10  Ibid., Recueil de Projets sur la Police Municipale, 1812, pp. 695–8, here p. 695.

11  Ibid., p. 697.

12  APP, Série DB 1, carton 40: Préfecture de Police, 2ème Division, 1er Bureau: Organization du nouveau service de nuit.

13  A. Durnatin, 'Les Français peints par eux-mêmes', in *Rapport des Gardiens de la Paix* for 1830–1848, pp. 112–14.

14  SBO, Rep. 01 HV, Nr. 2163: Letter from chair of the police authority, 15 March 1840.

15  SBO, Rep. 01 HV, Nr. 2163: Anweisung für Nachtwachtmeister und Nachtwächter in Berlin.

16  SAP, Rep. 30, Berlin C, Nr. 7402: Polizei-Sicherheits-Sachen 1854–95.

17  SAP, Rep. 30, Berlin C, Nr. 7347: Nachtwacht-Sachen 1845–95.

18  SAP, Rep. 30, Berlin C, Nr. 7426: Acta des Kgl. Polizei-Präsidii betr. den Sicherheitszustand Berlins und Umgegend. Bericht des Polizei-Hauptmanns Ahne vom 12. Januar 1862

19  SAP, Rep. 30, Berlin C, Nr. 7426: Brief des Magistrats vom 14. Februar 1862 an das Polizei-Präsidium.

20  See also Marie-Louise Plessen, 'Kommunale Selbstverwaltung und Polizei', in *Berlin, Berlin. Die Ausstellung zur Geschichte der Stadt*, exh. cat. by Gottfried Korff and Reinhard Rürup (Berlin, 1987), pp. 171–3.

21  See also Hans-Christian Täubrich, 'Industriestandort Berlin', in ibid., pp. 157–61.

22  SBO, Rep. 01 HV, Nr. 2164: Brief des Fabrikanten Heinrich vom 7 Juli 1861 an die Deputation für polizeiliche Angelegenheiten beim Magistrat der Haupt- und Residenzstadt Berlin.

23  SBO, Rep. 01 HV, Nr. 2165: Aufbringung der Nachtwachgelder, Vol. VI: 1860ff. Brief des Magistrats an das Ministerium des Innern, v. Dezember 1875.

24  Prussian Landtag, Chamber of Deputies, 38th session, 7 April 1875, Deputy Dr Weber (Erfurt).

25  *Verwaltungsbericht des Königlichen Polizei-Präsidiums Berlin für die Jahre 1871–1889* (Berlin, 1882), p. 15.

26  Dr X., *Berliner Prostitution und Zuhältertum* (Leipzig, n. d.), p. 30.

27  Philip John Stead, 'The New Police', in David H. Bayley, ed., *Police and Society* (Beverly Hills and London, 1977), pp. 73–84, here p. 74. In the [German] hardback edition of this book the magistrate was erroneously identified as Henry Fielding, and I would like to thank Günter Kunert for his correction; he also added that: 'John Fielding not only established the first police force, he also invented the "wanted" poster. It is said that being blind he was able to identify hundreds of people by their voices. He was essentially the first criminal investigator whose methods were at all scientific.'

28  *Verwaltungsbericht* (as n. 25), p. 14.

29  SBO, Rep. 00–02/1, Nr. 1060: Stadverordneten-Versammlung. Bericht der Deputation in bezug auf das Nachtwachtwesen. Vorlage 185 für die Sitzung vom 12.2.1874.

30  APP, Série DB 1, carton 40: Préfecture de Police. Secrétariat Général. Service de
    Rondes de Nuit (Paris, 28 June 1880).
31  APP, Série DB 1, carton 38: Kiosques Avertisseurs. Rapport à M. le Préfet de
    Police sur les Moyens d'augmenter la Sureté dans Paris (31 December 1881).
32  Max Ring, Berliner Leben. Kulturstudien und Sittenbilder (Leipzig and Berlin,
    1882), pp. 237–47, here p. 237.
33  Clive Emsley, The English Police, A Political and Social History (Hemel
    Hempstead, 1991).
34  Stefan Petrow, Policing Morals, The Metropolitan Police and the Home Office,
    1870–1914 (Oxford, 1994). See also Philip T. Smith, Policing Victorian London –
    Political Policing, Public Order, and the London Metropolitan Police (London and
    Westport, 1985).
35  Percy A. Harris, London and its Government (London and Toronto, 1933), p. 23.
36  Francis Sheppard, 'The Crisis of London's Government', in David Owen, The
    Government of Victorian London 1855–89, The Metropolitan Board of Works, the
    Vestries, and the City Corporation, ed. Ray MacLeod (London, 1982), pp. 23–30,
    here p. 24.
37  Berliner Börsen-Zeitung (1 September 1883).
38  Rixdorfer Zeitung 248 (1883).
39  Berliner Volksblatt (23 September 1885).
40  Staatsbürger-Zeitung (9 May 1884).
41  APP, Série BA 1, carton 567: Conseil Municipal de Paris (1891). Proposition de
    M. Georges Berry tendant à la création d'un service des gardiens de nuit.
42  Ibid., Statistiques de Crimes et Délits 1891–1903.
43  Luc Gersal, Spree-Athen. Berliner Notizen von einem Böotier (Leipzig, 1892).
    pp. 194ff.
44  SAP, Rep. 30, Berlin C, Nr. 7403: Polizei-Sicherheits-Sachen.
    Nachtwachtdienste der Grundbesitzervereine 1900–1909. Brief der
    'Wirtschaftsgemeinschaft Berliner Grundbesitzer' vom 22.9.1890.
45  SAP, Rep. 30, Berlin C, Nr. 7404: Wach- und Schließgesellschaften.
46  SAP, Rep. 30, Berlin C, Nr. 7403: Letter from the chairman and deputy chairman
    of 200th district of Berlin to the 16th police precinct, March 1907.
47  APP, Série DB 1, carton 242: Malfaiteurs divers; Apaches. La Presse (27 August
    1907).
48  Ernest Laroche, 'Parisiens, dormez!', L'Eclair (23 June 1906).
49  'Die 24 Stunden von Berlin', in Paul Lindenberg, Berlin in Wort und Bild (Berlin,
    1895), pp. 105–21, here p. 105.
50  Wolfgang Nahrstedt identifies the years around 1750 as the essential turning-
    point in the development of this feature of the 'modern', examining the
    relationship of tension between working and leisure time in the example of
    Hamburg in his Die Entstehung der Freizeit. Dargestellt am Beispiel Hamburgs
    (Göttingen, 1970).
51  Ulla Merle, 'Tempo! Tempo! – Die Industrialisierung der Zeit im 19.
    Jahrhundert', in Igor A. Jenzen, ed., Uhrzeiten. Die Geschichte der Uhr und ihres
    Gebrauches, Historisches Museum (Frankfurt a. M., 1989), pp. 161–217, here
    p. 161; see also Dietrich Mühlberg, ed., Proletariat. Kultur und Lebensweise im
    19 Jahrhundert (Leipzig, 1989); Udo Achten, Denn was uns fehlt ist Zeit.
    Geschichte des arbeitsfreien Wochenende (Cologne, 1988).
52  See also Utz Jeggle and Joachim Schlör, 'Stiefkinder des Fortschritts. "Kennt

Ihr die deutsche Provinz?"', in August Nitschke, Gerhard A. Ritter, Detlev J. K. Peukert and Rüdiger vom Bruch, eds, *Jahrhundertwende. Der Aufbruch in die Moderne 1880–1930*, Vol. I (Reinbek, 1990), pp. 56–74.

53 Jon Sternkopf, 'Kontinuierlicher Fabrikbetrieb', in *Jahrbücher für Nationalökonomie und Statistik*, 3rd ser., XXXIV / 1, ed. J. Conrad (Jena, 1907), pp. 80–103.

54 Dietrich Henkel et al., *Zeitstrukturen und Stadtentwicklung*, Vol. LXXXI of *Schriften der Dt. Instituts für Urbanistik* (Stuttgart, Berlin and Cologne, 1981), p. 11. See also Jürgen P. Rinderspacher, *Der Rhythmus der Stadt. Die Bedeutung der Zeit für die städtische Gesellschaft*, being *Materialien des DIfU* I/88 (Berlin, 1988).

55 'Nachtarbeit in der Großstadt. Eine Skizze von Ulfilas Müller', *Daheim* (27 November 1901). I would like to thank Bernd Jürgen Warneken for drawing this article to my attention.

56 Paul Lindenberg (as n. 49), p. 63.

57 Carol Hilarius, 'Wie das Berliner Pflaster entsteht', in *Berliner Pflaster. Illustrierte Schilderungen aus dem Berliner Leben* (Berlin, 1894), p. 343.

58 Klaus Neukrantz, *Barrikaden am Wedding. Der Roman einer Straße aus den Berliner Maitagen 1929* (1931) (Berlin, 1970), p. 9.

59 Ehm Welk, 'Das arbeitende Berlin', *Erste Beilage zur Vossischen Zeitung* (8 February 1927).

60 Louis Chevalier, *Montmartre du Plaisir et du Crime* (Paris, 1980), p. 151; Bob Landsberg, 'Negerball in der Rue Blomet', *Der Querschnitt* 3 (1929), pp. 107–9, here p. 109.

61 *Anfänge der Arbeiterfreizeit*, an exhibition organized by the Märkische Museum, at the former Museum 'Berliner Arbeiterleben um 1900', Berlin/GDR, 1987; catalogue, Berlin, 1989, p. 59.

62 Karl Marx and Friedrich Engels, *Die Deutsche Ideologie* (1848), in *Werke*, Vol. 3 (Berlin/GDR, 1959), p. 404.

63 See also Franz Dröge and Thomas Krämer-Badoni, *Die Kneipe. Zur Soziologie einer Kulturform oder 'Zwei Halbe auf mich!'* (Frankfurt a. M., 1987).

64 Cited without any further indication of source in *Anfänge der Arbeiterfreizeit* (as n. 61), p. 66.

65 E. Hirschberg, *Die soziale Lage der arbeitenden Klassen in Berlin* (Berlin, 1897), p. 267.

66 *Berlin für Kenner. Ein Bärenführer bei Tag und Nacht durch die deutsche Reichshauptstadt. Großstadtführer für Kenner*, Vol. I (Berlin, 1912), p. 157.

67 Cited in M. Rapsilber, 'Das Ende des Laternenanzünders', *Der Roland von Berlin*, VIII/40 (1910), pp. 1304–8, here p. 1305.

68 The essential document underlying all later considerations of this question was a 'Publicandum' of the King of Prussia, dated 12 May 1798, providing that 'tobacco divans and similar establishments' were to be *'closed in the evening at a certain time'*. This left to the police what it seldom failed to stress – its room for interpretation, its right to decide 'according to the circumstances of the case'.

69 SAP, Rep. 30, Berlin C, Nr. 19585: Polizeistunde (1816–80): Auszug aus dem Jahresbericht der Ordnungs- und Sittenpolizei, 11.9.1839.

70 Ibid: Anonymes Schreiben an das Polizei-Präsidium, 13.11.1843.

71 APP, Série DB 1, carton 194: Débits de Boissons, Bl. 89/90; letter of the Préfet de Police, 24 May 1841.

72  APP, DB 1, carton 194: Débits de Boisson. Ordonnance concernant les heures de fermeture, Paris le 1er novembre 1780, quoted in a letter from the Préfet, 6 May 1860.

73  Theodore Bade, *Über den Verfall der Sitten in den großen Städten, mit besonderer Berücksichtigung der Zustände in Berlin* (Berlin, 1857), p. 17.

74  SAP, Rep. 30, Berlin C, Nr. 19585: Police ordinance of 9 March 1866.

75  *Verwaltungsbericht* (as n. 25), p. 424.

76  Ibid., p. 427.

77  APP, Série DB 1, carton 194: Débits de Boisson. Heures de fermeture, ordinance of 28 July 1879.

78  Ibid., Police Municipale. Etablissements autorisés à ouvrir et à fermer à des heures non réglementaires (Paris, 11 April 1877).

79  SBO, Rep. 01 HV: Acta des Magistrats betr. Die Polizei-Verordnung betr. die anderweitige Festlegung der Polizeistunde, letter from Chief of Police to City Council (Berlin, 30 January 1891).

80  SAP, Rep. 30, Berlin C, Landtagsfascikel betr. Die Durchführung der Polizeiverordnung über die Polizeistunde. Nr. 1600: Bericht über die Polizeistunde der Nachtkafés und Bars. Zum Erlaß vom 27. Juli 1900. Berichterstatter: Polizeirath Rabbel (Berlin, 30 January 1901).

81  Ibid., Berichte der XI., XII. und V. Polizeihauptmannschaft.

82  'Bekanntmachungen des Kgl. Polizei-Präsidiums. Polizeiverordnung betr. Festlegung der Polizeistunde' (Berlin , 14 May 1901), signed by Police Chief von Windheim (as published in the *Norddeutsche Allgemeine Zeitung* of 18 May 1901, amongst others).

83  SBO, Rep. O1 HV, Nr. 2302: Amtlicher Stenographischer Bericht über die Sitzung der Stadtverordneten-Versammlung am 23. May 1901; ibid.: Eingabe betr. Protest-Versammlung gegen das neue Ortsstatut über den Schluß der Schankwirtschaften etc. früh 4–6 Uhr (Berlin, 15 July 1901).

84  Jules Huret, *Berlin* (Munich, 1909), repub. as *Berlin um 1900* (Berlin, 1979), p. 61.

85  *Berlin für Kenner* (as n. 66), pp. 179–85.

86  *Das Proletariat. Bilder und Studien von Werner Sombart*, Vol. I of *Die Gesellschaft. Sammlung sozialpsychologischer Monographien*, ed. Martin Buber (Frankfurt a. M., 1906), p.37.

87  Edmund Edel, 'Bars', in *Berliner Nächte*, with contributions by Edmund Edel and Hans Ostwald (Berlin, 1914), pp. 69–75, here p. 73.

88  APP, Série DB 1, carton 194: Préfecture de Police. Ordonnance concernant la fermeture des restaurants (Paris, 21 November 1914).

89  Magnus Hirschfeld and Andreas Gaspar, *Sittengeschichte des ersten Weltkrieges* (1929), repr. (Hanau, n. d.).

90  Sidney and Beatrice Webb, *The History of Liquor Licensing in England, principally from 1700–1830* (London, 1903).

91  T. R. Gourvish and R. G. Wilson (with Fiona Wood), *The British Brewing Industry, 1830–1980* (Cambridge, 1994).

92  Statutes of the United Kingdom, Vol. II, Geo. IV and Will. IV, 1830.

93  Gourvish and Wilson, *The British Brewing Industry* (as n. 91), p. 21.

94  The Greater London Record Office has put together its own information leaflet on the 'Licensed Victuallers' Records' available in its archives. This is very useful, although it may further increase the confusion of those unfamiliar with the administration of London.

95  Brian Harrison, 'Pubs', in *The Victorian City, Images and Realities*, Vol. I: *Past and Present/Numbers of People*, ed. H. J. Dyos and Michael Wolff (London, 1973), pp.161–90.

96  SBO, Rep. 01 HV, Nr. 2302: Der Minister des Innern. Runderlaß betr. Neuregelung der Polizeistunde in Preußen (Berlin, 19 August 1921).

97  *Wert und Wirksamkeit der Polizeistunde*, speech given by Oberverwaltungsgerichtsrat Dr Konrat Weymann (Berlin) on the occasion of the 16th International Congress Against Alcoholism in Lausanne (Berlin, 1922).

98  'Bacchanale gefällig?' in Egon Erwin Kisch, *Razzia auf der Spree. Berliner Reportage* (Berlin/GDR, 1986), pp. 43–6, here p. 43.

99  Egon Jacobssohn, 'Dunkles Berlin gefällig?', first published 26 May 1923, in Egon Jameson, *Augen auf! Streifzüge durch das Berlin der zwanziger Jahre*, ed. Walther v. La Roche (Frankfurt a. M., Vienna and Berlin, 1982); Carl Zuckmayer, *Als wär's ein Stück von mir. Horen der Freundschaft* (Frankfurt a. M., 1966), pp. 348–54.

100  LAB, Rep. 142, ST, B 1661: Einschränkungen der öffentlichen Tanzlustbarkeiten.

101  LAB, Rep. 142, ST, B 1238: Herabsetzung der Polizeistunde. Eingabe des Vereins gegen Mißbrauch alkoholischer Getränke (9.8.1920).

102  *Gastwirtsgehilfen-Zeitung* XXXVII/30 (29 July 1926).

103  Special number of the *Amtsblatt für den Landespolizeibezirk Berlin* (22 October 1926): *Bekanntmachungen des Polizeipräsidenten in Berlin. Verordnung betr. die Polizeistunde*.

104  Archiv des Diakonischen Werks der EKD (hereafter ADW), CA/GF 531/XII4: Polizeistunde. Survey by the Central Committee on the observation of closing time (Frl. Blücher); ibid., *Christliche Volkswacht* (January 1927): 'Die Polizeistunde'. Also a chapter on 'Wirtschaftsfreiheiten' in the submission of the Deutsche Frauen Bund für alkoholfreie Kultur to the Prussian Ministry of the Interior (18 October 1926), with a comment by chairman Gustel von Blücher.

105  Gustav Rasch, 'Eine Nacht in der Berliner Verbrecherwelt', in *Berlin bei Nacht. Schattenseiten einer Großstadt. Eine Auswahl aus den Schriften von Gustav Rasch*, ed. with annotations and a foreword by Paul Thiel (Berlin/GDR, 1986), pp. 74–105, here p. 74.

106  This section deals more with the *images* of crime than with the reality of criminal activity in the cities; on historical criminology see Dirk Blasius 'Kriminologie und Geschichtswissenschaft. Bilanz und Perspektiven interdisziplinärer Forschung', in *Geschichte und Gesellschaft* 14 (1988), pp. 136–49.

107  Adolf Heinzlmeier, Jürgen Menningen and Berndt Schulz, *Kino der Nacht, Hollywoods Schwarze Serie* (Hamburg and Zurich, 1985), p. 44.

108  Eugène Sue, *Les Mystères de Paris*, pub. 1843 as a serialized novel in *Le Journal des Débats*, new edn by F. Lacassin with an introduction by A. Lanoux (Paris, 1989), pp. 31–3.

109  Edgar Allen Poe, 'The Man of the Crowd', *Gentleman's Magazine* (1840), repr. in Poe, *The Complete Stories*, with an introduction by John Seelye (London, 1992), pp. 442–50, here p. 445.

110  Horst Conrad, *Die literarische Angst* (Düsseldorf, 1974), p. 174.

111  Rolf Lindner, 'Das Andere Ufer. Zwei-Kulturen-Metapher und

Großstadtforschung', in Theodor Kohlmann and Hermann Bausinger, eds, *Großstadt. Aspekte empirischer Kulturforschung* (Berlin, 1985), pp. 297–304, here p. 299.

112 *Das Arbeitshaus und seine Bewohner oder die Proletarier und Verbrecher der Residenz* (Berlin, 1846).

113 According to Robert D. Storch, there arose in the process of specialization 'a modern and generally effective technique of order-keeping; the installation of the eyes and ears of the ruling élites at the very centre of the working-class daily life'. Robert D. Storch, 'The Policeman as Domestic Missionary: Urban Discipline and Popular Culture in Northern England, 1850–80', in *Journal of Social History* IX/4 (June 1976), pp. 481–509, here p. 481.

114 Dirk Blasius, *Kriminalität und Alltag. Zur Konfliktgeschichte des Alltagslebens im 19. Jahrhundert* (Göttingen, 1978), pp. 71–3.

115 I am afraid that the printing of criminal statistics did not change this situation, but only further confused it.

116 From a letter by Dickens to Dr. G. D. Carrow, 1876, cited in Neil Philip and Victor Neuburg, eds, *Charles Dickens: A December Vision. His Social Journalism*, (London, 1986), p. 27.

117 Afterword to *Berlin bei Nacht* (as n. 105), pp. 219–27, here p. 219.

118 Gustav Rasch (as n. 105), p. 83ff.

119 'Das Elend und das Verbrechen – Die Berliner Unterwelt', in Victor Tissot, *Reportagen aus Bismarcks Reich. Berichte eines reisenden Franzosen, 1874–1876* (Stuttgart and Vienna, 1989), pp. 241–57. Tissot quotes Rasch once (p. 243), but then tells of his walk through exactly the same streets, where he meets the same characters – curiously enough, it is only the arrest of the prostitute 'Dora' that he misses.

120 W. G., 'Bilder aus der Berliner Verbrecherwelt', *Illustrirte Zeitung*, Leipzig (14 February 1885), p. 161.

121 Dr Bernhard Hesslein, *Berlins berühmte und berüchtigte Häuser aus der Vergangenheit und Gegenwart, in historischer, criminalistischer und socialer Beziehung dargestellt*, Vol. II (Berlin, 1881), pp. 443ff.

122 See also Daniel Pick, *Faces of Degeneration. A European Disorder* (Cambridge, 1990), and the review of the same work by Eugene Weber, 'Blemishes in the breed?', *Times Literary Supplement* 4539 (30 March–5 April 1990), pp. 335ff.

123 Rev. William Tuckniss, 'The agencies at present in operation within the Metropolis, for the suppression of Vice and Crime', in Henry Mayhew, *London Labour and the London Poor*, Vol. IV (London, 1861–2), repr. New York, 1968, pp. xiii–xl, here pp. xiii and xv.

124 Charles Booth, *Life and Labour of the People in London*, 17 vols (New York and London, 1902–4), 1st series: Poverty, Vol. I, Part I: 'East London', p. 39.

125 Jack London, *The People of the Abyss* (London, 1903).

126 Maxime du Camp, *Paris, ses organes, ses fonctions et sa vie dans la seconde moitié du XIX siècle* (Paris, 1884).

127 Paul Lindenberg, 'Straßenexistenzen', in *Berliner Pflaster. Illustrierte Schilderungen aus dem Berliner Leben* (Berlin, 1894), pp. 43–63, here p. 43.

128 Hesslein, *Berlins berühmte und berüchtigte Häuser* (as n. 121), p. 455.

129 J. H. Mackay, *The Anarchists* (Boston, 1891), cited in William J. Fishman, *East End 1888. A year in a London borough among the labouring poor* (London, 1988), p. 1.

130  Donald Rumbelow, *The Complete Jack the Ripper*, rev. edn (Harmondsworth, 1988), p. 37.

131  Ibid., p. 52 (from the letter of an 'unknown moralist to *The Times*').

132  *Le Matin* (16 January 1910).

133  'Comment on fait les Apaches', *Le Matin* (26 August 1908).

134  Leo Schidrowitz, ed., *Sittengeschichte von Paris. Die Großstadt, ihre Sitten und ihre Unsittlichkeit* (Vienna, n. d. [1927]), pp. 260, 264.

135  Cited in *Welt am Sonntag* (20 March 1955).

136  Egon Jacobssohn, 'Dunkles Berlin gefällig?' (as n. 99).

137  Siegfried Kracauer, *Die Angestellten. Aus dem neusten Deutschland* (1929/30), (Frankfurt a. M., 1971), p. 15.

138  See also Helmut Lethen, 'Chicago und Moskau. Berlins moderne Kultur der 20er Jahre zwischen Inflation und Weltwirtschaftskrise', in Jochen Boberg, Tilman Fichter and Eckhart Gillen, eds, *Die Metropole. Industriekultur in Berlin im 20. Jahrhundert* (Munich, 1986), pp. 190–213.

139  Fritz Giese, *Girlkultur: Vergleiche zwischen amerikanischen und europäischem Rhythmus und Lebensgefühl* (Munich, 1925), pp. 13, 49.

140  Stefan Zweig, 'Der Rhythmus von New York', in *Begegnungen mit Menschen, Büchern, Städten* (Frankfurt a. M., 1955), pp. 264–70, here p. 269.

141  Peter Conrad, *The Art of the City. Views and Versions of New York* (New York and Oxford, 1984), p. 199.

142  Josephine Baker and Joe Bouillon, *Josephine*, trans. Marianne Fitzpatrick (London, 1978), p. 58.

143  Peter Conrad (as n. 141), pp. 267–70.

144  See also Hélène Strohl, 'Ein gewisses Deutschland der zwanziger Jahre', in Ulrich Conrad, ed., *Panik-Stadt (Ville Panique)* (Paris and Berlin/Braunschweig, 1979), pp. 120–6.

145  'It is the unique quality of the poetry of Baudelaire that the images of woman and of death merge together in a third, that of Paris.' Walter Benjamin, 'Paris, Hauptstadt des 19. Jahrhunderts', in *Das Passagen-Werk*, Vol. I, ed. Rolf Tiedemann (Frankfurt a. M., 1983), pp. 45–59, here p. 55.

146  Gottfried Korff, 'Berliner Nächte. Zum Selbstbild urbaner Eigenschaften und Leidenschaften', in Gerhard Brunn and Jürgen Reulecke, eds, *Berlin. Blicke auf die deutsche Metropole* (Essen, 1989), pp. 71–103, here pp. 84–92.

147  Dr Bernhard Weiß, ' Die Berliner Polizei', in Berthold Hirschenberg, ed., *Berlin. Unter der Mitwirkung der Zentralstelle für Fremden-Verkehr Groß-Berlin und andere Verbände* (Berlin, 1925), pp. 57–61, here p. 61.

148  *In den Spuren des Verbrechertums. Ein Streifzug durch das großstädtische Verbrechertum und seine Schlupfwinkel*, by Ernst Engelbrecht, acting Chief Superintendent, formerly head of criminal investigation in Berlin (Berlin-Schöneberg, n. d. [1930] ), p. 98.

149  Ernst Engelbrecht, *Fünfzehn Jahre Kriminalkommisar. Ernstes und Heiteres aus meiner kriminalistischen Berufsarbeit* (Berlin-Schöneberg, n. d. [1928]), p. 66.

150  Ernst Engelbrecht and Leo Heller, *Berliner Razzien* (Berlin, 1924), chap. 1: 'Berlin W. bei Nacht', pp. 1–4, here p. 1.

151  'Das Berufsverbrechertum in der Großstadt' by Geh.-Rat Dr Robert Heindl (Berlin), in Dr Alfred Weise, ed., *Unser Berlin. Ein Jahrbuch von Berliner Art und Arbeit* (Berlin, 1928), pp. 140–57, here pp. 140ff.

152 H. A. Kober, 'Die Unterwelt der Großstädte', *UHU* V/12 (September 1929), pp. 72–9.
153 'Nachtelend in London', *Die Gartenlaube* 14 (1866), pp. 218–22, here p. 218.
154 Gustav Schubert, 'Das Asyl für Obdachlose', *Berliner Illustrirte Zeitung* (21 March 1885).
155 See also Norbert Preusser, *Überlebensstrategie der Armenbevölkerung in Deutschland seit 1807* (Munich, 1989); Lisgret Militzer-Schwenger, *Armenerziehung durch Arbeit. Eine Untersuchung am Beispiel des Württembergischen Schwarzwaldkreises 1806–1914* (Tübingen, 1979).
156 Ernst Willkomm, *Weiße Sklaven oder die Leiden des Volkes*, 5 vols (Leipzig, 1845), Vol. III, p. 40.
157 See also Bronislaw Geremek, *Geschichte der Armut. Elend und Barmherzigkeit in Europa* (Munich and Zurich, 1988), particularly pp. 286–300.
158 Gustav Rasch, 'Das Haus der Armen und Elenden', in Paul Thiel, ed., *Berlin bei Nacht. Schattenseiten einer Großstadt. Kriminalreportagen von Gustav Rasch* (Berlin/GDR, 1986), pp. 151–8, here p. 152.
159 Cited in C. J. Ribton-Turner, *A History of Vagrants and Vagrancy and Beggars and Begging*, repr. Montclair, N J, 1972, p. 255.
160 Report of Mr Grenvill Pigott to the Poor Law Board, 1848, cited in C. J. Ribton-Turner (as above), p. 261.
161 *The London City Mission Magazine* (1 December 1855), p. 280.
162 Louis Rivière, 'L'Hospitalité de Nuit en France. Son Développement, son état actuel, son avenir', *La revue philanthropique*, 2nd year, Vol. III (May–October 1898), pp. 417–28, here p. 420.
163 SBO, Rep. 03–732, Vol. I, 1816–61.
164 SBO, Rep. 03–959, 1825–56.
165 'Nachtelend in London' (as n. 153), p. 218.
166 Max Ring, 'Ein Abend im Asyl für Obdachlose,' *Die Gartenlaube* 2 (1870), pp. 54–6.
167 *Berlin und Seine Entwicklung. Städtisches Jahrbuch für Volkswirtschaft und Statistik* (Berlin, 1871), p. 206.
168 *Verwaltungsbericht* (as n. 25), p. 202.
169 As above.
170 Archives de l'Assistance Public, Paris, Asiles de Nuit: Rapport sur les Travaux de l'Oeuvre de l'Hospitalité de Nuit depuis le 2 juin jusqu'au 31 décembre 1878.
171 Lucius Mummius, 'Ein Besuch im Berliner Asyl für Obdachlose', *Illustrirte Volkszeitung* (Stuttgart, 1874), pp. 138ff.
172 Speech by Paul Singer at the opening of the men's shelter in the Wiesenstrasse on 13 December 1896, cited in *Wohnsitz nirgendwo. Vom Leben und vom Überleben auf der Straße*, Künstlerhaus Bethanien (Berlin, 1982), pp. 146ff.
173 Peter Schmandt, 'Armenhaus und Obdachlosenasyl in der englischen Graphik und Malerei (1830–1880)', doctoral thesis, University of Tübingen, 1986, p. 99.
174 Emil Ernst Ronner, *Der Mann mit der Laterne. Das Leben Thomas John Barnardos* (Wuppertal, 1961), pp. 48ff.
175 Karl Marx and Friedrich Engels, *Die heilige Familie* (1845), in *Werke*, Vol. 2 (Berlin/GDR, 1978), p. 206.

176 Françoise Coppée, *L'Asile de Nuit. Poésie dite par M. Coquelin Ainé à l'occasion du Centenaire de la Société Philantropique, le 9 mai, 1880* (Paris, 1880).

177 APP, Série DB 1, carton 88: Oeuvre de l'Hospitalité de Nuit. Asiles de Nuit. Conférence de M. le Duc de Broglie de l'Académie Française, le 27.4.1895.

178 SBO, Rep. 00–1388: Acta der Stadtverordneten-Versammlung betr. den Neubau eines Asyls für Obdachlose und einer öffentlichen Desinfektionsanstalt an der Prenzlauer Allee. Excerpt from the debate of 31 January 1884.

179 Ruth Köppen, *Die Armut ist weiblich* (Berlin, 1985), p. 21.

180 'Ein Weihnachtsabend im Frauenasyl', in Hans R. Fischer, *Was Berlin verschlingt* (Berlin, 1890), pp. 83–92.

181 E. Dely, 'Im Frauen-Asyl für Obdachlose in Berlin', *Die Frau* (1894/95), cited by Ruth Köppen (as n. 179), pp. 34–6.

182 Gert and Gundel Mattenklott, *Berlin Transit. Eine Stadt als Station* (Reinbek, 1987), p. 139.

183 Constantin Liebich, *Obdachlos. Bilder aus dem sozialen und sittlichen Elend der Arbeitslosen* (Berlin, 1901), p. 107.

184 Ibid., pp. 131ff.

185 Paul Grulich, *Dämon Berlin. Aufzeichnungen eines Obdachlosen* (Berlin, 1907), p.9.

186 Hermann Heijermann, *Berliner Skizzenbuch* (Berlin, 1908), p. 219.

187 Rosa Luxemburg, 'Im Asyl', *Leipziger Volkszeitung* (1907); cited in Klaus Bergman, ed., *Schwarze Reportagen. Aus dem Leben der untersten Schichten vor 1914: Huren, Vagabunden, Lumpen* (Reinbek, 1984), pp. 273–5.

188 Dr R. Burckhardt, 'Massenvergiftung. Ein Berliner Großstadtbild', *Basler Nachrichten* (10 January 1912).

189 SBO, Rep. 00–1461: Asyl-Verein, draft contract.

190 ADW, CA 1863 I: Obdachlosigkeit. 'Eindrücke im städtischen Asyl für Obdachlose', n. d., co-signed by Margarete Schneller.

191 'Eine Nacht in der "Palme"', *Rote Fahne* (9 May 1926).

192 'Die Abgebauten des Lebens. Nachtwanderungen durch den berliner Osten', *Die Welt am Abend* (8 October 1926).

193 'Das lockende Berlin', *Germania* (3 March 1929); 'Dämon Berlin', *Vorwärts* (16 March 1929). See also: 'Von der Straße zur Palme. Das Ofdachlosenasyl im neuen Gewande', *Deutsche Allgemeine Zeitung* (6 December 1926); 'Das Edelheim in der Fröbelstraße. Besuch im städtischen Obdachlosenasyl', *Tägliche Rundschau* (Berlin, 26 March 1927); 'Die armen "Warter" von Berlin. Unmögliche Zustände in den Wartesälen der Berliner Bahnhöfe', *Kleines Journal* (Berlin, 14 August 1927); 'Durchschnitt des Elends', *Tagblatt* (Köln, 12 November 1927); 'Im Keller der Entwurzelten. Menschen aus der Tiefe', *Der Abend* (Berlin, 18 February 1928); 'Nachts im Wartesaal', *Der Abend* (Berlin, 29 February 1928); 'Eine Nacht in "Fröbels Festsälen", Wie die Obdachlosen leben. "Palmkuhle" und Kasernenhofton', *Rote Fahne* (Berlin, 17 January 1929); Max Arthel, 'Die Palme am Strande der Armut. Besuch bei den Obdachlosen', *Der Abend* (Berlin, 22 January 1929), Egon Erwin Kisch, 'Das Obdach', *Rote Fahne* (1 July 1928); 'Fürsorgearbeit der Stadt Berlin', *Vorwärts (Stadtbeilage)* (Berlin, 26 May 1928); 'Und die Obdachlosen? Berlins Maßnahmen für die Asylisten', *Berliner Tageblatt* (12 February 1929); Hans Wesemann, 'Bei 20 Grad Kälte im Asyl für Obdachlose', *Welt am Montag* (Berlin, 18 February 1929).

194  Hermann Drechsler, *Aktenstaub. Aus dem Tagebuch eines Wohlfahrtsdezernenten* (Berlin, 1932), pp. 239ff.

IV  NIGHT AND MORALITY

1  Leopold von Riesbeck, *Salon-Gespräche. Achtzig anleitende Beispiele . . . Ein Rathgeber für unerfahrene und schüchterne junge Leute beiderlei Geschlechts* (Weimar, 1863), new edn with foreword by Wolfgang Max Faust (Munich, 1970), p. 100.

2  Ibid.

3  Wilhelm Rudeck, *Geschichte der öffentlichen Sittlichkeit in Deutschland* (Jena,1897), p. 1; for this concept see also Gottfried Korff, 'Kultur', in Hermann Bausinger, Utz Jeggle, Gottfried Korff and Martin Scharfe, *Grundzüge der Volkskunde* (Darmstadt, 1978), pp. 17–80, here pp. 19–26; Karl Heinz Ilting, 'Sitte, Sittlichkeit, Moral', in *Geschichtliche Grundbegriffe. Historisches Lexikon zur politisch-sozialen Sprache in Deutschland*, Vol. V, Pro–Soz, eds Otto Brunner, Werner Conze and Reinhart Koselleck (Stuttgart, 1984), pp. 863–921.

4  *Polizei und Sitte* by Albert Moll, Geheimer Sanitätsrat (Vol. IX of the series 'Die Polizei in Einzeldarstellungen', ed. W. Abegg, State Secretary in the Prussian Ministry of the Interior) (Berlin, 1926), pp. 9ff.

5  Ulrike Scholvin, *Döblins Metropolen. Über reale und imaginäre Städte und die Travestie der Wünsche* (Weinheim and Basel, 1985), pp. 6ff.

6  Wolfgang Schivelbusch, *Lichtblicke. Zur Geschichte der künstlichen Helligkeit im 19. Jahrhundert* (Munich and Vienna, 1983), p. 83.

7  Klaus Theweleit, *Male Fantasies – 1. Women, floods, bodies, history*, trans. S. Conway with E. Carter and C. Turner (Cambridge, 1987), pp. 229–94.

8  Undine Gruenter, *Ein Bild der Unruhe. Roman* (Munich and Vienna, 1986), pp. 45, 129.

9  On the historical formation of the street and the exclusion of women in the case of New York, see Christine Stansell, *City of Women. Sex and Class in New York 1789–1860* (Urbana and Chicago, 1982).

10  Janos Frecot, foreword to Nelly Rau-Häring, *Lichtungen. 66 Photographien der Nacht* (Nordlingen, 1987), p. 5.

11  Conversation with Louis Chevalier, 14 April 1989, Paris.

12  Hanne Bergius, 'Berlin als Hure Babylon', in Jochen Boberg et al., eds, *Die Metropole. Industriekultur in Berlin*, Vol. II (Munich, 1986), pp. 102–119, here pp. 102ff.

13  'One spoke of Berlin, as long as one did not possess her, as of a desirable woman.' Carl Zuckmayer, *Als wär's ein Stück von mir. Horen der Freundschaft* (Frankfurt a. M., 1967), p. 311.

14  Carola Lipp, 'Frauen auf der Straße. Strukturen weiblicher Öffentlichkeit im Unterschichtsmilieu', in C. Lipp, ed., *Schimpfende Weiber und patriotische Jungfrauen. Frauen im Vormärz und in der Revolution 1848/49* (Bühl-Moos, 1986), pp. 16–24, here p. 21.

15  Richard Sennett, *The Fall of Public Man* (London, 1977), p. 23.

16  Anne Friedberg uses the term *flâneuse*, but also notices that her field of movement was the department store rather than the street. Anne Friedberg, 'Les Flâneurs du Mal. Kino und die postmoderne Kondition': paper given at

'Amerikanische Hautpstädte' conference of the Deutscher Gesellschaft für Amerikaforschung, Bonn, 5–9 June 1990, unpublished.

17  Hans Ostwald, *Kultur- und Sittengeschichte Berlins* (Leipzig, n. d. [c.1925]), p. 10.

18  Ute Frevert, *Frauen-Geschichte. Zwischen bürgerlicher Verbesserung und neuer Weiblichkeit* (Frankfurt a. M., 1986), p. 86.

19  Ibid., p. 131.

20  Alfred Delveau, *Les Dessous de Paris* (Paris, 1861), p. 142.

21  Willy Hellpach, *Liebe und Liebesleben im 19. Jahrhundert*, cited in Ivan Bloch, *Das Sexualleben unserer Zeit* (Berlin, 1907), pp. 313ff.

22  Konstanze von Franken, *Handbuch des guten Tons und der feinen Sitten*, 23rd improved edn (Berlin, 1900), repr. Munich, 1977, p. 135.

23  Friedrich Naumann, 'Zum Geleit', in Schwester Henriette Arendt, *Menschen, die den Pfad verloren. Erlebnisse aus meiner fünfjährigen Tätigkeit als Polizei-Assistentin in Stuttgart* (Stuttgart, n. d. [c.1908]), p. 6.

24  Ernst von Salomon, *Die Geächteten* (Berlin, 1930), pp. 39ff.

25  Franz Hessel, 'Von der Mode', in *Spazieren in Berlin* (1929); reprinted as *Ein Flaneur in Berlin* (Berlin, 1984), p. 37.

26  Billy Schürer and Julie Martin, eds, *Kikis Paris. Künstler und Liebhaber 1900–1930* (Cologne, 1989).

27  'Die Frau die allein geht', *Vossische Zeitung* (19 January 1927); 'Polizeilicher Damenschutz. Von Regierungsdirektor Dr. Weiß, ibid.; contributions by Mady Christians, Dr Gertrud Haupt and Annemarie Horschitz, ibid.

28  Dr. Lotte Spitz, 'Die unbegleitete Dame', *Vossische Zeitung* (29 January 1927); contribution by Margarete Caemmerer, ibid.

29  See also Carole S. Vance, 'Pleasure and Danger: Toward a Politics of Sexuality', in C. S. Vance, ed., *Pleasure and Danger. Exploring female sexuality* (Boston, 1984), pp. 1–27.

30  Philippe Soupault, *Die letzten Nächte von Paris* (1928) (Heidelberg, 1982), p. 49.

31  Regina Schulte, *Sperrbezirke. Tugendhaftigkeit und Prostitution in der bürgerlichen Welt* (Frankfurt a. M., 1984), p. 11.

32  Wilhelm Joh. Stieber, *Die Prostitution in Berlin und ihre Opfer* (Berlin, 1846), p. 4.

33  SBO, Rep. 03–1059: Vol. I: 1792 bis Novbr. 1849.

34  *Berlins Licht- und Schattenseiten. Nach einem mehrjährigen Aufenthalte an Ort und Stelle skizziert v. Ad. von Schaden* (Dessau, 1822), p. 70.

35  Hans Ostwald, *Berliner Bordelle* (Leipzig, n. d. [1905]), pp. 15, 28.

36  SBO, Rep. 03–1059: Vol. I: Circular-Reskript an sämmtliche königliche Regierungen der Rheinprovinz, die Unterdrückung von Bordellen und unzüchtigem Treiben betreffend.

37  Dr Alexandre Parent-Duchâtelet, *De la prostitution dans la ville de Paris considérée sous le rapport de l'hygiène publique, de la morale et de l'administration* (Paris, 1836).

38  Alexandre Parent-Duchâtelet, *La prostitution à Paris au XIXème siècle. Présenté et annoté par Alain Corbin* (Paris, 1981), pp. 21 (commentary), 66 (quote). See also Alain Corbin, *Les Filles de Noce. Misère sexuelle et prostitution (19ème siècle)* (Paris, 1982), in English *Women for Hire, Prostitution and Sexuality in France after 1850*, trans. Alan Sheridan (Cambridge, MA, and London, 1990), pp. 3–18.

39  Alain Corbin, *Women for Hire* (as above), p. 9. Corbin also refers here to A. Béraud, *Les filles publiques et la police qui les régit* (Paris, 1839).

40  APP, Série: DA 1, carton 121: Préfecture de Police, 1ère division, 2ème bureau.

312

Circulaire No. 12: Manière de procéder à la répression des désordres causés par les filles publiques (Paris, 10 Febuary 1841).

41  Jill Harsin, *Policing Prostitution in 19th Century Paris* (Princeton, 1985), p. xviii.

42  *Haude- und Spenersche Zeitung* (5 October 1844).

43  On Stieber himself, see also SAP, Rep. 30, Berlin C, Nr. 8366: Geheime Personalregistratur: Polizeirat Stieber: 'In his employment as oscultator in the criminal tribunal he often came into contact with the heads of the criminal department at police headquarters, who often took him along on their expeditions in the investigation of crime and criminals.' L. Auerbach, 'Denkwürdigkeiten des Geh. Regierungsrathes Dr Stieber', *Berliner Tageblatt* (2 October 1882).

44  Wilhelm Joh. Stieber, *Die Prostitution* (as n. 32), p. 76.

45  Ibid., pp. 164ff.

46  Carl Röhrmann, *Der sittliche Zustand von Berlin nach Aufhebung der geduldeten Prostitution des weiblichen Geschlechts. Ein Beitrag zur Geschichte der Gegenwart unterstützt durch die vollständigen und freimüthigen Biographien der bekanntesten prostituierten Frauenzimmer in Berlin* (Leipzig, 1846).

47  Friedrech Saß, *Berlin in seiner neuesten Zeit und Entwicklung* (1846), reprinted with a foreword by Detlef Heikamp (Berlin, 1983), pp. 73ff., 79.

48  Ibid., p. 66.

49  Erlangen, 1850.

50  Ibid., pp. 203ff.

51  Berlin, 1857.

52  Ibid., pp. 17ff.

53  SAP, Rep. 30, Berlin C, Nr. 16927: Acta des Kgl. Polizei-Präsidii zu Berlin betr. die hiesigen sittlichen Zustände. Sittenpolizei 1857/1898.

54  Ibid., Stellungnahme des Polizeidirektors Hofrichter, Sittenpolizei, vom 30 Oktober 1857.

55  *Verwaltungsbericht des Kgl. Polizei-Präsidiums von Berlin für die Jahre 1871–1880* (Berlin, 1882), p. 430.

56  J. Werner, *Animir-Kneipen und Nachtcafés oder Polizei und Sittlichkeit* (Berlin, 1892), p. 10.

57  Theodor Bade, *Über Gelegenheitsmacherei und öffentliches Tanzvergnügen* (Berlin, 1858).

58  APP, Série DA 1, carton 122: Service des Moeurs. Pratique.

59  William Acton, *Prostitution* (London 1857), ed. and with an introduction and notes by Peter Fryer (London, 1968), p. 169.

60  *Hints to Men about Town or Water Fordiana* (London, 1851), cited in Ronald Pearsall, *The Worm in the Bud. The World of Victorian Sexuality* (Harmondsworth, 1971), p . 319.

61  Steven Marcus, *My Secret Life* (London, 1964).

62  'Zur öffentlichen Sittenlosigkeit. Die Verhandlungen im Preußischen Abgeordnetenhaus (26 November 1869)', in *Fliegende Blätter aus dem Rauhen Hause zu Horn bei Hamburg von Dr. Wichern. Organ des Centralausschusses der Inneren Mission der Deutschen Evangelischen Kirche* (Hamburg, 1870), pp. 11–21, here p. 13.

63  Excerpts from the debate, ibid., pp. 14, 20.

64  Josephine Butler, *Personal Reminiscences of a Great Crusade* (London, 1896), p. 18.

65  Dr X, *Berliner Prostitution und Zuhältertum* (Leipzig, n. d.), p. 10.

66  *Vossische Zeitung* (30 March 1873).

67  *Verwaltungsbericht* (as n. 55), p. 499.

68  *Les Deux Prostitutions. Par F. Carlier, ancien Chef du service actif des moeurs à la Préfecture de Police* (Paris, 1887), p. 19.

69  *Berliner Prostitution* (as n. 65), pp. 11ff.

70  Robert D. Storch, 'Police Control of Street Prostitution in Victorian London. A Study in the Contexts of Police Action', in David H. Bayley, ed., *Police and Society* (Beverly Hills and London, 1977), pp. 49–72, here pp. 50ff.

71  Friedrich Christian Benedict Avé-Lallement, *Physiologie der deutschen Polizei* (Leipzig, 1882), pp. 164ff.

72  Anonymous, *Naturgeschichte der Berlinerin* (Berlin, n. d. [1885]), p. 55.

73  *Die gefallenen Mädchen und die Sittenpolizei vom Standpunkte des praktischen Lebens. Von Kriminalkommissar v. Baumer* (Berlin, 1886).

74  ADW, CA/A 20/ III: Promemoria zur Gründung einer Gesellschaft für den Schutz und die Hebung der öffentlichen Sittlichkeit (January 1870).

75  *Edinburgh Medical Journal* XLVII (May 1859), p. 1088, cited in Eric Trudgill, 'Prostitution and Paterfamilias', in H. J. Dyos and Michael Wolff, eds, *The Victorian City. Images and Realities* (London, 1973), Vol. II, pp. 693–705, here p. 693.

76  S. E. Huppé, *Das sociale Deficit von Berlin in seinem Hauptbestandteil* (Berlin, 1871), p. 19.

77  'Landeszeitung, of last November' [1871], cited in Johannes Janssen, *Berlins sittliche und sociale Zustände, nach Berliner Berichten dargestellt* (Freiburg im Breisgau, 1872), pp. 34ff.

78  F. A. Hald, *Enthüllungen über Berliner Schwindel*, cited in Janssen (as above), pp. 38ff.

79  F. Oldenburg, 'Die Quellen der Sittenlosigkeit in Berlin', in *Fliegende Blätter* (as n. 62), p. 209.

80  Jill Harsin, *Policing Prostitution* (as n. 41), p. 307.

81  *Animir-Kneipen und Nachtcafés* (as n. 56), p. 10.

82  'Deutsche Bordellgassen. Studien von Hugo E. Lüdecke', in Friedrich S. Krauss, *Das Geschlechtsleben des deutschen Volkes*, new edn by Peter Schalk (Munich, 1977), pp. 140–75, here p. 140.

83  'Besuch im Nachtcafé', in Johanna Loewenherz, *Prostitution oder Production, Eigentum oder Ehe? Studien zur Frauenbewegung* (Neuwied, n. d. [1895]); see also Vera Konieczka, 'Arten zu sprechen, Arten zu schweigen: Sozialdemokratie und Prostitution im deutschen Kaiserreich', in Johanna Geyer-Kordesch and Anette Kuhn, eds, *Frauenkörper-Medizin-Sexualität* (Düsseldorf, 1986), pp. 102–26.

84  Hans v. B…r, *Ein Roman aus Berlin W.* (James Grunert, 1908), repr. Biblioteca Erotica et Curiosa (Munich, 1971), pp. 216, 270.

85  Alfred Blaschko, *Die Prostitution im 19. Jahrhundert* (Berlin, 1902), p. 38.

86  'Dienstanweisung über die Handhabung der Sittenkontrolle (Nach dem M.-Erl. vom 29.3.02 IIa 1077; 22.2.99; 11.12.09. M.-Bl. 1908, S.14–16)', in *Dienstanweisung für den Polizeibeamten*, ed. F. Metzlaff (Recklinghausen, n. d.), pp. 76ff.

87  O. Commence, *La prostitution clandestine à Paris* (Paris, 1904), p. 109.

88  *Schwester Henriette Arendt, Menschen die den Pfad verloren* (as n. 23), p. 49.

89  *Die Welt von der man nicht spricht! (Aus den Papieren einer Polizeibeamtin)*, compiled by Anna Pappritz (Leipzig, 1907), p. 5.

90  Abraham Flexner, *Prostitution in Europe* (1914) (Montclair, N J, 1969), p. 309.

91  Felix Block, 'Die nicht gewerbsmässige Prostitution, ihre Ursachen, Formen, und deren Bekämpfung', in *Zeitschrift für Bekämpfung der Geschlechtskrankheiten* III (1909), pp. 69–86, here p. 72.

92  Else Spiller, *Slums. Erlebnisse in den Schlammvierteln moderner Großstädte* (Aarau, Leipzig and Vienna, 1911), p. 9.

93  J. Ewing Ritchie, *The Night Side of London* (London, 1857).

94  Stephen Graham, *London Nights* (London, n. d. [*c*.1924–5]), p. 167.

95  Robert Murphy, *Smash and Grab, Gangsters in the London Underworld* (London and Boston, 1993), p. 9.

96  Gerrold Blanchard, introduction to *London: A Pilgrimage*, illustrated by G. Doré (1872) (New York, 1970).

97  Judith R. Walkowitz, *City of Dreadful Delight, Narratives of Danger in Late-Victorian London* (Chicago, 1992), p. 1.

98  Cited in Steve Jones, *London through the Keyhole* (Nottingham, 1991), p. 28.

99  George Reynolds, *The Mysteries of London* (London, 1846), p. 21.

100  Jost Hermand, 'Das Bild der "großen Stadt" im Expressionismus', in Klaus R. Scherpe, ed., *Die Unwirklichkeit der Städte. Großstadtdarstellungen zwischen Moderne und Postmoderne* (Reinbek, 1988), pp. 61–79, here p. 62.

101  Dominik Bartmann, 'Das Großstadtbild Berlins in der Weltsicht der Expressionisten', in *Stadtbilder. Berlin in der Malerei vom 17 Jahrhundert bis zur Gegenwart*, Berlin Museum (Berlin, 1987), pp. 243–59, here pp. 252ff.

102  Heinz Rölleke, *Die Stadt bei Stadler, Heym und Trakl* (Cologne, 1965), p. 96.

103  Jost Hermand (as n. 100), p. 67.

104  Edmund Edel, 'Berlin tanzt!', in *Berliner Nächte* (Berlin, 1914), pp. 77–102, here p. 99.

105  'Musikcafés', ibid., pp. 43–62, here p. 62; 'Nachtrestaurants', ibid., pp. 63–8, here pp. 64ff., 67; 'Bars', ibid., pp. 69–76, here p. 75.

106  J. Flemming, 'Das Nachtleben in deutschen Großstädten. Videant consules!', in *Zeitschrift für Bekämpfung der Geschlechtskrankheiten* XVI/7 (1915), pp. 202–16.

107  Ivan Bloch, *Das Sexualleben unserer Zeit in seiner Beziehung zur modernen Kultur* (1907) (Berlin, 10th–12th edns, 1919), p. 296.

108  Willy Hellpach, 'Unser Genußleben und die Geschlechtskrankheiten', in *Mitteilungen der Deutschen Gesellschaft zur Bekämpfung der Geschlechtskrankheiten 1905* II/5–6, pp. 103–5; cited in Ivan Bloch, *Das Sexualleben unserer Zeit* (as above), pp. 297–300, here p. 297.

109  Katharina Scheven, 'Die sozialen und wirtschaftlichen Grundlagen der Prostitution', in Anna Pappritz, ed., *Einführung in das Studium der Prostitutionsfrage* (Leipzig, 1919), pp. 139–175, here p. 164.

110  Charlotte Stemmler, 'Die Tätigkeit der Polizeipflegerin', in *Zeitschrift für Bekämpfung der Geschlechtskrankheiten* XVI/2 (1915), pp. 31–46, here p. 37.

111  See also Alfred Korach, *Über die Kommunalisierung der Prostituiertenfürsorge in Berlin. Veröffentlichungen aus dem Gebiete der Medizinalverwaltung*, XV/6 (Berlin, 1922).

112  Charlotte Stemmler (as n. 110), p. 35.

113  *Mitteilungen des Statistischen Amtes der Stadt Berlin*, No. 5, Pt 7 (August 1919): 'Die eingeschriebenen Prostituierten in Berlin 1925', pp. 7ff.

114  WEKA, *Prostitution und Verbrechen. Reportagen aus den Tiefen der Berliner Unterwelt* (Leipzig, 1930), pp. 100ff.

115  ADW, CA/GF 1737/4: Prostitution und das Straßenbild 1928–33; Brief des Referats Gefährdetenfürsorge an Pastor Licentiat Bohn (Plötzensee, 26 June 1928).

116  Ibid., Bericht aus Frankfurt, n. d.

117  *Stätten der Berliner Prostitution. Von den Elends-Absteigequartieren am Schlesischen Bahnhof und Alexanderplatz zur Luxus-Prostitution der Friedrichstraße und des Kurfürstendamms. Eine Reportage von WEKA* (Berlin, 1930), p. 7 and elsewhere.

118  Ibid., p. 51.

119  Wolfgang Mittermaier, 'Das Straßenbild nach Inkrafttreten des GBG', in *Der Abolitionist. Organ des Bundes für Frauen-und Jugendschutz* XXX/3 (Berlin, 31 May 1931); 'Sachverständigen-Konferenz am Mittwoch den 15 April 1931 in Berlin: Das Straßenbild nach Inkrafttreten des RGBG. Vorsitz: Frau Anna Pappritz', in *Mitteilungen der Deutschen Gesellschaft zur Bekämpfung von Geschlechtskrankheiten* XXIX/5–6 (May 1931), pp. 66–111; see also further reports in ADW, CA/GF 1637/4: 'Auswirkungen des GBG', n. d.

120  Oberverwaltungsgerichtsrat Dr Hagemann, Berlin, in 'Sachverständigen-Konferenz' (as above), p. 96.

121  Helga Bemmann cited this as the 'first German chanson', sung by Bozena Bradsky ('Adèle, la reine, la blonde') in the 'Überbrettl', the first German cabaret, which opened in Berlin on 18 January 1901: Bemman, *Musenkinder-Memoiren. Eine heitere Chronik von 1900 –1930* (Berlin/GDR, 1987), p. 9.

122  For this Alain Corbin cites various sources, some from literature, such as Léon Bloy and Guillaume Apollinaire, but also from the Socialist and Anarchist press, whose fight against the vice police led to a glorification of the prostitute as 'femme digne d'amour': Corbin, *Les Filles de Noce* (as n. 38), p. 358.

123  *50 Arbeitsjahre im Dienste des Glaubens und der Liebe. Jubiläumsschrift der Berliner Stadtmission* (Berlin, 1927), p. 14.

124  Johann Heinrich Wichern's 'Hamburgs wahres und geheimes Volksleben', a report on 'expeditions through the poor areas of Hamburg' published in 1832, is seen in Germany as the founding text for this type of missionary work; for the general history, practice and ideology of the Mission see also Christoph Sachße and Florian Tennstedt, eds, *Bettler, Gauner und Proleten. Armut und Armenfürsorge in der deutschen Geschichte. Ein Bild-Lesebuch* (Reinbek, 1981), and *Jahrbuch der Sozialarbeit 4: Geschichte und Geschichten* (Reinbek, 1981) (in particular Thomas Olk and Rolf G. Heinze, 'Die Bürokratisierung der Nächstenliebe. Am Beispiel von Geschichte und Entwicklung der "Inneren Mission"', pp. 233–71; and Hartmut Dießenbacher, 'Altruismus als Abenteuer. Vier biographische Skizzen zu bürgerlichen Altruisten des 19. Jahrhunderts', pp. 272–98); Florian Tennstedt, *Sozialgeschichte der Sozialpolitik in Deutschland. Vom 18. Jahrhundert bis zum Ersten Weltkrieg* (Göttingen, 1981); Volker Hentschel, *Geschichte der deutschen Sozialpolitik 1880 1980* (Frankfurt a. M., 1983); Christoph Sachße and Florian Tennstedt, eds, *Soziale Sicherheit und soziale Disziplinierung. Beiträge zu einer historischen Theorie der Sozialpolitik* (Frankfurt a. M., 1986).

125  Philip Magnus, *Gladstone. A Biography* (London, 1954), pp. 105ff.

126  William J. Fishman, *The Streets of East London* (London, 1979), pp. 64ff.

127  Tom Cullen, *The Prostitutes' Padre. The story of the famous rector of Stiffkey* (London, 1975).

128 John M. Weylland, *These Fifty Years, being the Jubilee of the City of London Mission* (London, 1884).

129 Harry Barnes, *The Slum, its Story and Solution* (London, 1931).

130 F. S. Schwarzbach, *Dickens and the City* (London, 1979) p. 118.

131 Gareth Stedman Jones, *Outcast London, A Study in the Relationship between Classes in Victorian Society* (Oxford, 1971), p. 257.

132 *The Bitter Cry of Outcast London, an inquiry into the condition of the abject poor*, reprinted with an introduction by Anthony S. Wohl (Leicester, 1970).

133 'The Midnight Meetings and their results', *The London City Mission Magazine* (1 October 1860).

134 John Ruskin, in E. T. Cook and A. Wedderburn, eds, *The Writings of J. R.*, (London, 1908), p. 205.

135 Robert Sandall, *The History of the Salvation Army*, Vol. I (1865–78), with a foreword by General Osborn (London, 1947), p. 1.

136 Hartmut Dießenbacher, 'Altruismus als Abenteuer' (as n. 124), p. 282.

137 See also Cornelia Carstens and Petra Heidebrecht, 'Der leichtsinnige Zug in die Großstadt. Dienstmädchen und Bahnhofsmission um 1900', in *Die Reise nach Berlin*, pub. Berliner Festspiele GmbH (Berlin, 1987), pp. 229–36.

138 Ernst Otto Hopp, *In der großen Stadt* (Berlin, 1885).

139 Pastor M. Gensichen, 'Die Nachtmission', *Blätter aus der Stadtmission* XXX/9 (Berlin, 1907), pp. 122–5, here p. 122.

140 Ibid., pp. 124ff. These fights too have 'another' side. In 1930 Egon Erwin Kisch described 'an amusing discussion on the street with missionaries from the Home Mission': 'Jiddisches Literaturcafé', in *Der rasende Reporter* (Berlin, 1930), pp. 347–51, here p. 348.

141 ADW, CA 912 I: Mitternachtsmission. Satzung des Vereins 'Deutsche Mitternachtsmission e.V.'

142 'Dresdner Nachtmission', a speech by P. Adolf Müller at a mission evening on 27 November 1911 in Dresden, in *Zeitschrift des deutsch-evangelischen Vereins zur Förderung der Sittlichkeit* XXVI/7–8 (15 July 1912).

143 ADW, CA 992 b: Zeitungsartikel, Flugblätter etc. der Mitternachtsmission: *Berliner Morgenpost*, n. d.

144 Ibid., H. Flemming, 'Die Nachtmission', manuscript, signed, n. d.

145 E. Heine, *Zertretene Blüten. Skizzen aus dem sittlichen und sozialen Elend der Großstadt* (Berlin, n. d.), pp. 5, 7.

146 ADW, CA 992 b: 'Erlebnisse aus der Nachtmission', manuscript, n. d.

147 Evangelisches Zentralarchiv (hereafter EZA), Berlin 7/XII–3808: Acta, die öffentliche Sittlichkeit betreffend: Brief der 'Volksgemeinschaft zur Wahrung von Anstand und guter Sitte' an den Reichsminister der Justiz, 1920.

148 Bernhard Duhr S. J., *Großstadt-Elend und Rettung der Elendesten* (Freiburg im Breisgau, 1920), pp. 21, 29ff.

149 EZA, Berlin, 7/XII–3808: Protokoll der Verfassunggebenden Preußischen Landesversammlung, 157. Sitzung am 23. September, 1920. P. 12408 (Mentzel), 12420 (Wegscheider, SPD), 12426 (Kilian).

150 See also ADW, CA/GF 992 a/5: Mitternachtsmission. Zeitungsartikel, Flugblätter etc. 1928–43: Heinz Cassier, Erlangen: 'Deutsche Mitternachtsarbeit! Aufruf zum Beitritt zur Deutschen Mitternachtsmission e. V.', n. d.

151 *Notizen. Weltstadtbetrachtungen* by Dr Carl Sonnenschein, issue 7 (17 April 1927).

152 'Die Menschen-Mühle Berlin. Eine Schilderung in Schildern von Hans Hyan', in *UHU* III/3 (March 1927), pp. 82–9, here p. 86.

153 Walter Benjamin, 'Berliner Kindheit um Neunzehnhundert', in *Gesammelte Schriften*, Vol. IV/1. *Kleine Prosa, Baudelaire-Übertragungen. Werkausgabe*, ed. Tillmann Rexroth (Frankfurt a. M., 1980) pp. 235–304.

154 Heinrich Berl, *Der Kampf gegen das rote Berlin* (Karlsruhe, 1932).

155 'Bahnhofsmission', *Märkische Volkszeitung* (12 February 1929); repr. in *Völkischer Beobachter*, 19 February 1929.

156 'Mitternachtsmission', *Kölner Lokal-Anzeiger* (5 June 1928).

V NIGHT-WALKING

1  In my doctoral thesis I was able to make this chapter longer than it is here, and will now therefore concentrate on a few fundamental aspects of the topic of 'walking'.

2  Wilhelm Heinrich Riehl, *Wanderbuch*, the second part of *Land und Leute*, Vol. IV of *Die Naturgeschichte des Volkes als Grundlage einer deutschen Sozialpolitik* (1852) (Stuttgart and Berlin, 1925), pp. 3, 5.

3  Ibid., p. 3

4  Walter Benjamin, *Das Passagen-Werk*, Vol. I, ed. Rolf Tiedemann (Frankfurt a. M., 1983), p. 533.

5  See also Arlette Farge, *Vivre dans la rue à Paris au XVIIIe siècle* (Paris, 1979); Manfred Gailus, ed., *Pöbelexzesse und Volkstumulte in Berlin. Zur Sozialgeschichte der Straße (1830–1880)* (Berlin, 1984); Gailus, *Straße und Brot. Sozialer Protest in den deutschen Staaten under bes. Berücksichtigung Preußens 1847–1849* (Göttingen, 1990).

6  See Johannes Willms, *Paris. Hauptstadt Europas 1789–1914* (Munich, 1988), pp. 343–370.

7  Gloria Levitas, 'Anthropology and Sociology of Streets', in Stanford Anderson, ed., *On Streets* (Cambridge, MA, and London, 1986), pp. 225–239, here p. 231.

8  Walter Benjamin, *Das Passagen-Werk* (as n. 4.), p. 531.

9  Richard Sennett, *The Fall of Public Man* (London, 1977).

10  Ibid., p. 27.

11  François Gasnault, *Guinguettes et Lorettes. Bals publics à Paris au XIXe siècle (1830–1870)* (Paris, 1986), p. 309.

12  M. von Reymond, 'Berliner Pflaster', preface to *Berliner Pflaster. Illustrierte Schilderungen aus dem Berliner Leben* (Berlin, 1894), p. 1.

13  Hermann Keller, 'Das Straßenbauwesen der Großstädte', in *Westermanns illustrierte deutsche Monatshefte* XXVII/53 (1883), pp. 637–656, here p. 638. I would like to thank Bernd Jürgen Warneken for the reference.

14  Peter Sloterdijk, *Der Zaubertraum. Die Entstehung der Psychoanalyse im Jahr 1785. Ein epischer Versuch zur Philosophie der Psychologie* (Frankfurt a. M., 1987), p. 184.

15  Karl Schlögel, *Jenseits des großen Oktober. Das Laboratorium der Moderne. Leningrad 1909–1921* (Berlin, 1988), p. 160.

16  Bernd Jürgen Warneken, 'Bürgerliche Gehkultur in der Epoche der Französischen Revolution', *Zeitschrift für Volkskunde* 2 (1989), pp. 177–187, here p. 187.

17  Laurence Sterne, *A Sentimental Journey through France and Italy* (1768), ed. and with an introduction by Ian Jack (Oxford and New York, 1964), p. 107.

18  Theodor W. Adorno, *Minima moralia. Reflexionen aus dem beschädigten Leben*, (Frankfurt a. M., 1969).

19  Paul-Ernest de Rattier, *Paris n'existe pas* (Paris, 1857), p. 12.

20  Jules Janin, *Un Hiver à Paris* (Paris, 1847), p. 210.

21  See also Wolfgang Griep, 'Die reinliche Stadt. Über fremden und eigenen Schmutz', in Konrad Wedemann, ed., *Rom – Paris – London. Erfahrungen und Selbsterfahrung deutscher Schriftsteller und Künstler in den fremden Metropolen* (Stuttgart, 1988 ), pp. 135–54.

22  'Das Verbrechertum in Berlin. Von A. Ragotzky, Prediger an der Stadtvogtei zu Berlin', in *Gartenlaube* 24 (1872), pp. 374–377, here p. 374 (continued in issue 25 [1872], pp. 390–2).

23  Katharina Oxenius, 'Vom Promenieren zum Spazieren. Eine ethnographische Studie Pariser Gärten', unpublished doctoral thesis, University of Tübingen, 1987, p. 126.

24  Eckhardt Köhn, *Straßenrausch. Flanerie und kleine Form. Versuch zur Literaturgeschichte des Flaneurs bis 1933* (Berlin, 1989), pp. 27–34: 'Der Flaneur. Sozialgeschichtliche Konturen einer Großstadtgestalt'.

25  Walter Benjamin, *Das Passagen-Werk*, Vol. I (as n. 4): 'Aufzeichnungen und Materialien. M: der Flaneur', pp. 525–569, here p. 526.

26  Walter Benjamin, 'Über einige Motive bei Baudelaire', in *Gesammelte Schriften*, Vol. I/2, eds Rolf Tiedemann and Hermann Schweppenhäuser (Frankfurt a. M., 1980), pp. 605–53, here p. 627.

27  Victor Fournel, *L'odyssée d'un flâneur ou ce qu'on voit dans les rues de Paris* (Paris, 1858), p. 2.

28  Ludwig Kalisch, 'Pariser Bilder und Geschichten. Die kleinen Rentiers', in *Gartenlaube* 21 (1872), pp. 346ff, here p. 347.

29  Siegfried Kracauer, *Ginster* (1928) (Frankfurt a. M., 1963), p. 24.

30  See also Eckhardt Köhn, *Straßenrausch* (as n. 24).

31  Victor Auburtin, 'Wie sie spazierengehen', *Berliner Tageblatt* I/5 (1911).

32  Julius Rodenberg, *Paris bei Sonnenschein und Lampenlicht. Skizzenbuch zur Weltausstellung* (Paris, 1867), p. 40.

33  J. H. Zedler, *Großes vollständiges Universal-Lexikon aller Wissenschaften und Künste* (Leipzig and Halle, 1790): 'Nachtschwärmer'.

34  Thomas Burke, *English Night Life. From Norman Curfew to Present Black-out* (London, 1941), p. v.

35  Theodor Fontane, *Wanderungen durch England und Schottland*, Vol. II, ed. Hans-Heinrich Reuter (Berlin/GDR, 1980), p. 525.

36  In particular, Louis Chevalier, *Montmartre du Plaisir et du Crime* (Paris, 1980); ibid., 'Les Ruines du Subure. Montmartre de 1939 aux Années 80 (Paris, 1985) ; see also Lothar Uebel, *Viel Vergnügen. Die Geschichte der Vergnügungsstätten rund um den Kreuzberg und die Hasenheide. Kreuzberger Hefte VIII* (Berlin, 1985), which provides further bibliographical references.

37  Ernst Günther, *Geschichte des Varietés* (Berlin/GDR, 1978), pp. 73ff.

38  Siegfried Kracauer, *Jacques Offenbach und das Paris seiner Zeit* (1937), ed. Karsten Witte (Frankfurt a. M., 1976), p. 32.

39  Maurice Talmeyr, 'Cafés-Concerts et Music-Halls', in *Revue des Deux-Mondes* 10 (1902), p. 159.

40  Johannes Willms, *Paris* (as n. 6), p. 454.

41  Edmund B. d'Auvergne, *The night side of Paris* (London, n. d. [after 1902]), p.

161. This book was modelled on Robert Machray, *The Night Side of London* (London, 1902).

42 Hans Ostwald, 'Dunkle Winkel und Menschen', in *Berliner Nächte* (Berlin, 1914), pp. 1–24, here p. 1.

43 In succession: Paul Lindenberg 'Die vierundzwanzig Stunden von Berlin', in Lindenberg, *Berlin in Wort und Bild* (Berlin 1895), p. 117; Hans Ostwald and Eberhard Buchner, *Berliner Nachtlebe. Lebeweltnächte – Berliner Clubs – Tanz – und Ballokale – Varietés und Tingeltangel – Kaffeehäuser und Nachtkneipen. Gesammelte Großstadt-Dokumente* (Berlin and Leipzig, n. d.), p. 10; *Berlin für Kenner. Ein Bärenführer bei Tag und Nacht durch die deutsche Reichshauptstadt,* Vol. I of *Großstadtführer für Kenner* (Berlin, n. d. [1912]), p. 10; Eugen Szatmari, *Das Buch von Berlin. Was nicht im 'Baedeker' steht,* Vol. I (Munich, n. d.), p. 139; Edmund Edel, 'Musikcafés', in *Berliner Nächte* (Berlin, 1914), pp. 43–62, here p. 43; Henry F. Urban, *Die Entdeckung Berlins* (Berlin, 1912), p. 39.

44 H. A. Kober, 'Was unsere Väter liebten. Abendbummel durch die Vergnügungs-Etablissements um 1900', *UHU* VI/6 (March 1930), pp. 39–46, here pp. 44–6.

45 Joseph Kessel, *Nuits de Montmartre* (Paris, 1971), p. 12.

46 John Gay, 'Trivia, or The Art of Walking the Streets of London (2nd Part: The Art of Walking the Streets by Night)', in *Poetry and Prose*, Vol. I, ed. Vinton A. Dearing, with the assistance of Charles E. Beckwith (Oxford, 1974), pp. 134–81.

47 'Paris la nuit', in Eugène de Mirecourt, *Paris Historique, Pittoresque et Anecdotique* (Paris, 1855), p. 17.

48 Ingrid Oesterle, 'Paris – das moderne Rom?', in Konrad Wiedemann, ed., *Rom – Paris – London* (as n. 21), pp. 375–419, here p. 376.

49 *Berliner Zeitung* (31 October 1903); see also the fine attempt at a definition by Roland Barthes: 'Night: any state which provokes in the subject the metaphor of the darkness, whether affective, intellective or existential, in which he struggles or subsides'; Barthes, *A Lovers' Discourse*, trans. Richard Howard (London, 1979).

50 Eduard Fuchs, *Die Frau in der Karikatur* (Munich, 1928), pp. 412ff.

51 See also especially Rolf Lindner, *Die Entdeckung der Stadtkultur. Soziologie aus der Erfahrung der Reportage* (Frankfurt a. M., 1990).

52 Cited in Raymond Williams, 'Cities of Darkness and Light', in *The Country and the City* (New York, 1973), pp. 215–32, here p. 228.

53 H. V. Morton, *The Nights of London* (London, 1926), p. 1.

54 Robert Machray, *The Night Side of London* (London, 1902), p. 9

55 Ibid., p. 10.

56 Donald Maxwell, *The New Lights o' London, being a series of impressions of the glamour and magic of London at night* (London, 1926).

57 Stephen Graham, *London Nights* (London, *c*.1924/25), p. 20.

58 Ibid., p. 1

59 Ibid., p. 5

60 Ralph Nevill, *London and Paris – Past and Present* (London, *c*.1920).

61 Karl Josef Friedrich, *Der Nachtwächter Gottes* (Dresden and Leipzig, 1939) [author's summary].

62 Harry Domela, *Der falsche Prinz. Mein Leben und meine Abenteuer* (Berlin, 1927), p. 53.

63 Pierre Sansot writes that there has to be a secret link, 'un lieu analogique,

secret, entre les chemins de la conscience et les avenues d'une ville'; he also says that the night-walkers were 'more alien' and 'closer' to each other at the same time; nobody knows the other person's intentions, whether or not he may be dangerous; nevertheless one tells him one's whole life history, to which he would never listen during the day: *Poétique de la Ville* (Paris, 1988) p. 153. Louis Aragon however says: '. . .they meet each other, the regulars of these nocturnal walks, scrutinizing each other as they pass with the suspicion of savages in the desert. They never speak. Yet they recognize each other, giving each other secret nicknames and never seeking any explanation for the constant presence of the others in the places where each wishes to maintain for himself alone the prerogative of a unique and threatening melancholy.' 'Le mauvais plaisant', in *Le mentir-vrai* (Paris, 1980), p. 82.

64  Louis Aragon, *Paris Peasant*, trans. with introduction by Simon Watson Taylor, (London, 1980), pp. 27–28.

65  Philippe Soupault, *Die letzten Nächte von Paris* (1928) (Heidelberg, 1982), p. 91.


VI  AN END: BIG CITY NIGHTS AROUND 1930

1  *L'Illustration* (4 March 1933).

2  Brassaï, *Le Paris secret des années 30* (Paris, 1976).

3  Brassaï, *Henry Miller in Paris* (Frankfurt a. M., 1981), p. 11.

4  H. von Wedderkop, 'Sous les toits de Paris', *Der Querschnitt* 9 (1930), p. 198.

5  Klaus Mann, *Der Wendepunkt Ein Lebensbericht* (Berlin/GDR and Weimar, 1979), p. 198.

6  Jean Giraudoux, Chas-Laborde, *Berlin. Straßen und Gesichter 1930*, eds Friederike Hassauer and Peter Roos (Nördlingen, 1987), p. 12.

7  Ivan Goll, 'Montparnasse à Berlin', *Vu* 213 (13 April 1932), pp. 534ff.

8  Pieter Lastman, '"Nana" unterm Stadtbahnbogen', *Die Weltbühne* (12 February 1929).

9  'Lebewelt. Aus den Berliner Gerichten', in the first supplement to *Vossische Zeitung* (2 August 1930).

10  Curt Moreck, *Führer durch das lasterhafte Berlin* (Leipzig, 1931) (repr. Berlin, 1987), p. 12.

11  Ibid., p. 75ff.

12  Siegfried Kracauer, 'Analyse eines Stadtplans', in *Straßen in Berlin und anderswo* (Frankfurt a. M., 1964), pp. 16–19, here p. 18.

13  Joseph Roth, 'Berliner Vergnügungsindustrie (1930)', in *Großstadt-Feuilletons*, Vol. IV of *Werke*, ed. Hermann Kesten (Cologne and Amsterdam, 1976), pp. 864–8, here p. 864.

14  Alain Corbin, *The Lure of the Sea, the discovery of the seaside in the Western world*, trans. Joscelyn Phelps (Cambridge, 1994), 'Considerations of Method', p. 279.

15  Hsi-hoey Liang, *Die Berliner Polizei in der Weimarer Republik* (Berlin, 1977), p. 181.

16  Joseph Goebbels, *Kampf um Berlin. I. Der Anfang (1926–1927)* (Munich, 1932), p. 27.

17  Ibid., p.33.

18  See also Utz Jeggle, 'Parteigenosse Feuer', in *Nationalsozialismus im Landkreis Tübingen. Eine Heimatkunde*, Ludwig-Uhland-Institut für Empirische Kulturwissenschaft der Universität Tübingen (Tübingen, 1988), pp. 167–71.

19  See also Gottfried Korff, 'Berliner Nächte. Zum Selbstbild urbaner

Eigenschaften und Leidenschaften', in Gerhard Brunn and Jürgen Reulecke, eds, *Berlin. Blicke auf die deutsche Metropole* (Essen, 1989), pp. 71–103; here pp. 92–100; Klaus Herding and Hans-Ernst Mittig, *Kunst und Alltag im NS-System. Albert Speers Berliner Straßenlaternen* (Giessen, 1975); Peter Reichel, *Der schöne Schein des Dritten Reiches. Faszination und Gewalt des Faschismus* (Munich, 1991).

20  'Unvermutete Besichtigungen. Gauleiter Dr. Goebbels fährt durch die Reichshauptstadt', *Völkischer Beobachter* (6 October 1934).

21  Marko Paysan, 'Zauber der Nacht', in Bernd Polster, ed.,'*Swing Heil'. Jazz im Nationalsozialismus* (Berlin, 1989), pp. 75–94, here p. 76.

22  'Ein Nazi reist um die Gedächtniskirche. Dupont wird stutzig', *Der Angriff* (30 November 1934).

23  Curt Moreck, *Führer durch das lasterhafte Berlin* (Leipzig, 1931) (repr. Berlin, 1987), p. 230.

24  Pierre Sansot, *Poétique de la Ville* (Paris, 1988), p. 146.

25  Robert Springer, *Berlin wird Weltstadt. Ernste und heitere Culturbilder* (Berlin, 1868), pp. 61ff.

26  Willy Hellpach, *Nervosität und Kultur* (Stuttgart, 1902), p. 90.

27  Heiner Schultz, 'Angst-Gewühl-Versicherung. Ein Versuch über Folgen der Industrialisierung für das Bewußtsein', *Kursbuch* 61 (1980), pp. 95–117, here p. 95.

28  Karl Scheffler, *Berlin. Ein Stadtschicksal* (Berlin, 1910), p. 107.

29  Magnus Hirschfeld, *Die Gurgel von Berlin*, Vol. XLI of *Großstadt-Dokumente* (Berlin and Leipzig, n. d. [after 1906]), pp. 130ff.

30  'Bericht der Gesellschaft für soziale Reform an den internationalen Kongreß für gesetzlichen Arbeiterschutz in Paris, 1900', cited in *Die Nachtarbeit in der Deutschen Metall und Maschinenindustrie* (Stuttgart, 1913).

31  Alexander v. Gleichen-Rußwurm, *Das Kulturbild des 19. Jahrhunderts*, Vol. 23/24: *Die geistige Entwicklung des modernen Europa. Die gesellschaftliche Struktur* (Hamburg, n. d.), pp. 574ff.

32  Karl Kautsky, *Vermehrung und Entwicklung in Natur und Gesellschaft* (Stuttgart, 1910), pp. 244ff.

33  Liliput, 'Vergnügen', *Die Weltbühne* (25 January 1923).

34  H. V. Morton, *The Nights of London* (London, 1926), p. 5.

# Bibliography

For reasons of space, I have not listed every individual archival file consulted. Precise references to sources are found in the notes to the individual chapters, where the following abbreviations are used:

APP    Archives de la Préfecture de Police
ADW  Archiv des Diakonischen Werkes, Evangelical Church, Berlin
EZA    Evangelisches Zentralarchiv, Konsistorium of the Evangelical Church, Berlin
LAB    Landesarchiv Berlin (West)
SBO    Stadtarchiv Berlin-Ost
SAP    Staatsarchiv der DDR, Potsdam

Achten, Udo, *Denn was uns fehlt, ist Zeit. Geschichte des arbeitsfreien Wochenendes* (Cologne, 1988)

Acton, William, *Prostitution. Considered in its Moral, Social and Sanitary Aspects, in London and other Large Cities* (London, 1857), ed. with introduction and notes by Peter Fryer (London, 1968)

Adan, Paul, *Badauderies Parisiennes. Les rassemblements. Physiologies de la rue observées et notées par P. A.* (Paris, 1896)

Adorno, Theodor W., *Minima Moralia. Reflections from a Damaged Life*, trans. E. F. N. Jephcott (London, 1974)

d'Allemagne, Henry-René, *Histoire du luminaire depuis l'époque romaine jusqu'au XIXe siècle* (Paris, 1891)

Allers, Christin W., *Spreeathener. Berliner Bilder* (Breslau, 1889)

Alphande, Adolphe, *Les Promenades de Paris*, 2 vols (Paris, 1868, 1873)

Anders N. J. (=Nathan Jacob), *Orpheum–Ballhaus. Berlins romantische Nächte! Humoristischer Führer durch die Feensäle der Norddeutschen Metropole* (Berlin, c.1878)

Anderson, Stanford, ed., *On Streets* (Cambridge, MA, London, 1986)

*Anfänge der Arbeiterfreizeit, Eine Ausstellung der Deutschen Demokratischen Republik*, catalogue of an exhibition organized by the Märkisches Museum, Museum 'Berliner Arbeiterleben um 1900', Berlin/GDR, 1987 (Berlin, 1989)

Anselm, Sigrun and Barbara Beck, eds, *Triumph und Scheitern in der Metropole. Zur Rolle der Weiblichkeit in der Geschichte Berlins* (Berlin, 1987)

Aragon, Louis, *Le Mentir–vrai* (Paris, 1980)

—, *Paris Peasant*, trans. with introduction by Simon Watson Taylor (London, 1980)

Archer, T., *The terrible sights of London and Labours of Love in the midst of them* (London, 1870)

Arendt, Schwester Henriette, *Menschen die den Pfad verloren. Erlebnisse aus meiner fünfjährigen Tätigkeit als Polizeiassistentin in Stuttgart* (Stuttgart, n. d. [1908])

de Arist, Paul, *La vie et le monde du boulevard* (Paris, 1930)

Armin, Bettine von, *Dies Buch gehört dem König* (1844), ed. Ilse Staff (Frankfurt, 1982)

Arndt, Ernst Moritz, *Pariser Sommer 1799*, new edn. with preface by Wolfgang Gerlach (Munich, 1982)

*Asiles de nuit pour femmes et enfants*. Inauguration (Paris, 1883)

Assessor, *Die Berliner Polizei, Großstadt-Dokumente*, Vol. XXXIV, ed. Hans Ostwald (Berlin, n. d.)

Atwood, Jane Evelyn, *Nächtlicher Alltag. Meine Begegnung mit Prostituierten in Paris. Eine fotografische Studie* (Munich, 1980)

d' Auvergne, Edmund B., *The night side of Paris* (London, n. d. [after 1902])

Avé-Lallement, Friedrich Christian Benedict, *Die Krisis der deutschen Polizei* (Leipzig, 1861)

—, *Physiologie der deutschen Polizei* (Leipzig, 1882)

—, *Das deutsche Gaunertum in seiner sozialpolitischen, literarischen und linguistischen Ausbildung zu seinem heutigen Bestande*, new edn. by Max Bauer, 2 vols (Munich and Berlin, 1914)

Ackroyd, Peter, *Evil London. The dark side of a great city* (London, 1973)

B...r, Hans von, *Ein Roman aus Berlin W.* (1908; Munich, 1971)

Bade, Theodor, *Ueber den Verfall der Sitten in den großen Städten. Mit besonderer Berücksichtigung der Zustände in Berlin und der betreffenden Polizei-Versuche während der letzten zehn Jahre* (Berlin, 1857)

—, *Über Gelegenheitsmacherei und öffentliches Tanzvergnügen (Neuer Beitrag zur Prostitutionsfrage)* (Berlin, 1858)

Baker, Josephine, and Jo Bouillon, *Josephine*, trans. Marianne Fitzpatrick (London, 1978)

de Balzac, Honoré, *Théorie de la démarche et autres textes*, ed. Jacques Bonnet (Paris, 1978)

Barnes, Harry, *The Slum. Its Story and Solution* (London, 1931)

Barthes, Roland, *A lover's discourse*, trans. Richard Howard (London, 1979)

Bastian, Ange, *Les mauvais lieux de Paris* (Paris, 1968)

Bausinger, Hermann, *Volkskultur in der technischen Welt* (Stuttgart, 1961; Frankfurt and New York, 1986)

—, *Volkskunde. Von der Altertumsforschung zur Kulturanalyse* (Darmstadt, 1971; Tübingen, 1979)

Bausinger Hermann, Utz Jeggle, Gottfried Korff and Martin Scharfe, *Grundzüge der Volkskunde* (Darmstadt, 1978)

Beer, Julius, *Die Schließung der öffentlichen Häuser und ihre sittlichen Folgen für die Stadt Berlin* (Berlin, 1856)

Behrend, Friedrich Jakob, *Die Prostitution in Berlin und die gegen sie und die Syphilis zu nehmenden Maßregeln* (Erlangen, 1850)

Beltran, André, 'La Fée Electricité, Reine et Servante', *Vingtième Siècle, Revue d'Histoire*, octobre–décembre 1987 (Paris, 1987)

Belyi, Andrej, *Im Reich der Schatten (Berlin 1921 bis 1923)*, with an essay by Karl Schlögel (Frankfurt, 1983)

Bemmann, Helga, *Musenkinder-Memoiren. Eine heitere Chronik von 1900 bis 1930* (Berlin/GDR, 1987)

Benjamin Walter, *Gesammelte Schriften*, eds Rolf Tiedemann and Hermann Schweppenhäuser (Frankfurt, 1972)

—, *Das Passagen-Werk*, ed. Rolf Tiedemann, 2 vols (Frankfurt, 1983)

Bennett, Arnold, *Paris nights and other impressions of places and people* (London, 1913)

Bergmann, Klaus, *Agrarromantik und Großstadtfeindschaft* (Meisenheim am Glan, 1970)

—, *Schwarze Reportagen. Aus dem Leben der untersten Schichten vor 1914, Huren, Vagabunden, Lumpen* (Reinbek, 1984)

Berl, Heinrich, *Der Kampf gegen das rote Berlin* (Karlsruhe, 1932)

*Berlin. Ein Verführer. Quartiermacher für erotisch interessierte Berlin-Besucher* (Berlin, 1973)

*Berlin. Eine entwicklungsgeschichtliche Darstellung von Friedrich Flierl u. Ulrich v. Uechtritz*, pub. on the occasion of the 25th World Advertising Congress (Berlin, 1929)

*Berlin. Unter Mitwirkung der Zentralstelle für den Fremdenverkehr Groß–Berlins u. a. Verbände*, ed. Berthold Hirschberg (Berlin, 1925)

*Berlin 1836. Wie Karl Marx es sah*, exhibition at the Märkische Museum (Berlin/GDR, 1953)

*Berlin, Berlin*, exhibition on the history of the city, catalogue eds Gottfried Korff and Reinhard Rürup (Berlin, 1987)

*Berlin 1910–1933. Die visuellen Künste, ed. Eberhard Roters* (Berlin and Fribourg, 1983)

*Berlin als Hauptstadt der Weimarer Republik 1919–1933*, ed. Arbeitsgruppe 'Berliner Demokratie' of the FB Geschichtswissenschaft at the Freie Universität Berlin (Berlin, 1987)

*Berlin als Vergnügungstadt*, supplement to *Sport im Bild* (Berlin, 1911)

*Berlin arbeitet!*, lecture series of the Reichsbund Deutscher Technik, Ortsgruppe Berlin 1929/30, reprinted from the journal *Technik voran* (Berlin, 1930)

*Berlin bei Nacht. Kaiserstädtische Kneipenstudien von Siegmund Haber* (Erfurt, 1881)

*Berlin bei Nacht in Wort und Bild*, Vols I–VI (Berlin, 1887)

*Berlin bei Nacht. Ein gründlicher Wegweiser durch das nächtliche Berlin vom frühen Abend bis zum späten Morgen* (Berlin, c.1896)

*Berlin bei Nacht. Erste Berliner illustrierte Nachtzeitung*, Vol. I, Nos 1–7 (Berlin, 1907)

*Berlin bei Tag. Ein Epos in Knüttelversen* (Hamburg, 1857)

*Berlin bei Tag und Nacht. Ein Führer durch die Theater, Conzert-, Tanz- und Vergnügungslokale, nebst Umgebung* (Berlin, 1883)

*Berlin für Kenner. Ein Bärenführer bei Tag und Nacht durch die Deutsche Reichshauptstadt von Ernst Boersche* (Berlin, 1912)

*Berlin im Keller und im ersten Stock* (Berlin, c.1860)

*Berlin im Licht. Festprogramm und Organisation der Arbeitsgemeinschaft 'Berlin im Licht'*, with a foreword by Oberbürgermeister Böss (Berlin, 1928)

*Berlin mit und ohne Gasbeleuchtung. Ein lustiger Führer durch das lustige Berlin für lustige Leute* (Altona, 1869)

*Berlin ohne Dach (Berliner Mysterien). Ein Sittengemälde der Neuzeit* (Berlin, 1854)

'Berlin um Mitternacht. Humoristisches Nachtstück von Dr B. Hesslein', *Berliner Stadtklatsch. Heitere Lebensbilder aus Berlin's Gegenwart* No. 5 (Berlin, n. d.)

*Berlin um 1900*, an exhibition at the Berliner Galerie (Berlin, 1984)

*Berlin und seine Entwicklung. Städtische Jahrbücher für Volkswirthschaft und Statistik*, pub. by the Statistisches Bureau der Stadt Berlin (Berlin, 1867ff.)

*Berlin unter dem Scheinwerfer*, ed. J. Landau (Berlin, 1924)

*Berlin wie es ist. Neuester Wegweiser für Einheimische und Fremde durch Berlin und Potsdam* (Berlin, 1840)

*Berlin wie es ist. Fortsetzung der Sitten- und Charaktergemälde von London, Madrid und Wien von C. v. K...y*, 2 vols (Leipzig, 1827)
*Der Berliner zweifelt immer. Seine Stadt in Feuilletons von damals*, presented by Heinz Knobloch (Berlin/GDR, 1977)
Berliner Asyl–Verein für Obdachlose, annual reports (1869ff.)
—, *Die Einweihung des Neuen Männer-Asyls, Berlin-N., Wiesenstraße Nr.55 am 13. Dezember 1896* (Berlin, 1897)
*Berliner Bauernfänger, oder, Die Geheimnisse der Residenz. Sittenroman aus Berlins Urzeit von A. Beyssel* (Berlin, 1869)
*Berliner Bilder, Berliner Nächte. Eine illustrierte Sammlung von Einzeldarstellungen aus allen Gebieten des Berliner Lebens* (Berlin, 1914)
*Berliner Bummel. Ein lustiger Bärenführer durch das amüsante Berlin*, with preface by Edmund Edel, ed. Felix Schloemp (Berlin, 1913)
*Berliner Gauner. Aus dem Tagebuche eines Berliner Kriminalbeamten von Oskar A. Klaussmann* (Leipzig, 1910)
*Berliner Mädchen. Erzählungen aus dem Leben der Großstadt von Renate Lindner*, Verlag der Berliner Stadtmission (Berlin, n. d.)
*Berliner Nächte*, with contributions by Edmund Edel and Hans Ostwald (Berlin, 1914)
*Das Berliner Nachtleben! Beschreibung und Führung durch das elegante Berlin von \*\*\** (Berlin-Charlottenburg, 1920)
*Berliner Nachtleben. Lebeweltnächte – Berliner Clubs – Tanz – und Ballokale – Varietés und Tingeltangel – Kaffeehäuser und Nachtkneipen. Gesammelte Großstadt-Dokumente von Hans Ostwald, Eberhard Buchner, Spektator und Satyr* (Berlin, Leipzig, n. d.)
*Berliner Nachtstunden. 12 Photos nach Originalen v. E. Urback* (Carlsruhe, 1892)
*Berliner Pflaster. Illustrierte Schilderungen aus dem Berliner Leben* (Berlin, 1894)
*Berliner Prostitution und Zuhältertum. Von Dr X* (Leipzig, n. d.)
*Berliner Wohlfahrtsblatt*, supplement to the official journal of the City of Berlin, special number on 'Fürsorge für Obdachlose', V/8 (14 April 1929)
*Berlins Aufstieg zur Weltstadt. Ein Gedenkbuch*, pub. Verein Berliner Kaufleute und Industrieller (Berlin, 1929)
*Berlins berühmte und berüchtigte Häuser aus der Vergangenheit und Gegenwart, in historischer, criminalistischer und socialer Beziehung dargestellt von Dr Bernhard Hesslein*, 2 vols (Berlin, 1881)
*Berlins Licht- und Schattenseiten. Nach einem mehrjährigen Aufenthalt an Ort und Stelle skizziert by Ad. von Schaden* (Dessau, 1882)
*Berlins sittliche und soziale Zustände. Nach Berliner Berichten dargestellt von Johannes Janssen* (Freiburg, 1872)
*Berlins Spelunken und Verbrecherkneipen. Beiträge zur Sittengeschichte der Residenz aus der Vergangenheit und Gegenwart* (Berlin, 1857)
Betraut, Jules, *Les belles nuits de Paris* (Paris, 1927)
Besant, Walter, *East London* (London, 1901)
Binder, Beate, '"Alles elektrisch!" Zur Metaphorik des Fortschritts, Der gesellschaftliche Diskurs um die Elektrizität im Deutschen Kaiserreich Ende des 19. Jahrhunderts', master's thesis, Tübingen, 1988
*The Bitter Cry of Outcast London. An Inquiry into the condition of the Abject poor. With leading articles from the* Pall Mall *gazette of October 1883 and articles by Lord Salisbury, Joseph Chamberlain and Forster Crocier*, introduction by Anthony S. Wohl (Leicester, 1970)

Blaschko, Alfred, *Die Prostitution im 19. Jahrhundert* (Berlin, 1902)
Blasius, Dirk, *Kriminalität und Alltag. Zur Konfliktgeschichte des Alltaglebens im 19. Jahrhundert* (Göttingen, 1978)
Bloch, Ernst, *Verfremdungen I* (Frankfurt, 1962)
Bloch, Iwan, *Das Sexualleben unserer Zeit* (Berlin, 1907)
Blumin, Stuart M., 'Explaining the New Metropolis. Perception, Depiction and Analysis in Mid-Nineteenth-Century New York City', *Journal of Urban History* 11 (1984), pp. 9–38
Boberg, Jochen, Tilman Fichter and Eckhart Gillen, eds, *Exerzierfeld der Moderne. Industriekultur in Berlin im 19. Jahrhundert* (Munich, 1984)
—, *Die Metropole. Industriekultur in Berlin im 20. Jahrhundert* (Munich, 1986)
Bodenschatz, Harald, *Platz frei für das neue Berlin! Geschichte der Stadterneuerung in der 'größten Mietskasernenstadt der Welt' seit 1871* (Berlin, 1987)
Bogdal, Klaus-Michael, *Schaurige Bilder. Der Arbeiter im Blick des Bürgers am Beispiel des Naturalismus* (Frankfurt, 1978)
Booth, Charles, *Life and Labour of the People in London*, 17 vols (New York and London, 1902–04)
Booth, William, *In Darkest London and the Way Out* (London, 1890)
Born, Paul, *Berlins dunkle Existenzen. Ernstes und Heiteres aus dem Leben und Treiben der Hauptstadt* (Berlin, 1893)
Bory, Jean Louis, *Eugène Sue, Dandy mais Socialiste* (Paris, 1962)
Bouman, Mark J., 'Luxury and Control. The Urbanity of Street Lighting in Nineteenth-Century Cities', *Journal of Urban History* XIV/1 (November 1987), pp. 7–37.
Bourdais, Jules, *Colonne-Soleil. Projet de phare électrique pour la ville de Paris* (Paris, 1885)
Brace, Charles Loring, *The Dangerous Classes of New York and Twenty Years Work among Them* (New York, 1890)
Brass, August Heinrich, *Die Mysterien von Berlin*, Vols I–V (Berlin, 1844–5)
Brassaï, *Paris de Nuit*, with text by Paul Morand (Paris, 1933)
—, *Henry Miller in Paris* (Frankfurt, 1981)
—, *Le Paris secret des années '30* (Paris, 1976)
Briffault, Edgar, 'La nuit de Paris', in *Le livre de cent-et-un*, Vol. II (Paris, 1831), pp. 127–50
Briggs, Asa, *Victorian Cities* (Harmondsworth, 1968)
Bruckner, Pascal, and Alain Finkielkraut, *Au coin de la rue, l'aventure* (Paris, 1976)
Brüggemann, Heinz, *'Aber schickt keine Poeten nach London'. Großstadt und literarische Wahrnehmung im 18. und 19. Jahrhundert. Texte und Interpretationen* (Reinbek, 1985)
—, *Das andere Fenster, Einblicke in Häuser und Menschen. Zur Literaturgeschichte einer urbanen Wahrnehmungsform* (Frankfurt, 1989)
Bruant, Aristide, *Am Montmartre. Chansons und Monologe*, ed. Walter Rösler (Berlin/GDR, 1986)
Buck-Morss, Susan, 'Le Flâneur, l'Homme-sandwich et la Prostituée, Politique de la Flânerie', in Heinz Wissmann, ed., *Walter Benjamin et Paris* (Paris, 1984), pp. 361–402
Burke, Thomas, *English Night-life from Norman Curfew to present Black-out* (London, 1941)
—, *Nights in Town* (London, 1915)

Burnat, André, *Police de Moeurs. Les dossiers excitants de la brigade des moeurs*
(Paris, 1977)

Butler, Josephine, *Personal Reminiscences of a Great Crusade* (London, 1896)

Cain, Georges, 'Paris la nuit', unpublished manuscript, Bibliothèque Historique
de Paris, Ms 1200, Fol. 176–81; 1909

du Camp, Maxime, *Paris, ses organes, ses fonctions et sa vie dans la seconde moitié du
XIXe siècle* (Paris, 1884)

Carco, Francis, *Nuits de Paris* (Paris, 1927)

Carlier, F., *Les deux Prostitutions (1860–1870)* (Paris, 1887)

Cauquelin, Anne, *La Ville la Nuit* (Paris, 1977)

—, *Cinéville* (Paris, 1979)

de Chambert, Paul, *Une nuit de Paris au pays du vice et de la misère* (Paris, n. d.)

Champier, Victor and Roger Sandoz, *Le Palais Royal d'après des documents inédits*,
2 vols (Paris, 1900)

Chancellor, John, *How to be happy in Berlin* (London, 1929)

Chesney, Kellow, *The Victorian Underworld* (London, 1970)

Chevalier, Louis, *Montmartre du Plaisir et du Crime* (Paris, 1980)

—, *Classes laborieuses et classes dangereuses à Paris pendant la première moitié du XIXe
siècle* (Paris, 1958)

—, *Histoires de la nuit parisienne* (Paris, 1982)

—, *Les ruines de Subure. Montmartre de 1939 aux années 80* (Paris, 1985)

*Chronik von Berlin* (Berlin, 1840)

*Cities of the Mind. Images and Themes of the City in Social Science*, eds Lloyd Rodwin
and Robert M. Hollister (New York and London, 1984)

Citron, Pierre, *La Poésie de Paris dans la littérature française de Rousseau à Baudelaire*,
2 vols (Paris, 1961)

Clemens, F. W., *Die Geheimnisse von Moabit. Auf seinen Kreuz- und Querzügen durch
Berlin und Umgebung entdeckt von F. W. Clemens* (Berlin, 1844)

Cobb, Richard, *The Police and the People* (London, 1970)

Commence, O., *La prostitution clandestine à Paris* (Paris, 1904)

Conrad, Horst, *Die literarische Angst* (Düsseldorf, 1974)

Conrad, Peter, *The Art of the City. Views and Versions of New York* (New York and
Oxford, 1984)

Conrads, Ulrich, ed., *Panik-Stadt* (Braunschweig, 1979)

Corbin, Alain, *Women for Hire, Prostitution and Sexuality in France after 1850*, trans.
Alan Sheridan (Cambridge, MA, and London, 1990)

—, *The Foul and the Fragrant, odour and the French social imagination* (Leamington
Spa, 1986)

—, *The Lure of the Sea, the discovery of the seaside in the Western world*, trans.
Joscelyn Phelps (Cambridge, 1994)

Crapsey, Edward, *The Nether Side of New York; or, the Vice, Crime and Poverty of the
Great Metropolis* (Montclair, NJ, 1969)

Cullen, Tom, *The Prostitutes' Padre. The story of the famous rector of Stiffkey*
(London, 1975)

Curvin, Robert and Bruce Porter, *Blackout Looting! New York City, July 13, 1977*
(New York, 1978)

de Dampmartin, Anne Henri, *Un provincial à Paris pendant une partie de l'année
1789* (Strassbourg, n. d. [1789])

Darzens, Rodolphe, *Nuits à Paris. Note sur une ville* (Paris, 1889)

Defrance, Eugène, *Histoire de l'éclairage des rues de Paris* (Paris, 1904)
Delpeche, René, *Les Dessous de Paris, Souvenirs reçus de l'ex-inspecteur de la brigade mondaine* (Paris, 1955)
Delvau, Alfred, *Les Dessous de Paris* (Paris, 1861)
—, *Les plaisirs de Paris. Guide prâtique et illustré* (Paris, 1867)
Desman, Charles, *Le crime et la débauche à Paris* (Paris, 1881)
Desmond, Shaw, *London Nights in the Gay Nineties* (New York, 1928)
*Der deutsche Nachtwächter in Paris. Im Jahr 1815*
*Deutsches Wörterbuch*, Jacob Grimm and Wilhelm Grimm (Leipzig, 1854ff.)
Devrient, Eduard, *Briefe aus Paris* (Berlin, 1840)
Diener, Gottfried, *Die Nacht in der deutschen Dichtung von Herder bis zur Romantik* (Bamberg, 1931)
Dickens, Charles, 'The Streets – Night', in *Sketches by Boz, Illustrative of Every-Day Life & Every-Day People* (London, 1836)
—, 'Night Walks', in *The Uncommercial Traveller and Reprinted Pieces* by Charles Dickens (London, 1860)
Domela, Harry, *Der falsche Prinz. Mein Leben und meine Abenteuer* (Berlin, 1927)
Drechsler, Hermann, *Aktenstaub. Aus dem Tagebuch eines Wohlfahrtsdezernenten* (Berlin, 1932)
Drexler, Peter, *Literatur, Recht, Kriminalität. Untersuchungen zur Vorgeschichte des englischen Detektivromans 1830–1890* (Frankfurt a. M. et al., 1991)
Dröge, Franz, and Thomas Krämer-Badoni, *Die Kneipe, Zur Soziologie einer Kulturform oder 'Zwei Halbe auf mich!'* (Frankfurt a. M., 1987)
Dronke, Ernst, *Berlin* (Berlin, 1846; Darmstadt and Neuwied, 1987)
Dyck, Margaret and Hedwig Stieve, *Ein Tag aus dem Leben einer Wohlfahrtspflegerin* (Berlin, 1926)
Edel, Edmund, *Neu-Berlin*, Vol. L of *Großstadt-Dokumente*, ed. Hans Ostwald (Berlin and Leipzig, n. d.)
—, *Die Pumpstation. Aus dem Abreißkalender einer Zeugin* (Berlin, 1911)
*Die Elemente der Bevölkerung Berlins mit Rücksicht auf die Prostitution* (Hamburg, 1869)
*Eldorado. Homosexuelle Frauen und Männer in Berlin 1850–1950. Geschichte, Alltag und Kultur* (Berlin, 1984)
Emsley, Clive, *The English Police. A Political and Social History* (Hemel Hempstead, 1991)
Endell, August, *Die Schönheit der großen Stadt* (Berlin, 1928)
Engelbrecht, Ernst, *Kinder der Nacht. Bilder aus dem Verbrecherleben* (Neu-Finkenkrug bei Berlin, 1925)
—, *Fünfzehn Jahre Kriminalkommissar. Ernstes und Heiters aus meiner kriminalistischer Berufsarbeit* (Berlin, n. d. [c .1928])
—, *In den Spuren des Verbrechertums. Ein Streifzug durch das großstädtische Verbrechertum und seine Schlupfwinkel* (Berlin, c.1930)
Engelbrecht, Ernst and Leo Heller, *Berliner Razzien* (Berlin, 1924)
Engler, Michael, and Günter Kunert, *Berliner Nächte. Laternenbilder* (Hamburg, 1986)
Farge, Arlette, *Vivre dans la rue à Paris au XVIIIe siècle* (Paris, 1979)
—, *La vie fragile. Violence, pouvoirs et solidarités à Paris au XVIIIe siècle* (Paris, 1986)
Fargue, Léon Paul, *Le piéton de Paris* (Paris, 1939)
Fechner, G. Th., *Die Tagesansicht gegenüber der Nachtansicht* (Leipzig, 1879)

Feval, Paul Henri C., *Les Nuits de Paris. Dramas et récits nocturnes* (Paris, 1851–2)

Fischer, Hans R., *Was Berlin verschlingt* (Berlin, 1890)

Fischer, Joachim, and Claudia Wagner, 'Sprachen der Nacht', *Nachtcafé* XII/26 (Autumn/Winter 1986/87), pp. 22–31

Fishman, William J., *The Streets of East London* (London, 1979)

—, *East End 1888. A year in a London borough among the labouring poor* (London, 1988)

Flemming, Hugo, *Nachtmission. Bilder aus der Stadtmission 14* (Berlin, 1913)

Flexner, Abraham, *Prostitution in Europe* (1913; Montclair, NJ, 1969)

Fontane, Theodor, *Wanderungen durch England und Schottland*, 2 vols, ed. Hans-Heinrich Reuter (Berlin/GDR, 1980)

Fournel, Victor, *L'odyssée d'un flâneur ou ce qu'on voit dans les rues de Paris* (Paris, 1858)

Frégier, H. A., *Des Classes dangereuses dans la population des grandes villes et des moyens de les rendre meilleures* (Brussels, 1840)

Frenilly, Baron François Auguste Fauveau, *Souvenirs (1768–1828)* (Paris, 1908)

Frevert, Ute, *Frauen-Geschichte. Zwischen bürgerlicher Verbesserung und neuer Weiblichkeit* (Frankfurt, 1986)

*Die Friedrichstraße. Geschichte und Geschichten*, with text by Peter Mugay, pub. Berlin-Information (Berlin/GDR, 1987)

Fuchs, Eduard, *Die Frau in der Karikatur* (Munich, 1928)

*Fünfzig Jahre im Dienst des Glaubens und der Liebe. Jubiläumsschrift der Berliner Stadtmission* (Berlin, 1927)

Gaillard, Jeanne, *Paris. La Ville (1852–1870)* (Paris, 1977)

Gailus, Manfred, *Straße und Brot. Sozialer Protest in den deutschen Staaten unter bes. Berücksichtigung Preußens 1847–1849* (Göttingen, 1990)

Gasnault, François, *Guinguettes et lorettes. Bals publics à Paris au XIXe siècle (1830–1870)* (Paris, 1986)

Gay, John, *Trivia, or The Art of Walking the Streets of London*, in *Poetry and Prose*, ed. Vinton A. Dearing (Oxford, 1974)

*Die Gefallenen Mädchen und die Sittenpolizei vom Standpunkte des praktischen Lebens. Vom Kriminalkommissar v. Baumer* (Berlin, 1886)

*Die Geheimnisse von Berlin. Aus den Papieren eines Berliner Kriminalbeamten von 1844*, ed. with afterword by Paul Thiel (Berlin/GDR, 1987)

*Die Geheimnisse von Stuttgart. Von Asmodeus II* (Stuttgart, 1878)

Geisel, Eike, *Im Scheunenviertel. Bilder Texte und Dokumente*, with a foreword by Günter Kunert (Berlin, 1981)

Gensch, Brigitte, and Veronika Zimmer, *Gewalt gegen Frauen. Stadtplanerische und bauliche Komponenten der nächtlichen Unsicherheit* (Kassel, 1981)

Gensch, Willy, *Der Berliner Osten* (Berlin, 1930)

Geremek, Bronislaw, *Geschichte der Armut. Elend und Barmherzigkeit in Europa* (Munich and Zurich, 1988)

Geroal, Luc, *L'Athène de la Spree par un béotien. Croquis berlinois* (Paris, 1892)

*Gesetz zur Bekämpfung der öffentlichen Unsittlichkeit und der venerischen Krankheiten* (Berlin, 1907)

Giese, Fritz, *Girlkultur, Vergleiche zwischen amerikanischem und europäischem Lebensgefühl* (Munich, 1925)

Giraudoux, Jean, *Berlin. Straßen und Gesichter um 1930*, eds Friederike Hassauer and Peter Roos (Nördlingen, 1987)

Girouard, Mark, *Cities and People, a social and architectural history* (New Haven and London, 1985)

Glassbrenner, Adolf, *Berlin, wie es ist – und trinkt* (Von Ad. Brennglas), 23 issues (Berlin 1832–50)

von Gleichen-Rußwurm, Alexander, *Die geistige Entwicklung des modernen Europa. Die gesellschaftliche Struktur*, Vols XXIII/XXIV of *Das Kulturbild des 19 Jahrhunderts* (Hamburg, n. d.)

Goebbels, Joseph, *Kampf um Berlin* (Munich, 1932)

Gourdon, Edouard, *Paris la nuit. Silhouettes* (Paris, 1842)

—, *Les Faucheurs de Nuit. Joueurs et Joueuses* (Paris, 1860)

Gourvish, T. R., and R. G. Wilson (with Fiona Wood), *The British Brewing Industry 1830–1980* (Cambridge, 1994)

Graham, Stephen, *London Nights* (London, *c*.1924/25)

Grant, James, *Lights and Shadows of London Life* (London, 1842)

Grauhan, Rolf Richard, ed., *Großstadt-Politik* (Gütersloh, 1972)

Greenwood, J., *The Policeman's Lantern. Strange Stories of London Life* (London, 1888)

Groschopp, Horst, *Zwischen Bierabend und Bildungsverein. Zur Kulturarbeit in der deutschen Arbeiterbewegung vor 1914* (Berlin/GDR, 1985)

*Großstadt, Aspekte empirischer Kulturforschung. 24. Deutscher Volkskunde–Kongreß in Berlin, 26–30 September 1983*, ed. on behalf of the Deutsche Gesellschaft für Volkskunde by Theodor Kohlmann and Hermann Bausinger (Berlin, 1985)

*Großstadt-Elend und Rettung der Elendesten*, Bernhard Duhr, S. J. (Freiburg i. Br., 1920)

Grothe, Wilhelm, *Berlin bei Nacht oder der Nachtgesellen Leben und Treiben in der Reichshauptstadt. Sensationelle Enthüllungen aus der Berliner Verbrecherwelt* (Berlin, 1893)

Gruenter, Undine, *Ein Bild der Unruhe. Roman* (Munich, 1986)

Grulich, Paul, *Dämon Berlin. Aufzeichnungen eines Obdachlosen* (Berlin, 1907)

Grünstein, Josef, *Babel-Berlin. Typen und Schicksale* (Berlin, 1907)

Günther, Ernst, *Geschichte des Varietés* (Berlin/GDR, 1978)

Gurk, Paul, *Berlin. Roman vom Sterben einer Stadt* (1925; Darmstadt, 1980)

Gutzkow, Karl, *Briefe aus Paris* (Leipzig, 1842)

Haber, Siegmund, *Berlin bei Nacht. Kaiserstädtische Kneipstudien*, 3rd edn (Leipzig, 1876)

*Hamburgische Nächte, oder Begebenheiten und Reflexionen des nächtlichen Wanderers über menschliche Situationen und Verhältnisse* (Altona, 1808)

*Handbuch des guten Tons und der feinen Sitten von Konstanze von Franken*, 22nd revised edn (Berlin, 1900; Munich, 1977)

*Handwörterbuch des deutschen Aberglaubens*, ed. Hans Bächtold-Stäubli with the help of Eduard Hoffmann-Krayer (1935), new edn with a preface by Christoph Daxelmüller (Berlin and New York, 1987)

Hanoteau, Guillaume, *Ces nuits qui ont fait Paris. Un demi-siècle de théâtre d'Ubu Roi à Huis clos* (Paris, 1971)

Harde, Maximilan, *Kaiserpanorama. Literarische und Politische Publizistik*, ed. with an afterword by Ruth Greuner (Berlin/GDR, 1983)

Harris, Percy A., *London and Its Government* (London and Toronto, 1933)

Harrison, Brian, 'Pubs', in eds H. J. Dyos and Michael Wolff, *The Victorian City. Images and Realities*, Vol. I: *Past and Present/Numbers of People* (London, 1973)

Harsin, Jill, *Policing Prostitution in 19th century Paris* (Princeton, 1985)

Harweck, L, *Berlin bei Tag und Nacht oder die Geheimnisse von Berlin* (Berlin, *c*.1866)

Hass, Hermann, *Sitte und Kultur im Nachkriegsdeutschland* (Hamburg, 1932)

Hegemann, Werner, *Das steinerne Berlin. Geschichte der größten Mietskasernenstadt der Welt* (1930; Braunschweig, 1979)

Heijermann, Hermann, *Berliner Skizzenbuch* (Berlin, 1908)

Heilborn, Ernst, *Zwischen zwei Revolutionen. Der Geist der Schinkelzeit (1789–1848)* (Berlin, 1927)

Heindl, Robert, *Polizei und Verbrechen* (Berlin, 1912)

Heinzlmeier, Adolf, Jürgen Menningen and Berndt Schulz, *Kino der Nacht. Hollywoods Schwarze Serie* (Hamburg and Zurich, 1985)

Heller, Leo, *Rund um den Alex. Bilder und Skizzen aus dem Berliner Polizei- und Verbrecherleben* (Berlin, n. d. [*c*.1925])

Heller, Reinhold, ' "The City is dark", Conceptions of Urban Landscape and Life in Expressionist Painting and Architecture', in *Expressionism Reconsidered. Relationships and Affinities*, eds Gertrud Bauer Pickar and Karl Eugene Webb (Munich, 1979), pp. 43–57.

Hellpach Willy, *Nervosität and Kultur* (Stuttgart, 1902)

—, *Mensch und Volk der Großstadt* (Stuttgart, 1939)

—, *Wirken in Wirren*, Vol. I, (Hamburg, 1948)

Herding, Klaus and Hans-Ernst Mittig, *Kunst und Alltag im NS-System. Albert Speers Berliner Straßenlaternen* (Giessen, 1975)

Herlaut, Colonel, *L'Eclairage de Paris à l'époque révolutionnaire* (Paris, 1932)

Hessel, Franz, *Spazieren in Berlin* (Berlin, 1929); reprinted as *Ein Flaneur in Berlin* (Berlin, 1984)

Hesslein, Bernhard, *Berliner Pickwickier. Fahrten und Abentheuer Berliner Junggesellen bei ihren Kreuz- und Querzügen durch das moderne Babylon*, Vols I–III (Berlin, 1854)

—, *Unter dem Schleier der Nacht, Sittenbild aus Berlins Gegenwart*, Vols I–IV (Berlin, 1857)

—, *Die Geheimnisse von Berlin. Sittenschilderungen aus der Vergangenheit und Gegenwart der deutschen Reichshauptstadt* (Magdeburg, *c*.1880)

Hildenbrandt, Fred, *Großes schönes Berlin* (Berlin, 1928)

Hirschberg, E., *Die soziale Lage der arbeitenden Klassen in Berlin* (Berlin, 1897)

Hirschfeld, Magnus, *Die Gurgel von Berlin*, Vol. XLI of *Großstadt-Dokumente* (Berlin and Leipzig, n. d.)

Hopp, Ernst Otto, *In der großen Stadt* (Berlin, 1885)

Huart, Louis, *Physiologie du flâneur* (Paris, 1841)

Humphreys, Anne, *Henry Mayhew* (Boston, 1984)

—, *Travels into the Poor Man's Country. The Work of Henry Mayhew* (London, 1977)

Huppé, S. E., *Das sociale Deficit von Berlin in seinem Hauptbestandteil* (Berlin, 1871)

Huret, Jules, *Berlin* (Munich, 1909), reprinted as *Berlin um 1900* (Berlin, 1979)

Husson, Friedrich, *Kurfürstendamm* (Berlin, 1934)

Huysmans, Joris-Karl, *Croquis Parisiens. Les Folies-Bergères en 1879*, Vol. VII of *Oeuvres complètes* (Paris, 1929)

Hyan, Hans, 'Die Menschen-Mühle Berlin. Eine Schilderung in Schildern', *UHU* III/3 (March 1927), pp. 82–9

*Ich weiß Bescheid in Berlin. Vollständiger systematischer Führer durch Groß-Berlin für Fremde und Einheimische, für Vergnügungs- und Studienreisende*, 1908/9 edn

*Isidors schwärmerische Nächte, oder romantische Darstellungen aus dem Gebiete der Phantasie und der Träume* (Leipzig, 1822)

*Jahrhundertwende. Der Aufbruch in die Moderne*, 2 vols, eds August Nitschke, Gerhard A. Ritter, Detlev J. K. Peukert and Rüdiger vom Bruch (Reinbek, 1990)

Jameson, Egon (=Egon Jacobssohn), *Augen auf! Streifzüge durch das Berlin der zwanziger Jahre*, ed. Walther von La Roche (Frankfurt, Vienna and Berlin, 1982)

Janin, Jules, *Un Hiver à Paris* (Paris, 1847)

Jansen, Wolfgang, *Glanzrevuen der zwanziger Jahre* (Berlin, 1987)

Jay, A. O. M., *Life in the Darkest London* (London, 1891)

Jeannel, Julien, *Die Prostitution in den großen Städten im 19. Jahrhundert* (Erlangen, 1869)

Jones, Steve, *London through the Keyhole* (Nottingham, 1991)

Jouhandeau, Marcel, *Images de Paris* (Paris, 1934)

Kahn, Gustave, *L'Esthétique de la rue* (Paris, 1901)

Kalisch, Ludwig, *Paris und London* (Frankfurt, 1851)

—, *Pariser Leben* (Mainz, 1880)

Karp, David Allan, *Public Sexuality and Hiding Behaviour. A Study of Times Square Sexual Community* (New York University, 1971)

Karsch-Haack, Ferdinand, *Erotische Großstadtbilder als Kulturphänomene, Wien und Berlin* (Berlin, 1926)

Kautsky, Karl, *Vermehrung und Entwicklung in Natur und Gesellschaft* (Stuttgart, 1910)

Keim, Dieter, *Stadtstruktur und alltägliche Gewalt. Fallstudie Wolfsburg-Westhagen*, Wolfsburger Beiträge zur Stadtgeschichte und Stadtentwicklung (Frankfurt a. M. and New York, 1981)

Kern, Elga, *Wie sie dazu kamen. Lebensfragmente bordellierter Mädchen*, ed. with a foreword by Hanne Kulessa (Darmstadt and Neuwied, 1985)

von Kertbeny, C., *Berlin wie es ist. Ein Gemälde des Lebens dieser Residenz und ihrer Bewohner, dargestellt in genauer Verbindung mit Geschichte und Topographie* (Berlin, 1831)

*Kikis Paris. Künstler und Liebhaber 1900–1930*, eds Billy Schürer and Julie Martin (Cologne, 1989)

Kisch, Egon Erwin, *Razzia auf der Spree. Berliner Reportagen* (Berlin/GDR, 1986)

Kläger, Emil, *Durch die Wiener Quartiere des Elends und Verbrechens. Ein Wanderbuch aus dem Jenseits* (Vienna, 1908)

Klein, Jean-René, *Le Vocabulaire des mœurs de la 'Vie Parisienne' sous le Second Empire, introduction à l'étude du langage boulevardier* (Louvain, 1976)

Kober, H. A., 'Die Unterwelt der Großstädte', *UHU* V/12 (September 1929), pp. 72–7.

—, 'Was unsere Väter liebten. Ein Abendbummel durch die Vergnügungs-Etablissments um das Jahr 1900,' *UHU* VI/6 (March 1930), pp. 39–46

de Kock, Paul, *La grande ville. Nouveau tableau de Paris* (Paris, 1842)

Köhn, Eckardt, *Straßenrausch. Flanerie und kleine Form. Versuch zur Literaturgeschichte des Flaneurs* (Berlin, 1989)

Köppen, Ruth, *Die Armut ist weiblich* (Berlin, 1985)

Korff, Goffried, 'Mentalität und Kommunikation in der Großstadt. Berliner Notizen zur "inneren" Urbanisierung', in *Großstadt. Aspekte empirischer*

*Kulturforschung*, eds Theodor Kohlmann and Hermann Bausinger (Berlin, 1985), pp. 343–61

—, 'Die Stadt aber ist der Mensch. . .', in *Berlin, Berlin. Die Ausstellung zur Geschichte der Stadt*, eds Gottfried Korff and Reinhard Rürup (Berlin, 1987), pp. 643–63

—, 'Berliner Nächte. Zum Selbstbild urbaner Eigenschaften und Leidenschaften,' in Gerhard Brunn and Jürgen Reulecke, eds, *Berlin. Blicke auf die deutsche Metropole* (Essen, 1989), pp. 71–103

Koschka, Emil, *Berliner Sitte(n)* (Berlin, 1981)

Kracauer, Siegfried, *Das Ornament der Masse* (Frankfurt, 1963)

—, *Straßen in Berlin und anderswo* (Frankfurt, 1964)

—, *Die Angestellten* (Frankfurt, 1971)

—, *Jacques Offenbach und das Paris seiner Zeit* (Frankfurt, 1976)

—, *Ginster* (1928; Frankfurt, 1963)

Krauss, Friedrich S., *Das Geschlechtsleben des deutschen Volkes*, new edn by Peter Schalk (Munich, 1977)

Krauss, Friedrich, ed., *Anthropophyteia. Jahrbuch für folkloristische Erhebungen und Forschungen zur Entwicklungsgeschichte der geschlechtlichen Moral*, Vols I–X (Leipzig, 1904–13)

Kretzler, Max, *Im Sündenbabel. Berliner Novellen und Sittenbilder* (Leipzig, 1886)

—, *Meister Timpe* (1888; reprinted Stuttgart, 1976)

Kreutzahler, Birgit, *Das Bild des Verbrechens in Romanen der Weimarer Republik. Eine Untersuchung vor dem Hintergrund anderer gesellschaftlicher Verbrecherbilder und gesellschaftlicher Grundzüge der Weimarer Republik* (Frankfurt a. M., Bern, New York and Paris, 1976)

Küchenmeister, Wera and Claus, *Der Lude. Roman* (Berlin/GDR, 1987)

Kuczynski, Jürgen, *Bürgerliche und halbfeudale Literatur aus den Jahren 1840 bis 1847 zur Lage der Arbeiter. Eine Chrestomathie*, Vol. IX of *Die Geschichte der Lage der Arbeiter unter dem Kapitalismus* (Berlin/GDR, 1960)

Kühne, Ferdinand Gustav, *Mein Carneval in Berlin 1843* (Braunschweig, 1843)

*Kulturleben der Straße. Vom Anfang bis zur großen Revolution* (Berlin, n. d. [c.1925])

Kupfer, Hugo, *Reporter-Streifzüge. Ungeschminkte Bilder aus der Reichshauptstadt* (Leipzig, 1889)

Ladoux, Gaston, *La vie des grandes capitales. Etudes comparatives sur Londres – Paris – Berlin* (Paris, 1908)

Laforgue, Jules, *Berlin. Der Hof und die Stadt* (1887; Frankfurt, 1970)

Landsberger, Arthur, *Die Unterwelt von Berlin. Nach den Aufzeichnungen eines ehemaligen Zuchthäuslers* (Berlin, 1929)

Lefèbvre, Henri, *La Révolution urbaine* (Paris, 1970)

Lemer, Julien, *Paris au gaz* (Paris, 1861)

Léon, Pierre, 'Du Monopole de l'Eclairage et de Chauffage par le gaz à Paris', doctoral dissertation, Paris, 1901

De Liancourt, Adolphe, *Le Rideau se lève sur les Mystères de Paris* (Paris, 1845)

Liang, Hsi-Huey, *The Berlin Police Force in the Weimar Republic* (Berkeley, 1970)

Von Lichtberg, Heinz, *Für 6 Mark Laster. Berliner Unterwelt-Reportage*. Berliner Lokalanzeiger, Collection Graeser, Landesarchiv, Berlin, n. d.

Lindau, Paul, *Im Fluge. Gelegentliche Aufzeichnungen* (Leipzig, 1886)

—, *Der Zug nach Westen. Roman* (Berlin, 1921)

Lindenberg, Paul, *Berliner Stimmungsbilder* (Leipzig, 1884)

—, *Berlin in Wort und Bild* (Berlin, 1895)

Lindner, Rolf, *Die Entdeckung der Stadtkultur. Soziologie aus der Erfahrung der Reportage* (Frankfurt, 1990)

Lipp, Carola, ed., *Schimpfende Weiber und patriotische Jungfrauen. Frauen im Vormärz und in der Revolution 1848/49* (Bühl-Moos, 1986)

Löffler, Karl, *Das galante Berlin*, 3rd edn (Berlin et al., 1856)

*Lokal-Termin in Alt-Berlin. Ein Streifzug durch Kneipen, Kaffeehäuser und Gartenrestaurants, unternommen von Paul Thiel* (Berlin/GDR, 1989)

London, Jack, *The People of the Abyss* (London, 1903)

Luginsland, G., *Großstädtischer Mädchenschacher* (Munich, 1886)

Machray, Robert, *The Night Side of London* (London, 1902)

Mackay, J. H., *The Anarchists* (Boston, 1891)

*Männerbund zur Bekämpfung der öffentlichen Unsittlichkeit. Die moralische Heilsarmee in Berlin. Ein Zeitbild* (Berlin, 1889)

Magnus, Philip, *Gladstone. A Biography* (London, 1954)

Maier, Hans, *Die ältere deutsche Staats- und Verwaltungslehre (Polizeiwissenschaft) Ein Beitrag zur Geschichte der politischen Wissenschaft in Deutschland*, Vol. XIII of *Politica* (Neuwied and Berlin, 1966)

Mann, Klaus, *Der Wendepunkt. Ein Lebensbericht* (1942; Berlin/GDR and Weimar, 1979)

Marcus, Max, *Führer durch Berlins Nachtlokale. Ein gründlicher Wegweiser durch das nächtliche Berlin* (Berlin, c.1880)

Mass Observation, *The Pub and the People. A Worktown Study* (London, 1943)

Mattenklott, Gert and Gundel, *Berlin Transit. Eine Stadt als Station* (Reinbek, 1987)

Maxwell, Donald, *The new lights o' London. Being a series of impressions of the glamour and magic of London at night* (London, 1926)

Mayhew Henry, *London Labour and the London Poor*, 4 vols (London, 1861)

McCabe, James D., *Lights and Shadows of New York Life; or the Sights and Sensations of the Great City* (New York, 1872)

—, *New York by Sunlight and Gaslight* (Philadelphia, 1881)

Mearns, Andrew, *The Bitter Cry of Outcast London* (1883), ed. Anthony S. Wohl (Leicester, 1970)

Meidner, Ludwig, *Im Nacken das Sternenmeer* (Leipzig, 1918)

*Memoiren eines Berliner Nachtwächters. Von D. Morvell (= W. F. A. Vollmer)* (Gdansk, 1845)

Mercy, Joseph Alois, *Berlinische Nächte* (Leipzig and Züllichau, 1803)

Mery, Joseph, *Les nuits parisiennes* (Paris, 1860)

Mirecourt, Eugène de, *Paris. Histoire Pittoresque et Anecdotique* (Paris, 1855)

Modrow, Hans O., ed., *Berlin um 1900. Querschnitt durch die Entwicklung einer Stadt um die Jahrhundertwende* (Berlin, 1936)

Montorgueil, Georges, *La vie des boulevards* (Paris, 1896)

Moreck, Curt, *Kultur- und Sittengeschichte der neuesten Zeit. Geschlechtsleben und Erotik in der Gesellschaft der Gegenwart* (Dresden, n. d.)

—, *Führer durch das 'lasterhafte' Berlin* (Leipzig, 1931)

*The Morning Chronicle Survey of Labour and the Poor, The Metropolitan Districts*, 6 vols, ed. with an introduction by Peter Razzell (London, 1980)

Morton, H. V., *The Nights of London* (London, 1926)

Mumford, Lewis, *The City in History* (London, 1961)

Murphy, Robert, *Smash and Grab. Gangsters in the London Underworld* (London and Boston, 1993)

*Eine Nacht in Berlin, oder Geheimnisse eines Viktualienkellers. Aus den Papieren eines Nachtwächters* (Dummin, 1844)

*Die Nacht in Berlin oder nächtlicher Spaziergang durch die Residenz. Von Clauren dem Jüngeren*, 1st–3rd edns (Berlin, 1856)

*Nachtseiten der Gesellschaft, eine Sammlung merkwürdiger Geschichten und Rechtsfälle aller Zeiten. Aus den Papieren eines Criminalbeamten* (Berlin, c.1840); pub. in 18 parts by A. Dietmann, W. Jordan and L. Meyer (Leipzig 1844–6)

*Die Nacht von Berlin*, Verlag der Lustigen Blätter (Berlin, 1912)

*Das Nachtwächterbüchlein*, eds Ludwig Bäte and Kurt Meyer-Rotemund (Göttingen, 1923)

*Der Nachtwächter Gottes. Ein seltsames Schicksal, erzählt von Karl Josef Friedrich* (Dresden and Leipzig, 1939)

'Eine Nachtwanderung durch die Verbrecherstätten Berlins. Von unserem Berichterstatter', illustrated by Ludwig Löfflin, *Daheim*, 1869/7 (14 November 1869), pp. 106–9.

Nahrstedt, Wolfgang, *Die Enstehung der Freizeit. Dargestellt am Beispiel Hamburgs* (Göttingen, 1970)

*Naturgeschichte der Berlinerin, von ***, 3rd edn (Berlin, 1885)

Nevill, Ralph Henry, *Night Life, London and Paris. Past and Present* (London, 1926)

*Night Side of New York*, pub. New York Press (New York, 1866)

*The Night Side of Paris, containing many curious revelations* (Paris, 1882)

*The Night the lights went out. By the staff of the New York Times*, eds A. M. Rosenthal and Arthur Gelb (New York, 1965)

Nizon, Paul, *Das Jahr der Liebe. Roman* (Frankfurt, 1984)

*Norddeutsches Babel. Ein Beitrag zur Geschichte, Characteristik und Verminderung der Berliner Prostitution, herausgegeben bei einem philanthropischen Verein* (Berlin, 1870)

*Les Nouveaux Mystères de Paris* (Paris, 1844)

Nuss, Emma, *Aus dem Tagebuch eines Tauentzien-Girls* (Charlottenburg, 1914)

*Obdachlos. Bilder aus dem sozialen und sittlichen Elend der Arbeitslosen. Von Constantin Liebich*

*Orpheums-Gestalten. Aus Berlins socialem Leben* (Altona, c.1870)

Osborn, Max, *Berlin, Ein Rundgang in Bildern durch das alte und neue Berlin* (Berlin, c.1913)

—, *Berliner Nachtbilder* (Berlin, n. d.)

—, *Berliner Tanzlokale*, Vol. IV of *Großstadt-Dokumente*, 2nd edn (Berlin, 1905)

—, *Das erotische Berlin. Der gesammelten Großstadt-Dokumente erster Band* (Berlin and Leipzig, n. d.)

—, *Das gallante Berlin* (Berlin-Grunewald, 1912)

—, *Die Berlinerin. Kultur- und Sittengeschichte Berlins* (Berlin, 1921)

—, *Dunkle Winkel in Berlin*, Vol. I of *Großstadt-Dokumente* (Berlin and Leipzig, 1904)

—, *Kultur- und Sittengeschichte Berlins* (Leipzig, n. d. [1925])

Oxenius, Katharina, 'Vom Promenieren zum Spazieren. Eine ethnographische Studie Pariser Gärten', doctoral dissertation, Tübingen, 1987

Painter, Kate, *Lighting and Crime Prevention, The Edmonton Project* (London, 1988)

Pappritz, Anna, *Die Welt, von der man nicht spricht. Aus den Papieren einer Polizeibeamtin* (Leipzig, 1907)
—, *Einführung in das Studium der Prostitutionsfrage* (Leipzig, 1919)
Parent-Duchâtelet, (Docteur) Alexandre, *De la prostitution dans la ville de Paris considérée sous le rapport de l'hygiène publique, de la morale et de l'administration* (Paris, 1836)
*Paris am Tage und bei Nacht. Eine Karikaturenfolge von Paul Gavarni* (Dortmund, 1979)
*Paris au clair de lune* (Paris, c.1878)
*Paris, Berlin*, exhibition catalogue, Centre Georges Pompidou (Paris, 1977)
*Das Paris der Surrealisten. Illustrierte Reisemontage zur poetischen Geographie einer Metropole*, ed. Pierre Gallissaire (Hamburg, 1986)
*Paris documentaire, par Ch. Virmaitre* (Paris, n. d.)
'Paris la nuit en 1901', *Naguère et Jadis*, 75 (February 1959)
*Paris la nuit. Journal-Guide de Joyeux Viveur à Paris pendant l'Exposition* (Paris, 1889)
*Paris la nuit*, No. 2 of *Le Panorama* (Paris, n. d.)
*Paris la nuit*, photographs by Michel Saloff, text by Jean-François Vilar (Paris, 1982)
*Paris le jour et la nuit. Histoires, galanteries, théâtres, etc.* (Paris, 1846)
*Pariser Nächte. Aus dem Franz. v. A. Schwarz* (Budapest, 1890)
*Pariser Nächte, Schattenbilder aus dem Leben und Treiben dieser Weltstadt. Frei nach dem Französischen*, in 18 parts (Vienna, 1847–8)
*Pariser Nächte. Wegweiser durch das nächtliche Paris*, ed. Doré Ogizek (Paris, 1941)
*Pariser Nachtfalter. Lebensbilder aus Neu-Babylon von Chevalier de Croix-Rouge* (Berlin, 1867)
Pearsall, Ronald, *The Worm in the Bud. The World of Victorian Sexuality* (Harmondsworth, 1972)
Pearson, Michael, *The Age of Consent, Victorian Prostitution and its Enemies* (Newton Abbot, 1972)
Petrow, Stefan, *Policing Morals. The Metropolitan Police and the Home Office, 1870–1914* (Oxford, 1994)
Philip, Neil, and Victor Neuburg, eds, *Charles Dickens, A December Vision, His Social Journalism* (London, 1986)
Pick, Daniel, *Faces of Degeneration. A European Disorder* (Cambridge, 1990)
Pivar, David J., *Purity Crusade and Social Control 1868–1900* (Greenwood, 1973)
Plantet, Eugène, *La charité à Paris au XIXe siècle* (Paris, 1900)
Platel, Félix (= Ignotus), *Paris secret* (Paris, 1889)
Poe, Edgar Allan, *The Complete Stories*, with an introduction by John Seelye (London, 1992)
*Pöbelexzesse und Volkstumulte in Berlin. Zur Sozialgeschichte der Straße*, ed. Manfred Gailus (Berlin, 1984)
*Police and Society*, ed. David H. Bayley (Beverly Hills and London, 1977)
*La Police des Moeurs. Lettres adressées au journal 'La Lanterne' par un ex-agent des mœurs et un médecin* (Paris, 1879)
*Polizei und Sitte. Von Dr Albert Moll, Geheimer Sanitätsrat*, Vol. IX of the series 'Die Polizei in Einzeldarstellungen', ed. W. Abegg, State Secretary in the Prussian Interior Ministry (Berlin, 1926)
Polster, Bernd, ed., *'Swing Heil'. Jazz im Nationalsozialismus* (Berlin, 1989)
Pontich, Henri, *Administration de la Ville de Paris et du Département de la Seine* (Paris, 1884)
Préfecture de Police. Service des Mœurs. *Règlement* (Paris, 1878)

—, Tableau de l'éclairage des rues de Paris pour l'année 1832 (Paris, 1832) and also for following years

Preston, William C., 'Light and Shade', Pictures of London Life (London, 1885)

—, The Bitter Cry of Outcast London (London, 1883)

Preusser, Norbert, Not macht erfinderisch. Überlebensstrategien der Armenbevölkerung in Deutschland seit 1807 (Munich, 1989)

Privat d'Anglemont, Alexandre, Paris anecdote. Les industries inconnues, les oiseaux de nuit, la ville des chiffoniers (Paris, 1854)

Das Proletariat, Bilder und Studien von Werner Sombart, Vol. I of Die Gesellschaft. Sammlung sozialpsychologischer Monographien, ed. Martin Buber (Frankfurt, 1906)

Proletariat. Kultur und Lebensweise im 19. Jahrhundert, ed. Dietrich Mühlberg (Leipzig, 1986)

Die Prostituierten in Berlin, deren Helfershelfer als Louis, Kupplerinnen, Lehnefrauen und ihr schädlicher Einfluß auf die Sittenzustände der Gegenwart (Berlin, c .1850)

Prostitution oder Production, Eigentum oder Ehe? Studien zur Frauenbewegung von Johanna Loewenherz (Neuwied, n. d. [1895])

Prostitution und Verbrechen. Reportagen aus den Tiefen der Berliner Unterwelt. Von WEKA (= Willy Pröger) (Leipzig, 1930)

Rancière, Jacques, La nuit des prolétaires. Archives du rêve ouvrier (Paris, 1981)

Rasch, Gustav, Die dunklen Häuser Berlins (Berlin, 1861)

—, Die dunklen Häuser von Paris (Berlin, 1871)

—, Berlin bei Nacht. Culturbilder (Berlin, 1871); repub. as Berlin bei Nacht. Schattenseiten einer Großstadt. Eine Auswahl aus den Schriften v. Gustav Rasch, ed. with annotations and an introduction by Paul Thiel (Berlin/GDR, 1986)

de Rattier, Paul-Ernest, Paris n'existe pas (Paris, 1857)

Rau-Häring, Nelly, Lichtungen. 66 Photographien der Nacht (Nördlingen, 1987)

Reichel, Peter, Der schöne Schein des Dritten Reiches. Faszination und Gewalt des Faschismus (Munich, 1991)

Reichhard, Hans J., Bei Kroll, exhibition catalogue, Landesarchiv Berlin (Berlin, 1988)

Reinbold, Ernst Thomas, Die Nacht im Mythos, Kultus, Volksglauben und in der transpersonalen Erfahrung. Eine religionsphänomenologische Untersuchung (Cologne, 1970)

Reynolds, George W., The Mysteries of London. 2 vols (London, 1846–8)

Die Reise nach Berlin, pub. Berliner Festspiele GmbH (Berlin, 1987)

Ribton-Turner, C. J., A History of Vagrants and Vagrancy and Beggars and Begging, reprinted (Montclair, NJ, 1972)

Rideamus (= Fritz Oliven), Berliner Bälle (Berlin, 1914)

Riehl, Wilhelm Heinrich, Die Naturgeschichte des Volkes als Grundlage einer deutschen Sozialpolitik (Stuttgart and Berlin, 1925)

—, Land und Leute (1854; Stuttgart, 1869)

von Riesbeck, Leopold, Salon-Gespräche. Achtzig einleitende Beispiele. Ein Ratgeber für unerfahrene und schüchterne junge Leute beiderlei Geschlechts (Weimar, 1863); ed. with introduction by Wolfgang Max Faust (Munich, 1970)

Riha, Karl, Die Beschreibung der 'Großen Stadt'. Zur Entstehung des Großstadtmotivs in der deutschen Literatur (c.1750 – c.1850) (Bad Homburg, Berlin and Zurich, 1970)

—, 'Berlin im Kopf. Die Stadt als literarisches Thema, zwischen Realität und

Imagination', in *Medium Metropole*, eds Friedrich Knilli and Michael Nerlich (Heidelberg, 1986)

Riis, Jacob A., *The Battle with the Slum* (1902; Montclair, NJ, 1969)

Rinderspacher, Jürgen P., *Der Rhythmus der Stadt – Die Bedeutung der Zeit für die städtische Gesellschaft* (Berlin, 1988)

Ring, Max, *Berliner Leben. Kulturstudien und Sittenbilder* (Leipzig and Berlin, 1882)

Ritchie J., *Days and Nights in London* (London, 1880)

—, *The Night Side of London* (London, 1857)

Rodenberg, Julius, *Tag und Nacht in London. Ein Skizzenbuch zur Weltausstellung* (Leipzig, 1867)

—, *Paris. Bein Sonnenschein und Lampenlicht. Ein Skizzenbuch zur Weltausstellung* (Leipzig, 1867)

—, *Bilder aus dem Berliner Leben* (1885, 1887), ed. Gisela Lüttig, with an introduction by Heinz Knobloch (Berlin/GDR, 1987)

Röhrmann, Carl, *Der sittliche Zustand von Berlin nach Aufhebung der geduldeten Prostitution des weiblichen Geschlechts. Ein Beitrag zur Geschichte der Gegenwart, unterstützt durch die vollständigen und freimüthigen Biographieen der bekanntesten prostituierten Frauenzimmer in Berlin* (Leipzig, 1846)

Rölleke, Heinz, *Die Stadt bei Stadler, Heym und Trakl* (Berlin, 1966)

Roessler, Julius, 'Berliner Vergnügungslokale 1830–1880', *Mitteilungen des Vereins für die Geschichte Berlins* XXI (1904), pp. 107–10

Roncayolo, Marie-Florence, 'Recherches sur la topographie des loisirs populaires de Paris au XIXe siècle', master's thesis with Maurice Agulhon, Université de Paris I, 1977

Ronner, Emil Ernst, *Der Mann mit der Laterne. Das Leben Thomas John Barnardos* (Wuppertal, 1961)

Roscher, G., *Großstadtpolizei* (Hamburg, 1911–14)

Rosenkranz, Karl, *Die Topographie des heutigen Berlin. Vortrag vor der Kgl. Dt. Gesellschaft zum Preußischen Krönungsfeste am 18 Januar 1850*

Rossi, Pietro, ed.,*Theorie der modernen Geschichtsschreibung* (Frankfurt a. M., 1987)

Roth, Joseph, *Großstadt-Feuilletons*, Vol. IV of *Werke*, ed. Hermann Kesten (Cologne and Amsterdam, 1976)

—, *Berliner Saisonbericht. Unbekannte Reportagen und journalistische Arbeiten*, ed. with an introduction by Klaus Westermann (Cologne, 1984)

Roz, Firmin, *La ville de la lumière* (Paris, 1933)

Rudeck, Wilhelm, *Geschichte der öffentlichen Sittlichkeit in Deutschland* (Jena, 1897)

Ruge, Arnold, *Zwei Jahre Paris. Studien und Erinnerungen* (Leipzig, 1846)

Rumbelow, Donald, *The Complete Jack the Ripper*, revised edn (Harmondsworth, 1988)

Rumpfs [Johann Daniel Fr.], *Neuester Fremdenführer in Berlin. Eine Beschreibung nebst einem Wanderungsplan durch Berlin* (Berlin, 1839)

von Sacher-Masoch, Leopold, *Die Messalinen Berlins. Realistische Novellen und Sittenbilder aus dem high life der Reichshauptstadt* (Berlin, 1887)

Sagave, Pierre-Paul, *1871. Berlin Paris. Reichshauptstadt und Hauptstadt der Welt* (Frankfurt, Berlin and Vienna, 1971)

von Salomon, Ernst, *Die Geächteten. Roman* (Berlin, 1930)

Sandall, Robert, *The History of the Salvation Army*, with a foreword by General Osborn, 3 vols (London, 1947)

Sansot, Pierre, *Poétique de la ville* (Paris, 1988)

Saß, Friedrich, *Berlin in seiner neuesten Zeit und Entwicklung* (1846); ed. with afterword by Detlef Heikamp (Berlin, 1983)

Satyr (= Richard Dietrich), *Lebeweltnächte der Friedrichstadt*, Vol. XXX of *Großstadt-Dokumente* (Berlin, c.1906)

Sauval, Henri, *La chronique scandaleuse de Paris ou histoire des mauvais lieux* (Brussels, 1883)

Schall, Georg, *Großstadtbenehmen* (Vienna, 1913)

Scheffler, Karl, *Berlin. Ein Stadtschicksal* (Berlin, 1910)

Scherpe, Klaus R., ed., *Die Unwirklichkeit der Städte. Großstadtdarstellungen zwischen Moderne und Postmoderne* (Reinbek, 1988)

Schivelbusch, Wolfgang, *Lichtblicke. Zur Geschichte der Künstlichen Helligkeit im 19. Jahrhundert* (Munich and Vienna, 1983)

—, 'Straßenlaternen und Polizei', in *Die nützlichen Künste. Gestaltende Technik und bildende Kunst seit der industriellen Revolution*, eds Tilmann Buddensieg and Henning Rogge (Berlin, 1981), pp. 104–8.

Schlögel, Karl, *Jenseits des großen Oktober. Das Laboratorium der Moderne* (Petersburg, 1909–21; Berlin, 1988)

Schmandt, Peter, 'Armenhaus und Obdachlosenasyl in der englischen Graphik und Malerei (1830–1880)', doctoral dissertation, Tübingen, 1986

Schneider, Louis, *Bilder aus Berlin's Nächten. Genre–Skizzen aus der Sage, Geschichte, Phantasie und Wirklichkeit* (Berlin, 1835); trans. as *Les nuits de Berlin* (Paris, 1840–1)

Scholvin, Ulrike, *Döblins Metropolen. Über reale und imaginäre Städte und die Travestie der Wünsche* (Weinheim and Basel, 1985)

Schrader, Bärbel and Jürgen Schebera, *Kunstmetropole Berlin 1918–1933. Die Kunststadt in der Novemberrevolution. Die 'Goldenen' Zwanziger. Die Kunststadt in der Krise* (Berlin/GDR and Weimar, 1987)

Schulte, Regina, *Sperrbezirke. Tugendhaftigkeit und Prostitution in der bürgerlichen Welt* (Frankfurt, 1984)

Schwabe, Hermann, 'Einblicke in das innere und äußere Leben der Berliner Prostitution', in *Berliner Städtisches Jahrbuch für Volkswirthschaft und Statistik* (Berlin, 1874), pp. 60–74

Schwarzbach, F. S., *Dickens and the City* (London, 1970)

Schweers, O., 'Prostituiertenüberwachung in Berlin nach dem neuen Gesetz zur Bekämpfung der Geschlechtskrankheiten', in *Ergebnisse der Socialen Hygiene und Gesundheitsfürsorge*, ed. A. Grotjahn et al. (Leipzig, 1930), pp. 360–91

*Selbstbekenntnisse einer Dirne oder ein Sittenbild aus dem Großstadtsumpf. Nach Tagebuchaufzeichnungen bearbeitet und hg. v. Ferdinand Rodenstein* (= Holzinger, Ferdinand Karl) (Dresden, 1927)

Sennett, Richard, *The Fall of Public Man* (London, 1977)

—, *The Uses of Disorder, personal identity and civic life* (New York and London, 1970)

*Sexualkatastrophen. Bilder aus dem modernen Geschlechts- und Eheleben*, ed. Ludwig Lewy-Lenz (Leipzig, 1926)

Sheppard, Francis, 'The Crisis of London's Government,' in David Owen, *The Government of Victorian London 1855–1889. The Metropolitan Board of Works, the Vestries, and the City Corporation*, ed. Ray MacLeod (London, 1982)

Siedler, Wolf Jobst, Elisabeth Niggemeyer and Gina Andreß, *Die gemordete Stadt. Abgesang auf Putte und Straße, Platz und Baum* (Berlin, Munich and Vienna, 1964)

Simmel, Georg, 'Die Großstädte und das Geistesleben', in *Die Großstadt. Vorträge und Aufsätze zur Städteausstellung. Jahrbuch der Gehe-Stiftung zu Dresden* IX (Dresden, 1903), pp. 185–206

*Sittengeschichte des Hafens und der Reise. Eine Beleuchtung des erotischen Lebens in der Hafenstadt, im Hotel, im Reisevehikel. Die Sexualität des Kulturmenschen während des Reisens und in fremdem Milieu* (Vienna, 1927)

*Sittengeschichte des Ersten Weltkrieges*, eds Magnus Hirschfeld and Andreas Gaspar (Hanau, n. d. [1929])

*Sittengeschichte des Lasters*, ed. Leo Schidrowitz (Vienna, 1927)

*Sittengeschichte von Paris. Die Großstadt, ihre Sitten und ihre Unsittlichkeit*, ed. Leo Schidrowitz (Vienna and Leipzig, 1926)

*Die öffentliche Sittenlosigkeit, mit besonderer Beziehung auf Berlin, Hamburg und die anderen großen Städte des nördlichen und mittlerern Deutschlands. Petition und Denkschrift des Central-Ausschusses für die Innere Mission der Deutschen Evangelischen Kirche* (Berlin, 1865)

*Die öffentliche Sittenlosigkeit. Entgegnung auf die gleichnamige Schrift des Central-Ausschusses für die Innere Mission*, 5th edn (Hamburg, 1870)

Sloterdijk, Peter, *Der Zauberbaum. Die Entstehung der Psychoanalyse im Jahr 1785. Ein epischer Versuch zur Philosophie der Psychologie* (Frankfurt a. M., 1987)

*Slums, Erlebnisse in den Schlammvierteln moderner Großstädte von Else Spiller* (Aarau, Leipzig and Vienna, 1911)

Smith, Philip T., *Policing Victorian London. Political Policing, Public Order, and the London Metropolitan Police* (Westport and London, 1985)

Sombart, Werner, *Luxury and Capitalism*, trans. W. R. Dittmar with an introduction by Philip Siegelmann (Ann Arbor, 1967)

Sommerfeld, Adolf, *Aus dem dunkelsten Berlin*, Vols I–VI (Berlin, n. d.)

Soupault, Philippe, *Die letzten Nächte von Paris* (1928; Heidelberg, 1982)

Spitthövel, Maria, 'Frauen und Freiraum. Zur Beanspruchung öffentlicher städtischen Freiraums durch Frauen', habilitation thesis, Oldenburg, 1988

Springer, Robert, *Berlins Straßen, Kneipen und Clubs im Jahre 1848* (Berlin, 1850)

—, *Berlin wird Weltstadt. Ernste und heitere Culturbilder* (Berlin, 1869)

*Stadtbilder. Berlin in der Malerei vom 17. Jahrhundert bis zur Gegenwart*, Berlin Museum (Berlin, 1987)

Stanjek, Klaus, ed., *Zwielicht. Die Ökonomie der künstlichen Helligkeit* (Munich, 1989)

Stansell, Christine, *City of Women. Sex and Class in New York 1789–1860* (Urbana and Chicago, 1987)

*Stätten der Berliner Prostitution. Von den Elends- und Absteigequartieren am Schlesischen Bahnhof und Alexanderplatz zur Luxusprostiution der Friedrichstraße und des Kurfürstendamms. Eine Reportage von WEKA* (= Willy Pröger) (Berlin, 1930)

*The Statutes of the United Kingdom* II Geo. IV. and Will. IV, 1830

Stedman Jones, Gareth, *Outcast London. A Study in the Relationship between Classes in Victorian Society* (Oxford, 1971)

Steffen, Katharina, *Übergangsrituale einer auto–mobilen Gesellschaft. Eine kulturanthropologische Skizze* (Frankfurt, 1990)

Steinert, Heinz, 'Nachtleben oder, Fragmente über die allgemeine Erniedrigung des Liebeslebens (2.)', in *Kriminalsoziologische Bibiliographie* 38/39 (Vienna, 1983), pp. 81–92

Sterne, Laurence, *A Sentimental Journey through France and Italy*, ed. with an introduction by Ian Jack (Oxford and New York, 1964)

Stieber, Wilhelm Joseph, *Die Prostitution in Berlin und ihre Opfer. In historischer, sittlicher und polizeilicher Hinsicht beleuchtet* (Berlin, 1846)

Stifter, Adalbert, *Die Mappe meines Urgroßvaters. Schilderungen. Briefe,* with an afterword by F. Krökel and notes by K. Pörnbacher (Munich, 1986)

Strohmeyer, Klaus, ed., *Berlin in Bewegung. Literarischer Spaziergang* – 1: *Die Berliner;* 2: *Die Stadt* (Reinbek, 1987)

Sue, Eugène, *Les Mystères de Paris,* ed. F. Lacassin with an introduction by A. Lanoux (Paris, 1989)

Szatmari, Eugen, *Das Buch von Berlin. Was nicht im Baedeker steht,* Vol. I (Munich, n. d.)

Talmeyr, Maurice, *Das Ende einer Gesellschaft. Neue Formen der Prostitution in Paris* (Berlin, 1910)

Theweleit, Klaus, *Male Fantasies* – 1. *Women, floods, bodies, history,* trans. Stephen Conway with Erica Carter and Chris Turner (Cambridge, 1987)

Thiele, Peter Ernst (= Carl Brandt), *Das moderne Berlin in seinen Tugenden und Lastern. Romantisch dargestellt* (Berlin, *c* .1852)

Thompson, E. P., and Eileen Yeo, *The Unknown Mayhew. Selections from the Morning Chronicle 1849–1850* (Harmondsworth, 1971)

Tissot, Victor, and Constant Améro, *Les Mystères de Berlin* (Paris, 1879)

Touchard-Lafosse, G., *Les Réverbères. Chroniques de nuit du vieux et du nouveau Paris* (Paris, 1844)

Tuan, Yi–Fu, *Topophilia. A Study of Environmental Perception. Attitudes and Values* (Englewood Cliffs, NJ, 1974)

Uebel, Lothar, *Viel Vergnügen! Die Geschichte der Vergnügungsstätten rund um den Kreuzberg und die Hasenheide, Kreuzberger Hefte* VIII (Berlin, 1985)

*Uhrzeiten. Die Geschichte der Uhr und ihres Gebrauchs,* ed. Igor A. Jenzen, Historisches Museum (Frankfurt, 1989)

Ulmer, Bruno, and Thomas Plaichinger, *Les Ecritures de la Nuit. Un siècle d'illuminations et de publicité lumineuse. Paris Ville Lumière* (Paris, 1987)

*Unser Berlin. Ein Jahrbuch von Berliner Art und Arbeit,* ed. Dr Alfred Weise (Berlin, 1928)

Urban, Henry F., *Die Entdeckung Berlins* (Berlin, 1912)

Vance, Carol S., ed., *Pleasure and Danger, Exploring female sexuality* (Boston, London, Melbourne and Henley, 1984)

Verein Dienst an Arbeitslosen e.V., *25 Jahre unter Obdachlosen. Festschrift zum 25 jährigen Bestehen des Vereins Dienst an Arbeitslosen e.V. zu Berlin* (Berlin, 1907)

*Eine verhängnisvolle Nacht. Wahre Begebenheit aus dem Leben einer Weltstadt* (London, 1905)

*Vergnügungsgewerbe rund um den Bülowbogen. Streifzug duch die Geschichte der Großstadtprostitution von Reingard Jäkl,* pub. Bezirksamt Schöneberg (Berlin, 1987)

*Versuch einer medicinischen Topographie und Statistik von Berlin. Von Dr H. Wollheim* (Berlin, 1844)

*Verwaltungsbericht des Königlichen Polizei-Präsidiums zu Berlin für die Jahre 1871–1880* (Berlin, 1882)

*The Victorian City. Images and Realities,* 2 vols, eds H. J. Dyos and Michael Wolff (London, 1973)

Virmaitre, Charles, *Paris – Impur; Les maisons de rendez-vous* (Paris, 1898)

*Vorschriften für die jenigen Frauenspersonen, welche, der dringlichsten Abmahnung ungeachtet, von ihrer unzüchtigen Lebensweise nicht ablassen wollen, und deshalb unter polizeiliche Aufsicht gestellt sind*, Kommission für Sittenpolizei (Berlin, 1852)

Walkowitz, Judith R., *Prostitution and Victorian Society: Women, Class and the State* (Cambridge, 1980)

—, *City of Dreadful Delight. Narratives of Danger in Late-Victorian London* (Chicago, 1992)

Walser, Karin, 'Prostitutionsverdacht und Geschlechterforschung. Das Beispiel der Dienstmädchen um 1900', *Geschichte und Gesellschaft* 2, (1985), pp. 99–111

Warnod, André, *Bals, Cafés et Cabarets* (Paris, 1913)

*Was die Frau von Berlin wissen muß. Ein praktisches Frauenbuch für Einheimische und Fremde*, ed. Eliza Ichenhaeuser (Berlin and Leipzig, 1912)

Webb, Beatrice, *My apprenticeship* (London, 1926)

Webb, Sidney and Beatrice, *The History of liquor licensing in England, principally from 1700 to 1830* (London, 1903)

Werner, J., *Animir-Kneipen und Nachtcafé oder Polizei und Sittlichkeit* (Berlin, 1892)

Werthauer, Johannes, *Sittlichkeitsdelikte der Großstadt* (Berlin, 1907)

Weylland, John M., *These Fifty Years. Being the Jubilee of the London City Mission* (London, 1884)

Wichern, Johann Heinrich, *Hamburgs wahres und geheimes Volksleben* (Hamburg, 1832)

Wiedemann, Konrad, ed., *Rom – Paris – London. Erfahrung und Selbsterfahrung deutscher Schriftsteller in den fremden Metropolen* (Stuttgart, 1988)

Willms, Johannes, *Paris. Hauptstadt Europas 1789–1914* (Munich, 1988)

de Wissant, Georges, *Cafés et Cabarets* (Paris, 1928)

Wohl, Anthony S., *The Eternal Slum. Housing and Social Policy in Victorian London* (London, 1977)

*Wohnsitz Nirgendwo. Vom Leben und vom Überleben auf der Straße*, pub. Künstlerhaus Bethanien (Berlin, 1982)

Yonnet, Jacques, *Rue des Maléfices. Chronique secrète d'une ville* (Paris, 1987)

Zanthe, Thilo, *Der Berliner Prater. Streiflichter aus der Geschichte einer Freizeit- und Vergnügungsstätte* (Berlin/GDR, 1987)

Zapp, Arthur, *Vom Babel an der Spree. Sittenbilder aus dem neuen Berlin* (Leipzig, 1887)

*Zertretene Blüten. Skizzen aus dem sittlichen und sozialen Elend der Großstadt von E. Heine* (Berlin, n. d.)

Zuckmayer, Carl, *Als wär's ein Stück von mir. Horen der Freundschaft* (Frankfurt a. M., 1966)

Zweig, Stefan, *Begegnungen mit Menschen Büchern Städten* (Frankfurt a. M., 1955)

—, *Die Welt von Gestern* (Frankfurt a. M., 1970)

# Index

347

350